Volunteers
for
Learning

norc

NATIONAL OPINION RESEARCH CENTER
MONOGRAPHS IN SOCIAL RESEARCH

Volunteers
for
Learning

———

A Study of the Educational
Pursuits of American Adults

———

By

JOHN W. C. JOHNSTONE

and

RAMON J. RIVERA

ALDINE PUBLISHING COMPANY
Chicago

*The study reported in this volume was supported
by a grant from the Carnegie Corporation of New York,
whose generosity and interest is hereby gratefully
acknowledged. The Corporation is not responsible,
however, for any of the statements made in this volume.*

*First published 1965 by
ALDINE Publishing Company
64 East Van Buren Street
Chicago, Illinois 60605*

*Library of Congress Catalog Card Number 64-15606
Designed by Greer Allen
Printed in the United States of America*

Preface

This volume is about one of the quieter sectors of America's educational establishment. Adult education does not figure in our current controversies: no one has raised the issue "why Uncle John can't read." Adult education has no football or basketball teams, no panty raids or sit-in demonstrations. School bond or school board elections do not center around whether there are frills or essentials in the evening classes given in the local high school; indeed, adult education is largely financed out of tuition. National leaders do not hold conferences on where we are going to get the teachers to run our Bible classes. And there is no problem of dropouts in adult education. Dropouts are expected.

Yet, adult education, as this volume relates in considerable detail, is a major part of our total educational effort. In one year some twenty-five million American adults undertook to learn some topic. Three out of five Americans engaged in one or more educational activities since finishing their more formal schooling. American adults continue their education, and continuing education shows many signs of becoming an even more important (at least in terms of coverage) component of the total American educational system.

The major forces behind the heavy participation of adults in educational activities are the demands for adequately prepared workers generated by our highly industrialized and technologically sophisticated occupational system. In traditional or stable industrial societies individuals can for the most part live out their working lives on the basis of what they know and know how to do by the time they reach adulthood. In contrast, societies experiencing rapid technological and organizational changes require that their workers constantly learn new skills and tasks. The major portion of adults participating in learning experiences were doing just that.

v

However, American adults in their educational activities are not merely puppets moved by an inexorable economic determinism. Having learned to learn as students in their earlier years, they turn again and again to educational activities in seeking a variety of non-occupational skills and information. Through formal courses, correspondence schools, and disciplined self-study they can and do learn how to play, how to relate to their fellow men, how to understand the traditions of their religions, and how to perform as responsible citizens in our democratic society.

Although Americans who have learned as adults are in the majority, there is a sizable minority whose adult learning has never taken the form of systematic application. David Riesman's principle of "the more, the more" applies to adult education as well as to other areas of life. The more educated one is, the more likely he is to have engaged in educational activities as an adult. Ironically, adult education is used most by those who need it least.

This overview of contemporary adult education arises out of the research reported in this volume where adult education learning in the United States today is examined by means of a national sample survey. The time orientation of Dr. Johnstone's study is the present and the immediate future, rather than historical. Adult learning is approached mainly from a social-psychological vantage point, on the needs, motives, and satisfactions which impelled adults to seek to learn some subject. It is concerned with the organization of adult education only insofar as such organization facilitates or hinders individuals in the pursuit of learning.

This monograph reviews the extent and nature of adult participation in continuing education, identifies the people who engage in these pursuits, reconstructs the situations, circumstances, and personal goals which influenced people to become involved in educational endeavors, looks at the national climate of opinion regarding education for adults, and, to a lesser degree, investigates the range of facilities currently available for the instruction of the adult population.

The design, execution, and analysis of a national sample survey on the scale involved in the research reported in this volume requires the highest level of skill and social science competence. There is no doubt that the reader will see ample evidence throughout the volume that Dr. Johnstone commands an enviable technical and social science competence.

The efforts of a great many persons went into the development and conduct of this investigation. The study is indebted to all these persons, although it is not possible to mention each contributor by name.

First and foremost, thanks are due to the Carnegie Corporation of New York, who stimulated our interest in this project and then fully supported the research proposal which we devised. The complete freedom which they granted us in developing and carrying out the study created an ideal situation in which to conduct sponsored social inquiry, and is greatly appreciated.

Several persons outside NORC contributed valuable ideas to the original study plan: these were Florence Anderson, Cyril O. Houle, Eugene I. Johnson, Sloan Wayland, Rose Cologne, Malcolm Knowles, Thurman White, Fred Harrington, Leonard Stein, and Philip Ennis. Professors Houle, Stein, and Ennis also offered helpful suggestions during later stages of the study.

Within NORC, the investigation was directed by John Johnstone throughout all its stages. Ramon Rivera joined the project staff during the fall of 1962, acted first as co-director on the community studies, and then analyzed and wrote up the section dealing with the post-school educational pursuits of young adults. In the present volume Chapters 1 through 16 were written by Johnstone and Chapters 17 through 20 by Rivera.

Many other NORC staff members also made important contributions to the study. James A. Davis, Norman Bradburn, Seymour Sudman, Harold Levy, Seymour Warkov, and Jacob J. Feldman (former Director of Research at NORC) contributed helpful ideas during all stages of the study. Feldman and Sudman also designed and supervised the sampling and wrote Appendix 1 of the present monograph.

Field work on the study was directed by Galen Gockel, who in turn was ably assisted by Eve Weinberg, Miriam Kaplan, and Branson Frevert. It was only through the tireless efforts of the entire NORC Field Department, however, that the massive data collection demands imposed by the study were so efficiently organized and completed. The field workers responsible for tracking down information on community adult education facilities were Joan Romine, Shirley Breuer, Dean Long, and John Carver.

Three persons were employed as research assistants on the project. Bryan Roberts assisted in the design of the survey instruments and acted as coding supervisor during the first phase of the study. Paul M. Siegel supervised coding and assisted in the analysis of the data reported in Part II of this volume. Gerald McWorter then assisted on the community studies.

Approximately twenty-five University of Chicago students worked as coders and clerical assistants during different stages of the project. Of the original staff, Judy Green, Diana Glaberson, and Frank Stafford stayed with the project the longest, and Stafford later assisted Rivera in the analysis of the youth data. Nella Siefert, Joanne Hesslink, and Lillian Rochon did most of the typing for the study, and Jean Block provided excellent editorial assistance in the preparation of the final manuscript and also prepared the index.

This volume attempts to be a contribution to the professional educator concerned with the field of adult education, to the social scientist concerned with contemporary American society, and to the general reader with some curiosity and concern with the problems of continuing education. We hope that these three audiences are served well by Dr. Johnstone's work.

PETER H. ROSSI
Director
National Opinion Research Center

Contents

List
of
Tables

TABLE

List
of
Illustrations

General Introduction

This monograph is the final report on the National Opinion Research Center's general inquiry into the nature of adult education in America. The investigation, which was begun in January, 1962, and sponsored throughout by the Carnegie Corporation of New York, focused on the educational experiences of the American population following termination of regular, full-time school attendance.

The best way to introduce the contents of this volume is to begin with a brief description of the study as a whole. The investigation took shape around four distinct phases of inquiry, and it is these which delimit the four sections in this monograph.

The first phase of the study sought to provide a general description of the nature and scope of adult participation in formal and informal educational pursuits of all kinds. The rapid expansion in adult education has created an acute need for comprehensive information about the learning habits and practices of adults. Except for one study conducted under the auspices of the Department of Health, Education and Welfare (1959) and a couple of Gallup polls, reported respectively in the *Adult Education Journal* (1945) and by London *et al.* (1963), this behavior has never before been examined on a national scale in this country. The first purpose of the NORC study was to try to remedy this informational need by providing a comprehensive overview of the numbers and characteristics of adults engaged in studies of various subjects, the methods of study employed, and the institutional settings within which such instruction was received. Part I of the monograph presents a detailed behavioral inventory of the educational experiences of American adults over a twelve-month period.

Part II then turns to somewhat broader considerations. At this point in the study we sought to assess attitudes and opinions held by adults concerning education, and in so doing tried to evaluate the nature of potential audiences for various programs of adult learning. This section of the report, therefore, goes considerably beyond the measurement of actual learning experiences and focuses on the general question of how different segments of the population perceive and evaluate educational experiences. In addition, this section also investigates the situations under which adults typically enter into formal learning pursuits, the reasons they have in mind when they enroll, and the general impact of adult education experiences on their lives.

Part III considers a quite different type of question, the extent and nature of facilities for adult learning in "typical" urban communities. Our main goal in this phase of the study was a better understanding of the ranges of educational programs currently available to adults, the kinds of institutions engaged in providing the programs, and the nature of public knowledge of and dispositions toward such facilities.

In the fourth and final phase of the study, our attention was focused exclusively on one special segment of the population: adolescents and young adults between the ages of seventeen and twenty-four. Our main purpose here was to trace the educational and occupational experiences of young people during the years immediately following termination of regular schooling, with a special emphasis on the experiences of high-school and college drop-outs. Part IV of the monograph, therefore, first presents a descriptive overview of the schooling of young adults and then focuses specifically on the readiness of out-of-school youth to seek further education.

In combination, these four phases of inquiry represent a broadly based investigation of the activities and sentiments of the American public regarding continuing education, and, except for the community resources phase of the study, the focus throughout is national in scope.

In general design, the study took shape as a national sample survey consisting of successive waves of data collection. In the initial wave, an extremely large number of households were "screened" in order to derive basic information on the educational activities of adults during the previous twelve-month period. A probability sample of 13,293 households was drawn for this stage of the study, and successful contacts were subsequently made in 11,957 (90 per cent) of these households. Altogether, this field operation netted us information on the activities of 23,950 adults, and, in addition, on 1,928 unmarried youths between the ages of seventeen and twenty, and 11,554 children between the ages of three and sixteen. This field work took place during May and June, 1962, and it is from this body of data that the contents of Part I of the monograph are derived.

For the second phase of the study, personal interviews of approximately one hour's length were conducted with special subsamples of adults drawn from the aggregate of individuals enumerated in the survey of households. Interviews were completed with a total of 2,845 persons in this part of the study; 1,808 from a sample representing the total adult population of the United States and 1,037 from a special subsample drawn to represent those who had participated in some type of educational activity during the previous year. The first wave of this interviewing was conducted during May and early June, 1962, and the second wave during July and August of the same year.

Field work for the third phase of the study was organized as a completely independent operation and consisted of two quite distinct field tasks. First, data on community resources for adult education were collected by field representatives who contacted officials in local schools, industries, churches, government agencies, voluntary organizations, and other community institutions in four middle-sized American cities. From these contacts, exhaustive lists were prepared covering all instructional offerings available to local adults between September and December, 1962. Next, two of these four cities were selected for further study, and personal interviews were subsequently completed with random samples of adults in these cities. Altogether 545 interviews were completed in the two cities during April and May, 1963.

For the fourth and final phase of the study, a special sample of 865 young people was drawn to represent the total population of persons between the ages of seventeen and twenty-four, and personal interviews were subsequently completed with 697, or

81 per cent, of those selected. These interviews were conducted during September and October, 1962.

To summarize, the nature and goals of the over-all study may be described as consisting of the following phases and research steps:

Phase   I: A national survey of the educational activities of the adult population, based on a survey of the activities of members of some 12,000 American households

Phase II: An intensive study of the reactions of adults to continuing education, based on personal interviews with national samples of approximately 1,800 randomly selected adults, plus 1,000 recent adult education participants

Phase III: Case studies of adult education facilities in four middle-sized American cities, and of the impact of these facilities on the residents of two of these cities, based on information collected through field inventories of educational resources and personal interviews with roughly 550 adults

Phase IV: An inquiry into the post-school educational experiences of youth, based on personal interviews with a national sample of approximately 700 young adults

A more detailed description of the contents of specific chapters is provided in the introduction to each section of the report, and, as a further guide to the reader, a survey of the principal findings of the study is presented in Chapter 1. A more technical description of the nature of the sampling procedures employed is presented in Appendix 1, and copies of all survey materials and interview schedules used in the study are reproduced in Appendix 2.

1

Principal Findings of the Study

In this overview, we discuss the main findings in relation to the chief questions about adult learning behavior to which we addressed our attention at different points in the study. Happily, most of the questions are the ones we identified at the beginning of our inquiry, although a few represent problems which did not become apparent until we were well immersed in the analysis of the data. Throughout this review, the reader is guided to the specific chapter or chapters in which the pertinent data are discussed in full detail.

1. *How many adults engage in educational activities after they terminate their formal schooling? (Chaps. 3 and 6)* — The answer to this question ultimately hinges on the definition one applies to the concept of an "educational activity." In this study educational activities were defined very broadly. The investigation was concerned with all activities consciously and systematically organized for purposes of acquiring new knowledge, information, or skills; therefore, it covered a much wider range of behavior than is usually associated with the term "adult education."

We estimated that approximately 25 million American adults, more than one person in five, had been active in one or another form of learning during the twelve-month period just prior to June, 1962. Fifteen per cent, or more than 17 million persons, had been enrolled in courses on a part-time basis, 2.5 million were full-time students, and close to 9 million had engaged in independent study. These estimates refer to just the adult population of the country, that is, to persons either twenty-one or over, married, or the head of a household.

Many more adults than this become active in learning pursuits over longer periods of time. To estimate cumulative exposure in a cross-sectional study, of course, it is necessary to ask people about events that may have taken place many years earlier in their lives, and there is therefore some question about the accuracy of estimates based on such information.

Nonetheless, when people were asked whether or not they had ever taken an educational course since leaving school, as many as 47 per cent said that they had, and 38 per cent recalled at least one occasion on which they had tried to teach themselves something on their own. All told, 61 per cent of the adults we interviewed had been involved in one or the other of these forms of learning activity at some time during their adult lives. Most had been involved just once or twice, but about one in six listed at least three separate occasions on which instruction had been received, and about one in one hundred reported being active on nine or more occasions.

It is probably safe to conclude, then, that just about as many adults as not become involved at least once in a systematic attempt to acquire new knowledge, information, or skills after they leave school.

2. *What types of subjects do adults study?* (*Chap. 3*) – An analysis of the subjects people had studied during the year prior to our inquiry indicated that adult studies differ quite markedly from those in formal schooling. Not only were these studies primarily non-credit in nature, but their subject matter was overwhelmingly non-academic. Thirty-three per cent of the learning activities recorded in our inventory were vocational, and 20 per cent were in recreational learning. By comparison, only 12 per cent of all studies were in academic subjects.

One of the more revealing findings in this regard was that as few as 3 per cent of the total studies were in public affairs or current events. On the basis of popular stereotypes about adult education, one might have expected a considerably stronger representation from courses of this type. If any single preconception is inappropriate, however, it is that which equates the field of adult education with Great Books classes or current events study groups. Even in combination the adults involved in these activities made up but a tiny fraction of the total participants.

It was quite clear from the results of our study that the major emphasis in adult learning is on the practical rather than the academic; on the applied rather than the theoretical; and on skills rather than on knowledge or information. Subject matter directly useful in the performance of everyday tasks and obligations accounted for the most significant block of the total activities recorded. Together, the vocational and home and family life categories alone represented 44 per cent of all formal courses studied and 47 per cent of the subjects people had studied on their own. By comparison, the academic, religious, and public affairs categories—areas one might consider more concerned with ideas and values—made up just 30 per cent of the courses and 22 per cent of the independent studies. These figures illustrate the predominantly pragmatic quality of adult learning.

3. *What types of things do adults try to learn on their own? (Chaps. 3 and 10)*—Adults do not typically study vocational subjects on their own, nor are religion and public affairs frequently subjects for independent study. Learning efforts in the home and family life area, on the other hand, were undertaken independently more often than with instruction.

There was evidence, too, that some independent learning activities may be a quite recent development. A number of the subjects people had frequently studied on their own were in areas influenced by changes in patterns of leisure-time use, by recent innovations in teaching methodology, or by entry of commercial interests into the field of adult instruction. Eighty per cent of those who had studied gardening had done so without formal instruction; this was also true of 61 per cent who had studied a foreign language, 50 per cent who had studied music, and 44 per cent who had taken a course in speed reading.

4. *What methods of study do adults employ? (Chaps. 3 and 11)*—Just as the content of adult learning differs markedly from

that of an academic curriculum, so too the methods deviate from the more conventional forms. Leaving aside independent self-education, almost one-half of the courses people had taken during the previous year were outside of classroom settings. Although no single method was extensively employed, the combined use of the group discussion, the public lecture, correspondence study, private instruction, and on-the-job training accounted for 45 per cent of the activities reported by adults.

One of our more surprising results in this regard was that television has apparently failed to make much of an impact as a medium of adult instruction. Only 1.5 per cent of all courses studied during the previous year had been through television and only 290,000 adults were estimated to have followed an educational course on television during this time. From some points of view, this would represent a sizeable number of adult students, but it by no means came close to the 1,750,000 adults estimated to have taken correspondence courses over the same period of time. Indeed, when we evaluate the major home-study forms, television classes are still very much overshadowed by correspondence courses.

Adult audiences of more general programs on educational television stations are much larger than those attracted to formal courses of instruction on television, however, and these two aggregates must not be confused with one another. From other data collected in the study, we estimated that there are over 6 million "regular" and 12 million "occasional" viewers of educational television. These latter figures correspond closely with other estimates of the national audience for educational television stations.

5. *What methods of study do adults prefer? (Chap. 10)* – On the whole, adults do seem to prefer formal methods of study over informal ones, although quite striking differences were noted among different sectors of the population. When given a choice, older adults were much less likely to select formal classroom settings for their instruction and showed a relatively greater tendency to choose both private instruction and home-study methods.

In addition, persons of middle socio-economic circumstances

were found to be most likely to prefer the formal classroom, while those in lower positions were least likely to do so. Although our evidence was far from conclusive on this point, it was nonetheless consistent with the interpretation that people from lower echelons of the social class hierarchy feel a certain reluctance to expose themselves to formal learning situations.

Interestingly, no consistent differences were found in the methods of study preferred by men and women.

6. *Where do adults go to take courses? (Chap. 3)* — Although high schools, colleges, and universities are highly influential in adult instruction, our inventory of learning activities revealed that more adults study outside the regular school system than within it — by a ratio of about two to one. Moreover, we estimated that 56 per cent of all studies involving attendance at classes, lectures, or group discussions took place in institutions whose primary functions were not educational, such as churches and synagogues, private businesses, YMCA's, government agencies, the armed forces, and community institutions other than schools or adult education centers. In terms of over-all number, more adults had studied in churches and synagogues than in any other type of institution. As one would expect, of course, this instruction was confined almost exclusively to religious training.

One important feature of the learning experience of adults, then, is that it takes place chiefly in institutions whose main concerns are with functions other than education.

7. *In what types of institutional settings do adults prefer to study when given a choice? (Chaps. 10 and 16)* — When we asked people how they would go about learning a foreign language if they had to, some quite revealing findings emerged concerning both the methods of study they would use and the institutions to which they would turn. Although many more persons indicated they would seek out instruction than said they would try to learn on their own, a large number were unclear about what they would actually do. Fifteen per cent had no idea whatever of what to do, and 39 per cent made casual references to "lessons" or "classes," but were unable to identify any specific facility or resource to which they would turn.

The most striking finding, however, was that fewer than one adult in five would turn to the regular school system to develop proficiency in a foreign language. Substantially more adults were aware of foreign language instruction in the schools in their communities than were ready to use these facilities: for example, 28 per cent knew about language courses in a local high school, but only 7 per cent said they would go there to learn a foreign language; and while 33 per cent knew of such instruction in a local college, university, or university extension, only 12 per cent said this was where they would go for it. Thus very few adults viewed the formal school system as the most appropriate place to go to learn a new language, even though this kind of instruction is in rather abundant supply in these schools.

From the community studies, we learned that secondary schools were on the whole more attractive than universities to persons without much formal schooling, while the converse was true of those who had completed high school or better. We found too that a university setting is more important to men than to women, and, more generally, that the prominence and prestige an educational institution enjoys in a community is also of considerable importance to men.

8. *What are adult education participants like?* (*Chaps. 4 and 5*) — After investigating a large number of personal, social, and ecological characteristics, three factors emerged that persistently distinguished participants from non-participants: they differed in age, in the amount of formal schooling they had had, and in where they lived.

The first distinctive feature of the participant is that he is younger than the average American adult. The median age of those who had studied during the previous year was 36.5 — over six years younger than the median age of the sample. Over one-half of all participants were under forty, and nearly four in five were under fifty. In terms of rates of participation, moreover, there were vast differences between persons in different age brackets: the rates fell from a high of 29 per cent among adults in their twenties to 4 per cent among persons seventy or over.

Other than age, however, there were no other personal or life-cycle characteristics that set the adult student apart from the general population. The participants were about equally divided between men and women, and there were only slight discrepancies in religious background between participants and the general population. A slight underrepresentation of Negroes among participants completely disappeared when Negroes were compared with whites of similar educational background. A slight overrepresentation of married persons and underrepresentation of widows and widowers was explained by the different ages of persons in these statuses.

The second outstanding feature of the participant is that he is better educated than the average adult. The participants had attended school 12.2 years on the average, compared with 11.5 years for all adults in the sample, but the importance of this factor is much more sharply expressed when one compares rates of participation. During the previous year, these ranged from 4 per cent among persons with no formal schooling to 47 per cent among those who had attended for more than sixteen years.

Participants were also more likely to hold white-collar than blue-collar jobs and, in addition, had median family incomes almost $1,200 higher than the average. Of the three indicators of socio-economic position, however (education, occupation, and income), formal schooling was found to have by far the most powerful influence on rates of learning activity. Taken together, the impact of all three factors was enormous: a person who had been to college, who worked in a white-collar occupation, and who made more than $7,000 a year was about six times more likely to have been engaged in learning pursuits during the previous year than a person who had never gone beyond grade school, who worked in a blue-collar occupation, and whose family income was less than $4,000 a year.

Although to a somewhat lesser degree than by age or education, the participants could also be differentiated from the general population by their geographical location. First, residents of large metropolitan areas were overrepresented among participants, while those living in small cities, small towns, or rural areas were underrepresented. Within the large urban areas, however, only those living in suburbs or on the outskirts were overrepresented; those located within the central cities were not. This discrepancy was found both among persons who had completed high school and those who had not.

Participants also differed in their representation by region. Among both graduates and non-graduates of high school, rates of study were considerably higher among residents of Western states than among those in other regions.

In overview, then, one might compose the following social profile: The adult education participant is just as often a woman as a man, is typically under forty, has completed high school or more, enjoys an above-average income, works full-time and most often in a white-collar occupation, is married and has children, lives in an urbanized area but more likely in a suburb than a large city, and is found in all parts of the country, but more frequently in the West than in other regions.

9. *How do family responsibilities affect rates of learning activity?* (*Chap. 5*) — Only slight differences were found in the over-all rates of study of men and women: 21 per cent of men and 19 per cent of women had been active during the previous year, and although this difference is statistically significant, it certainly does not appear to have much practical significance. When rates of study were examined among men and women of different ages, however, some quite revealing differences emerged. We found that among persons under thirty-five, rates of study were substantially higher among men than women (33 per cent compared with 25 per cent), while older men and women had virtually identical rates of involvement in organized studies.

This result reflects the differential impact of family life on younger men and women. When we compared rates of study among young adults with and without children, we found substantial differences between young fathers and young mothers (34 and 23 per cent, respectively), but no differences at all between young men and women who did not have children (29 per cent each). Parenthood, in other words, appears to have exactly opposite effects on the educational behavior of young men and women; rates of study among mothers were lower than among non-mothers, but they were higher among fathers than non-fathers. Moreover, when we compared the subjects studied by fathers and non-fathers we discovered that the over-all difference could be attributed primarily to vocational learning—fathers were much more likely than non-fathers to take vocational courses. The best explanation for the general result, then, is that because men who have children also have increased financial responsibilities, they turn more frequently to adult education for knowledge and skills that will help them supplement their incomes.

10. *When and how do people first come to enroll in adult education courses?* (*Chaps. 6, 7, 19, and 20*)—When we interviewed our participants about this, we learned that initial contacts with adult education typically occur quite early in adult life. Two of three adults who had ever taken a course had done so before their thirtieth birthday, and seven of eight had done so before they were forty.

We also found, however, that men were more likely than women to have taken their first course during their twenties, while proportionately more women had done so both before twenty and after forty. This probably reflects two tendencies. First, since more girls than boys drop out of school before reaching twenty, the pool of teen-agers from which adult education recruits could be drawn would be disproportionately female. But second, since women who have families are less likely to take courses during their twenties and thirties, the proportionately higher rates of initial recruitment among women over forty probably reflects enrollment that would have taken place earlier had family responsibilities not intervened.

When we asked participants to tell us in their own words how they first came to enroll in an adult education course, a majority recalled some kind of occupational reason. First, about 33 per cent mentioned preparation for a new job: a first job after leaving school, a new job to replace one already held, or vocational training encountered either upon entry into or discharge from the armed forces. A second group of about 20 per cent mentioned additional training in a line of work they had already entered.

In addition, however, about 30 per cent of the participants talked about their initial recruitment to continuing education as a result of some interpersonal influence. Although these influences were recalled about equally often by men and women, more women mentioned family members or friends, while men were much more likely to attribute their initial enrollment to employers or co-workers. Thus, while other people could be said to play a quite significant role in the recruitment of both men and women to adult education, it appears that for women these influences come mainly from the primary social environment, while for men they are produced more often by secondary social contacts.

Finally, about one participant in ten recalled some change in family status which prompted his or her first ventures into continuing education. Family expansion and the lessening of family responsibilities were given as reasons about equally often.

The main things people remembered about how they first came to enroll in courses, then, were preparation for new jobs, advancement in present jobs, relationships with other people, and changes in the status or composition of their families.

Additional insights into the process of recruitment to continuing education emerged from our study of young people aged seventeen to twenty-four. We found, first, that a successful adjustment to high school (as measured by an index combining academic performance and involvement in student activities) was associated with rates of exposure to learning experiences over and above regular schooling. This association was stronger among young women than young men. It was also found, however, that school adjustment was related to the types of supplementary studies engaged in by young men; those who had done less well in high school were much more likely to concentrate their studies on blue-collar vocational skills.

We found, too, that experiences with supplementary learning were more common among young men with high mobility expectations. Interestingly, however, these young people, especially the mobile youngsters from high-status backgrounds, were not particularly inclined to use these studies for vocational training. When young men without high mobility goals became involved in extra-curricular studies, on the other hand, they were much more likely to take vocational courses, and, in particular, those giving training in blue-collar skills.

The supplementary learning activities of young women are also closely connected with career goals. We found that girls who were able to cite specific employment expectations were much more likely to become involved in the informal school system.

Finally, we found that rates of exposure to supplementary education were much higher among young persons relatively dissatisfied with their early employment experiences, and this was particularly true of dissatisfied workers from more modest social origins. For disadvantaged young persons, then, the main route to continuing education would appear to be a rocky one; they are much more likely to return to education when disappointing experiences in the world of work bring them to reappraise the adequacy of their education.

11. *Why do adults take courses?* (*Chap. 8*) — While job-centered reasons lead younger adults to take courses, the enrollment goals of older adults are much less pragmatic and utilitarian. We found that older adults were much less likely to have occupational goals in mind when they enrolled and much more likely to take courses simply for general knowledge.

The importance of leisure-centered goals was also seen to vary dramatically among persons of different ages. Among men, for example, just 10 per cent who took courses in their twenties had done so with spare-time interests in mind, as compared with 16 per cent in their thirties, 19 per cent in their forties, and 28 per cent of those fifty or over.

At all ages, more men were concerned with vocational goals while women enrolled relatively more often in response to home and family life and leisure-time interests. In addition, women were also more likely to take courses to expand their social horizons or to get away from the daily routine. Among participants under thirty, for example, the goal "meet new and interesting people" was named by 23 per cent of women compared with just 11 per cent of men; among those in their forties, 15 per cent of women compared with 4 per cent of men agreed they had enrolled to "get away from the daily routine." The results suggest that a fairly sizeable minority of women who take courses do so either to cultivate new social relationships or simply to escape.

People in different socio-economic positions were also found to have quite different reasons for taking courses. First, a relationship was discovered between socio-economic level and the types of vocational motives which led people to enroll in courses. Men and women from lower socio-economic positions were much more likely to take courses to prepare for jobs than to advance on them, while the opposite was true of participants from higher social positions.

A second difference was that spare-time interests were given more importance by participants from higher socio-economic positions. There were virtually no men at all from the lowest third of the socio-economic continuum who had enrolled in their most recent course for leisure-time enjoyment. Higher on the socio-economic ladder, however, the incidence of this goal increased from 6 to 12 to 18 per cent among men, and from 16 to 21 to 31 per cent among women. Among women from the upper two-thirds of the continuum, in fact, use of leisure was cited more frequently than either job preparation, job advancement, or homemaking goals.

The uses of adult education differ most markedly across the social class spectrum in that at lower levels people take courses chiefly to learn skills necessary to cope with everyday living, while at higher levels there is a shift away from learning for basic life adjustment and an accompanying increase of concern with less pressing needs, such as the enrichment of spare time.

12. *How much do people gain from the courses they take?* (*Chap. 8*) — People evidently gain quite a bit. When we asked participants how much they had benefited from the courses they had taken most recently, 63 per cent said "a great deal," 23 per cent said "some," and only 13 per cent said "not very much."

There are many more stringent criteria by which to evaluate the effectiveness of adult studies, of course; at the very minimum, one might ask whether courses help people satisfy the goals that led them to enroll in the first place. When our data were examined from this perspective, they indicated that adult education experiences are much more effective in satisfying some goals than others. We found that courses were most effective when people had enrolled to learn more about their jobs and least effective in preparing people to enter new jobs or occupations. Moreover, the discrepancy here was quite striking. As many as 90 per cent who took courses for purposes of job advancement agreed this was one of the ways in which the courses had actually helped them. On the other hand, just 57 per cent of those who had enrolled to "prepare for a new job or occupation" cited getting a new job as one of the positive consequences of having been enrolled.

13. *What factors are associated with the persistence of learning interest during adult life? (Chap. 9)* — Age and years of formal schooling were the characteristics most strongly related to whether or not a person manifested any interest at all in learning new things. Learning interest was found to decrease sharply with increasing age and to be significantly more prevalent among persons in higher educational brackets.

With regard to age, we found that the incidence of learning interest not only fell off continuously in each older age group, but that the rate of this decrease was an accelerating one. Up until the fifties, there was no appreciable drop-off; rates of interest were only 7 per cent lower among persons in their forties than among those in their twenties (76 and 83 per cent, respectively). By the fifties, however, the incidence had fallen to 65 per cent, and it then tumbled to 53 per cent and 35 per cent among persons in their sixties and seventies.

The effect of education on learning interest was equally dramatic. Among those with less than five years of schooling, only 43 per cent could think of something they wanted to learn more about as compared with 87 per cent among those who had attended school for sixteen years or more.

Next, we looked at rates of learning interest in relation both to a person's own educational attainment and to that of his parents. Some quite interesting results emerged from this analysis. We found that regardless of whether or not a person had gone very far in school himself, the fact that his father or mother had done so increased the likelihood of his being favorably disposed toward learning as an adult. At the same time, however, the effect of one's own schooling was found to be approximately twice as powerful as the influence of having well-educated parents.

Two unanticipated secondary findings also emerged from this section of the analysis. We found that parental influences on learning interest were somewhat stronger on sons than on daughters and that the influence of mothers was more powerful than that of fathers. Moreover, when relationships were examined individually, it turned out that the influence of the mother's education on sons was slightly stronger than that of the son's own education.

When we looked more carefully at the impact of aging on learning interest, we found that in the later decades of adult life favorable attitudes toward learning were closely associated with a number of other dispositional states. Among men, particularly among older and less well-educated respondents, learning interest was strongly related to whether or not the the occupational future looked promising. Perceptions of future economic prospects were also tied in closely with a readiness to learn, people who were optimistic in this regard being also more likely to want to learn new things. This was again especially true of older adults who had not gone very far in school. Finally, an interest in learning was also related to expectations concerning residential mobility, those expecting to move in the near future being more likely to manifest an interest in learning.

Together, these results suggested that favorable dispositions toward learning among adults—and particularly among older adults—are part of a much wider psychological outlook having to do with optimism about the future and general readiness to accept change.

14. *How large is the potential audience for programs of adult learning? (Chap. 10)*—We approached this question by considering a potential participant as someone manifesting two fundamental dispositions: an interest in knowing more about something and a readiness to engage in systematic study in order to satisfy his interest. This notion, in turn, led us to conceive of the

total population as containing three aggregates of individuals: those both interested in learning and favorably disposed toward taking courses, those interested in learning but not prepared to take courses, and those uninterested in learning anything new at all. Of the total sample interviewed, 44 per cent showed favorable dispositions of both types, 26 per cent identified something they wanted to know more about but showed no readiness to take courses, and 29 per cent were unable to think of anything at all they wanted to know more about. As a very rough approximation, then, we concluded that as many as seven adults in ten may have interests that could conceivably lead them into some type of learning situation, but that less than one-half of the population could be seriously regarded as potential adult education participants.

15. *What types of people think about taking courses? (Chap. 10)* — As expected, younger and better-educated persons were the ones most likely to consider the possibility of taking courses to satisfy their learning interests. In addition, however, women were more likely to do so than men, and when we followed up on this we found that even though men and women were about equally well disposed toward learning per se, women very definitely had more favorable attitudes than men toward the idea of taking courses. Paradoxically, fewer women than men actually did end up taking courses, but this tendency can probably be explained by the fact that men have more opportunities and are relatively freer to do so when the opportunity arises.

There is also a fairly widespread impression that classes are attended primarily by women. For most adults, in fact, the idea of "adult education classes" implies feminine rather than masculine behavior. It is difficult to say what effect this has on the motivation of men (or women) to enroll in courses, but if participation is indeed defined as a feminine thing to do, then we would suspect that considerably more men than women would say "adult education classes are not for me." It was revealing, in any event, that significantly fewer men than women agreed that participation in an adult education class would be an interesting thing to do.

16. *How much do adults know about the educational facili-*

ties available to them? (*Chaps. 10 and 16*)—In the national survey, 55 per cent said they knew of at least one place where adults in their community could go to receive instruction, 33 per cent did not know whether or not such resources were available, and 12 per cent said there were no such places.

Our main findings on this question, however, emerged from the third phase of the study, when adults in two middle-sized cities were interviewed on their awareness of educational facilities after information had been collected on the actual resources available. Our findings here indicated, first, that public awareness of facilities varies quite markedly with the type of subject matter under consideration. Large majorities of adults in both communities knew of facilities for learning skills such as swimming, dancing, or typing, but considerably fewer than half knew of places to study auto mechanics, speed reading, or more esoteric subject matter such as comparative religion.

Second, it was quite evident that knowledge about such resources is unequally distributed throughout the adult public. Persons who had been to school longer were much more knowledgeable about local facilities than those with less education; although these discrepancies were widest in subject fields of little interest to persons without much schooling, they were sharply evident, too, in fields of genuine interest and relevance to the lower- and lower-middle-class adult.

Third, evidence was also found which indicated that when the very same instructional courses are offered in different institutional settings they come to the attention of quite different segments of the population. We found that people without much education were much more likely to know about courses in secondary schools than about similar instruction elsewhere in the community.

Finally, a kind of informational halo effect appeared to surround the most active institution in each city. In cases where instruction in a given subject (such as typing or shorthand) was available in a number of places, adults were much more likely to know about the instruction offered at the largest institution in the community than about identical courses offered in less prominent settings.

17. *What obstacles prevent adults from taking courses?* (*Chap. 10*) — The barriers to participation most frequently cited by persons classified as members of the "potential audience" were financial (43 per cent), busy schedules (39 per cent), and a lack of sufficient physical energy at the end of the day (37 per cent).

On the whole, women identified more obstacles to enrollment than men, older adults identified more than younger adults, and persons in lower socio-economic positions mentioned many more than those in higher positions. However, there were also differences in the types of barriers identified by persons in these different categories. Many more women than men, for example, said they would find it difficult to get away from home in the evening, and women were also somewhat more likely to say they lacked the energy to take courses. Financial constraints were cited more frequently by younger adults than older, but older persons were much more likely to feel certain personal qualms about taking courses; for example, they were much more likely to feel "too old to learn" or that it would be "childish" to enroll in courses. Interestingly, however, we discovered that these two latter reactions were confined almost exclusively to persons of lower socio-economic background.

Finally, it was significant that large majorities of potential participants from lower socio-economic backgrounds said lack of money prevented their enrollment in courses.

18. *How plentiful are adult education facilities today?* (*Chaps. 10, 14, and 15*) — Resources for the instruction of adults were quite abundant in the four cities that we studied in detail. We found that vocational courses were especially plentiful, although in all four cities considerably more places offered instruction in white-collar than in blue-collar occupational skills. We found too that educational facilities for adults were distributed widely throughout the institutional structure of these communities, with government agencies, proprietary schools, and private businesses playing a highly active role along with the local secondary schools and colleges.

To illustrate the variety of instructional settings in these centers, we shall summarize briefly the resources in the two largest cities we studied. The main difference between these two cities was that one had an extensive secondary-school adult education program and the other an equally extensive program in the evening college of the local university. It was this difference, in fact, which prompted us to address our primary attention to these two cities.

Outside of courses offered in the regular school system, we found almost identical resources in these two communities. With respect to proprietary schools, for example, each city contained one large electronics college, one or two colleges of business and commerce, and numerous dancing, music, and hairdressing schools. Agencies representing all levels of government (federal, state, and municipal) provided in-service training courses for their employees, and the state and local agencies also offered courses to members of the general public in such fields as homemaking, nursing, first aid, civil defense, arts and crafts, driver training, and soil conservation. The instructional programs of private businesses, by comparison, were confined exclusively to employee training. We found, in addition, that company training programs were much more prevalent in large companies than in small ones, and that this was also true of tuition reimbursement programs for employees.

The YMCA's in both cities were also active in providing courses for adults; interestingly, in both cities these courses were concentrated in the same three fields: swimming, dancing, and contract bridge. We found, too, that a majority of the churches in each city provided religious instruction for adults, but that only about one in ten sponsored programs in other fields of learning. Hospitals and medical centers were relatively inactive, although they did provide in-service training for medical technicians and hospital service workers and on occasion sponsored courses in practical nursing for members of the general public. No programs of instruction were found in the public libraries in these cities; one of the cities, however, did house a fairly large municipal art center.

Finally, we discovered that the instructional offerings of voluntary organizations and associations were particularly sparse in these communities. Although many groups scheduled speakers or lecturers for their meetings, very few programs had sufficient continuity to be meaningfully classified as formal instruction. During the period of our inventory, just 12 per cent of the organizations in one city and 7 per cent in the other had sponsored or conducted programs which satisfied even the minimal criteria for classification as instructional activities.

19. *To what extent do the educational facilities available in a community influence the educative behavior of adults? (Chap. 16)* — Our results indicated that when educational facilities are more plentiful and accessible, more adults use them. We also found, however, that the nature of the educational resources in a community has very little effect on people's general readiness to take courses. When instructional facilities are more plentiful, then, there appears to be a deeper penetration into what we have termed the "potential audience" for programs of adult instruction: that aggregate of adults with a previously developed readiness to engage in formal learning pursuits as a means of acquiring new knowledge, information, or skills. The institutional environment appears to be influential in bringing persons of this type into structured learning situations, but it appears to have almost no effect at all in arousing interests among adults who never had them in the first place.

20. *What is the outlook for adult education in the future?* — The most important conclusion to be derived from this study is that America is likely to experience an adult education explosion during the next few decades. The typical adult student today is young, urban, and fairly well-educated, and this is exactly the type of person who will be around in greatly increased numbers in the very near future. While the population as a whole will grow by about 33 per cent over the next two decades, the increase in the number of adults under thirty-five will be much greater than this, probably close to 70 per cent. In place of a pool of some 33 million "young" adults in 1962, there will be some 57 million by 1982.

The changes which will occur in the educational composition of the population will also have a powerful effect on adult education. Even very conservative projections[1] suggest that within two decades the population will contain as many as 64 per cent more adults who have been to college, 59 per cent more who have attended high school, and by contrast, some 15 per cent fewer with only a grade-school education.

All in all, then, the changes which will occur in the composition of the American population over the next two decades are all changes which will work substantially to increase the categories from which adult education participants emerge most frequently today. It should be abundantly clear, then, that the potential audience for adult education is increasing at a much faster rate than the population as a whole. Just as in the fifties and sixties the regular school system had to tool up rapidly to accommodate the greatly increased numbers of young persons in the population, so too in the seventies and eighties adult education will be subject to greatly increased demands as this group moves into the social categories where greatest uses are made of adult education. Moreover, the prospects for increased numbers of older participants are also very good. More persons aged fifty, sixty, and seventy will engage in educational pursuits twenty years from now because at that time the average educational attainment of people in these brackets will be considerably higher than it is today. Population projections again suggest that by the early eighties there will be nearly three million fewer persons aged fifty-five or over with only a grade-school education, and close to four million more who have been college educated.

What will our future adults want to study? There is no meaningful way in which to answer this question precisely, but if the increased amounts of leisure time which have been heralded actually do come to characterize American life in the future, we

[1]These estimates are based on the following assumptions: (*a*) that persons under thirty-five in 1982 will have the same levels of educational attainment as persons under thirty-five today; (*b*) that adults who are now twenty-five or older will not increase their formal educational attainment in the next twenty years; and (*c*) that only one-quarter of those now fifty-five or above will still be alive in 1982. In view of these assumptions, the projections will tend to be on the conservative side. The authors are indebted to Seymour Sudman for valuable assistance in the derivation of these figures.

can expect considerable increase in the use of adult education for recreation. On the other hand, the trend toward even greater specialization of occupational skills in our society shows no prospect of reversal. It seems likely, therefore, that learning-for-work and learning-for-leisure will together come to dominate the adult education scene to an even greater extent than they do today.

By far the most persistent finding in our investigation was that formal educational attainment plays a highly crucial role in determining whether or not one enters the ranks of adult students. Better educated adults were found not only to be more active in learning pursuits, but also to be more interested in learning per se, more ready to turn to formal instruction to satisfy interests, and much more knowledgeable about the existence of resources for continuing education. Adult education today does not cater primarily to those who are trying to complete an unfinished formal education; only a small fraction of those who take courses do so to receive formal credit for their studies. In this sense, the field cannot be said to play a primarily remedial or rehabilitative role on the American educational scene today. Most people who turn to adult education have at least average, and in many cases above-average educational credentials. Because it is much more than remedial education, adult learning in America today can be better characterized as "continuing education" — continuing in the sense of applying systematic learning processes to the particular demands and interests of adult life rather than in the sense of extending a formal education.

Continuing education is quite clearly a middle- and upper-middle-class phenomenon in our society. There are very few continuing learners in our lower classes. Part of this tendency can be explained by the fact that learning and education are perceived and evaluated in radically different ways by persons on different rungs of the social ladder. Lower-class adults not only value high educational attainment less, but they assess the worth of education strictly in terms of the tangible advantages which can be gained from having it. They see little value in obtaining knowledge for its own sake. Our findings of the existence of distinct middle-class and lower-class orientations to education are hardly revolutionary, of course, but they have extremely important implications for adult education today. One consequence of the fact that the lower-class adult does not conceive of education in terms of personal growth or self-realization, for example, is that he is much less ready to turn to continuing education for recreational learning than for vocational learning. Lower-class adults realize fully that education can lead to employment opportunities and job security but education is in no sense defined as pleasurable. Indeed, for the typical lower-class adult, the concepts of "learning" and "spare-time enjoyment" convey quite opposite meanings.

Yet at the same time, there is a reasonably strong case for the contention that the lower classes in our society could benefit the most from instruction for use of leisure. What little objective evidence there is indicates that lower-class adults now have as much spare time as persons in higher social positions, but in our study we found that they also have greater difficulty in finding things to do with it and are considerably less enthusiastic about the prospects of having more (Chap. 12). The paradox is that the segment of the population which may realize the greatest increment of free time in an age of automation is, on the one hand, the least well-prepared to handle it, and on the other, the least likely to turn to continuing education to develop and expand its spare-time interests. And it is this, perhaps, that constitutes the most critical challenge to the adult educators of the future.

Part I

The Educational Experiences of American Adults: June 1961 — June 1962

Introduction
to
Part I

The first section of this report deals with the educational activities of American adults over a one-year period. The section begins, in Chapter 2, with a discussion of the general problem of trying to isolate and define the concept of an "educational activity" and proceeds to the working definitions and operational measures used in the present study.

Chapter 3 introduces the first results of the study and presents a lengthy description of national patterns of participation in continuing education. National estimates are made of the number of adults who engaged in educational pursuits during the previous year, and the main concern of the chapter is the identification of the types of subject matter which adults study either with instruction or independently. Estimates are also made of the total number of courses studied over the year, of the duration of people's learning efforts, the study methods employed, the different institutions they turned to for instruction, and the enrollment status (credit or non-credit) of their studies.

Following this, Chapter 4 turns to the question of who engages in these pursuits. The adults who were active during the previous year are compared with the total adult population in terms of a number of different background characteristics: age, sex, years of formal schooling, family income, labor force status and occupation, race, religion, and geographic location.

Chapter 5 concludes the first section of the monograph. In this chapter statistical controls are used to isolate the background factors most strongly associated with participation in continuing education. These factors are of two main types: those related to life-cycle position and those reflecting position in the socio-economic hierarchy.

2
Concepts, Definitions, and Measures

THE DEFINITION OF AN EDUCATIONAL ACTIVITY

In initiating this inquiry the first issue which had to be settled was which activities were to be considered educational — what to include and to exclude from a national inventory of educational activities.

This question soon proved one for which there was no clear-cut or widely accepted answer, but it was quite apparent that the scope of the investigation was going to vary radically depending on how this question was resolved. The main problem was to avoid both a too narrow and a too broad conceptualization of an educational activity. At the one extreme it was tempting to equate educational activities with pursuits carried on in formal institutions of learning, but it was also obvious that this type of formal restriction was exactly what we did not want, since it excludes some of the most typical situations in which adults do encounter such learning experiences as on-the-job training or lessons with private instructors. Indeed, the whole institutional approach to the development of a definition was out of keeping with the spirit of a behavioral inventory of adult learning.

At the other extreme, of course, it was possible to formulate a definition strictly on the basis of the formal characteristics of an activity itself, or in terms of the consequences of an activity for the individual. While this strategy had more intrinsic appeal, the overwhelming problem here was that there was virtually no way

to exclude from consideration a host of activities whose consequences would certainly be educational (such as a visit to an
aquarium) yet which clearly would fall beyond the range of any
reasonable or workable definition of adult education.

The approach finally adopted, however, was closer to the
behavioral than the institutional formulation. It was based on
two considerations: the basic purpose of an activity and the
nature of its organization. The first criterion was that we would
restrict the study to activities in which the main purpose was to
acquire some type of knowledge, information, or skill. Activities
with central functions more closely akin to recreation, fellow-
ship, or remuneration were not to be included in the inventory
even though they might have as by-products the acquisition of
knowledge, information, or skill.

This criterion, then, allowed us to focus on the rationale of the
activity itself rather than on the motives of the people who
engaged in it. Thus "Bible class" or "Sunday school classes"
were defined as educational since their main function is to teach
about a religion; but "going to church" was not, on the grounds
that its main purpose is worship. Similarly, "golf lessons" are
educational, whereas "playing golf" is not.

The second criterion was that an activity had to be organized
around some form of instruction. No restrictions were made as to
the form the instruction could take, however. Whether it was
received through classes, lecture series, discussion groups, private lessons, workshops, seminars, conferences, correspondence
lessons, educational television programs, or on-the-job training,
an activity was counted in the inventory as long as its central
purpose was to impart some sort of knowledge, information, or
skill.

Finally, we felt it was important not to exclude certain types
of self-instruction from the study, especially in the light of recent
innovations in teaching machines and other home-study techniques. Accordingly, independent self-instruction was also
examined in all situations where an individual consciously and
systematically organized a program of study for himself and
followed it for a period of not less than one month. Thus persons
teaching themselves a foreign language by tapes or recordings,

or a musical instrument through home-study courses, were also counted in the inventory. General reading and other forms of casual information intake were by the same token excluded, except in cases where a person might claim that the reading was part of an organized program of study on some subject.

Together, these criteria cover a wide range of behavior. Indeed, the definitional boundaries adopted in this study are perhaps wider than most uses of the term "adult education" suggest, and they are considerably wider than those adopted in the Office of Education's survey of adult education (U.S. Department of Health, Education and Welfare, 1959). In that study only activities experienced within the context of "adult education classes or group meetings" were enumerated. All correspondence studies, on-the-job training, private lessons, television courses, and other home-study activities were explicitly excluded from the study. For this reason as well as other methodological considerations the results of our present study can be compared only conditionally with those of the Office of Education survey.

OPERATIONAL MEASURES

Three types of educational involvement were measured in the present study: involvement as a full-time student, as a participant in adult education activities, and as a participant in independent self-education. Since separate measures were employed to enumerate activities in each of these categories, the statuses are not mutually exclusive; indeed a number of persons were located who were active within two different educational categories, and a few who were classified as active within all three categories.

The status of full-time students

The identification of full-time students in the study was based on the responses provided by household informants to the following question:

[Question 6] Are there any adult members of this household who were enrolled in some type of school or college as full-time students this past school year—that is, since last September? (IF YES: Who?)

Although ultimate classification thus rested on respondent identification, in situations of ambiguity interviewers were instructed to define full-time students as persons who carried the full load of courses normally required by the program of studies in which they were enrolled. In most cases, but not necessarily in all, this covered persons enrolled in courses leading to some sort of degree, certificate, or diploma in a college, university, high school, trade school, or business school. It was also possible within the definition, however, to be a full-time student in non-credit courses offered by other sponsoring institutions, such as industry or the armed forces.

Interviewers were also instructed to disregard labor-force status when deciding whether or not an adult was a full-time student. There was no guarantee that this separation was always clear in the mind of the respondent, of course, and a few cases were discovered in which persons carrying a full load of college courses were not classified as full-time students by the household informants, presumably because these persons also held full-time jobs. For this reason persons reported during the previous year as having taken more than three adult education courses for credit toward some sort of degree, certificate, or diploma in a high school or college were reclassified as full-time students. In addition, hospital interns or residents who reported courses relating to a medical specialty were also reclassified into this category.

In spite of the relative lack of ambiguity surrounding this category, there are a number of ways in which the status measured here differs from the Bureau of the Census concept of school enrollment in its 1961 report (U.S. Department of Commerce, Bureau of the Census, 1962*a*). In census usage, school enrollment statistics are based on the numbers of persons enrolled in "any type of graded public, parochial, or other private school in the regular school system." Thus while persons attending trade schools or business colleges could not be classified by the census as enrolled in school, they could be included as full-time students in the present study. Furthermore, the Census Bureau's enrollment figures include persons attending school on either a full-time or part-time basis. The classification of full-time students in the present study quite clearly omits the latter.

Participation in adult education activities

Adult education activities were enumerated in the following way: first, the informant was handed a flash card listing ten general categories of subject matter with representative topics in seven of these categories. The purpose of this card was to aid recall and to provide the respondent with a clear understanding of the range of learning experiences being measured in the survey. At the same time, the following question was asked:

[QUESTION 7] Here is a list of subjects and skills that people sometimes study after they have left school. Would you please read this over and tell me whether during the past twelve months any adult member of the household has received instruction in any of these things — or in any other subjects or skills not listed here? Please include evening classes, correspondence courses, private lessons, lecture series, courses given over television — or anything else like that. How about yourself? (How about _____?)

While this complete question was normally asked just once at each household, a specific probe was asked for each adult so that interviewers could obtain a "yes" or "no" answer for each adult in the household.

When an adult education activity was reported, it was recorded in two ways; first, the specific name of the subject was entered, and second, with the aid of the respondent, the interviewer recorded the flash-card category into which the subject best fitted. All subjects reported were recorded in this same way. When the same individual had studied more than one subject during the previous year, the additional subjects were listed in a special recording space at the back of the interview form.

In this way, a single measure was developed to screen all adult education subjects which involved instruction, all adults in each selected household, and all subjects studied by a given individual.

Once a subject had been properly identified, information was collected concerning the method of study employed, the sponsorship of the instruction (providing it was received through attendance at classes, discussion groups, talks, or lectures), the duration of the studies, and the credit status of the studies.

Independent self-education

Information on activities carried out independently, without an instructor, was collected by asking the following question:

[QUESTION 8] During the past twelve months, has any adult living here been engaged in learning some new subject or skill by means of independent study strictly on his or her own? How about yourself? (How about _____?)

Here again, the interviewer used a probe question to extract specific coverage for each adult member of the household. No more than two self-taught subjects were recorded for any one individual, however.

Courses involving instruction and self-taught courses were differentiated by whether or not the activity involved any form of relationship between student and teacher. In general, wherever any kind of teacher-student relationship existed, even if it was only rudimentary (as in the case of correspondence lessons), the activity was classified as involving instruction. There are a number of marginal situations here, of course; the two most ambiguous are probably educational television courses and instruction by recordings or tapes. It was between these two types of educational activity, in fact, that the threshold between the presence and absence of a teacher-student relationship was considered to lie. In the case of educational television, we felt that even though in most cases the direction of communication would be one way only, at least the possibility usually existed for the student to make some contact with the instructor if he so desired. On television, instructors are usually identified by name and whereabouts. In instruction by recordings, on the other hand, we felt that even the possibility of communication between student and teacher would in most cases be nonexistent.

In any event, all home-study methods involving actual or potential contact between the student and the teacher were classified with those involving instruction. And all those involving no actual contact, or considered to have little or no possibility of any such contact, were classified under independent self-education.

Definition of sampling universe

Throughout this section the discussion is restricted to the adult population of the United States, an adult being defined as anyone either twenty-one or over, or married, or the head of a household. Although our sampling universe was formally defined as the non-institutionalized adult population, an attempt was also made to include armed forces personnel in the survey in order to include any educational activities experienced within that context. Householders were asked to provide data about any members of the household who, at the time of the interview, were living in armed forces bases, camps, or barracks. In effect, then, the survey covered all servicemen who were reported as members of a household.[1] While there is no way of knowing precisely which categories of personnel this procedure picks up and excludes, it probably results in better coverage of younger short-term servicemen than of older career soldiers, since more of the younger men could be expected to be reported as children or husbands. The younger members of the armed forces, of course, are most likely to be involved in the various vocational training programs which are available in the services. Informants were also asked to provide information on any member of the household who at the time of the survey was living in a school residence or dormitory.

In review, then, the estimates made in this chapter are based on a definition of the non-institutionalized adult population, which includes the following aggregates: (*1*) all householders twenty-one years of age or over; or (*2*) under twenty-one but married; or (*3*) under twenty-one but the head of a household; plus (*4*) all persons twenty-one or over who live on an armed

[1] In order to avoid the problem of having some persons reported as members of more than one household, informants were instructed to give information only on those out-of-residence household members whose closest family ties were with members of that household.

forces base and have close family ties with some adult member of an American household; and (5) anyone twenty-one or over and living in a school residence or dormitory and closely related to some household member.

Our estimate of this population as of June 1, 1962, was 114 million persons, and accordingly, all projections made in this section are made to that figure.

With the operational measures thus described, we now turn to the results of the study. The following chapter examines the activity patterns of the total sample on the types of behavior identified in this chapter.

3

Adult
Participation
in Educational
Activities

In this chapter the chief findings of our national inventory of educational activities are presented, and from them projections are made of the number of American adults who were active in various categories of educational involvement between June, 1961, and June, 1962. The chapter first assesses membership in the three types of educational groups discussed in Chapter 2 and then proceeds to a more detailed consideration of the types of subjects studied, the methods of study, the sponsorship of classes, and finally the number of persons who studied for various types of credit.

NUMBERS OF PERSONS IN THE BASIC EDUCATIONAL CATEGORIES

The overall response patterns to the questions measuring the educational status of full-time students, adult education participants, and self-education students and their translations into population projections are shown in Tables 3.1 through 3.4 and 3.6. Tables 3.1, 3.2, and 3.3 show that 2.3 per cent are full-time students, 15 per cent are adult education participants, and 7.9 per cent are in independent studies. When projected to the total population in Table 3.4, these proportions resolve into estimates of 2,650,000 full-time students, 17,160,000 adult education participants, and 8,960,000 persons engaged in self-education.[1]

[1]Table A-1.1 in Appendix 1 provides a set of standard errors which can be applied to these and other estimates made in this chapter.

Table 3.1   Number of Full-Time Students in Sample

Status	Number	Per Cent
Full-time students	549	2.3
Not full-time students	23,105	97.7
Total	23,654	100.0
No information	296	
Total adults	23,950	

Table 3.2   Participation in Adult Education Courses Involving Instruction of Any Type

Status	Number	Per Cent
Participated	3,534	15.0
Did not participate	19,953	85.0
Total	23,487	100.0
No information	463	
Total adults	23,950	

Table 3.3   Participation in Independent Studies of Any Type

Status	Number	Per Cent
Engaged in independent studies	1,808	7.9
Did not engage in independent studies	21,181	92.1
Total	22,989	100.0
No information	961	
Total adults	23,950	

Table 3.4   Estimated Number of Adults Active in Different Educational Categories*

Type of Educational Activity	Estimated Number†
Enrolled in adult education courses (June, 1961, to June, 1962)	17,160,000
Engaged in independent self-education (June, 1961, to June, 1962)	8,960,000
Enrolled as full-time students (September, 1961, to June, 1962)	2,650,000

*At any time during specified periods.
†Based on an estimated total adult population of 114 million persons as of June 1, 1962, and rounded to the nearest 10,000.

Full-time students

Some of the problems involved in comparing the NORC estimate of full-time students with census statistics on school enrollment were outlined in Chapter 2. In spite of these difficulties, it is worthwhile to attempt at least an approximate comparison between these two sources of figures, if only to test the reliability of our present sample by comparing its results with the results of a much larger survey, based on a sample of 35,000 households.

The most relevant figures for this comparison are those in the October, 1961, report on school enrollment, issued by the Bureau of the Census (U.S. Department of Commerce, Bureau of the Census, 1962*a*, p. 7). There, for the civilian non-insitutionalized population in the twenty — thirty-four age group, a total of 2,154,000 persons were estimated as enrolled in school. To make a meaningful comparison between this estimate and the results of the present survey, however, it was necessary to introduce the following changes in the composition of our category of full-time student: (*1*) We added all persons reported enrolled for credit in high school, college, or university on a part-time basis. (*2*) We omitted all persons enrolled as full-time students in trade schools, business schools, and other institutions outside the regular school system. (*3*) We dropped all persons not between the ages of twenty and thirty-four. (*4*) We added all unmarried youth aged twenty who were enrolled either as full-time or part-time students in high schools, colleges, or universities. (*5*) Finally, we omitted from our category any full-time students living on an armed forces base.

Even with these adjustments, the two measures still do not designate identical phenomena since the census figures focus on school enrollment at a specific point in time (October, 1961), while the NORC measure covers persons enrolled in school at any time between September, 1961, and June, 1962. Nonetheless, the figures are much more closely comparable with the adjustments made in Table 3.5. It is obvious that when reduced to comparable bases, the two measures agree closely. What differences remain show the NORC estimates to be slightly higher, but these discrepancies could very easily reflect the longer time period covered in the NORC measure of enrollment.

Participation in adult education activities

The estimate that 17,160,000 persons received some kind of part-time instruction between June, 1961, and June, 1962, is an extremely impressive figure, and indicates that in a study of the educational pursuits of American adults we are by no means dealing with rare phenomena. The estimate is nearly twice that of the Department of Health, Education and Welfare (HEW) figure of 9,212,000 active participants (U.S. Department of Health, Education and Welfare, 1959), although direct comparisons between these two groups of figures are probably more misleading than illuminating. While some of this discrepancy might reflect a genuine increase in the incidence of these activities over the five-year interval in question, most of it would be a function of the radically different ways in which educational activities were defined in the two studies. For example, these definitions differed on at least the following points: (*1*) As noted earlier, the NORC study covered many more forms of activity than did the HEW survey. All on-the-job training, correspondence studies, educational television courses, and lessons from private teachers and tutors were omitted from the earlier study. (*2*) The NORC estimate includes part-time credit courses taken within the regular school system, whereas the HEW figure omits these. (*3*) The NORC figure covers religious study; the HEW estimate does not. (*4*) The NORC figure includes some persons who were enrolled in courses for just one or two sessions. In the HEW survey, all activities attended for fewer than three sessions were excluded. (*5*) Finally, the NORC estimate covers adults only (in the main persons aged twenty-one and over) while the

Table 3.5 Estimates of School Enrollment

Source of Information	Age		
	20 – 24	25 – 29	30 – 34
Bureau of the Census: per cent enrolled in school, October, 1961	13.7	4.4	2.0
NORC: per cent enrolled in school, September, 1961 – June, 1962	14.6	5.6	2.4

HEW estimate is based on all persons aged fourteen to thirty-four not regularly enrolled in school, plus everyone thirty-five years of age and above.

It should be clear, then, that any real changes which may have occurred in the incidence of participation over the years 1957–62 would be completely obscured by these discrepancies in measurement. Because these differences are fundamental, moreover, it makes little sense to try to reconstruct our present category in order to make it comparable to the 1957 measure. One should simply note that all these differences, except possibly the last, work in the direction of increasing the relative size of the NORC figure.

Participation in self-education

Perhaps the most surprising of the three figures is the estimate of close to nine million persons who were active in independent studies. To the author's knowledge, this type of measure has never before been extracted from a national sample of the population—which in itself suggests that self-instruction is probably the most overlooked avenue of activity in the whole field of adult education. Even in the present study, these activities were from the beginning regarded as a residual category of adult studies, and for this reason no additional information was collected concerning the learning materials and methods employed. In a later section of this chapter, however, information is presented on the types of subject matter studied in this manner. About the only comment that can be made at this point is that the incidence of self-education throughout the adult population is much greater than we had anticipated.

Overlapping statuses

Table 3.6 completes our introductory examination of rates of participation by presenting estimates of the number of adults active in various combinations of the three categories. This table also gives two summary estimates, which indicate that close to 25 million adult Americans (more than one in five) were active within some educational category between June, 1961, and June, 1962, and that over 23 million were active other than as full-time students. These numbers are roughly equivalent to the total number of paid attendances at major league baseball games during a season,[2] represent about one-third the number of persons who voted in the 1960 presidential election,[3] and constitute considerably more Americans than have their teeth cleaned by a dentist over the period of a year.[4] Moreover, the number of different adults active in some type of educational pursuit in a one-year period is over one-half as large as the total number of persons under twenty who are enrolled in school in a year.[5] The numbers, in short, are substantial and would merit attention in any complete study of American education.

[2]The total paid attendances at major league baseball games during 1960, including the World Series games, was 20,261,000 (U.S. Department of Commerce, 1962, p. 206).

[3]Some 68,836,000 votes were cast for Presidential nominees in the 1960 election (U.S. Department of Commerce, 1962, p. 361).

[4]Between July, 1957, and June, 1958, adult Americans made a total of 17.7 million visits to dentists during which a teeth-cleaning was performed (U.S. Department of Health, Education and Welfare, 1958, p. 34).

[5]A total of 44,118,000 persons between the ages of five and twenty were enrolled in school in 1960 (U.S. Department of Commerce, 1961, p. 105).

Table 3.6 Estimated Number of Adults Active in Different Combinations of Educational Experience

Type of Educational Experience			Estimated Number of Persons*
Full-Time Students	Adult Education Students	Independent Studies	
yes	yes	yes	140,000
yes	yes	no	450,000
yes	no	yes	270,000
yes	no	no	1,790,000
no	yes	yes	2,960,000
no	yes	no	13,610,000
no	no	yes	5,590,000

Number of different adults active in any educational category	24,810,000
Number of different adults active either in adult education courses or in independent self-education	23,020,000

*Based on an estimated total adult population of 114 million persons as of June 1, 1962, and rounded to the nearest 10,000.

TOTAL COURSES REPORTED

All courses which involved instruction were recorded in the inventory, and Table 3.7 shows that a considerable number of persons did report more than one course for the year. The largest number of courses studied by any one part-time student was six, and a simple calculation reveals that close to one-quarter (23 per cent) of those who received instruction at all received it in more than one subject. From these data, then, it is possible by means of direct projection to arrive at an estimate of 22,650,000 total course enrollments over the period measured.

In regard to independent studies, only two different subjects

Table 3.7   Estimates of Total Adult Education Courses Studied

a. Courses in Which Instruction Was Received

Number of Courses Reported	Number of Persons	Number of Courses
One	2,715	2,715
Two	602	1,204
Three	151	453
Four	39	156
Five	20	100
Six	7	42
Total	3,534	4,670

Estimate of total courses in which
instruction was received   22,650,000*

b. Self-Education Courses

Number of Courses Reported	Number of Persons	Number of Courses
One	1,392	1,392
Two	416	832
Total	1,808	2,224

Estimate of total self-education
courses studied   11,020,000†

Estimate of total courses studied
by all methods   33,670,000

*An average of 1.32 courses studied by an estimated 17,160,000 persons, and rounded to the nearest 10,000.
†An average of 1.23 courses studied by an estimated 8,960,000 persons, and rounded to the nearest 10,000.

were recorded for any one person, although undoubtedly some people studied more courses than this on their own. A close examination of the figures in Table 3.7*b* shows that 23 per cent (416 of 1,808) of those active at all in self-education studied more than one subject. In view of this similarity to the results from Table 3.7*a*, it is not unlikely that a complete enumeration of independent studies would have uncovered a distribution of multiple activities very much the same as that found for courses involving instruction. However, a complete enumeration was not made, and therefore it is possible to estimate only that a minimum of about 11 million courses were studied through self-instruction.

Not counting the regular school work of full-time students, then, Table 3.7 estimates the total number of educational courses studied between June, 1961, and June, 1962, at 33,-670,000.

DURATION OF STUDIES

For each activity involving some form of instruction, information was collected either on the number of sessions attended or the number of weeks of study, depending on which method of study was employed. This information was not collected for self-instructed subjects, although interviewers had been told not to record them where it was clear that the period of study had been less than one month.

The data on duration of study are summarized in Table 3.8, where we note immediately that nine courses in ten involved studies of not less than four weeks or four sessions. It is not clear from these figures whether courses which were studied for shorter periods than this were bona fide short courses, seminars, or workshops lasting only from one to three sessions or weeks, or whether these were situations where participants dropped out soon after starting. In any event, neither of these conditions could account for more than 10 per cent of all activities, and the much more important finding is that a vast majority of the courses involved enough continuity to be meaningfully labeled as "courses of study." Of the estimated 22,650,000 total course enrollments, probably about 20,400,000 were of at least one month's duration.

TYPES OF SUBJECT MATTER STUDIED

Clearly the most relevant estimates in the study are those pertaining to the types of subjects studied. We shall, therefore, deal with these at some length.

At the time subjects were reported, two recording procedures were employed: first, the name of the course was entered, and then it was classified by the respondent into one of the subject categories on the flash card (see Appendix 2). The reason for having respondents themselves classify subjects was that some of the categories reflected the function of an activity for the participant and not simply the substantive content of the course. Thus it was not always possible for an independent observer to make a valid classification on the basis of the course titles alone. For example, it is not at all clear whether a subject such as "radio technology" should be grouped with vocational subjects or with hobbies and recreations. In this case only the respondent himself can decide, making it absolutely essential that the respondent rather than the analyst make the initial classification.

Table 3.8 Duration of Studies in Courses Involving Instruction

Duration of Studies	Number of Courses	Per Cent
One session only, or one week or less	135	3.3
Two sessions only, or two weeks or less	125	3.1
Three sessions, or not more than three weeks	142	3.5
Four or more sessions, or one month or more	3,649	90.1
Total	4,051	100.0
Information not given	619	
Total reported courses in which instruction was received	4,670	
Estimated number of courses involving outside instruction which were studied for a minimum of four sessions or four weeks	20,410,000*	

*90.1 per cent of an estimated 22,650,000 courses in which instruction was received, to the nearest 10,000.

The subsequent analysis of adult education subjects, then, was guided fundamentally by the categories on the flash card presented to all household informants.[6] The classification finally adopted involved a two-stage system of identification: subjects were described by the general categories and then were further subdivided within each of those categories.

The dimensions of the entire classification scheme are described in detail as the results are examined. The relevant data are presented in Table 3.9 in the form of estimates of the number of different persons who studied each type of subject matter. These estimates exclude courses taken as part of a full-time course load, but they cover all part-time studies of both a credit and non-credit nature, studies carried on for varying lengths of time, and courses taken on through all study methods, including self-instruction.

Within this table, the subject categories are listed in the order of their magnitude, which indicates immediately that by far the most frequent studies are in job-related subjects and skills. Over nine million persons are estimated to have studied some type of vocational topic during the time period covered by the survey.

By formal definition, this category covered the following range of subjects:

1. *Job-related subjects and skills*
All courses dealing with subjects and skills used in the professional, technical, business, office, and sales spheres of white-collar occupations, and in the skilled trades, semi-skilled, and service spheres of blue-collar occupations.

Within this general category, further subdivisions were made to relate subjects and skills to the specific occupations in which they are used. These subcategories closely follow the census classification of occupations.

[6]It should be noted that not all of these categories actually describe subject matter per se. The third, on-the-job training, refers to a form of learning rather than to a body of subject matter, and it was listed on the card mainly to remind respondents that this type of learning experience was also being enumerated in the inventory.

a) Technical-professional courses—health professions: subjects such as eye testing, Public Health nursing, or X-ray equipment.

b) Technical courses—all other spheres: the standard range of technical courses and skills; the main entries here are courses in electronics, tool design, and blueprint reading.

c) Teacher training courses: chiefly courses in teaching methods, but also includes training to become driving instructors, ski instructors, and the like.

d) Professional courses—all other spheres: chiefly courses in accounting and law, but subject matter such as library science or industrial relations is also classified here.

e) Business administration or management: courses in executive training, life insurance management, real estate, and securities and finance.

f) Sales and advertising skills: by far the most frequent courses classified here are in salesmanship, but courses in advertising or distributive skills are also included.

g) Office management: including personnel management.

h) Office machines: excluding typing, chiefly courses on data-processing machines and conventional business machines.

i) General office skills: traditional office skills—mainly courses in typing, shorthand, and bookkeeping.

j) Auto mechanics and other machine skills: all subjects pertaining to skilled trades of a mechanical nature, mainly auto mechanics, but also courses in the repair or installation of television sets.

k) Other skilled trades: courses in foreman training as well as any of the skills performed in occupations classified by the Census as "craftsmen, foremen and kindred workers."

l) Operative skills: all subjects pertaining to occupations classed as "operatives and kindred workers" by the Census. Typical course titles here are welding, millinery, and truck driving.

m) Service skills in the health professions: practical nursing or first aid.

n) Service skills in the protection and security field: most frequently courses in basic police work or in fire fighting.

o) Personal service skills: barbering and hairdressing, waiting, and training courses for service station attendants.

p) All other job-related subjects and skills: residual category for unclassifiable vocational subjects.

Although the number of persons studying any of these groups of subjects is fairly sizeable, the three which stand out particularly are technical, business, and general office skills courses. Together, these three areas represent over one-third of the total entries in the vocational field.[7]

2. *Hobbies and recreation*

The second largest category of subject matter is that of subjects and skills used in leisure-time pursuits. Approximately 5.5 million adult Americans are estimated to have studied such material over the year. A detailed description of this category follows.

   a) Athletics: mainly golf, swimming, and bowling lessons.
   b) Decorative arts and crafts: typically ceramics, flower arranging, cake decorating, leather crafts, and jewelry making.
   c) Dancing: chiefly social dancing. The very few adults found to be studying ballet are classified with "other recreation."
   d) Bridge lessons.
   e) Music (performing): learning how to play a musical instrument or taking singing lessons.
   f) Music (non-performing): chiefly music appreciation.
   g) Art (performing): painting, drawing, or sketching.
   h) Art (non-performing): art appreciation.
   i) Technical arts and hobbies: typically photography and hi-fi equipment.
   j) All other hobbies and recreation. Because they turned out to be so few in number, persons studying performing arts other than music and painting (such as ballet, sculpture, or acting) were ultimately classified here along with other miscellaneous subject matter of a recreational type.

[7]For the exacting reader who might take the trouble to match the totals in the subcategories with the overall category totals and thus find discrepancies in addition, the explanation is that some persons may have studied more than one type of subject matter within the same category. This same reader would also discover that the sum of the numbers in the category titles is less than the total number of courses estimated in Table 3.7. This discrepancy is again explained by the fact that the estimates in Table 3.9 are of the number of different persons studying different subjects, while those in Table 3.7 are for total courses studied. Thus, the total person-courses in Table 3.9 would be reduced by the number of second and subsequent courses on the same subjects studied by the same people.

3. *Religion, morals, and ethics*

a) Traditional religious training: standard training in the basic teachings of any religion in the Christian or Hebrew traditions, most commonly "Bible study," "prayer study," or simply "religion." This subcategory contains the largest single number (3,480,000) of persons found in any subcategory of the entire classificatory system.

b) Religion applied to everyday life: any subject concerned with the functions of religion in relation to common human problems. The most typical subject matter classified here focused on the role of religion in family life.

c) All other subjects on religion, morals, or ethics: such topics as religious history and courses in the basic teachings of religions outside the Hebrew-Christian traditions.

4. *General education*

Academic subjects of the sort normally studied as part of a high school or college education, but excluding all business, trade, vocational, technical, professional, or other job-related courses.

a) Foreign languages.

b) Mathematics and statistics.

c) English literature and composition: excluding courses in speech, basic English for immigrants, and elementary reading and writing proficiency. These particular subjects are all classified in Category 6.

d) History: any historical course except the history of art, music, or religion.

e) Sciences: both the physical and biological sciences.

f) Psychology.

g) Social sciences: mainly courses in sociology and economics. Shortly after the subject coding was begun, it was decided that all political education courses would be excluded from this category—including political science courses. This was done because it soon became evident that political courses of a non-academic nature were too often being labeled as political science. Hence all courses in political education were reclassified under Category 7 (*a*).

h) Great Books courses: purposely restricted to courses bearing the specific title of "Great Books." As it turned out, the num-

ber of persons who reported these courses was too small to
allow a meaningful estimate to be made.

i) Other general education subjects: primarily unspecified regular
school subjects.

5. *Home and family life subjects*

Topics pertaining to the establishment, maintenance, and
improvement of a home, or to the carrying out of household
duties and family responsibilities.

a) Sewing or cooking.
b) Home improvement skills: most frequently interior decorating
and do-it-yourself building or repairing skills.
c) Gardening.
d) Child care: courses in parent training, excluding child psychology, which is classified in Category 4.
e) All other home and family life subjects: courses in homemaking,
budgeting, consumer education, and family or marital relations.

6. *Personal development courses*

Miscellaneous subjects all aimed at helping people expand
themselves in the areas of physical fitness, health, personality
development, interpersonal and social skills, or basic reading,
writing, and language skills. The category is therefore organized
in terms of the functions or consequences of studies, and not at
all on the basis of any substantive connection between the subjects. The general notion of physical or social adjustment provided the organizing rationale linking together these otherwise
quite unconnected subjects.

a) Physical fitness: exercising, body building, yoga, dieting and
weight control.
b) Speed reading: also courses labeled as "reading improvement,"
but not courses in fundamental reading skills for illiterates.
c) Dale Carnegie courses or other leadership training courses: also
subjects which prepare for leadership responsibilities in service
organizations such as the Boy Scouts or 4-H Clubs.
d) Speech or public speaking: also courses in vocabulary building
and debating.
e) All other personal development subjects. Although three other

categories of personal development subjects were originally identified, these turned out to be so thinly represented that they were subsequently abandoned. This residual category therefore includes a few recent immigrants taking courses in English, a few illiterates studying elementary reading and writing, and a few persons studying charm, etiquette, or "personality" courses. Some of the additional types of subject matter included here are exemplified by the following interviewer note: From Household 02447 – "The entire family uses the sleep-teaching method of learning. They have it connected to all three of the family's pillows, and have records on physical well-being, true relaxation, decisive will power, perfect memory, self-confidence, magnetic personality, restful sleep, financial abundance, abundant vitality, self-mastery, power of praise, disciplined imagination, complete success, dynamic concentration, hidden power of the subconscious mind, gratitude, and meditation. They play these regularly during sleep."

7. *Current events, public affairs, and citizenship*

Topics dealing with current social, political, and economic affairs; courses in Americanization and citizenship, in civic responsibilities, and in general political education.

- *a*) General political education: political science, courses labeled "government," "civics," "democracy," and "public law."
- *b*) Current events: courses focusing specifically on contemporary international, national, regional, or local affairs.
- *c*) Courses on communism: any course titles making reference to the nature or threat of communism – including those with obvious religious contents.
- *d*) Civil defense.
- *e*) Americanization and citizenship: excluding courses in the English language for immigrants, but as Table 3.9 shows, there were not enough persons found to be studying these topics to allow national estimates to be made.
- *f*) All other public affairs courses: a residual category which, as the results also indicate, contained very few persons.

8. *Agriculture*

All topics dealing with farming and commercial gardening. In overall terms, this category contains surprisingly few persons, an estimated 320,000. Indeed, this is the only major category in which the NORC figures turn out to be lower than those estimated in the HEW survey (U.S. Department of Health, Education and Welfare, 1959, p. 13), where a total of 352,000 persons were estimated to be studying agricultural courses. While no direct attempt has been made to make the two sets of figures comparable, it is clear that if this were done, it would further reduce the size of the NORC estimate. In other words, it would probably be concluded that the number of adults studying agricultural subjects through adult education was lower in 1962 than in 1957. One explanation for this, of course, is that since the number of persons employed in agriculture in the United States is currently declining, there were simply fewer farmers in 1962 than in 1957 to study agricultural topics.[8]

Within the agricultural category, only two subcategories were used:

> *a*) Farming and market gardening: topics such as "soils and fertilizers," new farm equipment, dairy farming, fruit growing, cranberry farming, and mink raising.
> *b*) Other agricultural topics: a residual category which turned out to contain almost no entries.

9. *Miscellaneous subject matter*

Two types of courses which appeared with enough frequency to warrant separate classification, yet could not be meaningfully fitted into any other general category. These are

> *a*) Driver training.
> *b*) Military science courses with titles such as "Atomic Warfare" or "Military Procedures and Tactics."

Two additional categories rounded out the classificatory scheme by covering

---

[8]In 1957, there were 6,222,000 persons employed in agriculture; in 1961 there were 5,463,000 (U.S. Department of Commerce, 1961, p. 219).

    c) General miscellany (such as Siamese cat raising).
    d) Uncodeable subject titles, or subjects where course titles were
        not given.

Happily, the incidence of the latter was rare.
    While Table 3.9 contains a large number of interesting facts

Table 3.9 Estimated Number of Different Adults Who Studied Subjects of Various Types through Adult Education Instruction or Independent Study

Type of Subject Matter	Estimated Number of Persons*
1. Job-related subjects and skills	9,020,000
a) Technical courses: health professions	350,000
b) Technical courses: all other spheres	1,500,000
c) Teacher training courses	500,000
d) Professional courses: all other spheres	710,000
e) Business administration or management	1,160,000
f) Sales or advertising skills	620,000
g) Office management	300,000
h) Office machines (excluding typewriter)	380,000
i) General office skills (including typing)	1,030,000
j) Auto mechanics and other machine skills	690,000
k) Other skilled trades	810,000
l) Operative skills	400,000
m) Service skills in the health professions	590,000
n) Service skills in the protection and security field	330,000
o) Personal service skills	300,000
p) All other job-related subjects and skills	†
2. Hobbies and recreation	5,470,000
a) Athletic recreations	1,360,000
b) Decorative arts and crafts	780,000
c) Dancing lessons	760,000
d) Bridge lessons	640,000
e) Music (performing)	680,000
f) Music (non-performing)	230,000
g) Art (performing)	560,000
h) Art (non-performing)	320,000
i) Technical arts and hobbies	530,000
j) All other hobbies and recreations	370,000
3. Religion, morals, and ethics	3,820,000
a) Traditional religious training	3,480,000
b) Religion applied to everyday life	180,000
c) All other subjects on religion, morals or ethics	220,000

*These estimates are based on 22,648 adults (94.5 per cent of sample) for whom information was available on adult education courses involving both instruction and independent studies.
†Less than 180,000.

(Table 3.9 continued)

Table 3.9 *Continued*

Type of Subject Matter	Estimated Number of Persons*
4. General education	3,500,000
a) Foreign languages	970,000
b) Mathematics or statistics	700,000
c) English literature or composition	630,000
d) History (excluding history of religion, art, or music)	490,000
e) Sciences	300,000
f) Psychology	300,000
g) Social sciences (excluding political science)	240,000
h) Great Books courses	†
i) All other general education subjects	200,000
5. Home and family life	3,440,000
a) Sewing or cooking	1,890,000
b) Home improvement skills	690,000
c) Gardening	490,000
d) Child care	400,000
e) All other home and family life subjects	270,000
6. Personal development	1,700,000
a) Physical fitness	380,000
b) Speed reading	360,000
c) Dale Carnegie or other leadership training courses	340,000
d) Speech or public speaking	330,000
e) All other personal development subjects	390,000
7. Current events, public affairs, and citizenship	1,080,000
a) General political education (including political science)	310,000
b) Current events	280,000
c) Courses on communism	250,000
d) Civil defense	190,000
e) Americanization and citizenship	†
f) All other public affairs courses	†
8. Agriculture	320,000
a) Farming or market gardening	280,000
b) All other agricultural topics	†
9. Miscellaneous subject matter	970,000
a) Driver training	370,000
b) Military science	180,000
c) Miscellaneous other	310,000
d) Subject matter not reported or uncodeable	†

*These estimates are based on 22,648 adults (94.5 per cent of sample) for whom information was available on adult education courses involving both instruction and independent studies.
†Less than 180,000.

concerning the subjects studied by American adults, the very presence of such a large number of figures tends to obscure the underlying pattern. To provide a more manageable reference point for discussion, therefore, essentially the same data are presented in a different form in Table 3.10. Here, a slight modification is made in that the figures represent the total courses studied, and not the total persons in each category. The only effect of this modification is that in the rank ordering of subject categories, general education subjects move into a tie with religious studies. In the overall pattern of results, of course, this slight shift makes no difference whatsoever.

From Table 3.10 one gains a much better view of the distribution of emphasis in adult studies. Vocational education is by far the most significant segment for 32 per cent of all courses studied. It is also significant that almost 20 per cent of the activities are related to leisure time use and together, these two categories account for over 50 per cent of all adult studies. It is obvious, therefore, that the post-school educational energies of American adults are directed primarily to vocational and recreational concerns.

General education, religion, and home and family life each claim about 12 per cent of the total activities, while all other

Table 3.10 Types of Subject Matter Studied through Adult Education Methods

Category of Subject Matter	Total Courses Reported	Per Cent of Total Courses
Vocational	2,224	32
Hobbies and recreation	1,322	19
General education	850	12
Religion	810	12
Home and family life	796	12
Personal development	377	5
Public affairs and current events	236	3
Agriculture	73	1
Miscellaneous	182	3
Total	6,870	99
No information	24	
Total courses reported	6,894	

categories have a relatively minor position in the overall pattern. Somewhat surprisingly, only 3 per cent of the total courses were in public affairs and current events. On the basis of popular notions about adult education, one might have expected considerably more in this field.

It is quite clear that the major emphasis of adult education is on the practical rather than the academic, on the applied rather than the theoretical, and on skills rather than knowledge or values. Subjects closely related to performance in work, family, and social-personal adjustment, for example, represent a significant proportion of the total. Taken together, the vocational, agricultural, home and family life, and personal development categories total 50 per cent of all subjects studied. By comparison the academic, religious, and public affairs categories, which are much more concerned with ideas and values, make up just 27 per cent of the total courses. These results point up markedly the pragmatic quality of adult education in the United States.

METHODS OF STUDY

Information was also collected on the method or methods of study employed in all courses involving a relationship between student and instructor. To collect this information, respondents were shown a set of categories listed on the back of the flash card containing the course titles.

The basic findings on method of study are summarized in Table 3.11, which contains estimates of both the total number of courses studied by each method and the total number of persons who studied in each way. Thus an estimated 12,730,000 courses were studied through attendance at classes by an estimated 10,450,000 different persons.

The results show that a majority of the courses involved attendance at classes, and that the relative frequency of other methods of study was as follows: group discussions, lectures and talks, correspondence study, private instruction, on-the-job training, and finally educational television.[9]

[9]In the rank ordering of the number of different persons who used each method, it should be noted that private instruction and on-the-job training change places.

Table 3.11 Methods of Study in Adult Education Courses

Method of Study	Total Courses Reported	Per Cent	Estimated Number of Courses Studied by This Method	Total Persons Who Reported Courses	Estimated Number of Different Persons Who Studied Courses by This Method
			a. Courses in Which Instruction Was Received		
Attended classes	2,528	56.2	12,730,000	2,076	10,450,000
Attended group discussions	486	10.8	2,450,000	457	2,300,000
Attended lectures or talks	471	10.5	2,380,000	439	2,220,000
Correspondence study	377	8.4	1,900,000	347	1,750,000
Private teachers	351	7.8	1,770,000	332	1,670,000
On-the-job training	347	7.7	1,740,000	335	1,680,000
Educational television	68	1.5	340,000	59	290,000
All other methods	17	0.4	*	9	*
Total	4,497†	103.3†	22,650,000†	3,534†	17,160,000†
Information not given	173				
Total	4,670				
			b. Courses in Which No Instruction Was Received		
Total independent study	2,224	100	11,020,000	1,808	8,960,000
			c. Total of All Methods		
Total	6,894	100	33,670,000	4,724†	23,020,000†

*Too few to estimate.
†Does not total 100 per cent (or the sum of the figures in the column) because some courses were studied by more than one method.

None of these figures should come as much of a surprise, except perhaps the estimate that only 290,000 persons studied some 340,000 courses by educational television. At the time of this survey there were some sixty-three educational television stations in this country, and at least twenty of the forty-three large urban areas covered by the NORC sample had an educational television station. Virtually all these stations, moreover, telecast formal courses of instruction as at least a part of their programming activities. Many more of the sample households, too, were located within the reception range of commercial television stations which carried early morning educational courses. In view of this, it is quite surprising that only 59 adults out of 23,950 screened in this study (some 0.02 per cent) had followed an educational course on television during the previous year.[10]

Although there have been some studies recently of educational television audiences (Schramm, Lyle, and Pool, 1963), still very little is known about the audiences of formal courses of instruction on these stations. What information does exist, moreover, tends to be confined to case studies of audiences for particular courses on particular stations;[11] there has not been as yet, at least to our knowledge, any systematic study of national exposure to educational courses on open-circuit television.

From some points of view, of course, 290,000 students would represent a sizeable achievement for a relatively new medium of adult instruction. On the other hand, television's impact does not even come close to that of correspondence study, in which 1,750,000 adults were estimated to have taken courses over the same period of time. Indeed, as a method of home-study televi-

[10]These figures in no way reflect on the size of audiences for general programming on educational television stations, since formal courses represent only a tiny fraction of the overall offerings of ETV stations. In the second phase of our study, more general information was collected on people's exposure to these stations, and these data are reported in Chapter 11.

[11]For example, it was estimated that 120,000 persons in the New York Metropolitan Area followed the NYU and WCBS-TV program "Sunrise Semester" in 1957 (*RCA ETV News,* 1958). In an attempt to bring together diverse sources of information on this question, a 1955 report estimated that approximately 335,000 persons had followed telecourses (Schramm, 1955).

sion is still very much overshadowed by correspondence study. This is surprising mainly because in discussions of television audiences one usually deals with figures at least ten and often several hundred times this large.[12] The question is why a medium capable of attracting the largest audiences of all times should attract so few followers in its formal educational efforts.

Although open-circuit instructional television is still very much in a developmental stage in this country, there may be reason to believe that factors other than sheer availability are behind this result. In the conclusions of a recent study of the uses of television, for example, Steiner (1963) describes the "average American viewer" as follows:

> He would like TV to be more informative and educational but certainly not at the expense of entertainment. Aside from the day's news and weather—which he watches regularly—he rarely uses the set as a deliberate source of information, and he is extremely unlikely to turn on serious and informative public affairs presentations, even if he is watching while they are on the air. . . . Television, among the home sources of mass communication, has its greatest comparative advantage in the field of entertainment. . . . It is television, by a wide margin, that is turned to for relaxation and diversion (pp. 228–29).

It may be that television has come to be identified by the American public almost exclusively as a medium of light entertainment, and, if this is true, then it might also be that no matter how much instructional fare were made available on the medium, it would still be preferred for other purposes, and other sources would still be regarded as more appropriate for systematic learning.

Some further insight into the uses of different study methods is gained from Table 3.12, which presents a distribution of the methods of instruction employed within each major subject area.

These data reveal that methods of study do vary quite noticeably in different areas of subject matter. The traditional class-

---

[12]For example, it is estimated that some 70 million U.S. adults watched or listened to the first Kennedy-Nixon television debate in the 1960 presidential campaign (Katz and Feldman, 1962, p. 130).

Table 3.12 Methods of Study for Different Types of Subject Matter

Method of Study	Type of Subject Matter								
	General Education (Per Cent)	Vocational Subjects (Per Cent)	Agriculture (Per Cent)	Hobbies and Recreation (Per Cent)	Home and Family (Per Cent)	Personal Development (Per Cent)	Religion (Per Cent)	Public Affairs (Per Cent)	All Other (Per Cent)
Attended classes	44	42	16	34	26	45	40	26	28
Self-education	40	25	59	43	59	30	13	23	15
Discussion groups	2	3	10	2	8	7	30	16	3
Talks or lectures	3	8	10	1	6	8	12	30	8
Correspondence	8	10	*	2	1	6	2	3	16
Private teacher	1	1	3	18	1	1	5	*	24
Educational TV	2	*	*	*	*	6	*	6	1
On-the-job training	1	14	3	*	1	1	*	1	7
All other methods	*	*	*	*		*	*	*	*
Total	101†	103†	101†	100	102†	104†	102†	105†	102†
Number of courses for which information was available	841	2,166	73	1,296	785	353	790	227	190

*Less than 1 per cent.

†Does not total 100 per cent because some courses were studied by more than one method.

room form is the method most frequently used in four fields
— academic, vocational, personal development, and religious
— but self-instruction is most frequent in agricultural, recreational,
and home and family life studies. Persons who study public affairs
and current events, moreover, do so most frequently through
attendance at lectures and talks.

Correspondence study appears to be used most often for
academic and vocational courses, although even here it is used in
only a small proportion of the total courses studied. The more
frequent incidence of correspondence study in the miscellaneous
subject category is attributable chiefly to courses on military
topics sponsored by the armed forces.

The only frequent use of private instruction is in recreational
studies (18 per cent) and in the miscellaneous category (24 per
cent). This latter figure is influenced by the number of persons
who took driving lessons from private teachers.

Finally, television appears to have little impact in any subject
area, while on-the-job training, understandably, is confined to
the vocational sphere, where it accounts for approximately one
course in seven.

These data yield most interesting results when we examine
the kinds of subject matter most frequently handled in independent study. Table 3.13 orders forty-nine specific titles according to the proportion of courses of each type which were
studied without any formal instruction. The table also estimates
the number of different persons who studied each subject in this
way. Although the middle range of this array of figures does not
tell us much, the figures at the top and bottom of the list are
quite revealing.

First, it is interesting to note that there are some subjects
which were almost always self-taught and others for which no
cases at all of independent study were reported. It is in relation
to the types of subject matter at the extremes of the array that
the most interesting results emerge, however. The top three
subjects are all basically leisure-time pursuits of the do-it-yourself variety, and it is not too surprising, therefore, to find do-it-
yourself methods of study applied to this brand of subject matter. What is more surprising, however, is that 61 per cent of all

courses in foreign languages were studied without formal instruction. Indeed, all together more than 500,000 American adults studied some foreign language independently during the year, and this figure is certainly impressive. While there is no direct evidence here which would help to account for this, it is undoubtedly related, at least in part, to the influence of recent newspaper campaigns to promote subscriptions through offers of foreign-language instruction by low-cost, long-play recordings.

The case of speed reading is also an interesting one, since nearly one-half of the persons who took courses in this were self-instructed. This undoubtedly reflects the strong influence which innovations in teaching machines have exerted on pro-

Table 3.13 Types of Subject Matter Studied Independently

Subject	Per Cent of Courses of This Type Studied Independently	Estimated Number of Persons Who Studied This Subject Independently
1. Technical arts and hobbies	86	460,000
2. Gardening	83	410,000
3. Home improvement skills	80	550,000
4. Foreign languages	61	590,000
5. All agricultural subjects	59	190,000
6. Sewing and cooking	55	1,040,000
7. Music (performing)	50	340,000
8. Speed reading	44	160,000
9. Vocational: skilled trades other than mechanics	43	350,000
10. Decorative arts and crafts	41	320,000
11. Bridge lessons	41	260,000
12. Great Books courses	41	*
13. Sciences	39	*
14. Athletic recreations	37	500,000
15. Art (non-performing)	36	*
16. General office skills	36	370,000
17. Physical fitness	34	*
18. Child care	34	*
19. History	33	160,000
20. Mathematics and statistics	32	220,000
21. General political education	30	*
22. Americanization and citizenship	29	*
23. Technical: health professions sphere	28	*
24. Vocational: auto mechanics, etc.	28	190,000

*Less than 160,000.

Table 3.13 *Continued*

Subject	Per Cent of Courses of This Type Studied Independently	Estimated Number of Persons Who Studied This Subject Independently
25. English literature and composition	28	180,000
26. Current events and public affairs	26	*
27. Vocational: skills for operatives	26	*
28. Courses on the nature of communism	25	*
29. Music (non-performing)	24	*
30. Technical courses other than in the health professions	24	360,000
31. Social sciences	24	*
32. All professional courses other than teacher training	23	160,000
33. Psychology	22	*
34. Business administration or management	21	240,000
35. Sales and advertising skills	19	*
36. Vocational: personal service skills	17	*
37. Teacher training	16	*
38. Driver education	16	*
39. Speech and public speaking	15	*
40. Vocational: service skills in the health professions	15	*
41. Vocational: service skills in the protection and security fields	13	*
42. Traditional religious training	12	420,000
43. Religion and problems of everyday life	11	*
44. Dale Carnegie or leadership training courses	11	*
45. Office machines (other than typewriter)	11	*
46. Office management	11	*
47. Dancing	7	*
48. Military science	0	*
49. Civil defense	0	*

*Less than 160,000.

grams of home study. Further developments in educational technology will probably have an additional impact on home studies.

From the number of self-taught courses in music, too, one might guess that a substantial number of Americans no longer laugh when their friends sit down at the piano. Of course, it may be they are laughing all the harder, for it is almost impossible to evaluate the quality of the learning experiences people get from independent study methods. In terms of quantity of activity, however, the findings are impressive.

Each of these activities reflects the influence which recent events on the American scene have had on adult education. These influences have stemmed from diverse sources: changes in patterns of leisure time use; innovations in educational technology, particularly teaching machines and instructional recordings; and from the direct entry of commercial interests into the educational field. Moreover, all these independent study courses are the result of an approach to adult education as a consumer market. The growth of interest in each of these areas of study has undoubtedly been stimulated, at least in part, by the use of professional marketing skills and mass advertising.

At the bottom of Table 3.13 are examples of subjects which seem to be least amenable to independent study. Happily, perhaps, no persons were found who were studying military science other than with presumably qualified instructors; civil defense courses, too, had no students without instructors. Finally, it would appear that it is difficult to learn how to dance unless one has a partner who does know how.

SPONSORSHIP OF STUDIES

Following the investigation of methods of study, information was collected on the institutions sponsoring all courses studied in classes, lectures, talks, or group discussions — those activities in which people made a direct contact with some institution in order to receive instruction. All on-the-job training activities are omitted from the totals shown, however, and because these, as well as correspondence and educational television courses, are excluded, the analysis covers only about 80 per cent of the courses where there would be a meaningful question of sponsorship to be asked.

With these qualifications outlined, we examine the results presented in Table 3.14. This table provides estimates both of courses and people; the most striking finding is that on both measures churches and synagogues turn out to be the institutions most often attended. In descending rank, the remaining institutions are ordered as follows: colleges and universities;

Table 3.14 Estimates of Courses Attended at Different Sponsoring Institutions*

Sponsoring Institution	Number of Courses Reported	Per Cent	Estimated Number of Courses Attended at Different Institutions	Number of Different Persons Who Reported Courses	Estimated Number of Different Persons Who Attended Classes, Lectures, Talks, or Discussion Groups
Churches and synagogues	692	21	3,460,000	652	3,260,000
Colleges and universities	689	21	3,440,000	528	2,640,000
Community organizations	488	15	2,450,000	446	2,240,000
Business and industry	406	12	2,040,000	370	1,860,000
Elementary and high school	383	12	1,920,000	347	1,740,000
Private schools	246	7	1,220,000	226	1,120,000
Government (all levels)	235	7	1,180,000	210	1,050,000
Armed forces	116	4	580,000	96	480,000
All other sponsors	50	2	250,000	49	240,000
Total	3,305	101	16,560,000	2,667†	13,360,000†
Don't know or no answer	83			60	
Total courses	3,388		16,560,000	2,727	

*Includes only those courses studied by attending classes, talks, lectures or discussion groups.

†Does not total number of persons listed in column because some persons studied at more than one sponsoring institution.

community organizations; business and industry; elementary and secondary schools; private schools; government; and finally the armed forces.

Some of these categories require further definition. The category "colleges and universities," for example, includes only non-profit institutions of higher learning, and thus excludes business colleges, barber colleges, or any other profit-making schools which might be called colleges. The category "private schools" consists of profit-making institutions of all types. By the same token, however, it does not include schools which are non-public but non-profit as well, such as parochial secondary schools. Institutions of this latter type are included in the regular school system, either with elementary and secondary schools or with colleges and universities.

The category "community organizations" brings together all civic and community service organizations where instruction is offered to the general public, rather than privately to members only. The category includes community centers, adult education centers, YMCA's, libraries, museums, and other related institutions. The governmental category, finally, is composed of all federal, state, or local government agencies engaged in educational instruction (such as the Co-operative Extension Service). All branches of the armed forces, however, are classified separately.

It is clear from the results in Table 3.14 that the regular school system accounts for considerably less than one-half of all adult education activities. Together, colleges and universities and elementary and secondary schools sponsored only one-third of the courses reported. Furthermore, if private schools are added to this total, as well as all courses studied in community adult education centers (approximately one-quarter of the courses grouped together in the "community organizations" category —perhaps 4 per cent of all courses), it is still true that less than one-half the courses reported were sponsored by institutions whose primary function is education. A majority of adult education studies, in other words, are taken in institutions whose main functions are other than educational.

This discovery is revealing, and leads one to inquire further into the kinds of subjects being studied in these different institutions. Since there are two meaningful questions to ask of the relationship between subject matter and sponsoring institutions, Table 3.15 is presented in two ways: in part *a* the information is organized to answer the question "Where are courses of various types studied?" while part *b* more directly answers "What types of courses do various institutions sponsor?"

Table 3.15*a* yields a number of interesting findings.

1. General education subjects are studied primarily in the regular school system. Some 66 per cent of all general education courses were studied in colleges or universities, and a total of 79 per cent in either colleges, universities, elementary schools, or secondary schools.

2. Vocational subjects, however, are split between business and industry and the regular school system. The largest single category is business and industry, with 29 per cent of the courses, but together the three levels of the regular school system account for 38 per cent of all vocational subjects.

3. Although few in number, those courses in agricultural subjects in an institutional context were taken most frequently from the government. These were mainly courses sponsored by the Co-operative Extension Service.

4. Recreation subjects were studied most frequently in community organizations (40 per cent). Only 23 per cent of these courses were studied in the regular school system.

5. Similarly, home and family life subjects were studied more often in community organizations than in any other institution (28 per cent), although 25 per cent were taken at elementary or secondary schools.

6. Personal development subjects, also, were studied most frequently in community organizations (27 per cent), with another 20 per cent studied in colleges and universities.

7. Churches and synagogues account for practically all religious studies (96 per cent).

8. Finally, public affairs were studied most often in community organizations (36 per cent), and second most often in colleges and universities (20 per cent). More courses of this type were taken in community organizations than in all levels of the

Table 3.15 Institutional Sponsorship and Subject Matter Studied*

a. Where Are Courses of Various Types Studied?

Sponsoring Institution	Type of Subject Matter								
	General Education (Per Cent)	Vocational Subjects (Per Cent)	Agriculture (Per Cent)	Hobbies and Recreations (Per Cent)	Home and Family (Per Cent)	Personal Development (Per Cent)	Religion (Per Cent)	Public Affairs (Per Cent)	All Other (Per Cent)
Elementary, secondary	13	14	4	13	25	8	†	10	12
Colleges, universities	66	24	21	10	8	20	1	20	16
Private schools	3	9	4	20	3	12	†	1	6
Business, industry	4	29	17	2	6	10	†	7	12
Churches, synagogues	3	2	†	5	4	6	96	11	3
Armed forces	1	6	17	1	1	7	2	4	22
Community organization	5	7	37	40	28	27	1	36	17
Government	3	9	†	3	21	8	†	11	12
All other	1	†		5	4	2	†	1	1
Total	99	100	100	99	100	100	100	101	101
Number of courses for which information was available	403	1,105	24	459	287	193	619	146	69

*Covers only those subjects studied by attending classes, lectures, talks or group discussions.

†Less than 1 per cent.

Table 3.15 Continued

b. What Types of Courses Do Various Institutions Sponsor?

Type of Subject Matter	Sponsoring Institution								
	Elementary and Secondary (Per Cent)	Colleges and Universities (Per Cent)	Private Schools (Per Cent)	Business and Industry (Per Cent)	Churches and Synagogues (Per Cent)	Armed Forces (Per Cent)	Community Organizations (Per Cent)	Government (Per Cent)	All Other (Per Cent)
General education	13	38	5	4	2	5	4	5	12
Vocational subjects	41	39	39	79	2	52	16	42	6
Agriculture	1	1	*	1	*	*	1	4	*
Hobbies, recreations	16	6	38	2	4	2	38	6	48
Home and family	19	3	4	4	2	2	16	26	22
Personal development	4	6	10	5	2	11	11	6	6
Religion	*	1	1	*	86	9	1	*	2
Public affairs	3	4	1	2	2	5	11	7	2
All other	2	2	2	2	*	13	2	3	2
Total	99	100	100	99	100	99	100	99	100
Number of courses for which information was available	383	689	246	406	692	116	488	235	50

*Less than 1 per cent.

regular school system combined (36 per cent and 30 per cent, respectively).

To summarize further, let us consider that any institution which sponsors at least 20 per cent of all courses in a given category plays a major role in relation to those studies.

On this criterion, elementary and secondary schools can be said to play a major role only in home and family life subjects; colleges and universities in academic, vocational, agricultural, public affairs, and personal development subjects; private schools in hobbies and recreations only; business and industry in vocational education only; churches and synagogues in religious education only; community organizations in recreational, home and family life, personal development, and public affairs subjects; government in agricultural and home and family life subjects; and the armed forces in none of the main categories identified here.

The organization of Table 3.15*b* offers a better framework from which to generalize concerning the emphasis on adult education in various institutions. From this part of the table, the following inferences might be drawn.

1. The adult education concerns of colleges and universities are evenly split between academic (38 per cent of courses) and vocational (39 per cent).

2. Elementary and secondary schools, on the other hand, emphasize the vocational field much more than the academic (41 per cent to 13 per cent, respectively). Thirty-five per cent of elementary and secondary-school adult education courses, moreover, were in recreation and home life.

3. Private profit-making schools are clearly most active within two subject categories—vocational education and recreation.

4. Not surprisingly, the adult education activities of business and industry are overwhelmingly vocational (79 per cent), while those of churches and synagogues are almost exclusively confined to religious education (86 per cent of courses).

5. The majority of courses studied from the armed forces were vocational (52 per cent), with the remainder distributed widely throughout other categories.

6. Community organizations diversify their emphasis in a

number of different subject areas, with education for leisure apparently the main one (38 per cent of the courses).

7. Governmental activity is concentrated within two subject areas which account for two-thirds of the courses studied in that context—vocational (42 per cent) and home and family life (26 per cent).

To conclude, it is evident that some types of institutions, such as business and industry and churches and synagogues, play highly specialized roles in adult education, while others, such as community organizations and elementary and secondary schools, play much more diversified roles.

NATURE OF REGISTRATION

We conclude with a brief examination of the ways in which people were registered for adult education studies. For each activity in which instruction was received, information was collected concerning any "credit" which may have been gained from the course. Because the terms "credit" and "non-credit" were found during the pretest to be confusing to a considerable number of respondents, the question finally used was phrased as follows:

Was that instruction taken for "credit"—that is, for some type of degree, diploma, or certificate—or was it "non-credit"?

For present purposes a credit course is defined as any course leading to a certificate, degree, or diploma of any type. Names of specific degrees, diplomas, or certificates were asked for whenever a credit course was reported.

The results are reported in Tables 3.16 and 3.17. The main finding of these tables is simple and clear: by far the majority of adult education activities are non-credit activities. Of all courses, including those in the independent study group, which are non-credit by definition, only 17 per cent were credit courses. Even when we omit independent studies, however, only 26 per cent of the remaining courses were taken for credit (not shown in tables). This is quite revealing, for it is sometimes assumed by practitioners in the field that it is difficult to increase attendance at adult education courses unless some form of credit is offered for the activity. While in some cases this may be true, these results indicate that in the main, the earning of formal credit is not an important motive in the educational behavior of American adults.

Table 3.16 estimates, nonetheless, that some 4,360,000 different persons did take adult education courses for credit, and, if full-time students are added to this number, the total number of adult Americans studying for some type of credit would be estimated at approximately 6,800,000.[13]

Table 3.17 describes the types of credit which were reported. These credits were classified first according to whether or not they were received in the regular school system, and if they were, then, according to the level of the school system within which they would count. All certificates and diplomas received outside the regular school system were grouped together in a single category. By far the majority of these latter credits were vocational certificates of one sort or another.

Table 3.17 indicates that the split between credit courses in and outside of the regular school system was an even fifty-fifty.

[13]The sum of the full-time students estimated in Table 3.4 and the part-time credit students estimated in Table 3.16 is 7,010,000. A small number of these persons, however (estimated at 210,000), were the same people reported twice —that is, persons who were both full-time students and, independently, studying some adult education subject for credit.

Table 3.16 Credit Status of Adult Education Studies

Credit Status	Number of Courses Reported	Per Cent	Estimated Number of Courses	Number of Persons Reporting Courses	Estimated Number of Different Persons
Credit	1,084	17	5,660,000	836	4,360,000
Non-credit	5,385	83	28,010,000	3,913	20,350,000
Total	6,469	100	33,670,000		23,020,000*
Information not given	425				
Total courses	6,894				

*Does not total numbers in column because some persons studied some courses for credit and others not for credit.

Table 3.17 Types of Credit Sought

Type of Certificate, Degree, or Diploma	Number of Courses Reported	Per Cent of Courses Reported	Estimated Number of Courses Taken for This Type of Credit	Number of Different Persons Who Reported Credit	Estimated Number of Different Persons Who Took Courses for This Type of Credit
Elementary school certificate	3	*	†	3	*
High school diploma	78	8	420,000	55	300,000
First college degree	236	23	1,280,000	168	910,000
Higher college degree	200	19	1,090,000	153	830,000
All other certificates or diplomas	525	50	2,850,000	442	2,400,000
Total	1,042	100			
Information not given	42				
Total credit courses reported	1,084				

*Less than 1 per cent.
†Too few to estimate.

Of all credit courses, 23 per cent led to some first college degree, 19 per cent to higher college degrees, and 8 per cent to high-school diplomas. Only three persons were found to be studying courses leading to an elementary school certificate.

To conclude, it is clear that of the educational activities under examination in this study, less than one course in five was taken for any kind of credit, and less than one in ten for credit within the regular school system.

4
Characteristics
of
Participants

We now turn to a description of what the adults who engage in educational pursuits are like. There are two main sections to this chapter; in the first, participants as an aggregate are examined on a wide range of social and demographic factors; in the second, attention is narrowed to an examination of the sex, age, and educational composition of subgroups who took different subjects, used different methods of study, attended institutions of various sorts, and studied under different types of registration.

Throughout this discussion participants will be compared with the total sample of adults, and thus, in effect, with the total adult population of the United States.

WHO THE PARTICIPANTS ARE

The category of "participants" examined in this first section consists of all persons who were active in any way in part-time educational pursuits. It does not include full-time students unless a full-time student was also active in adult education. In sum, the aggregate represents some 20 per cent of the adults screened in the survey, and an estimated total of 23,020,000 American adults.

A general description of these people is provided in Tables 4.1, 4.2, and 4.3, which present information on eleven different background characteristics. These characteristics are clustered into three general classes:

1. Personal characteristics (Table 4.1). Sex, age, life-cycle position (marital status and number of children under twenty-one), race and religion.
2. Socio-economic characteristics (Table 4.2). Labor-force status, occupation, family income, and education.
3. Ecological characteristics (Table 4.3). Size and type of community, and region.[1]

Although Tables 4.1 – 4.3 contain a considerable amount of detail, the distinguishing features of adult education participants can be extracted and summarized rather quickly. They are as follows:

1. Personal characteristics
   a) Sex. Equal numbers of men and women participate in adult education, but because there are more women than men in the total adult population, there is a slight overrepresentation of men among participants.
   b) Age. A majority of participants (57 per cent) are under the age of forty, and over three-quarters (79 per cent) are under fifty. This constitutes a considerable overrepresentation of younger persons among participants, and as Table 4.1a indicates, participants are on the average more than six years younger than the "average" American adult.
   c) Marital status and number of children under twenty-one. Although some 83 per cent of adult education participants are married, this represents just 4 per cent more married adults than in the population as a whole. However, 60 per cent of all participants have at least one child under twenty-one, and this constitutes a six-to-five overrepresentation of parents. Widows and widowers, on the other hand, are represented at just half their population proportion.
   d) Race. Ninety per cent of the participants are white, just 2 per cent more than the total adult population. Negroes are underrepresented by a factor of three to four.

[1]The presentation is made in terms of the proportion of persons within each category. The reader who would like to convert these proportions to actual numbers of people could derive approximate estimates by applying any proportion describing the participants to the figure of 23,020,000 (estimated in Table 3.6 as the number of different persons active in adult education), or any proportion describing the total adult population to the figure of 114 million persons.

e) Religion. There are only slight differences between the religious preferences of participants and those of the general population. Protestants are present among participants in exactly their population proportion; Catholics are slightly underrepresented at a twenty-three to twenty-five ratio; and Jews are slightly overrepresented at four to three. Thus participants, like the total population, are about 66 per cent Protestant, 25 per cent Catholic, and less than 5 per cent Jewish.

2. Socio-economic characteristics

a) Labor-force status. Nearly 75 per cent of all participants are in the labor force, and 62 per cent held full-time jobs at the time of the survey. Compared with the total adult population, this indicates an overrepresentation of persons who work, a slight underrepresentation of housewives, and a considerable underrepresentation of retired persons.

Table 4.1 Personal Characteristics of Participants in Adult Education Compared with Total Sample

a. Sex	Participants*	Total Sample
Male	50%	47%
Female	50%	53%
Total	100%	100%
Base	4,724	23,947
No information	0	3
Total persons	4,724	23,950

b. Age	Participants*	Total Sample
Under 20	1%	1%
20–29	28	19
30–39	28	22
40–49	22	21
50–59	13	16
60–69	6	12
70 and over	2%	9%
Total	100%	100%
Base	4,678	23,677
No information	46	273
Total persons	4,724	23,950
Median age	36.5 years	42.8 years

*Persons who studied any subject by any method.
Note: Subcategories do not always add up to totals because of rounding.

(Table 4.1 continued)

Table 4.1   *Continued*

c. Marital Status and Number of Children under 21	Participants*		Total Sample	
Married		83%		79%
No children under 21	22%		29%	
1–2 children under 21	39		31	
3 or more children under 21	21%		19%	
Single		9		9
Widowed		4		8
Divorced or separated		4%		4%
Total		100%		100%
Base		4,717		23,831
No information		7		119
Total persons		4,724		23,950

d. Race	Participants*	Total Sample
White	90%	88%
Negro	9%	12
Other	†	1%
Total	99%	101%
Base	4,681	23,728
No information	43	222
Total persons	4,724	23,950

e. Religion	Participants*		Total Sample	
Protestant		66%		66%
Baptist	21%		24%	
Methodist	13		14	
Lutheran	9		9	
Presbyterian	7		6	
Episcopalian	4		3	
Congregational	2		2	
Other denomination	7		6	
Denomination not given	4%		4%	
Catholic		23		25
Jewish		4		3
Mormon		2		1
Christian Science		1		†
Unitarian		1		†
None		2		3
All other religions		1%		1%
Total		100%		99%
Base		4,692		23,608
No information		32		342
Total persons		4,724		23,950

*Persons who studied any subject by any methods.

†Less than 1 per cent.

b) Occupation. Among those in the labor force, a majority of participants (58 per cent) compared with a minority of all adults (43 per cent) hold jobs in the white-collar occupations (the first four categories on the list). Moreover, nearly one participant in four who works at all is employed in a professional or technical occupation, and persons in these occupations are overrepresented by a ratio of almost two to one. The other white-collar occupations, on the other hand, are repre-

Table 4.2 Socio-Economic Characteristics of Participants in Adult Education Compared with Total Sample

a. Labor-Force Status	Participants*		Total Sample	
Total in labor force		72%		61%
Work full-time	62%		51%	
Work part-time	9		9	
Unemployed	1		1	
Total out of labor force		28%		39%
Keep house only	25		30	
Go to school only	1		1	
Retired	2%		7	
Disabled	†		1%	
Total		100%		100%
Base		4,689		23,742
No information		35		208
Total persons		4,724		23,950

b. Occupation (of Those in Labor Force)	Participants*	Total Sample
Professional, technical and kindred	23%	12%
Managers, officials and proprietors	12	11
Clerical and kindred	15	13
Sales workers	8	7
Craftsmen and foremen	18	16
Operatives and kindred	10	17
Service workers	10	13
Farmers and farm managers	2	4
Farm laborers	1	2
Other laborers	2%	5%
Total	101%	100%
Base	3,321	14,265
No information	49	286
Total persons in labor force	3,370	14,551

*Persons who studied any subject by any method.
†Less than 1 per cent.

(Table 4.2 continued)

Table 4.2 *Continued*

c. Family Income	Participants*	Total Sample
Under $1,000	2%	5%
$1,000 – $1,999	4	8
$2,000 – $2,999	6	9
$3,000 – $3,999	8	10
$4,000 – $4,999	10	12
$5,000 – $5,999	12	13
$6,000 – '6,999	12	11
$7,000 – $7,999	11	9
$8,000 – $9,999	13	9
$10,000 – $14,999	15	9
$15,000 and over	6%	4%
Total	99%	99%
Base	4,637	23,123
No information	87	827
Total persons	4,724	23,950
Median family income	$6,600	$ 5,410

d. Years of Schooling	Participants*	Total Sample
Never attended school	†	1%
1 – 4 years	1%	4
5 – 7 years	3	10
8 years	6	15
9 – 11 years	15	20
12 years	36	31
13 – 15 years	20	11
16 years	11	6
More than 16 years	7%	3%
Total	99%	101%
Base	4,681	23,299
No information	43	651
Total persons	4,724	23,950
Median years of schooling	12.2 years	11.5 years

*Persons who studied any subject by any method.
†Less than 1 per cent.

sented at just about their incidence within the total labor force. Within the blue-collar group, craftsmen and foremen are over-represented by a factor of nine to eight, while all others are underrepresented — persons in agriculture in a ratio of one to two, and non-farm unskilled laborers by as much as one to two and one-half.

c) Family income. The median income of persons active in adult education was $6,600 a year, nearly $1,200 per annum higher than the average. More than one participant in five had an annual family income of $10,000 or more.

d) Education. In terms of formal education, participants went to school 12.2 years on the average, compared with 11.5 years for all adults in the sample. The magnitude of this discrepancy is more sharply expressed by the fact that participants are over-represented with persons who had been to college by a ratio of

Table 4.3 Ecological Characteristics of Participants in Adult Education Compared with Total Sample

a. Size of Community	Participants*		Total Sample	
Large metropolitan areas (2,000,000 or more)		25%		23%
Central city	11%		11%	
Suburbs and outskirts	14		11	
Small metropolitan areas (under 2,000,000)		45		40
Central city	21		21	
Suburbs and outskirts	25%		18%	
Small cities (10,000 – 50,000)		13		14
Small town and rural		16%		23%
Total		99%		100%
Base		4,710		23,840
No information		14		110
Total persons		4,724		23,950

b. Region	Participants*		Total Sample	
Total Northeast		21%		24%
New England	4%		5%	
Middle Atlantic	16		19	
Total North Central		27		29
East North Central	17		18	
West North Central	10		11	
Total South		29		31
South Atlantic	11		14	
East South Central	6		6	
West South Central	12		12	
Total West		23%		16%
Mountain	3		2	
Pacific	20%		14	
Total		100%		100%
Base		4,724		23,950
No information		0		0
Total persons		4,724		23,950

*Persons who studied any subject by any method.

almost two to one, and underrepresented with persons holding only a grade-school education by a factor of one to three.

3. Ecological factors

   a) Size and type of community. Table 4.3*a* shows that people living in large metropolitan areas are slightly overrepresented among the active, while those in small cities, small towns, and rural areas are underrepresented. Within large metropolitan areas, however, only those living in suburbs or outskirts are overrepresented; those in the central cities are not. Thus some 39 per cent of participants (compared with 29 per cent of the population) live in suburbs or outskirts of cities over 50,000 in size; in actual numbers, it works out that more participants live in the outlying areas of cities than live in the cities themselves (39 per cent to 32 per cent). On the other hand, those living in rural areas or in cities under 50,000 make up 37 per cent of the total (adult) population, but only 29 per cent of participants in adult education.

   b) Region. Although more participants live in the South than in any of the other three major regions of the country, only those participants living in the West are overrepresented. The regional imbalance is particularly strong on the West Coast, however. Persons living in the three Pacific states make up only 14 per cent of the total population, but represent 20 per cent of adult education participants.

In summary, one might compose a sort of profile of the "typical" adult education participant: The participant is just as often a woman as a man, is typically under forty, has completed high school or better, enjoys an above-average income, works full-time and most often in a white-collar occupation, is typically white and Protestant, is married and a parent, lives in an urbanized area (more likely in the suburbs than in a large city), and is found in all parts of the country, but more frequently on the West Coast than would be expected by chance.

VARIATION IN CHARACTERISTICS BY TYPE OF PARTICIPATION

While this profile represents a valid modal characterization of the adults who are active in educational pursuits, at the same time it obscures the fact that important differences exist among people who are active in different ways. One would inquire immediately, for example, whether these characteristics hold equally well for persons who study in different subject fields, use different methods, attend different institutions, or are in different classes of registration. To clarify these questions, the remainder of the chapter deals with variations in the characteristics of people in these different subgroups. Although the full range of background factors could also be utilized for this further inquiry, the discussion can be meaningfully restricted to just three factors: sex, age, and education.

Variation by subject matter studied

The first of these breakdowns is shown in Table 4.4, and it describes the characteristics of persons who studied different kinds of subjects. These data indicate marked differences on all three factors being considered.

First of all, men are seen as heavily overrepresented in the vocational and agricultural categories, while women are overrepresented in the family life, recreational, and religious categories. The first three of these discrepancies should come as no surprise, for one could hardly expect not to find learning-for-work predominantly masculine, or learning-for-home predominantly feminine. It is a little surprising, however, that women are as heavily represented as they are among those studying leisure-time subjects and religion.

Certain categories are also heavily age-dominated. Although persons under thirty-five are found in at least their population incidence in all subject categories, they are much more heavily represented in some than in others. One-half of those in academic subjects, for example, are under thirty-five, as are just under one-half of those in vocational or home and family subjects. These results again reflect only what might be expected, of course, since it would have been surprising indeed not to find large numbers of young persons among those who study to complete a formal education, make a living, or establish a home.

Nonetheless, there are distinct age differences across different subject fields, and although persons aged fifty-five and above are

Table 4.4 Sex, Age, and Education of Persons Studying Different Types of Subject Matter

Characteristic	Type of Subject Matter									
	Vocational Subjects (Per Cent)	General Education (Per Cent)	Hobbies and Recreation (Per Cent)	Home and Family (Per Cent)	Personal Development (Per Cent)	Religion (Per Cent)	Public Affairs (Per Cent)	Agriculture (Per Cent)	All Other (Per Cent)	Total Sample (Per Cent)
Sex										
Male	68	53	39	23	50	38	54	71	53	47
Female	32	47	61	77	50	62	46	29	47	53
Total	100	100	100	100	100	100	100	100	100	100
Age										
Under 35	47	50	43	48	42	35	31	38	45	31
35–54	46	40	44	37	49	42	46	43	48	41
55 and over	7	10	13	14	9	24	22	19	6	28
Total	100	100	100	99	100	101	99	100	99	100
Education										
Grade school	7	6	5	12	8	20	8	15	7	29
High school	53	37	52	57	48	52	36	50	59	51
College	40	58	43	30	44	28	56	35	34	20
Total	100	101	100	99	100	100	100	100	100	100
Total N	1,910	706	1,110	701	342	774	217	73	166	23,950

not found at their population proportion in any subject category, they come close to being proportionally represented among those who study religion or public affairs. Persons who study these subjects, in other words, tend on the average to be older than those who study in other areas.

With regard to educational background, Table 4.4 indicates that persons who have been to college are heavily overrepresented in all subject fields. At the same time, however, there are large differences in the extent of this overrepresentation: at one extreme, a majority of those taking academic and public affairs courses had attended college (58 and 56 per cent respectively), while at the other, only 30 per cent of those taking homemaking and 28 per cent of those studying religion had gone beyond high school.

The main finding here, however, is that all spheres of study tend to have more persons of above-average education, and it is particularly revealing to find persons without much formal education so noticeably absent from the vocational and academic categories—that is, from areas of study which would help extend a minimal formal education or widen a perhaps limited vocational horizon.

One question, also relevant to the present discussion, concerns the representation of members of different religious faiths among those engaged in organized religious study. This information is brought together in Table 4.5. Here a striking imbalance may be noted. Although they constitute two-thirds of the total population, Protestants account for as many as eight of every nine persons studying religion. Among the Protestants, moreover, Baptists and members of smaller denominations and sects dominate in these studies. Together, the Baptists and members of "other denominations"[2] constitute 59 per cent of all persons studying religion, but make up only 30 per cent of the total population.

All other faiths are underrepresented here except the Mormons, who, although located in only small numbers, are nonetheless overrepresented among those studying religion by a factor of three to one.

[2]This category consists mainly of Quakers, Seventh Day Adventists, Mennonites, Brethren, and Jehovah's Witnesses.

Variation by method of study

Next, Table 4.6 compares the background characteristics of persons who used different methods of study.

At this point, it is important to re-emphasize that our purpose in this chapter is to describe the characteristics of subgroups of participants, not to explain participatory behavior. These results cannot be interpreted here as demonstrating or even reflecting cause-and-effect relations between characteristics of people and dimensions of adult education.

As noted earlier, in Table 3.12, the methods of study employed vary considerably according to subject. Because of this, any statement about the relationship between background characteristics and study method could not be meaningfully explored unless at the very least, methods of study were controlled by the subject matter studied.

At the same time, however, the topics under discussion are important substantive questions in their own right, and an examination of the types of people who channel their studies into different methods or institutions has intrinsic descriptive merit

Table 4.5 Religious Background of Persons Who Studied Religion

Religion	Persons Who Studied Religion (Per Cent)	Total Sample of Adults (Per Cent)
Protestant	87	66
Baptist	43	24
Methodist	12	14
Lutheran	6	9
Presbyterian	6	6
Episcopalian	2	3
Congregational	1	2
Other denomination	16	6
Denomination not given	2	4
Catholic	6	25
Jewish	1	3
Mormon	3	1
All other	2	4
Total	99	99
Total N	774	23,950

Table 4.6 Sex, Age, and Education of Persons Employing Different Methods of Study

Characteristic	Method of Study								Total Sample (Per Cent)
	Attended Classes (Per Cent)	Talks or Lectures (Per Cent)	Discussion Groups (Per Cent)	Correspondence Study (Per Cent)	Private Teachers (Per Cent)	Educational Television (Per Cent)	On-the-Job Training (Per Cent)	Independent Study (Per Cent)	
Sex									
Male	48	53	40	75	36	25	75	50	47
Female	52	47	60	25	64	75	25	50	53
Total	100	100	100	100	100	100	100	100	100
Age									
Under 35	47	33	31	55	39	30	59	43	31
35 – 54	44	51	45	39	49	.44	37	44	41
55 and over	10	15	24	6	12	25	4	14	28
Total	101	99	100	100	100	99	100	101	100
Education									
Grade school	6	7	21	7	9	7	6	10	29
High school	51	40	47	52	52	58	58	52	51
College	43	53	32	41	40	36	36	37	20
Total	100	100	100	100	101	101	100	99	100
Total N	2,076	439	457	347	332	59	335	1,808	23,950

even if unknown explanatory value. In the remaining parts of this chapter, too, the reader will note that the question constantly asked is "What are the people like who engage in different types of adult education?" and not "What are the types of adult education that different kinds of people engage in?" Although both of these are descriptive questions, a focus on the latter has clearly more relevance when one's task is to explain why people participate in educational pursuits. All questions of this latter type will be reserved for later chapters.

With this note of caution, we may proceed to examine Table 4.6. From these figures the following points appear worthy of comment:

1. Two forms of study, on-the-job training and correspondence study, are heavily dominated by men. Women, on the other hand, make up three-quarters of those who study by educational television and substantial majorities of those studying with private instructors or in discussion groups. It is noteworthy that of the three major forms of home study, one is heavily dominated by men (correspondence study), one by women (educational television), while the third, independent study, is characterized by an exact fifty-fifty split between men and women.

2. In addition, the on-the-job training and correspondence categories have many more persons under thirty-five than do the others. By comparison, those studying by educational television or in discussion groups are somewhat older than average.

3. Finally, the table shows little variation in the educational levels of persons using different methods of study. Lectures and talks are the forms most heavily dominated and group discussions are the least dominated by persons who had attended college.

Variation by institution attended

Data on the sex, age, and educational characteristics of persons who attended classes, lectures, talks, or group discussions at different institutions are presented in Table 4.7. Although these results reflect differences largely attributable to the kinds of subject matter offered by different institutions, there are nonetheless characteristic differences in the types of people who receive instruction at different institutions.

Table 4.7 Sex, Age, and Education of Persons Attending Classes, Lectures, Talks, or Group Discussions at Different Institutions

Characteristic	Elementary and Secondary (Per Cent)	Colleges and Universities (Per Cent)	Private Schools (Per Cent)	Business and Industry (Per Cent)	Churches and Synagogues (Per Cent)	Armed Forces (Per Cent)	Community Organizations (Per Cent)	Government (Per Cent)	Total Sample (Per Cent)
				Sponsoring Institution					
Sex									
Men	35	57	43	74	35	92	32	53	47
Women	65	43	57	26	65	8	68	47	53
Total	100	100	100	100	100	100	100	100	100
Age									
Under 35	47	54	46	40	34	73	40	38	31
35–54	46	39	48	53	42	27	45	48	41
55 and over	7	7	7	7	24	0	15	14	28
Total	100	100	101	100	100	100	100	100	100
Education									
Grade school	8	1	4	5	20	2	6	10	29
High school	63	24	57	54	53	60	49	49	51
College	29	75	39	40	27	37	44	41	20
Total	100	100	100	99	100	99	99	100	100
Total N	347	528	226	370	652	96	446	210	23,950

1. Some institutions clearly have chiefly male clientele (business and industry, and the armed forces), while in others (elementary and secondary schools, churches and synagogues, and the various classes of institutions included in the "community organizations" category) large majorities of the participants are women.

2. Persons attending courses sponsored by the armed forces are by far the youngest, while those who go to churches and synagogues to receive instruction are, on the average, the oldest. It is interesting, too, that in their adult education programs colleges and universities attract a slightly younger adult than do lower levels of the formal education system (54 per cent of persons at colleges and universities, compared to 47 per cent at elementary and secondary schools, are under thirty-five).

3. As might be expected, those attending colleges and universities are overwhelmingly (75 per cent) persons who have already had some college experience while virtually none (1 per cent) are persons with only a grade-school education. Community organizations also have high proportions of college educated, while the institutions with the lowest proportions of persons who have been to college are the religious institutions (27 per cent) and the elementary and secondary schools (29 per cent).

In overview, then, it is clear that different institutions vary considerably in the types of adult students they instruct.

Variation by nature of registration

The final section of this chapter compares the characteristics of persons who participated in educational activities for various types of credit. The comparisons along this dimension are shown in Table 4.8.

1. First, it is clear from these data that both categories of credit students have considerably more men than women, while non-credit enrollees are represented with just about the expected numbers from each sex. This suggests that the slight overrepresentation of men among adult education participants as a whole is primarily an overrepresentation of men seeking formal credit for their studies.

2. Credit participants are not only more likely to be men, but are much more likely to be younger adults. A substantial majority, 62 per cent of those studying for high-school and college credit, were under thirty-five years of age, as were exactly 50 per cent of those seeking other types of credit for their studies. By comparison, only 42 per cent of those not seeking credit of any kind were under thirty-five. Clearly, adults enrolled for credit are younger than those who are not, and in addition, those seeking college degrees or high-school diplomas are younger than those striving for other kinds of certification.

3. It is significant, finally, that as many as 76 per cent of those taking credit courses within the regular school system were persons who had already had at least some college education. By contrast, only one-half this number (37 per cent) in the other two categories were college educated.

Table 4.8   Sex, Age, and Education of Persons Engaged in Credit and Non-Credit Studies

| Characteristics | Type of Registration | | | Total Sample of Adults (Per Cent) |
| | Credit Students | | Non-Credit Students (Per Cent) | |
	Credit within Regular School System (Per Cent)	Other Kinds of Credit (Per Cent)		
Sex				
Male	59	61	48	47
Female	41	39	52	53
Total	100	100	100	100
Age				
Under 35	62	50	42	31
35–54	33	44	45	41
55 and over	5	7	13	28
Total	100	101	100	100
Education				
Grade school only	2	8	10	29
High school	22	55	53	51
College	76	37	37	20
Total	100	100	100	100
Total N	374	442	3,913	23,950

5

Factors
Related
to
Participation

Up to this point, we have examined the social composition of adult education participants in terms of eleven different background characteristics. These same factors will now be re-examined, but for the express purpose of isolating the extent to which they affect participation of educational pursuits. This chapter, then, reverts to a consideration of participation rates, and will be concerned throughout with two indices: the overall rates of activity in studies of any type, and the rates of study within particular subject areas.

THE INFLUENCE OF LIFE-CYCLE POSITION

The first characteristics to be examined in this connection are sex and age. Chart 5.1 shows the overall rates of participation for men and women, and then, separately, for persons in three major age groupings. This chart indicates that men participate slightly more often than women and that a strong relationship exists between age and rates of participation.[1] These do not constitute new findings, of course, since it was noted in Chapter 4 that men were slightly overrepresented and younger persons heavily overrepresented among participants in adult education. In order to provide continuity to the present discussion, how-

[1] Readers who wish to evaluate the statistical significance of any differences contained in these tables or charts may do so by referring to Table A-1.2 of Appendix 1.

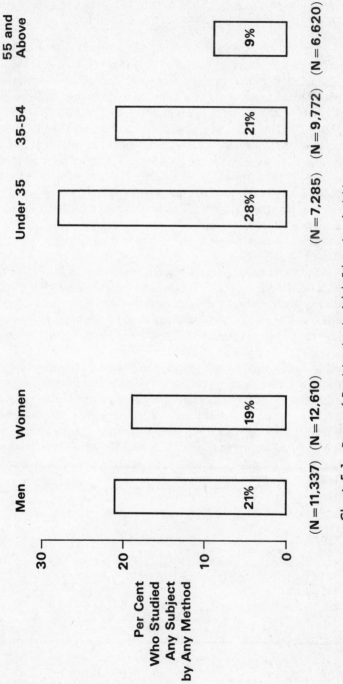

Chart 5.1 Rates of Participation in Adult Education Activities, by Sex and Age

ever, it will be necessary at several points to return to results which have been examined in a less direct fashion in Chapter 4.

A much more revealing insight into the relative influence of these factors emerges when rates of participation are examined in relation to sex and age simultaneously. Table 5.1 demonstrates that the slight overall difference in rates of study between the sexes stems solely from the youngest age-group. While men under thirty-five participate quite a bit more often than do women in this group, in the second age-group the difference is erased completely, and among persons aged fifty-five and over it is even reversed slightly. Thus, while among both sexes the incidence of study drops off with increasing age, the rate of decrease is much more precipitous among men than among women.

This suggests that educational behavior may be strongly influenced by life-cycle position, and raises the specific question of why the sex-linked difference found among younger persons does not persist into middle age. One possible explanation is that the finding reflects differences in the life-cycle roles of young men and young women.

The differential occurs during the period in which young couples are establishing homes and having their children, when sex differential in family obligations and responsibilities probably reaches a peak. In other words, the finding might be completely explained by the fact that young wives' activities away from home are more greatly curtailed than those of their husbands.

Table 5.1 Rates of Participation in Educational Activities, by Sex and Age

	Men			Women		
Rate	Under 35 (Per Cent)	35–54 (Per Cent)	55 and Over (Per Cent)	Under 35 (Per Cent)	35–54 (Per Cent)	55 and Over (Per Cent)
Per cent who studied any subject by any method	33	21	9	25	21	10
N	3,287	4,684	2,920	3,847	4,900	3,420

While we might explore this possibility through a comparison of rates of participation among married and single persons, a much more reasonable strategy is to examine the influence of parenthood. In Table 5.2, respondents are classified not only by sex and age, but also according to whether or not they are parents. Clearly, the presence of children affects the participation rates of men and women quite differently. There is no difference at all between the activity rates of young men and women without children (29 per cent each), but very substantial differences may be noted between the rates of young fathers and young mothers (34 per cent and 23 per cent, respectively). The original difference appears to be explained completely by the fact that women are more tied down with young children than are men.

In fact, parenthood seems to have quite opposite effects on the educational activities of fathers. Whereas rates of study were lower among mothers than among non-mothers, they were actually higher among fathers than among non-fathers. In seeking to explain one result, then, we have uncovered a second for which further explanation appears necessary.

Why is it that fathers engage in adult education studies more frequently than non-fathers? The most likely interpretation seems connected in some way to economic considerations. For example, if it can be reasonably assumed that fathers have heavier financial obligations than non-fathers, then they might take courses more often in order to acquire skills or knowledge which can help them supplement their incomes.

On the other hand, perhaps, since parenthood probably commits a man more firmly to a home and family role, the accelerated rates of study could be accounted for primarily through increased participation in courses pertaining to home and family life subjects and skills. Or, indeed, perhaps the explanation is that enrollment in educational courses constitutes a socially acceptable way for a man to gain respite from the confusion in his home. In any event, at least as far as men are concerned, adult education activities do not attract primarily the lonely or the isolated; if anything, the results indicate quite the opposite.

Although motives for studying will not be systematically considered until Part II of this monograph, examination of the

Table 5.2 Life-Cycle Position and Participation in Adult Education

Rate	Age under 35				Age 35–54				Age 55 and Over			
	Men		Women		Men		Women		Men		Women	
	Number of Children under 21				Number of Children under 21				Number of Children under 21			
	One or More (Per Cent)	None (Per Cent)	One or More (Per Cent)	None (Per Cent)	One or More (Per Cent)	None (Per Cent)	One or More (Per Cent)	None (Per Cent)	One or More (Per Cent)	None (Per Cent)	One or More (Per Cent)	None (Per Cent)
Per cent who studied any subject by any method	34	29	23	29	24	16	22	18	14	8	8	10
N	2,036	1,349	2,893	993	3,072	1,714	2,877	2,098	333	2,727	131	3,421

different kinds of subject matter studied by fathers as compared with non-fathers — and for that matter, by mothers compared with women who have no children — is rather revealing. These data are presented in Table 5.3. In trying to find out which subjects account for the overall difference in the rates of activity of men in different positions of family responsibility, we find that the results clearly point to vocational learning. In all age-groups men with children study job-related subjects and skills more frequently than their counterparts who do not have children, and the differences, although not spectacular, are larger than those related to any other area of subject matter. This suggests that the first interpretation, that men who support larger families have greater economic needs and therefore turn more often to adult education, is probably most accurate.

Although this is the main finding in Table 5.3, other differences also reflect the influence of life-cycle position. For example, the table also shows that family responsibilities have the strongest effect on the vocational and academic studies of young mothers. In these areas, the rates of study of young women without children exceed those of young mothers by ratios of about three to one and two to one, respectively. In all other subject areas, however, there are virtually no differences between the two categories.

It is interesting, too, that the differences in vocational learning completely disappear among women in the thirty-five – fifty-four age group. Moreover, while vocational studies among non-mothers fall off precipitously after the age of thirty-five, among the mothers they do not — and in fact even increase slightly. A difference of 1 per cent does not constitute much absolute increase in activity, but because it occurs during a period when rates of activity in most other subject areas fall off sharply among both men and women, it is extremely meaningful. This finding, of course, reflects the return to the labor force of married women whose children no longer demand their full-time attention.

In the main, then, family responsibilities seem to have strong effect on vocational learning. For men, parenthood works to accelerate participation, while for women it practically extin-

Table 5.3 Per Cent Who Studied Subject Matter of Each Type, by Life-Cycle Position

Subjects	Age under 35				Age 35–54				Age 55 and Over			
	Men		Women		Men		Women		Men		Women	
	Number of Children under 21				Number of Children under 21				Number of Children under 21			
	One or More (Per Cent)	None (Per Cent)	One or More (Per Cent)	None (Per Cent)	One or More (Per Cent)	None (Per Cent)	One or More (Per Cent)	None (Per Cent)	One or More (Per Cent)	None (Per Cent)	One or More (Per Cent)	None (Per Cent)
Vocational	21	17	5	14	14	9	6	6	7	3	1	2
Academic	5	8	3	6	3	3	2	4	1	1	1	1
Recreational	6	5	7	8	4	4	6	5	1	2	*	3
Home and family	2	1	7	6	1	1	4	3	2	*	2	2
Religion	4	2	4	4	3	2	5	3	2	2	6	3
All other	5	3	4	4	4	3	4	2	2	1	2	1
N	2,036	1,349	2,893	993	3,072	1,714	2,877	2,098	333	2,727	131	3,421

*Less than 1 per cent.

guishes it, at least during the childbearing years. In home and family life subjects, only small differences are found between parents and non-parents, suggesting that one's role as a father or mother has little direct impact on this sphere of adult education. The category of religious study, however, is interesting in this connection; even though the rates are small among persons in all categories, whatever differences do exist are all in the direction of higher rates of study among persons with children.

THE IMPACT OF SOCIO-ECONOMIC FACTORS

This section examines the ways in which socio-economic factors influence rates of participation in adult education. Information was collected on education, occupation, and family income, the three indicators usually combined in social research to measure social class position. For present purposes, however, these factors are examined separately, and our central task is to determine which if any of them have an effect on participatory behavior. Throughout this analysis, the comparisons are made between persons in three educational groupings (grade-school, high-school, and college educated), two classes of occupation (white collar and blue collar), and three categories of family income (under $4,000, $4,000 – $6,999, and $7,000 and over).

First, Chart 5.2 shows how each of these factors is related individually to rates of educational participation, and it indicates that all three are indeed effective in producing differences in rates of activity. In education the differences are particularly large, with a range from 6 per cent among those with only a grade-school education to 38 per cent among those who had been to college. As survey research results go, these are exceptionally large differences; in fact, they suggest that participation in adult education is probably as much affected by formal schooling as practically any other type of social behavior one might think of. At the same time, however, substantial differences are also produced by the other two background factors. Rates of study among persons in white-collar jobs are almost twice as high as among those in the blue-collar category (32 per cent to 17 per cent); and the incidence of activity is also seen to rise from 12 to 20 to 29 per cent as one scans upward through the income scale.

Although each of these factors produces substantial differences on its own, it is questionable whether the genuine influence of each is as strong as indicated in Chart 5.2. Since level
of education has a direct influence on occupation, and occupation is a major determinant of income, it is necessary to examine
more carefully the influence order among these factors as they
affect adult education participation. In other words, in order to
isolate the independent impact of any one factor, appropriate
statistical controls must be imposed on the other two. While all
three factors can be examined simultaneously, the relationships
can perhaps be demonstrated more clearly if the factors are first
looked at two at a time.

Since education and income come first in the theoretical
influence chain, these should be the first two to be examined in
combination. Table 5.4 isolates the activity rates for persons in
the two types of occupations within each of the educational
groupings. It should be noted that this table deals only with
members of the labor force; housewives are not assigned the
occupations of their husbands, unlike the usual practice of allocating social status on the basis of occupation.

Table 5.4 clearly describes the relative impact of education
and occupation on rates of participation. Although differences
between occupations are found in each educational category, the
much more powerful influence stems from educational background. Regardless of class of job, participation in educational
activities is greater if formal education is higher. This holds just
as effectively between the grade-school and high-school categories as between the high-school and college levels, and the
overall range in levels of activity varies from a low of 8 per cent
among those with a grade-school education who work in blue-
collar occupations to 43 per cent among those with a college
education who work in white-collar occupations. Between educational background and type of occupation, then, education has
clearly the more dominant influence on participatory behavior.

The two other sets of comparisons are presented in Tables 5.5
and 5.6. The first isolates the relative impact of occupation and
income; the second, educational attainment as compared with
family income. As between type of occupation and level of

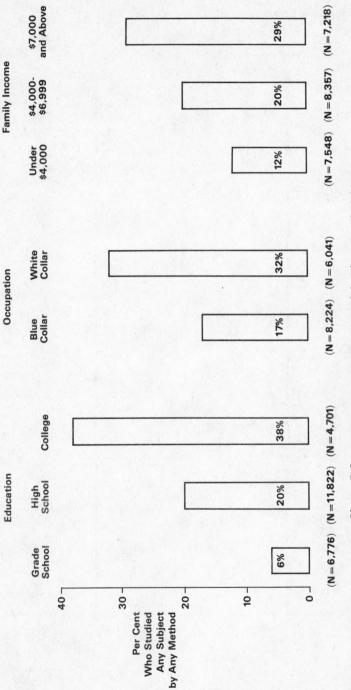

Chart 5.2 Rates of Participation in Adult Education Activities, by Education, Occupation, and Family Income

Table 5.4 Rates of Participation in Adult Education, by Education and Occupation

Rate	Education					
	Grade School		High School		College	
	Blue Collar (Per Cent)	White Collar (Per Cent)	Blue Collar (Per Cent)	White Collar (Per Cent)	Blue Collar (Per Cent)	White Collar (Per Cent)
Per cent who studied any subject by any method	8	11	21	25	38	43
N	2,914	444	4,397	2,877	655	2,647

Table 5.5 Rates of Participation in Adult Education, by Occupation and Income

| Rate | Blue-Collar Occupations | | White-Collar Occupations | | |
| | Family Income | | Family Income | | |
	Under $4,000 (Per Cent)	$4,000–$6,999 (Per Cent)	$7,000 and Over (Per Cent)	Under $4,000 (Per Cent)	$4,000–$6,999 (Per Cent)	$7,000 and Over (Per Cent)
Per cent who studied any subject by any method	14	18	22	24	29	36
N	2,098	3,257	1,788	698	1,984	3,190

Table 5.6 Rates of Participation in Adult Education, by Education and Family Income

Rate	Grade School			High School			College		
	Under $4,000 (Per Cent)	$4,000 – $6,999 (Per Cent)	$7,000 and Over (Per Cent)	Under $4,000 (Per Cent)	$4,000 – $6,999 (Per Cent)	$7,000 and Over (Per Cent)	Under $4,000 (Per Cent)	$4,000 – $6,999 (Per Cent)	$7,000 and Over (Per Cent)
Per cent who studied any subject by any method	6	8	9	17	19	26	28	38	41
N	3,791	1,901	831	2,920	4,860	3,680	574	1,410	2,594

income, Table 5.5 clearly demonstrates that the former makes more difference than the latter. No matter what one's income is, one is more likely to participate in adult education if one works in a white-collar rather than in a blue-collar job. However, income still seems to have some effect, since within each occupational category the rates increase by about one-half their original size as one moves from the lowest to the highest levels (from 14 to 22 per cent in the blue-collar group and from 24 to 36 per cent in the white-collar group).

On the other hand, type of occupation clearly dominates over level of income, and a comparison of any two cells at the same income level shows that the rates of white-collar persons are higher than those of blue-collar persons by a factor of approximately 1.6 or 1.7 to 1.

Table 5.6 rounds out the set of comparisons, and, as could be anticipated from the results of Tables 5.4 and 5.5, confirms that the influence of education is clearly dominant over that of income. No matter what one's economic level, a higher education is still a more important determinant of whether one participates in educational activities. It is quite revealing that those in the lowest income category who had been to college participate about three times more frequently than those with only a grade-school education but who are in the highest income category (28 per cent compared with 9 per cent). Nonetheless, within the educational categories, family income does appear to make a difference, since rates for the highest income cells exceed those for the lowest income cells by ratios of almost exactly three to two.

Although further clarification of these influence relations is hardly necessary, the analysis is technically more complete if the factors are examined simultaneously. The results of Table 5.7, therefore, add little new information, but do show conclusively that education is the prime determinant among the three. According to Table 5.7, no combination of income or occupational conditions contributes an effect which supercedes that of having more education. The rates fall into three distinct ranges clustered around the three educational categories: for the grade-school category they all fall between 7 and 14 per cent;

Table 5.7 Rates of Participation in Adult Education, by Education, Occupation, and Family Income (Per Cent Who Studied Any Subject by Any Method)

Occupation	Grade School			High School			College		
	Under $4,000	$4,000 – $6,999	$7,000 and Over	Under $4,000	$4,000 – $6,999	$7,000 and Over	Under $4,000	$4,000 – $6,999	$7,000 and Over
Blue collar	7 (1,463)	8 (964)	11 (389)	20 (1,207)	21 (1,937)	23 (1,126)	37 (136)	40 (269)	37 (229)
White collar	9 (125)	11 (176)	14 (122)	22 (371)	21 (1,081)	29 (1,340)	37 (190)	45 (704)	43 (1,698)

for the high-school group between 20 and 29 per cent; and for the college group between 37 and 45 per cent.

At the same time, however, the results in Table 5.7 tend to obscure the influence relations between occupation and income. Although occupation does account for a slight difference in seven of the nine conditions in which the effects can be assessed, occupation no longer seems to make more difference than income under all conditions. For example, in both the grade-school and high-school groups, those in the favored income categories who hold blue-collar jobs have slightly higher rates of participation than do persons with white-collar jobs who are found in the low-income cells.

In addition, the influence of income itself disappears under certain conditions, in particular among the college educated. In both categories of occupation here, the rates tail off in transition from the middle to the highest income levels. The highest rate of all, therefore, is not found in the category where all three factors would be most "favorable," but rather among the college-educated who hold white-collar jobs and are in the middle-income brackets.

In summary, the most powerful factor by far is educational attainment, and although occupation and income do count for a little, their effects are quite secondary by comparison. Taken together, of course, the effect of all three factors is enormous, and through their combined influence, rates of activity emerge from levels of virtual nonexistence to levels which include close to one person in two. A person who has been to college, works in a white-collar occupation, and makes more than $7,000 a year is about six times more likely to have been active in adult education pursuits during the previous year than a person who has never been beyond grade school, works in a blue-collar occupation, and whose family income is less than $4,000 a year.

These effects, in short, appear to be cumulative and to have a kind of spiraling effect not dissimilar to the way a capital investment accumulates with increasing magnitude under a compound interest structure.

It is clear, too, that formal schooling tells much of the story in the overall appraisal of participatory behavior. Somewhere in the process of getting an education, it seems people learn either that education itself is a continuing life experience, or that the way to acquire new skills and knowledge in life is to engage in formal or informal programs of study.

Because the average education of the American public has been increasing steadily over the past few decades, wide discrepancies currently exist between the educational achievements of different age-groups in the population. Young adults today are, on the average, better educated than their parents and have a considerably higher formal education than their grandparents. In view of this, it is necessary to reconsider the relationship between age and participation in adult education in order to make sure that the differences originally attributed to the influence of age are not in reality a function of differences in education. Table 5.8, therefore, examines the relative influence of both age and education on the participation rates of both men and women.

On this point the evidence is clear-cut: formal education does not erase the influence of age, and in all educational categories among both men and women the rates of activity fall off, in some cases quite sharply in the older age groups. On the other hand, age does not destroy the strong differences produced by education, and thus both factors can be said to influence participatory behavior. Just how important this influence is can be seen by comparing the rates of the oldest and least well-educated with those of the youngest and best-educated in the extreme cells of Table 5.8. These extremes range from 5 to 47 per cent among

Table 5.8 Rates of Participation in Adult Education, by Age, Sex, and Education (Per Cent Who Studied Any Subject by Any Method)

Education	Men			Women		
	Under 35	35–54	55 and Over	Under 35	35–54	55 and Over
Grade school	9 (394)	8 (1,257)	5 (1,692)	11 (369)	9 (1,190)	6 (1,82
High school	29 (1,813)	20 (2,349)	12 (834)	21 (2,635)	20 (2,904)	11 (1,1
College	47 (1,080)	38 (1,078)	18 (394)	42 (843)	40 (806)	25 (4

men (a factor of more than nine to one) and from 6 to 42 per cent among women (a factor of seven to one).

What can be said about the relative effect of age and education on rates of participation in adult education? One way to answer this is to examine the discrepancies in rates which each factor produces across its various conditions. For example, there are six observations which can be made on the influence of each factor, and although the percentage differences are by no means constant on each condition they nonetheless work out to averages of 27 per cent for education and 14 per cent for age. Other quick tests of the relative impact of each factor confirm this general result and suggest that education contributes approximately two-thirds of the impact and age about one-third. The more important conclusion, however, is that both age and education play a major role in relation to rates of participation in adult education.

Before turning to other background factors, we will examine the ways in which educational background affects the types of subject matter people study. Table 5.9 shows the rates at which men and women with differing amounts of schooling studied subjects of various types. These results indicate quite clearly that persons without much formal schooling do not study anything very frequently, and that as education increases so do rates of study in all subject areas.

Table 5.9 Type of Subject Matter Studied, by Sex and Education (Rates of Participation: Per Cent Who Studied Subject Matter of Each Type)

Subjects	Men			Women		
	Grade School	High School	College	Grade School	High School	College
Vocational	3	14	22	1	5	11
Academic	1	2	9	*	2	8
Recreational	1	4	8	1	5	13
Home and family	1	2	2	2	5	7
Religion	2	3	4	3	4	6
All other	1	3	8	1	3	7
N	3,343	4,996	2,552	3,387	6,698	2,082

*Less than 1 per cent.

However, these data also suggest that the selection of some types of subject matter may be much more affected by education than may the selection of others. For example, among both men and women, rates of vocational, academic, and recreational studies seem to reflect much more pronounced increases across the three educational groupings than do studies in the other categories. The findings suggest, in other words, that persons with differing amounts of formal schooling emphasize quite different types of subjects in their post-school learning experiences.

This tendency is much more directly expressed in Table 5.10, where the same results are presented as profiles of the total activities of different categories of persons. By far the most impressive figures here are those showing the relative place of religious study in the total activities of these different groups. Among women, religious studies constituted 34 per cent of all courses reported by grade-school educated; 16 per cent of those mentioned by high-school educated; and only 11 per cent of those who had been to college. For men, the comparable percentages were 23, 10, and 7, respectively. But, even more significantly, religion was the most frequently studied subject among women with little education, and the least frequently studied among those who had been to college. Home and family life subjects and skills also received more emphasis among women of low rather than high educational attainment. Moving from low to high across the educational continuum, these studies made up, respectively, 24, 20, and 14 per cent of all courses undertaken.

Balancing these tendencies, academic and recreational subjects were much more prominent in the profiles of persons higher up the educational continuum, and among college-educated women, studies related to spare-time employment predominated.

Together, then, Tables 5.9 and 5.10 illustrate two important features of the relationship between educational background and participation in continuing education. They demonstrate, first, that people who have more formal education are more likely to study in all subject areas, but second, that the increases in these rates of study are quite uneven across different categories of subject matter.

DIFFERENCES BY REGION AND TYPE OF COMMUNITY

In Chapter 4 it was noted that persons living in the Western states and also in the suburbs and outskirts of large and middle-sized cities were overrepresented among adult education participants. This next section will re-examine these trends and attempt to isolate more carefully the influence of region and type of community on educational behavior.

Chart 5.3 points quite clearly to the main ways in which the incidence of educational participation differs in various geographical settings. With respect to region, the chart shows that rates of study are very much the same in the Northeast, the North Central states, and the South, but that they are, at 28 per cent, about one and one-half times higher in the West. With respect to size and type of community, the results indicate first, that rates of activity are slightly higher in large urban centers than in small communities, and second, that within standard metropolitan areas they are considerably higher among suburbanites than among those living within the central cities.

While these trends are quite revealing, one must again ask whether the differentials genuinely reflect regional or community

Table 5.10 Profiles of Subject Matter Studied, by Sex and Education (Per Cent of Total Subjects Reported)

Subjects	Men			Women		
	Grade School	High School	College	Grade School	High School	College
Vocational	39	50	42	16	22	21
Academic	10	8	17	6	9	16
Recreational	10	15	15	11	22	26
Home and family	8	6	5	24	20	14
Religion	23	10	7	34	16	11
All other	11	11	15	10	11	13
Total	101	100	101	101	100	101
N	250	1,375	1,332	274	1,588	1,082

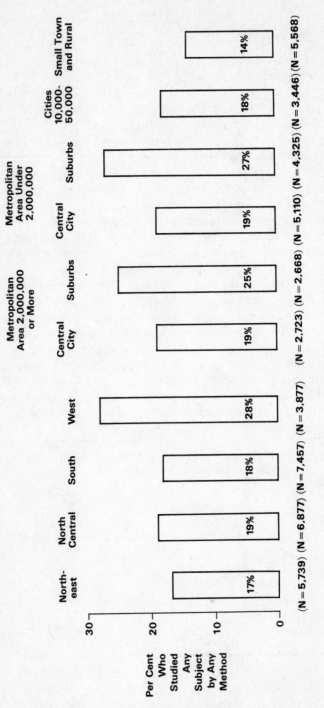

Chart 5.3 Rates of Participation in Adult Education Activities, by Region and Size of Community

effect, or simply those effects produced by differences in the composition of these particular segments of the population. For example, the median years of schooling in the West is known to be higher than in other regions of the country,[2] and, in addition, educational levels are usually higher among persons who live in the suburbs of large cities than among those living within the city limits.[3] One should inquire, therefore, whether the overall differences are produced simply because Western states and the suburbs of large cities have, on the average, better-educated segments of the population.

This possibility is examined first, in Table 5.11, in relation to regional differences. This table divides the population into those who completed high school and those who did not and then presents overall rates of participation and rates of study within specific subject areas for both groups.

From part *a* of the table it is clearly evident that the regional differences do in fact persist after an educational control is imposed. If anything the differences become sharpened, and particularly so among the non-high-school graduates, where they range from 6 per cent in the Northeast to 18 per cent in the West. Among the high-school graduates, the discrepancies are of about the same magnitude of absolute percentage difference, but because participation rates are generally higher among these segments of the public, the overall impact of region is not nearly so dramatic. In the West, however, even non-high-school graduates participate in educational activities at a level close to the national average of 20 per cent.

In ranking by region, then, the highest rates of activity are clearly found in the West, the second highest in the South, the third highest in the North Central region, and the lowest in the Northeast. This ranking is rather surprising when one compares it with the rank order of overall educational attainment by re-

[2]In 1960 the median years of schooling completed by persons aged twenty-five and over in different regions was 12.0 in the West, 10.7 in both the Northeast and North Central regions, and 9.1 in the South (U.S. Department of Commerce, Bureau of the Census, 1962*b*, Table 115, pp. 1–260).

[3]In 1960 the median years of schooling for persons aged twenty-five and over living in the fringes of urbanized areas was 12.0 years—as compared with 10.7 years for persons living within central cities (U.S. Department of Commerce, Bureau of the Census, 1962*b*, Table 151, pp. 1–316).

Table 5.11 Rates of Participation in Adult Education, by Region and Education

Activity	Completed High School or More				Did Not Complete High School			
	Northeast (Per Cent)	North Central (Per Cent)	South (Per Cent)	West (Per Cent)	Northeast (Per Cent)	North Central (Per Cent)	South (Per Cent)	West (Per Cent)
a. Overall Activity								
Per cent who studied any subject by any method	26	27	30	37	6	9	10	18
b. Activity by Subject Area								
Vocational	13	12	12	17	3	4	3	7
Academic	4	4	4	6	1	1	*	3
Recreational	7	8	7	9	1	2	1	4
Home and family	4	5	3	5	1	2	1	3
Religion	1	3	7	5	*	1	5	2
All other	4	4	5	7	1	1	1	2
N	3,135	3,468	3,032	2,209	2,472	3,252	4,174	1,555

*Less than 1 per cent.

gion. The percentages of high-school graduates in different regions in 1960, for example, were 51 in the West, 42 in the North Central states, 41 in the Northeast, and 35 in the South (U.S. Department of Commerce, Bureau of the Census, 1962*b*, Table 115, pp. 1 – 260). Thus, although the West has both the highest percentage of high-school graduates and the highest rates of adult education participation, a comparison of the other three regions on these rankings reveals a far from consistent pattern. Southerners, while lowest in overall educational attainment by a considerable margin, have the second highest rate of participation in adult education activities.

Some insight into this imbalance is gained from an examination of the rates at which different types of subject matter are studied in the different regions. From Table 5.11*b* a comparison of the Northeast, North Central, and Southern regions indicates that rates of activity are identical within one percentage point in all areas of study except religion. Among both high-school graduates and non-graduates, however, rates of religious study are considerably higher in the South than in either Northern region — in fact, they are higher in the South than in the West. This explains why the incidence of total activity is greater in the South than in the North. The difference is entirely a function of the more frequent religious study in the South, a sphere of learning not nearly so much affected by educational background as other areas of subject matter.

One can also isolate from these data the areas of subject matter which produce the elevated rates of overall study in the West. Here, however, the discrepancies are not concentrated within one field, but apparently within three. The principal differences are found in vocational studies, but important secondary differences are found in academic and recreational categories. Together, these three categories account for most of the differences between the West and the remainder of the country.

In summary, these data indicate two important differences between regions insofar as adult education behavior is concerned. The West has definitely higher rates of study in the vocational, academic, and recreational spheres, while Southerners are considerably more likely to study religion.

Next, a similar control is imposed, in Table 5.12, on the comparison of rates between communities of different types. Stratification by education again fails to erase the main patterns of difference originally noted, the highest rates are consistently found among the suburbanites, and the lowest among those in small towns and rural areas. In addition, the city-suburban differences persist, since in the four comparisons of persons in these locales rates of activity among the latter are all higher than among the former. These differences are by no means gross, but because they exist within both educational groupings, they are quite meaningful.

A more detailed scrutiny of these community effects is undertaken in Table 5.13, where rates of activity are shown for specific subject fields. Here, the large and middle-sized cities are grouped together in order to emphasize more clearly the urban-suburban comparison. However, the results are inconclusive. Among those who completed high school, the main difference can be attributed easily enough to recreational learning, but this tendency is not reflected by the non-high-school graduates, where there are no differences at all between city dwellers and suburbanites in relation to learning for leisure. In fact, among non-high-school graduates there does not seem to be any single subject area in which urban and suburban groups differ very much: the home and family, and religious categories produce

Table 5.12 Rates of Participation in Adult Education, by Size and Type of Community and Education (Per Cent Who Studied Any Subject By Any Method)

Education	Large Cities		Middle-Sized Cities		Small Cities	Small Town and Rural
	Central City	Suburbs	Central City	Suburbs		
Persons who completed high school	28 (1,413)	34 (1,655)	29 (2,501)	35 (2,478)	30 (1,644)	22 (2,117)
Persons who did not complete high school	9 (1,210)	12 (967)	10 (2,440)	16 (1,761)	8 (1,731)	8 (3,275)

large ratio differences, but these do not mean very much in terms of absolute numbers.

Among those in the higher educational group, it is again in recreational studies that residents of small towns and rural areas appear to differ most from persons living in the larger centers. Again, however, the discrepancies are only slight and the trend is only minimally supported among persons in the lower education category.

In conclusion, it appears that while size and type of community do make a slight difference in overall rates of participation in educational activities, it is only among persons with a somewhat higher than average education that the effects become channeled in any specific way. Among the better educated segments of the population, however, there does appear to be a slight tendency for recreational studies to be undertaken more frequently by suburban dwellers and less frequently by residents of small towns and rural areas.

DIFFERENCES RELATED TO RACE

In this final section, a brief examination is made of differences between whites and Negroes in participation in adult education.

Table 5.13 Kinds of Subject Matter Studied, by Education and Type of Community (Per Cent Who Studied Subject Matter of Each Type)

Subjects	Completed High School or More				Did Not Complete High School			
	Large and Middle-Sized Cities		Small Cities	Small Town and Rural	Large and Middle-Sized Cities		Small Cities	Small Town and Rural
	Central City	Suburbs			Central City	Suburbs		
Vocational	13	15	13	11	4	5	3	3
Academic	5	6	4	3	2	1	1	1
Recreational	6	11	8	4	2	2	2	1
Home and family	4	5	3	3	1	3	2	2
Religion	4	4	4	4	2	4	2	2
All other	5	6	5	3	1	2	1	1
N	3,914	4,133	1,644	2,117	3,650	2,728	1,731	3,275

In Chapter 4 it was found that Negroes were underrepresented among adult education participants by a factor of about three to four. This underrepresentation is reflected in the slight differential found in the top line of Table 5.14, where activity rates for whites are shown to be 20 per cent and for Negroes 16 per cent.

The interesting feature about this difference, however, is that it completely disappears once an educational control is introduced. The second and third lines of the table show identical rates of participation for whites and Negroes within each educational category. Thus the differences between races in the overall incidence of educational activity can be completely explained by the fact that, on the average, whites have a better education than Negroes.

Table 5.14 Rates of Participation in Adult Education, by Race and Education (Per Cent Who Studied Any Subject by Any Method)

Category	White	Negro
Total population	20 (20,844)	16 (2,730)
Persons who completed high school or more	30 (10,791)	30 (856)
Persons who did not complete high school	10 (9,579)	10 (1,724)

Table 5.15 Kinds of Subject Matter Studied, by Race and Education (Per Cent Who Studied Subject Matter of Each Type)

Subjects	Completed High School or More		Did Not Complete High School	
	White	Negro	White	Negro
Vocational	13	13	4	2
Academic	5	6	1	1
Recreational	8	4	2	1
Home and family	4	4	2	1
Religion	4	5	2	5
All other	5	7	1	1
N	10,791	856	9,579	1,724

Finally, Table 5.15 compares the activities of whites and Negroes in specific subject areas. The main finding here is that within the higher educational grouping, whites participate twice as often as Negroes in studies of recreational subjects (8 per cent compared with 4 per cent), and although in the lower educational grouping the rates are simply too small to be definitive, at least the same two-to-one ratio may be noted on studies of this type.

The overall balance in rates seems to be restored primarily through the influence of religious study. Although differences in studies of this type are almost nonexistent among high-school graduates, they emerge sharply within the lower educational grouping and are particularly strong there if one takes into account the levels of activity generally found among persons who did not complete high school. Indeed, for Negroes of lower education, religion clearly represents the most frequent category of study.

To conclude, then, a comparison of subject emphasis between whites and Negroes shows that whites, particularly the better-educated ones, study hobbies and recreations more frequently, while Negroes, particularly the less well-educated ones, study religion more frequently. Taken in sum, however, there are no overall differences in rates of activity which can be attributed to the influence of race.

Part II

Cumulative Experience
and the
Potential Audiences
for
Programs of
Continuing Education

Introduction
to
Part II

In Part II we consider adult education participation in a much wider perspective; the scope of our study is expanded from learning activities over one year to experiences encountered at any time since leaving school. This section also deals with people's attitudes, opinions, beliefs concerning learning, and their motivation to participate in systematic programs of continuing education. Throughout, the approach is in the main analytic rather than descriptive, and the chief goal of the analysis is to spell out the ways in which social and social-psychological factors work to propel some adults, but not others, into educational pursuits.

In Chapter 6 we trace people's educational experiences back to the point at which they stopped their formal schooling. We first consider the cumulative incidence of learning experiences during people's post-school lives and then compare the types of studies undertaken, both formally and informally, during these extended periods.

In Chapter 7 the circumstances under which participants were initially recruited into adult education pursuits are reconstructed. Information is reviewed concerning the ages and life-cycle stages at which people first enrolled and the kinds of subject matter they studied during these initial encounters.

In Chapter 8 the analysis turns more directly to the question of why adults enroll in courses, reasons people have for enrolling in courses of different types, and the motives which different kinds of people have for engaging in educational activities. This chapter also reviews evidence on the benefits people say they derive, and these are examined in relation to the motives which led them to enroll in the first place.

In Chapters 9 and 10 attention is then shifted to the question of the nature of "potential audiences" for programs of continuing education. The act of educational participation by adults is viewed here as the end result of at least two quite fundamental processes: first, the emergence of some minimal desire for new knowledge, information, or skills, and second, the development of a capacity to convert a learning interest into actual behavior. In Chapter 9 we trace the social origins of dispositions favorable to continued learning during adult life and also discuss the conditions under which these dispositions either persist or decline. The main focus of Chapter 10, on the other hand, is on those conditions which both facilitate and block the translation of interests into actions: there we identify the types of individuals most ready to take action in relation to their interests, examine levels of public awareness of facilities for continuing education, analyze people's reactions to different types of study methods, and evaluate the kinds of barriers different people face when they attempt to activate their educational interests.

Chapter 11 deals with the very specialized topic of national audiences for educational television stations. It reviews what very well may be the only information currently available for making relatively precise national estimates of the number of American adults who are aware of educational television stations and who have watched their programs.

Finally, Chapter 12 presents a general discussion of the premises and definitions from which adults perceive and evaluate education, and it attempts to determine how these influence the educational behavior of different sectors of the population. The chapter then concludes with a discussion of the adult education implications of increased amounts of leisure time in American life.

All the data examined in this section are derived from personal interviews with adults selected from the households screened in the first phase of the study. Technical details on the sampling procedures employed are discussed in Appendix 1, and a copy of the interview schedule (the Long-Form Personal Interview) is reproduced in Appendix 2.

6

Patterns
of Experience
with
Continuing
Education

Since the first phase of this investigation dealt exclusively with participation in educational pursuits over one year, the most natural way to initiate the second phase was to inquire about how many additional adults participated over longer periods of time. Here we are concerned with the general problem of estimating the cumulative incidence of course-taking, and in this connection we will review evidence pertaining to three specific questions: (*1*) How many different adults take educational courses of one type or another at some time after leaving school? (*2*) How frequently do people typically engage in learning pursuits after leaving school? (*3*) What is the cumulative incidence of adult exposures to different fields of subject matter?

THE CUMULATIVE INCIDENCE OF COURSE-TAKING

Because answering these questions requires that people recall events which may have taken place many years ago, there are quite serious problems concerning the accuracy of the reports which people can be expected to provide. Probably the best we can hope for is an approximate rather than a precise estimate of the incidence of cumulative experiences with adult education.

In order to maximize recall of experiences, respondents were handed a card with a long list of examples of different types of subjects and then were asked the following question:

[QUESTION 17] Thinking back over the time since you left school, have you at any time since then taken an educational course of any sort—including things like evening classes, correspondence courses, lecture series, discussion groups, courses given over television, home studies, courses given by the armed services, or anything like that?

Table 6.1 indicates that 47 per cent of the sample said they had had experiences of this type, while 53 per cent said they had not. As expected, many more adults had been enrolled in adult education courses at some time in their lives than had done so during the previous twelve months, and Table 6.1 also provides some indication of the rate of development of this level of cumulative exposure. Thus, while at the time of the interview the number enrolled was only 7 per cent, it was 14 per cent during the previous year,[1] 21 per cent over the previous two years, 27 per cent over five years, 33 per cent over ten years, and 40 per cent over the previous twenty years.

[1]In Part I of the study the proportion who had taken a course during the previous year was estimated to be 15 per cent (see Chapter 3, Table 3.2).

Table 6.1 Prior Experience with Adult Education Courses (Per Cent Who Had Taken an Adult Education Course)

Yes		47%
Currently enrolled	7%	
Enrolled in past year	7	
Enrolled 1–2 years ago	7	
Enrolled 3–5 years ago	6	
Enrolled 6–10 years ago	6	
Enrolled 11–20 years ago	7	
Enrolled more than 20 years ago	6	
Time of enrollment unknown	1%	
No		53
Total		100%
Base (weighted)	9,784	
No information	29	
Still in school	151	
Total sample (weighted)*	9,964	

*An explanation of the weighting procedures employed in this section of the study is presented in Appendix 1.

In interpreting these figures it is important to bear in mind that the estimates are only approximate and that they pertain only to the experiences of the current population of adults. Because the American population is undergoing radical changes in its age and educational composition, it is safe to surmise that this particular level of cumulative exposure will not be applicable at all to future generations of adults. Indeed, since the population is becoming both younger and better educated, the overall incidence of experiences with continuing education will undoubtedly be found to be higher if the same question is asked of a national sample ten or twenty years from now.

Some evidence suggests that the total exposure of the population to educational pursuits has already increased appreciably in recent years. While a one-time cross-sectional survey is by no means the appropriate vehicle with which to study change, it is at least possible to compare the overall rates of exposure of persons of different ages in the current adult population. While such a comparison for rates of activity over the previous year tells us only that younger people are more active than their elders, a comparison of the proportion of persons in different age groups who have ever taken an adult education course should reflect generational changes in exposure, if in fact any exist. In other words, if it were found that the overall exposure to adult education courses is already higher among younger than among older persons, there would be good reason to believe that rates of participation in educational pursuits have increased in recent decades.

That this is in fact the case is revealed in Table 6.2. Here we note that 49 per cent of those under age thirty had already taken at least one course, and that the rate rises to 57 per cent for persons now in their thirties and then falls off to progressively lower levels among those in the older age brackets. Thus, even though people who had lived longer had a greater length of time over which to have taken a course, the cumulative incidence of exposure among those over forty was lower than for younger adults. Moreover, if current rates of activity were to remain unchanged, and if no new persons were recruited to educational pursuits after their thirties, it should be obvious that the overall level of exposure to adult education would rise to at least 57 per cent within about a generation.

Next, rows 2 and 3 of Table 6.2 reveal another interesting pattern. The most surprising aspect of these findings is not so much that there are tremendous differences in the exposure rates of the two educational groupings, but rather that the over-all drop-off in the incidence of exposure after the thirties is produced almost completely by the less well-educated sector of the population. Among those who had at least completed high school, 66 per cent of those in their thirties had taken a course, but so had 64 per cent of those aged sixty or over. However, among adults who had not completed high school, the incidence of exposure drops from 39 to 25 per cent across the comparable age-span.

In other words, younger adults without high-school diplomas are already considerably more likely to have had post-school educational experiences than are their counterparts in older age groups, but this same generational difference does not hold among the high-school graduates. This would suggest, then, that the differential exposure of better-educated and less well-educated adults to continuing education is much less pronounced today than it has been in the past. The gap is still a pretty large one, of course, but the discrepancy in rates of experience between persons in the two educational brackets has narrowed from 39 per cent among persons currently aged sixty and over to 24 per cent among those still under thirty years of age. These findings suggest a comparatively heavier recent recruitment to the ranks of continuing learning from the less well-educated segments of the population.

Another way of measuring recent changes in rates of activity from these same data is to see how many persons in different age brackets today had taken adult education courses by the time they had reached specified ages. For example, we might ask how many adults now sixty or over had taken a course by the time they were thirty, and then examine how this rate compares with that for persons now in their thirties.

The major weakness in conducting an analysis of this type is that older people have had a much longer period of time to forget

Table 6.2 Prior Experience with Adult Education Courses, by Age and Education (Per Cent Who Have Taken an Adult Education Course)

Category	Under 30	30–39	40–49	50–59	60 and Over
All adults (1)	49 (1,953)*	57 (2,100)	49 (2,192)	45 (1,542)	35 (1,932)
Adults who completed high school or more (2)	57 (1,254)	66 (1,370)	65 (1,126)	66 (597)	64 (489)
Adults who did not complete high school (3)	33 (698)	39 (730)	32 (1,057)	32 (929)	25 (1,432)

*All bases are weighted.

Table 6.3 Cumulative Experience with Adult Education Courses at Various Ages

Per Cent Who Had Taken an Adult Education Course by the Age Of	Current Age of Respondent				
	Under 30 (N = 1,953)*	30–39 (N = 2,100)	40–49 (N = 2,192)	50–59 (N = 1,542)	60 and Over (N = 1,932)
20	17	12	5	5	5
30		42	27	21	15'
40			39	32	20
50				41	26
60					31

*All bases are weighted.

about any courses they may have taken, and even if there were no real differences at all between generations we might still expect younger people to report more activities, if only because the events are more recent. On the other hand, since considerable care was taken to provide cues which covered a wide variety of subjects, there is a basis for having at least some confidence that the information reported is not entirely inaccurate.

Table 6.3 reorganizes the results to show the cumulative exposure levels at specific ages, and these figures certainly suggest that exposure to adult education courses has increased greatly in recent years. Because some unknown portion of the differences must be attributed to differential loss of memory, however, the figures can hardly be presented as a precise reflection of growth. About the only conclusion which can really be made here is that the results are consistent with other evidence indicating that rates of exposure to activities of this type have been rising recently.

FREQUENCY OF COURSE-TAKING

Also relevant here is the question of how often adults engage in formal educational pursuits. Table 6.4 presents the number of different courses people reported they had taken since leaving school. The table shows that in the total adult population, 18 per cent had been involved just once, 11 per cent twice, and some 17 per cent three or more times. Thus a sizable proportion of American adults—better than one in four—had been exposed more than once to continuing learning.

These figures also indicate that about one adult in a hundred had taken a minimum of nine courses. Altogether, we interviewed a total of forty-nine persons who had taken nine or more courses since leaving school,[2] and some quite interesting variations were found in the patterns of course taking in this small group of extremely active individuals. The first and most common pattern was that of the individual who engaged in part-time education as an adult to complete a college degree.

[2]These forty-nine individuals represent eighty-five weighted cases, and in relation to the weighted base of 9,784 constitute 0.87 per cent of all adults. In Table 6.4 this proportion is rounded up and reported as 1 per cent.

Mr. X was a thirty-one-year-old suburban New York school teacher who had never stopped or even interrupted his own formal schooling. Ever since leaving school as a full-time student some five years previously, he had been enrolled in courses which would eventually lead him to a Ph.D. in modern languages. In the previous year he had taken three different courses in French literature, and at the time of the interview had worked off some eighty-four credit hours toward his Ph.D. He had never been enrolled in a non-credit adult education course (Case No. 6031).

This pattern of learning activity can be distinguished easily from a second type in which enrollments were confined to studies having no relation to any formal degree requirements.

Mrs. Y was a forty-one-year-old Seattle resident, a college graduate, wife, and mother, who had been a school teacher prior to the birth of her first child. Her first adult education instruction was a course in sewing which she took when she was twenty-six. At twenty-eight she took a mathematics course for credit—presumably a credit which she could apply toward a promotion on her job. At the age of thirty she took a course in infant and child care and also began a series of courses in international affairs which she continued off and on until she was

Table 6.4 Number of Adult Education Courses Ever Taken

Number of Courses		
One or more		47%
One only	18%	
Two	11	
Three	7	
Four	3	
Five	3	
Six	1	
Seven	1	
Eight	1	
Nine or more	1	
Number undetermined	1%	
None		53
Total		100%
Base (weighted)	9,784	
No information	180	
Total sample (weighted)	9,964	

thirty-five. At thirty-four she took another credit course — this time in history, and at thirty-five a course in public speaking. For the next four years she was not active in courses at all, but she became active again at age thirty-nine when she attended a series of *National Geographic* lectures in Washington, D.C. During the previous year she had enrolled in a course titled "Christian Education" (Case No. 0029).

In this pattern of study the courses for the most part were non-credit, and none was connected with the requirements for any academic degree. Mrs. Y's studies, rather, were related to a much wider variety of life roles: to those of homemaker, parent, member of the community, and member of the labor force. Her experiences also differed in that they were characterized by periodic rather than uninterrupted involvement.

A third pattern was that of the participant whose first experiences with continuing education were in degree-connected courses, but who later branched out into other types of studies.

Mr. Z was a thirty-nine-year-old Palo Alto electronics engineer who between his mid-twenties and mid-thirties spent a total of eleven years as a part-time credit student and eventually obtained both a Bachelor's and Master's degree in engineering. After completing the Master's degree, he began to enroll in courses outside the degree program. At thirty-six he took a course in analog computers and another in digital computer mathematics; at thirty-seven, courses in electronic timing circuits and statistics; at thirty-eight, courses in literature, Zen Buddhism, psychology, digital computer programming, and management development. Most recently, at thirty-nine, he had joined a Great Books group (Case No. 0476).

In this particular case the habit of continuous study became established through formal degree studies, and, when the degree requirements were completed, a well-entrenched study habit was extended into completely new fields of learning. This particular respondent had been continuously engaged in educational courses for fifteen years.

These three examples represent interesting profiles, but they are rather atypical cases, since it was much more common for a participant to have been active just once or twice.

EXPOSURE TO DIFFERENT TYPES OF SUBJECT MATTER

In the final section of this chapter we examine evidence concerning the number of adults who accumulate experiences with different types of subject matter. From Table 6.5, we note that a majority of the 47 per cent who had taken an adult education course at all had taken some kind of vocational course. In total, as many as one adult in three had taken a job-connected course since leaving school—some 22 per cent in subjects related to white-collar occupations; 15 per cent in blue-collar subjects and skills; and 1 per cent in agricultural topics. By comparison, only 11 per cent had ever studied an academic subject; 10 per cent a course related to leisure-time enjoyment; and 7 per cent subject matter in the home and family life field. All together, in fact, a larger number of persons had studied vocational subjects than all other areas combined (33 versus 29 per cent).

These findings are quite revealing. They not only illuminate the central character of adult studies, but quite clearly indicate that formal vocational training following full-time schooling is a

Table 6.5 Total Exposure to Adult Education Courses in Different Subjects

Category of Subject		
Total who have taken a course in any subject		47%
Job-related skills, white collar occupations	22%	
Job-related skills, blue collar occupations	15	
Job-related skills, agriculture	1	
Total vocational	*33*	
Academic subjects	11	
Hobbies and recreation	10	
Home and family life	7	
Personal development	5	
Religion, morals, and ethics	3	
Current events and public affairs	2	
Miscellaneous other	3	
Total non-vocational	*29%*	
Total who have taken a course in any subject		53
Total		100%
Base (weighted)	9,784	
No information	180	
Total sample (weighted)	9,964	

widespread practice in America. Although no information was collected on the occupational histories of our respondents, we did ask about their current labor-force status, and among persons in the labor force,[3] a total of 41 per cent reported that they had at some time taken a vocational adult education course. This is an impressive statistic. Indeed, if as many as two of every five members of the labor force have as adults sought out training in relation to their employment, it is clear that adult education plays a highly significant role in relation to American manpower needs. And, with the prospect of continually increasing demands for specialized skills in the labor force, the practice of acquiring these skills through adult education will undoubtedly continue.

Following the question on experiences with formal courses, the respondents were asked the following:

[QUESTION 23] Up to this point, we've been talking about enrollment in courses and attendance at classes. Have you ever tried to teach yourself some subject by means of independent study strictly on your own?

Table 6.6 indicates that some 38 per cent had been involved at some time in the past in independent education, and this again represents a substantial increase over the number of persons (estimated in Part I) who engaged in independent studies during the previous year.[4]

Next, for subject matter studied, the table shows that a total of 17 per cent reported studies related to some kind of vocational concern, while 26 per cent reported essentially non-vocational subject matter. This represents a sharp reversal from the pattern

[3]In the total sample 60 per cent were employed either full time or part time, or were unemployed and presumably looking for a job.

[4]Our general reservations about the precision of estimates presented in this chapter apply even more strongly to these data. Since independent studies would tend to lack any temporal, geographic, or social points of reference, the accuracy of people's memory concerning them would probably become seriously impaired with the passing of time. In view of this, we shall present only a limited discussion of the overall exposure of the population to these types of learning experiences.

found for formal courses of instruction, where the incidence of vocational studies predominated over all others.

A more thorough scrutiny of Tables 6.5 and 6.6, moreover, reveals that while in most subjects a larger number of persons studied by taking courses than independently, the form of study did differ considerably from field to field. A more direct way to report these tendencies is through ratio scores. For example, since the cumulative exposure to formal courses was 47 per cent, and to independent studies 38 per cent, we could say that for every 100 persons who had ever studied on their own, some 124 had taken a formal course. When ratio scores were computed for each category of subject matter, the pattern of results in Table 6.7 emerged.

These figures indicate that the extent to which different kinds of subjects were studied with formal instruction varied consid-

Table 6.6 Total Exposure to Independent Studies in Different Subjects

Category of Subject		
Total who have ever studied something on their own		38%
Job-related skills, white-collar occupations	9%	
Job-related skills, blue-collar occupations	8	
Job-related skills, agriculture	1	
Total vocational	*17*	
Academic subjects	9	
Hobbies and recreation	8	
Home and family life	9	
Personal development	3	
Religion, morals, and ethics	2	
Current events and public affairs	*	
Miscellaneous other	*	
Total non-vocational	*26%*	
Total who have never studied anything on their own		62
Total		100%
Base (weighted)		9,958
No information		6·
Total sample (weighted)		9,964

*Less than 1 per cent.

erably. While it is not surprising to find the two main classes of vocational education relatively high on this listing, we might not have anticipated that public affairs and religious studies would be in first and third places. Indeed, one might have considered that studies in both of these fields could be conducted as readily on one's own as through formal courses, whereas the results clearly indicate that these fields are relatively more likely than most to be studied in a structured setting.

The results also show that two fields of study were undertaken independently more often than in formal courses: in home and family studies, there were only 69 course-takers for every 100 who had studied independently, and in agriculture the comparable ratio was 91 to 100.

Our final concern is with the incidence of combined exposure through both formal and informal channels. The data are brought together in Table 6.8, which shows that a majority of adults (61 per cent) reported prior experiences with some kind of study. Although not shown in the table, this figure is made up of 23 per cent who had studied both formally and informally, 24 per cent who had taken courses only, and 14 per cent who had been engaged in independent studies only.

Some of the findings in Table 6.8 are quite revealing when compared with the estimates examined in the first phase of this

Table 6.7 Comparative Exposure to Courses and Independent Studies, by Subject Field

Subject Category	Number of Persons Who Had Taken a Course for Every 100 Who Had Studied Independently
Public affairs and current events	264
White-collar occupational skills	227
Religion	212
Blue-collar occupational skills	183
Personal development	180
Hobbies and recreation	129
Academic	121
Agricultural topics	91
Home and family life	69

study. For example, in Part I, 3,820,000 persons were estimated to have studied religious subject matter during the previous year, or about 3.4 per cent of the adult population (see Table 3.9). In Table 6.8, however, we see that only 5 per cent of adults (actually it was 4.6 per cent) had ever engaged in religious study as adults, which indicates that the combined exposure to religious study over time was only about 35 per cent higher than the exposure during the previous year. By itself this does not represent a very large factor of accumulation, and in comparison with the other categories of subject matter it turns out to be very slight indeed. From a similar comparison, for example, we can determine that a maximum of 8.2 per cent of the population had studied some kind of vocational subject during the previous year, while a total of 41.6 per cent reported these studies at some time or other after leaving school. The accumulation factor here, in other words, works out to 507 per cent.

For the complete range of major subject categories, moreover,

Table 6.8 Combined Exposure, through Either Adult Education Courses or Independent Studies, to Different Types of Subjects

Category of Subject	
Total who have either taken an adult education course or been engaged in independent study	61%
Job-related skills, white-collar occupations	27%
Job-related skills, blue-collar occupations	21
Job-related skills, agriculture	2
Total vocational	42
Academic subjects	17
Hobbies and recreation	16
Home and family life subjects	14
Personal development	7
Religion, morals and ethics	5
Current events and public affairs	3
Miscellaneous other	4
Total non-vocational	43%
Total who have neither taken courses nor engaged in independent study	39
Total	100%
Base (weighted)	9,779
No information	185
Total sample (weighted)	9,964

Note: Subtotals do not add to totals because some persons had studied more than one type of subject matter.

these ratios were as shown in Table 6.9. In interpreting these figures, a low ratio score probably indicates one of two things. The first possibility is that subjects of that type had only recently begun to be studied by adults and that practically everyone who had ever studied the subject at all had studied it during the previous year. While this might indeed be a reasonable assumption for certain studies, such as speed reading, it would obviously not explain the low ratio score found in relation to religious study. A much more likely possibility is that a low score reflects some sort of continuity measure in people's patterns of study. For example, it might very well be that most adults who engage in religious studies continue to do so on a fairly regular basis, and if this were indeed the case, most people who had ever studied religion as adults would be found studying it during any given twelve-month period.

Interestingly, the field of public affairs also shows a relatively low accumulation ratio, and the third lowest on this tendency is the field of recreational studies. Of course, the continuity-of-studies interpretation is not an unreasonable explanation for these particular findings either, since current events has a constantly replenishing field of material to keep up with, and leisure-time studies—at least in the performing arts and perhaps athletics as well—involve persistence, improving skills through continued study over a fairly lengthy period.

By the same token, academic studies and vocational training

Table 6.9 Comparison of Rates of Study since Leaving School with Rates of Study during Previous Year, by Subject Field

Subject Category	Number of Persons Who Had Ever Studied This Subject for Every 100 Who Studied It the Previous Year (Rounded to Nearest Five)
Academic subjects	550
Vocational subjects	505
Personal development	485
Home and family life	480
Hobbies and recreation	335
Public affairs	280
Religion	135

are much more readily characterized in terms of discrete temporal commitments. Academic education usually terminates with a high-school diploma or college degree; vocational training, too, has a natural closure with finding a job or winning a promotion.

SUMMARY

To sum up, then, if an inventory of educational activities is extended to cover a longer period of time, the number of American adults with some relevant experience to report is considerably expanded. Post-school learning pursuits are, on the whole, quite common experiences in the United States and, although they are not regular activities for must adults, nonetheless in the current population any given adult is just about as likely as not to have been exposed at least once to some systematic learning experience since leaving school.

7

The Initial Exposure to Post-School Learning

Because of the special nature of the sampling design of the second phase of this study, a quite substantial number of interviews were completed with persons who had been enrolled in adult education courses at one time or another since leaving school.[1] For these persons a considerable portion of the interview schedule was devoted to questions relating to prior experiences with continuing education; information was collected concerning how they originally came to enroll, the purposes they had in mind when they enrolled in their most recent course, and the benefits, if any, they felt they derived from being enrolled.

The findings on these topics are reported in the next two chapters in this section. In this chapter the life situations in which people first came to have experiences with adult education are examined, while the next deals more directly with questions of why people enrolled in courses and how much they got out of them when they did.

[1] A total of 1,759 respondents had taken one or more adult education courses since leaving school. Although these people constitute some 62 per cent of all those interviewed, they represent only 47 per cent of the adult population. Altogether, these 1,759 persons become a weighted aggregate of 4,603 persons in the tables which follow.

Our main task here is to reconstruct the circumstances under which people first came to enter into educational pursuits as adults, and we consider first ages at which people most typically become involved, if indeed they ever do. Table 7.1, accordingly, shows that a majority of those who became participants did so quite soon after leaving school.

Most frequent recruitment took place in the twenties, almost half of all introductory courses being taken during these ten years. The median age of initial enrollment was 25.9 years. By thirty, over two-thirds had already enrolled; by forty about seven of eight had been recruited. In other words, not many people were found who had begun their adult education studies for the first time after forty.

Table 7.1 also reveals some quite important differences in the recruitment ages of men and women: men were more likely than women to have taken their first course while in their twenties, but proportionately more women were recruited both before twenty and after forty. This probably reflects two tendencies. First, since more girls than boys drop out of school before twenty, the pool of teen-agers from which adult education re-

Table 7.1 Age at First Enrollment in Adult Education Courses, by Sex

Age	Men (Per Cent)	Women (Per Cent)	All Participants (Per Cent)
Under 20	17	22	20
20–29	52	43	48
30–39	19	18	19
40–49	9	11	10
50–59	1	5	3
60 or over	1	2	1
Total	99	101	101
Base	2,270	2,271	4,541
No information	26	36	62
Total (weighted)	2,296	2,307	4,603
Median age	25.7	26.1	25.9

cruits could be drawn would be disproportionately female.[2] Second, since women who have families are likely to experience rather severe restrictions on their freedom during their twenties and thirties, their proportionately higher recruitment after forty probably reflects enrollment which might have taken place earlier had family considerations not interfered.

The types of subjects studied during first encounters with continuing education are shown in Table 7.2. Here we note from the right-hand column that a majority (55 per cent) of all first courses were vocational while only 13 per cent were academic; 11 per cent were recreational and 8 per cent pertained to home and family life. Thus considerations about making a living appear to play by far the most significant role in first bringing people into adult education situations. Among men, some 65 per cent of all first courses were vocational, and a total of 80 per cent were either vocational or academic. Even among women, moreover, some 46 per cent were directly job connected while another 10 per cent were academic; by comparison, only 16 per

[2]For example, among eighteen- and nineteen-year-olds in the United States population in 1960, the proportion no longer in school was 70 per cent of girls and 52 per cent of boys (U.S. Department of Commerce, 1961, p. 105).

Table 7.2 Subject Matter Studied in First Adult Education Courses, by Sex

Type of Subject	Men (Per Cent)	Women (Per Cent)	All Participants (Per Cent)
Vocational	65	46	55
Academic	15	10	13
Hobbies and recreation	6	16	11
Home and family life	1	14	8
Personal development	3	5	4
Religion	2	6	4
Public affairs	2	2	2
Miscellaneous	5	2	4
Total	99	101	101
Base	2,296	2,296	4,592
No information	0	11	11
Total (weighted)	2,296	2,307	4,603

cent of women first enrolled to study subjects connected with enjoyment of leisure, and only 14 per cent to study homemaking.

Our main findings about initial entry stem from a pair of free-answer questions which were asked of all participants. These were:

[QUESTION 17-I] Thinking back to the first course you took, the (SUBJECT) course, could you tell me how you happened to enroll in that?

[QUESTION 17-J] Why do you think you hadn't enrolled in any courses before that time?

Participants were thus given the opportunity to identify, in their own terms, the situations and influences which they remembered as most relevant to their initial recruitment to formal learning experiences as adults; it is on the responses elicited by these questions that our discussion focuses throughout the remainder of this chapter.

Table 7.3 summarizes the answers given by both men and women, although we shall first discuss the types of contexts identified by the total sample of participants. From the right-hand column in the table, it is clear that the most frequent reference was to some vocational context. Indeed, over one-half (54 per cent) of all participants recalled that it was some occupational contingency which first led them to enroll in further studies. Thirty-six per cent described their initial enrollment as preparation for new employment, while 20 per cent indicated they first had turned to adult education to gain advancement in a job already held. Within these main categories, moreover, a number of more specific initiating situations were also identified: for example, 7 per cent indicated they enrolled first in a course when they left school and were looking for a job; 9 per cent more did so when they were getting ready to change from one job to another; another 10 per cent became involved either upon entry into or discharge from the armed forces.

As expected, these results closely parallel the findings concerning the content of first adult education courses, and together they establish that initial recruitments are most frequently based

on considerations regarding role as a member of the labor force.
Certain other clusters of answers are also of interest here,
however. For example, as many as three respondents in ten
mentioned some interpersonal influence: 10 per cent said that
their employers had had something to do with their enrollment,
12 per cent mentioned their family or friends, and 8 per cent
identified some other person who had played a role in their
recruitment. (One woman said she had been talked into taking
piano lessons by a salesman.) That social contacts should have
been spontaneously identified this often suggests that interper-

Table 7.3 Context of Enrollment in First Adult Education Course, by Sex

Context of Entry into First Course	Men (Per Cent)		Women (Per Cent)		Total (Per Cent)	
All job-connected situations		68		40		54
Job preparation	*46*		*27*		*36*	
Transition from school to first job	6		8		7	
Changing from one job to another	11		7		9	
Entry into armed forces	16		†		8	
Discharge from armed forces	5		†		2	
Unemployment	2		1		1	
Other	8		11		9	
Job advancement	*24*		*16*		*20*	
Self-initiated	12		9		11	
Employer initiated	12		7		10	
Other job-connected situation	*2*		*1*		*2*	
Personal influence other than from employers		15		24		20
Friends, relatives, and acquaintances	7		18		12	
Other sources	8		7		8	
No situational factors mentioned: general interest in learning only		12		25		19
Changes in family situation		2		19		10
Decrease in family responsibilities	†		10		5	
Family expansion	1		6		4	
Death or family dissolution	†		2		1	
Other family contingencies	†		3		2	
Finishing off an incomplete education		5		3		4
All other factors, situations, influences		8		8		8
No answer		3		4		3
Total		113*		123*		118*
Base (weighted)		2,296		2,307		4,603

*Does not total 100 per cent because some persons mentioned more than one factor.
†Less than 1 per cent.

sonal influence may play a very important role in making new recruits.

Among the remaining response clusters, 10 per cent remembered that some change in family composition had prompted their initial enrollment, either change brought about by family expansion, such as marriage or the birth of children, or change in which responsibilities were lessened, by children growing up, or by family disintegration through death or separation.

Finally, we might note in passing that about one participant in five—some 19 per cent—made no mention at all of any situation or factor other than simply a desire to learn more about the subject, and that only 4 per cent reported the completion of their formal education as the circumstance which first led them to engage in continuing education as adults.

In overview, then, there are four main contexts which people remember as having been particularly important in their initial recruitment: job preparation, job advancement, personal relationships, and changes in family status or composition.

Next, there were a number of interesting differences between the situations of entry identified by women and men. First, many more men than women referred to job-related contexts, and, while hardly unexpected, it is nonetheless instructive that as many as two-thirds (68 per cent) of all male participants identified one or another vocational context with their original enrollment. Moreover, the table also shows that as many as 16 per cent of the men had their first adult education experiences while in the armed forces, while another 5 per cent became involved at the time of their discharge from the services.

The second important sex-linked difference is that practically all the persons who mentioned family contingencies were women. Altogether, 19 per cent of the women identified some situation which involved their families, while only 2 per cent of the men reported influences of this type. It is revealing, too, that as many as 10 per cent of all the women who had ever taken a course said their original enrollment took place at a time when household duties and responsibilities had lessened.

While both these differences are just about what we might

have expected, given the central life roles of men and women in our society, it is somewhat more surprising to find that women were more likely than men to mention the influence of family and friends on recruitment: a total of 18 per cent of the women compared with just 7 per cent of the men said that either family members or friends had had something to do with how they first came to take a course. At the same time, however, this difference was not found in interpersonal influences originating from secondary social relationships; indeed, some 12 per cent of men compared with just 7 per cent of women mentioned the influence of employers, and about equal proportions (8 and 7 per cent, respectively) said that individuals other than family members, friends, or employers had influenced them to enroll.

In summary, it would appear that initial contacts with adult education typically occur quite early in adult life, and that most people who become participants do so before reaching thirty. The first concerns adults have with continuing education are typically job-related, and this is particularly true among men, with four out of five having taken their first courses in either vocational or academic subjects—fields which have a direct bearing on occupational placement. Vocational and academic studies also led a majority of women into continuing education for the first time, but sizeable minorities of women became adult students in order to learn more about home and family skills or subjects connected with the use of leisure. All in all, many more men than women talked about occupational concerns in connection with their first enrollment, and they recalled job preparation situations over job advancement ones by a ratio of about two to one. On the other hand, practically all the participants who first turned to adult education in relation to some family situation were women.

Finally, a good number of both men and women reported that other people had had some kind of influence on their original recruitment. In this connection, however, women were more likely to mention influences from primary social relationships, and men to mention contacts with persons in secondary social settings.

8

Why
People Take Courses
and
What They Get
from Them

At this point we turn to a direct examination of the goals people have when they enroll for adult education courses, the reasons they have for taking courses, and the benefits they feel they derive from them. Although most of the discussion is concerned with the reasons people give, near the end of the chapter an attempt is made to assess the effectiveness of their studies by analyzing to what extent their experiences proved helpful.

REASONS FOR TAKING COURSES

We approached the investigation of why adults enroll in studies by asking participants about the goals they had in mind at the time of their most recent enrollment. First, a number of popular interpretations of why adults enroll were translated into a series of eight statements about how courses could be helpful, and participants were asked directly whether any of these considerations had had a bearing on their most recent enrollment. Following this, they were asked to identify any other purposes they had had at the time of their most recent course enrollment (see Questions 17-F and 17-H).

Answers to these questions are reported in Table 8.1. Part *a* orders the statements according to the frequency with which each

Why People Take Courses and What They Get from Them

was endorsed and part *b* indicates how often additional goals were identified by the participants themselves. We first note that even though just eight reasons for enrollment were shown to respondents, only 7 per cent failed to find at least one which was applicable to their own situation, and only 10 per cent were able to think of any others. For the most part it seems that the goals listed in Table 8.1*a* represent the most typical purposes adults have in mind when they enroll for adult education courses.

Table 8.1 Reasons for Taking Adult Education Courses

a. [Question 17-F(2)] In which of the following ways had you hoped the course would be helpful to you?

Become a better informed person	37%
Prepare for a new job or occupation	36
On the job I held at that time	32
Spend my spare time more enjoyably	20
Meet new and interesting people	15
In carrying out everyday tasks and duties around home	13
Get away from the daily routine	10
In carrying out everyday tasks and duties away from home	10
None of these, or don't know	7
Total	180%*
Base	4,175
No information	428
Total participants (weighted)	4,603

b. [Question 17-H] Were there any other ways not listed here in which you had hoped the course would be helpful?

Yes	10%
Other work or job-related reasons	3%
Improve skills or increase knowledge (general)	3
Increase income	1
Home or family life role	1
Personality or interpersonal relations	1
Other personal development	1
All other	2%
No	90
Total	100%
Base	4,419
No information	184
Total participants (weighted)	4,603

*Does not total 100 per cent because some persons endorsed more than one reason.

Three statements in Table 8.1*a* were selected considerably more often than the others, but none was picked by a majority of the participants. First, 37 per cent of all participants said they had enrolled in order "to become a better informed person," this statement being endorsed more frequently than any other. Since becoming better informed could be a meaningful rationale for studying practically anything, of course, the meaning of the responses to this item is not too clear. The statement would seem to be more relevant for persons seeking knowledge or information, rather than skills, but it probably has meaning, too, for those who enter learning pursuits without well-defined goals. Endorsement of this purpose might also reflect at least some modicum of intrinsic intellectual commitment to a subject. If it does, it is certainly revealing that more than one-half the participants failed to identify this purpose as one of the goals they had hoped to achieve.

The two other goals endorsed by sizeable numbers of participants were both vocational: some 36 per cent indicated they had enrolled to prepare for a new job, while 32 per cent said they had done so to learn more about the job they already held. Over and above the desire to become better informed, then, vocational goals most frequently direct adults into continuing education, and, on the basis of the relative frequency of response to the two job-connected items included in the list, it appears that slightly more adults take courses for job preparation than for job advancement.

In descending frequency the other goals were endorsed as follows: 20 per cent confirmed they had taken their most recent course to help them enjoy their leisure; 15 per cent said they had hoped to expand their social contacts through attendance in classes; 13 per cent said they enrolled to learn homemaker skills; 10 per cent had other everyday tasks in mind when they enrolled; and another 10 per cent agreed that they had enrolled to escape the confines of everyday routine.

For the most part, these results are quite in keeping with our earlier findings on the types of subjects people study, and they add few new insights to what has already been presented. For example, even though we now may conclude quite legitimately that reasons for enrollment in adult education courses are more often vocational than recreational, this could have been quite easily predicted from the fact that the number of adults in vocational studies was much larger than that in the recreation category.

At the same time, however, a knowledge of titles of courses people study is by no means a completely reliable indicator of the reasons why they study, and it is altogether likely that different people study the very same subjects for quite different reasons. The results in Tables 8.2 and 8.3 illustrate this point quite vividly: the first of these tables gives a breakdown of the reasons people gave for taking courses in various categories, and the second shows similar information for a selected number of specific subjects.

The most important finding in Table 8.2 is that, regardless of the category of subject studied, each reason was selected by at least some of the participants. Indeed, 9 per cent of those who took vocational courses said they did so with leisure time in mind, and 5 per cent of those who studied religion said the main reason they did so was to prepare for a new job. These latter results are curious, but they are not at all beyond the realm of feasibility. For example, it is quite conceivable that some people who took vocational subjects (such as auto mechanics) did so purely for pleasure, and that some who studied religion did so to become Sunday School teachers, missionaries, or perhaps even ministers of their religion.

Although these deviant cases are interesting, our more central concern at this point is with the main patterns of answers, and here the results suggest a number of specific conclusions about why people study different types of subjects. For example, if we assume that any statement which was endorsed by at least 20 per cent of the participants represents a "typical" usage of that subject area, we can then summarize the results of Table 8.2 as follows:

1. The most typical function of vocational education is preparation for new employment—although sizeable numbers of persons also studied to become better informed and to advance in their present jobs.

2. Persons who studied academic subjects also expressed these same three goals (general information, job advancement,

Table 8.2 Reasons for Taking Courses, by Type of Subject Matter Studied

Reasons	Type of Subject Matter						
	Vocational (Per Cent)	Academic (Per Cent)	Hobbies and Recreation (Per Cent)	Home and Family (Per Cent)	Personal Development (Per Cent)	Religion (Per Cent)	Public Affairs (Per Cent)
Prepare for a new job	52	25	14	17	26	5	14
Help on present job	42	37	9	9	37	10	11
Become better informed	44	42	21	41	55	74	67
Spare-time enjoyment	9	20	58	32	35	24	6
Home-centered tasks	12	8	4	40	20	21	3
Other everyday tasks	11	9	2	5	18	19	8
Meet new people	13	17	25	12	25	18	4
Escape the daily routine	6	11	25	14	21	17	1
None of these or don't know	4	8	7	5	7	12	21
Total	193*	177*	165*	175*	244*	200*	135*
Base	2,224	510	505	304	182	165	72
No information	290	48	65	30	12	23	14
Total (weighted)	2,514	558	570	334	194	188	86

*Does not total 100 per cent because some persons gave more than one reason.

job preparation) and in addition, about one in five studied these subjects purely for pleasure.

One interesting feature of these findings is the relative incidence of job preparation and job advancement goals. Since the pursuit of an academic education is normally associated with periods of life which precede rather than follow entry into the labor force, it would follow that adults who enroll in academic courses would more often be concerned with seeking new employment than with trying to get ahead on jobs already held. This turned out not to be the case, however, since 37 per cent had enrolled in response to advancement goals while just 25 per cent were concerned with job preparation.

3. The reason most frequently given by persons who took courses in recreation was, not surprisingly, to increase spare-time enjoyment. However, sizeable minorities also enrolled in these courses to meet new people, to escape daily routines, and simply to become better informed.

4. Although the main reasons for taking home and family life courses were to become more informed, and to improve performance in household and family tasks, almost as many participants who took these courses did so with spare-time interests in mind.

5. As explained in Part I, the "personal development" category houses a large number of different subjects, all of which seem to be aimed at improving either physical, psychological, or social well-being. Not unexpectedly, Table 8.2 indicates that persons who enrolled in these subjects did so for a wide variety of reasons. Seven of the eight statements were checked by at least 20 per cent of the participants, and the eighth—the acquisition of skills related to everyday tasks performed outside the home—was relevant for 18 per cent. The main functions of these studies, however, were to help people become better informed, to help them advance on their jobs, and to help them enjoy their spare time more.

6. People who studied religion overwhelmingly chose "becoming better informed" to explain their enrollment, although smaller numbers—between one-fourth and one-fifth—justified

their enrollment in terms of benefits related to leisure-time use and to home and family life tasks.

7. Finally, and again not unexpectedly, those who studied public affairs described their motivation almost exclusively as acquisition of new information.

It is clear that while in some areas of study people seek fairly obvious goals, in others goals are not at all obvious on the basis of course titles alone. That academic courses and home and family life topics are frequently studied for spare-time enjoyment, as well as for their more apparent functions, illustrates this quite well.

Considerable variation may also be noted in the kinds of benefits sought by persons who studied specific subjects within these general categories. Table 8.3, for example, arrays all the individual course titles which were reported by at least twenty respondents, and a total of twenty-seven fields of subject matter are presented here, along with the reasons people chose to explain how they wanted to be helped by these courses. The main cluster of subjects shown pertains to different vocational spheres, and this part of the table in itself reveals a wide diversity of expectations — particularly in the relative frequency with which job preparation and job advancement goals were endorsed.

First, an impressive variance may be noted in the extent to which different vocational subjects were studied for job preparation. The proportion who endorsed this goal ranged from 85 per cent among those who took courses on specialized office machines (such as the IBM keypunch) to 26 per cent among those who studied teaching on a part-time basis. Other vocational courses in which a substantial majority enrolled for job preparation dealt with personal service skills such as barbering, hairdressing, and waiting, and general office skills such as typing, shorthand, and bookkeeping. At the other extreme, neither salesmanship nor practical nursing were studied very often by persons looking for new jobs.

The highest incidence of job advancement expectations was found in relation to courses chiefly in teaching (64 per cent), courses in non-technical and non-teaching professions (chiefly

Table 8.3 Reasons for Taking Selected Adult Education Courses

Reasons	Technical Courses (Per Cent)	Teacher Training (Per Cent)	Other Professions (Per Cent)	Business Management (Per Cent)	Salesmanship (Per Cent)	Office Machines (Per Cent)	General Office Skills (Per Cent)	Mechanics (Per Cent)	Other Skilled Trades (Per Cent)	Operatives Skills (Per Cent)	Practical Nursing and Related Skills (Per Cent)	Personal Services (Per Cent)
				Vocational								
Prepare for a new job	45	26	51	44	31	85	65	45	61	63	36	71
Help on a present job	55	64	62	59	59	21	25	53	33	46	21	30
Become better informed	38	59	36	58	20	27	24	37	17	14	54	43
Spare-time enjoyment	10	16	6	3	13	8	8	12	11	3	7	1
Home-centered tasks	9	16	–	1	13	9	7	11	14	18	42	14
Other everyday tasks	5	26	6	4	21	3	7	11	11	10	26	15
Meet new people	5	24	8	9	25	1	11	11	12	1	21	24
Escape the daily routine	3	7	–	5	2	12	8	–	10	–	9	11
None of these or don't know	3	10	1	6	7	1	3	1	5	1	1	8
Total per cent*	173*	248*	170*	189*	191*	167*	158*	180*	174*	156*	217*	217*
Base	291	81	134	153	97	72	401	120	273	77	150	133
No information	25	13	13	22	18	8	56	25	25	11	24	12
Total (weighted)	316	94	147	175	115	80	457	145	298	88	174	145

*Does not total 100 per cent because some persons gave more than one reason.

(Table 8.3 continued)

Table 8.3 Continued

Reasons	Academic				Hobbies–Recreation							Other			
	English (Per Cent)	Foreign Languages (Per Cent)	Mathematics or Statistics (Per Cent)	Natural Sciences (Per Cent)	Athletics (Per Cent)	Bridge (Per Cent)	Dancing (Per Cent)	Music (Performing) (Per Cent)	Art (Painting) (Per Cent)	Art Appreciation (Per Cent)	Decorative Arts (Per Cent)	Sewing–Cooking (Per Cent)	Child Care (Per Cent)	Traditional Religious Training (Per Cent)	Driving Lessons (Per Cent)
Prepare for a new job	23	11	26	50	13	–	12	23	31	20	1	3	49	5	3
Help on present job	45	26	61	33	7	–	13	2	8	40	1	14	4	11	19
Become better informed	31	54	27	38	15	12	6	26	18	40	33	30	56	75	7
Spare-time enjoyment	29	28	9	25	56	67	73	74	46	48	59	32	19	27	41
Home-centered tasks	13	1	2	14	–	–	–	–	–	–	29	44	41	23	41
Other everyday tasks	9	13	12	14	–	2	–	2	2	3	1	8	2	22	35
Meet new people	19	37	1	5	20	58	37	12	29	12	35	6	17	15	3
Escape the daily routine	15	7	2	8	33	27	25	6	19	15	33	8	4	18	4
None of these or don't know	16	8	7	–	15	15	8	21	5	–	6	9	–	14	9
Total per cent*	200*	185*	147*	187*	159*	181*	174*	166*	158*	178*	198*	•154*	192*	210*	162*
Base	92	103	99	38	98	43	64	66	65	33	71	182	49	138	70
No information	6	8	14	3	0	1	18	8	6	1	20	24	1	18	2
Total (weighted)	98	111	113	41	98	44	82	74	71	34	91	206	50	156	72

*Does not total 100 per cent because some persons gave more than one reason.

law and accounting, 62 per cent), and courses in business management and salesmanship (59 per cent each). On the other hand, practical nursing, general and specialized office skills, and personal service skills were infrequently studied for purposes of advancement.

A more direct way to appraise the relative incidence of these two goals in vocational studies is to examine the ratio of preparation to advancement goals among persons taking different types of vocational courses. When these measures were derived, the twelve vocational titles identified in Table 8.3 were ranked as shown in Table 8.4. This listing indicates, first, that courses in both general and specialized office skills were heavily dominated by people seeking new employment rather than job advancement. Persons with preparation goals outnumbered those with advancement goals by better than 4 to 1 in courses on specialized office equipment, and by 2.60 to 1 in the field of general office studies. Interestingly, however, these two fields are in sharp contrast with the other white-collar fields represented on the list, and the contrast with courses in salesmanship is particularly striking. In studies of this latter type, persons seeking new jobs were outnumbered by 52 to 100. Thus, while training for clerical posts is typically taken in advance of employment, sales training is typically received after one has actually been employed as a salesman.

Table 8.4 Ratio of Job Preparation to Job Advancement Goals among Persons Taking Vocational Courses

Subject Matter	
Office machines (other than typewriter)	4.05
General office skills	2.60
Skills used in personal service occupations	2.37
Skilled trades	1.85
Practical nursing and related skills	1.71
Skills for operatives	1.37
Auto mechanics and other machine skills	0.85
Technical-professional courses	0.82
Courses in non-technical, non-teaching professions	0.82
Business management	0.75
Salesmanship	0.52
Teaching	0.41

Despite the fact that Table 8.4 is topped with two types of white-collar studies, the next five subjects all represent skills used in blue-collar occupations, while the five fields at the bottom of the list again relate to the white-collar sector of the labor force. With the exception of office skills, then, the data indicate a general tendency for vocational training in white-collar occupations to take place subsequent to entry into an occupational field, and for training courses in blue-collar lines of work to precede actual employment.

Table 8.3 also sheds interesting light on certain of the supplementary goals in vocational studies. In addition to the people who mentioned "becoming better informed," there were sizeable numbers who selected clearly non-vocational goals from the list of statements offered. For example, among those who took courses in practical nursing and related medical service skills, more did so to use these skills in their own homes than because they sought employment. Moreover, of those who took courses in teacher training and salesmanship, between one-quarter and one-fifth identified help with everyday tasks outside the home or new social contacts as reasons for taking the instruction. Thus, while it is not possible to reconstruct a complete description of these supplementary contexts for study, it is clear that they at least represent non-vocational uses of essentially job-related subject matter.

Only a limited range of non-vocational subjects is represented in Table 8.3, but eleven different academic or recreational subjects were reported by enough persons to allow a meaningful investigation to be made of the reasons for study.

The four academic subjects represented in the table include two from the humanities (English literature and composition, and foreign languages), and two from the technical branches of knowledge (mathematics and statistics and natural sciences). An examination of the reasons people gave for studying in these areas reveals a number of interesting points of contrast. First, mathematics and statistics were taken primarily by persons seeking to get ahead on their jobs; only small numbers were concerned with preparation for new employment or with other goals. Among those who enrolled for courses in the natural sciences, on the other hand, the relative incidence of the two types of vocational concerns was just the reverse: more persons were concerned with occupational preparation than with advancement. In addition, 25 per cent of those who took science courses did so with spare-time interests in mind, considerably more than the 9 per cent who had studied mathematics or statistics for these reasons.

Next, and in contrast with both these subjects, vocational concerns were of only secondary importance to those studying foreign languages. Over one-third of these students had enrolled to develop new social contacts — presumably with members of other nationality groups rather than simply with classmates — and, in addition, more mentioned spare-time interests than mentioned either of the vocational considerations. The main goals of foreign-language studies among adults appear to be social and recreational rather than vocational.

The pattern is different again for those who studied English literature. Here there were sizeable clusters of individuals who enrolled, both in order to advance on their jobs (45 per cent) and to satisfy spare-time interests (29 per cent).

In both English and foreign languages some people appear to enroll for vocational and others for recreational reasons. As such these fields of study probably attract a more heterogeneous student body than most other adult education programs.

Reasons given for recreational learning are more unexpected. Large numbers of those who studied art or music, for instance, did so for vocational reasons. One-fifth or more of all those who studied a musical instrument, took art lessons, or attended art appreciation classes did so in preparation for new employment, and as many as 40 per cent of those in art appreciation classes mentioned getting ahead on their jobs as a motive for enrollment. Although we do not have complete data on the occupations of these particular persons when they entered these courses, a good number of them were elementary school teachers at the time they were interviewed. Three other occupations represented here were those of sign painter, laboratory technician in a paint factory, and blueprint draftsman. Thus, while the results are surprising, they are not at all implausible.

If one were asked to think of an area of instruction completely unambiguous in its functions, one might suggest bridge lessons as being prototypically recreational. At least we would not expect to find many persons taking bridge lessons for vocational, domestic, or informational reasons. These expectations are borne out in Table 8.3, which shows that the motives for bridge studies were almost exclusively leisure-time enjoyment and meeting new people. Of all the courses listed, this had the heaviest concentration of persons who enrolled to expand their social contacts.

Hobbies and recreation, as might be anticipated, drew a preponderance of persons who enrolled to get away from daily routines. One-third of those who took courses in athletics or the decorative arts gave this as a reason.

One final comment is in order concerning the rather improbable finding that more persons had enrolled in child-care courses to prepare for new jobs than to carry out their home and family life tasks and duties. We suspect that expectant mothers probably interpreted the phrase "prepare for a new job or occupation" as referring to their own imminent motherhood rather than to paid employment taking care of other people's children; most of these women mentioned preparation for the birth of a child when they were asked for information on how they happened to enroll in the course.

Although useful insights into the functions of adult education for persons in different phases of the life cycle were gained from an examination of which courses people studied at different ages, a more direct appraisal is possible when we examine the actual reasons people gave for taking courses. In this next section we shall examine briefly the expectations men and women of different ages had when they enrolled in their most recent courses. The ages presented here are those at which the enrollments took place—not the current ages of the respondents.

The most prominent results in Table 8.5 tend to be the more obvious ones: vocational considerations are of more importance to men than to women, and people turn less and less frequently to adult education for job preparation as they grow older. However, the findings also indicate that the downward trend in the

Table 8.5 Reasons for Taking Most Recent Adult Education Course, by Sex and Age at Time of Enrollment

Reasons	Men				Women			
	Under 30 (Per Cent)	30–39 (Per Cent)	40–49 (Per Cent)	50 and Over (Per Cent)	Under 30 (Per Cent)	30–39 (Per Cent)	40–49 (Per Cent)	50 and Over (Per Cent)
Prepare for new job	48	39	29	33	41	27	24	17
Help on present job	40	50	48	37	19	20	25	18
Become better informed	35	40	27	57	31	41	41	47
Spare-time enjoyment	10	16	19	28	24	30	24	29
Home-centered tasks	7	15	6	2	13	24	21	16
Other everyday tasks	10	16	7	3	9	9	8	22
Meet new people	11	16	12	19	23	20	15	22
Escape the daily routine	6	8	4	8	13	16	15	16
None of these, or don't know	7	4	6	6	4	5	9	4
Total	174*	204*	158*	193*	177*	192*	182*	191*
Base	1,010	578	320	144	842	548	420	223
No information	98	70	34	28	125	24	36	58
Total (weighted)	1,108	648	354	172	967	572	456	281

*Does not total 100 per cent because some persons gave more than one reason.

job preparation goal stops after fifty among men—a result which suggests that some men may turn to adult education to learn new vocational skills after they retire or are perhaps displaced from obsolescent jobs.

Moreover, during the thirties the main vocational reason men give for taking courses shifts from job preparation to job advancement. This switch in vocational emphasis does not occur until the forties among women, however.

In the main, job-centered reasons most frequently propel younger adults into education and, by comparison, the uses made of education by older adults are much less pragmatic and utilitarian. For example, the proportion who endorsed the goal "to become a better informed person" was considerably higher among those over fifty. This general shift away from a pragmatic orientation is also reflected in the extent to which leisure-centered goals were endorsed by persons in different age groups. Among the men, at least, the emphasis on learning for spare-time enjoyment was greater in each successively older group. In fact, the statement "spend my spare time more enjoyably" was selected almost three times more often by men over fifty than by those under thirty (28 per cent compared with 10 per cent). A similar shift was not found among women, but a substantial number of the younger women had already used adult education for leisure-time interests.

More generally, of course, these results may only reflect the fact that the learning concerns of younger men are strongly influenced by considerations about making a living, while those of older men are not.

It is interesting that women were more likely than men to use adult education not only to learn home and family life skills, but also to meet new people and to get away from the daily routine. With respect to making new social contacts, the difference between men and women was particularly wide among participants under thirty: in this age bracket the statement "meet new and interesting people" was selected by 23 per cent of the women and only 11 per cent of the men. The greatest sex-linked difference in the endorsement of the goal "to get away from the daily routine," on the other hand, occurred among persons in their forties (15 per cent of the women but only 4 per cent of the men). This suggests, in any event, that not insignificant numbers of women use adult education both to cultivate new social relationships and to escape from the repetitiveness of everyday experiences.

To sum up, it is evident that vocational considerations propel younger adults into educational participation more frequently than they do older adults, and also that vocational motives for learning change over time from concerns about entering occupations to concerns about advancement within jobs already held. By comparison, older people, more often than younger, have as goals general information, social contacts, and spare-time enjoyment. Finally, it appears that more women than men turn to adult education not only to learn how to be more competent at home, but also to learn things which will help them make a more challenging use of their extra time.

Findings about how adult education is used by persons situated at different levels of the social hierarchy are quite revealing. In the first phase of the study, it was found that the socio-economic indicators (income, occupation, and, in particular, years of formal schooling) all were related positively with rates of participation in educational pursuits over one year. In addition, however, socio-economic level can be shown to be quite strongly related to the types of goals people have in mind when they enroll in adult education courses.

First, in Table 8.6 a direct relationship may be noted between socio-economic levels[1] and the vocational reasons which were stressed. Men and women of lower socio-economic status, for

[1]Table 8.6 is restricted to courses taken during the previous five years, so that we can be better assured that the respondents' socio-economic levels did not change since they were last enrolled in a course. The measure of socio-economic status employed here combines the factors of education and family income to produce three groups of persons: these are identified simply as representing "low," "medium," and "high" levels of socio-economic position. In the sample as a whole the index scores divided the population roughly into thirds. It is evident from the bases in the cells, however, that the groupings are not of equal size among respondents who had been enrolled in an adult education course during the previous five years. The explanation for this, of course, is that persons of higher education and income were much more likely to participate in educational pursuits.

Table 8.6 Reasons for Taking Courses Studied during Previous Five Years, by Sex and Socio-Economic Status

Reason	Men			Women		
	Socio-Economic Status			Socio-Economic Status		
	Low (Per Cent)	Medium (Per Cent)	High (Per Cent)	Low (Per Cent)	Medium (Per Cent)	High (Per Cent)
Prepare for new job	59	39	34	41	29	20
Help on present job	44	43	50	13	18	24
Become better informed	25	38	45	39	39	40
Spare-time enjoyment	6	12	18	16	32	31
Home-centered tasks	2	8	8	26	21	13
Other everyday tasks	8	12	8	18	12	7
Meet new people	9	11	13	23	16	21
Escape the daily routine	*	7	7	16	20	15
None of these, or don't know	4	8	3	7	2	7
Total	157†	178†	186†	199†	189†	178†
Base	212	375	650	207	427	628
No information	23	31	70	41	46	56
Total (weighted)	235	406	720	248	473	684

*Less than 1 per cent.
†Does not total 100 per cent because some persons gave more than one reason.

example, were much more likely to use adult education for job preparation than for advancement, while the opposite was true for participants of higher socio-economic status. In lower social class positions, in other words, it appears that the main function of vocational education is to place people into new jobs; at higher levels, on the other hand, vocational education functions much more to advance one's position on a job already held.

A second important difference was that, among both men and women, learning in relation to spare-time enjoyment was more emphasized at the higher socio-economic levels. In fact, there were virtually no men in the lower third of the socio-economic continuum who had enrolled in their most recent course for purposes of leisure-time enjoyment. Across the middle and upper thirds of this distribution, however, the endorsement of spare-time goals trebled: it moved from 6 to 12 to 18 per cent. Among women these reasons were also endorsed more frequently in the upper socio-economic levels (from 16 to 32 to 31 per cent in the low, middle, and upper thirds, respectively). Moreover, for women of middle or higher socio-economic status, leisure-time considerations were motives for enrollment more frequently than either job preparation, job advancement, or homemaking. In addition, among women adult education for homemaking was negatively related to socio-economic level. The proportion of women who enrolled in courses to learn how to carry out tasks around the home dropped from 26 to 21 to 13 per cent across the three socio-economic levels.

To sum up, there are very pronounced ways in which the uses of adult education differ across the range of social classes. At lower socio-economic levels adult education is used primarily to learn the skills necessary for coping with everyday life. Among men, learning concerns are almost exclusively vocational, and particularly strong emphasis is placed on preparing for jobs. Among women of lower socio-economic status, adult education is used primarily for vocational and homemaking purposes.

As one moves up in social class, vocational concerns not only become less prevalent, they shift from finding employment to getting ahead in a line of work already entered. In general, however, there is an overall shift away from learning for purposes of basic life adjustment, and an accompanying increment of concern with less pressing contingencies such as the enrichment of spare time.

THE IMPACT OF ADULT EDUCATION COURSES

How much do people benefit from the courses they take? Do they find these experiences at all useful? In general, our results indicate that they do. When asked how much they had gained from the courses they had taken most recently, 63 per cent said "a great deal," 23 per cent said "some," and only 13 per cent said "not very much" (see Table 8.7). However, there was considerable variation in the benefits attributed to different types of studies: Table 8.7 also shows that 83 per cent of those who studied religion and 75 per cent of those who studied agricultural subjects said they benefited "a great deal," while in the academic and public affairs areas the corresponding figures were barely over 50 per cent.

A more stringent criterion by which to evaluate the effectiveness of adult studies, of course, is whether courses are helpful in the ways people want them to be. In other words, while a person

Table 8.7 Amount of Benefit Derived from Most Recent Adult Education Course

[Question 17-E] How much do you feel you benefited from the course you took most recently — would you say a great deal, some, or not very much?

Amount of Benefit	A Great Deal (Per Cent)	Some (Per Cent)	Not Very Much (Per Cent)	Total (Per Cent)	Base (Weighted)
Total, all subjects	63	23	13	99	4,462
Religion	83	17	0	100	183
Vocational (agriculture)	75	25	0	100	79
Vocational (blue collar)	71	15	13	99	956
Personal development	62	28	10	100	193
Vocational (white collar)	62	23	15	100	1,394
Home and family life	62	19	19	100	315
Hobbies and recreation	59	26	15	100	562
Academic	52	35	13	100	550
Public affairs – current events	51	40	9	100	84
Miscellaneous other	64	27	9	100	146

might be able to say a course had helped him in a number of ways, the crucial question should be whether or not it satisfied the goals which led him to enroll in the first place.

To evaluate course-taking by this criterion, an "effectiveness index" was worked out for each of the different reasons people gave for taking courses. These scores are shown in Table 8.8 and represent the proportion of those expressing specific purposes for whom the courses were helpful in achieving them. Two other measures are also shown in Table 8.8: a column of scores labeled "unanticipated effectiveness" and an "overall impact" measure.

Although we are most concerned here with the left-hand column of scores, we may quickly sum up the main findings from the other two measures presented. In terms of both "overall impact" and "unanticipated effectiveness" adult education courses were helpful to people in two principal ways, making them feel better informed and helping them perform better on their jobs.

The figures in the left-hand column of scores, however, suggest that adult education courses may be considerably more effective in satisfying some goals than in satisfying others. The two most important findings here are (*a*) that adult education

Table 8.8 Effectiveness of Adult Studies

Ways in Which Course Was Helpful	Index of Effectiveness* (Per Cent)	Unanticipated Effectiveness† (Per Cent)	Overall Impact‡ (Per Cent)
Help on present job	90 (1,330)§	21 (2,845)	40 (4,505)
Home-centered tasks	87 (554)	11 (3,621)	20 (4,505)
Become better informed	86 (1,528)	38 (2,647)	51 (4,505)
Meet new people	80 (635)	17 (3,540)	25 (4,505)
Spare-time enjoyment	77 (837)	16 (3,338)	26 (4,505)
Escape the daily routine	73 (434)	11 (3,741)	17 (4,505)
Other everyday skills	72 (435)	08 (3,740)	14 (4,505)
Prepare for a new job	57 (1,492)	12 (2,683)	26 (4,505)

*Proportion of those who expressed purpose and found course helpful in achieving it.
†Proportion for whom course was helpful this way who did not give this as a purpose.
‡Proportion of all participants who said their most recent course was definitely helpful in this way.
§All bases are weighted.

courses were most effective when people enrolled to learn more about their jobs; and (*b*) that they were least effective in preparing people to enter a new job or occupation. This is not a minor difference: as many as 90 per cent of those who took a course for job advancement agreed that this was one of the ways the course had actually helped them, but only 57 per cent of those who had enrolled to "prepare for a new job or occupation" also identified this as one of the positive consequences of enrolling.

One might conclude that vocational education for adults is highly effective when it takes place after one has already entered an occupation or job, but that it is much less effective when its purpose is to lead to initial placement. In fact, the results indicate that when it comes to actually finding employment related to the training received, almost as many participants are unsuccessful as are successful.

What is not completely clear, however, is whether this occupational placement rate indicates a high or a low measure of success. Certainly the task of training adults so they can find new jobs represents a much more difficult assignment than that of extending the skills of those already employed. Indeed, one would expect that persons who require vocational training as adults in order to find employment would in large measure be persons in disadvantaged positions vis-à-vis the labor market. Although this group would include some skilled members of the labor force trying to switch from one occupation to another, it would also include large numbers of persons seeking to acquire enough basic skills to be employable in the first place. Thus it is not altogether clear whether the finding that adult education courses were "57 per cent effective" in the function of occupational placement is one which should be interpreted with optimism or pessimism.

On all other functions examined, the effectiveness scores ranged between 72 and 87 per cent, indicating that, in the main, participants were successful in getting the kind of help they wanted from adult education experiences. By far the most important findings, however, are those pertaining to the effectiveness of adult education studies in relation to vocational considerations.

9

Potential Audiences for Programs of Adult Learning I. Interest in Continuing Learning

At this point we shift our attention away from an analysis of persons who take adult education courses to a broader and somewhat less visible aggregate of individuals — that which might be defined as the "potential audience" for programs of adult learning. Although one might think of any number of personal traits which would identify a potential adult-education participant, there are two general characteristics such a person should be expected to possess as a very minimum. He should show at least some interest in learning more about a subject or skill, and he should display some readiness to take action to satisfy his learning interests. The disposition to learn and the readiness to act are examined in the next two chapters.

Our first problem is to discover how a generalized interest in learning new things is distributed throughout the adult population. Following this, we inquire into the origins of favorable dispositions toward learning. This chapter concludes with a discussion of some of the factors which have a bearing on whether or not these dispositions persist throughout adult life. However, a distinction should be made between people who want to learn and people who actually take adult education courses. These two aggregates are by no means identical; the most obvious way in which they differ is that only some segment of all adults who have things they would like to learn more about actually engage in organized learning. That the converse is also true — not all persons who take courses necessarily have learning interests — is not quite so obvious, since it is tempting to reason that enrollment in an educational course represents prima facie evidence of a favorable disposition toward learning. On the basis of the data examined in the previous chapter, however, there is good reason to suspect that at least some participants take courses for reasons which have little to do with learning interest. For example, it is probably safe to conclude that people who enroll in adult education courses solely to expand their social horizons possess little or no intrinsic commitment to the learning process. Indeed, for these people participation in any one of a number of different social activities would probably serve the same function.

This particular segment of adult education participants, in fact, is closely akin to what Cyril Houle (1961, pp. 15–16) identifies as the "activity-oriented," persons who find in the courses they take "a meaning which has no necessary connection . . . with the content or the announced purpose of the activity." Houle distinguishes these participants from two other types: the "learning-oriented" persons who seek knowledge for its own sake and the "goal-oriented" persons who use education in order to accomplish fairly clear-cut objectives. Both these latter types fall within the boundaries of our working definition of a potential audience, of course, since the "learning-oriented" are obviously interested in learning new things, and the "goal-oriented" seek an increased knowledge of some subject or skill as a channel to the particular goals they have in mind.

Thus our general approach to the study of potential audiences for programs of adult learning probably includes a fairly sizeable number of adults who do not take courses, and at the same time it excludes a small number of persons who do. From the viewpoint of the field of adult education, however, the definition which has been adopted here can be defended quite readily.

Adults who want to learn new things should certainly represent a major target for educators faced with the task of fitting programs of study to community needs; from this same perspective, adults who attend classes for other reasons must be considered of lesser interest. The audience of prime interest in this connection, of course, would be those who have definite learning interests, but have never had their interests channeled into formal educative behavior.

THE INCIDENCE OF LEARNING INTERESTS

The existence of learning interests among the adult population was measured by the following question:

[QUESTION 24] Most people have things they'd like to learn more about or would like to be able to do better. Is there anything in particular that you'd like to know more about, or would like to learn how to do better?

Since the discussion which follows is based on the way this question was answered, first we should clarify what the answers probably reflect. This question was purposely phrased to catch even the faintest glimmer of a learning interest if any existed at all. Because of the way it was worded, however, the most valid interpretation of the responses it elicited is not to treat positive answers as indications that a person is likely to engage in organized studies, but rather to consider that negative answers represent a strong indication that there would be little hope of ever attracting that individual into an adult education situation. In effect, then, we treat the difference between a positive and negative answer to this question as a threshold which differentiates persons who conceivably might be attracted to learning endeavors from those who, for all practical purposes, could probably never be attracted.

On this basis, then, the most revealing findings in Table 9.1 are that nearly one adult in four (23 per cent) claimed there was nothing he or she wanted to know more about, and a total of 29 per cent of the adult population failed to give a positive response to this question. While it is encouraging that seven adults in ten (71 per cent) did answer in the affirmative, one should perhaps be more impressed by the fact that this majority was not considerably larger.

Our discussion in this section is built on the rather fundamental premise that the presence of a learning interest represents a necessary—though not necessarily sufficient—precondition to participation in adult education. Before broadening the discussion, therefore, it is useful to review evidence which has at least some bearing on the validity of this assumption. Table 9.2 presents data which indicate the extent to which the presence of

Table 9.1 Incidence of Learning Interests among American Adults

[Question 24] Most people have things they'd like to learn more about, or would like to be able to do better. Is there anything in particular that you'd like to know more about, or would like to learn how to do better?

Yes	71%
No	23
Don't know	6
Total	100%
Number who answered	9,945
No information	19
Total (weighted)	9,964

Table 9.2 Relation of Learning Interests to Various Measures of Educational Behavior

Measures of Educational Behavior	Persons Who Would Like To Learn More about Something	Persons Who Do Not Want To Learn More about Anything	Strength of Association (Q)
Per cent who have taken an adult education course during the past five years	35 (6,729)*	11 (2,804)	+.64
Per cent who have engaged in independent study during the past five years	33 (6,874)	10 (2,820)	+.65
Per cent who have recently thought they might like to take an (another) adult education course	63 (6,689)	21 (2,816)	+.73

*All bases are weighted and include only persons who provided information on both questions.

learning interests overlapped with other measures of educational behavior. These data reveal that strong relationships do indeed exist between learning interests and educative behavior. The *Q* values of association indicate that if we were predicting who had taken part or thought of taking part in learning activities, our predictions would be improved by the following amounts if we knew whether or not a person was currently interested in learning something new: (*a*) by 64 per cent, if we were predicting who had taken an adult education course during the previous five years; (*b*) by 65 per cent, if we were predicting who had engaged in independent self-education during the previous five years; and (*c*) by 73 per cent, if we were predicting who had thought recently about taking an adult education course.

The existence of these rather sizeable relationships, then, suggests that learning interests do in fact represent important preconditions to enrollment in adult education courses. That they fail as sufficient preconditions is demonstrated by the fact that only one-third of those with learning interests had participated in either formal or informal educational pursuits during the previous five years, and, in addition, by the fact that more than one-third of those with learning interests had not even thought recently about taking a course.

LEARNING INTERESTS AMONG DIFFERENT POPULATION AGGREGATES

In view of our earlier findings concerning participation in educational activities, the next step is to examine learning interests in relation to the basic background factors of sex, age, and formal schooling. These results are presented separately in Table 9.3. Here we note that there was virtually no difference between men and women in the incidence of learning interests; this parallels our earlier results, which showed closely corresponding rates of participation between the sexes.

However, Table 9.3 also shows that age and education each have a particularly strong influence on learning interests, and in directions which would be anticipated on the basis of our earlier findings. Learning interests decrease rapidly with increasing age and rise just as sharply in the higher educational brackets. In relation to age, it can also be noted that interest not only falls off continuously in each succeeding decade, but that the rate of the decrease itself appears to be an accelerating one. This tendency is highlighted if we look at the percentage drop-off across each pair of decades.

Decades Compared	Per Cent Drop-off in the Incidence of Learning Interest
20's and 30's	2
30's and 40's	5
40's and 50's	11
50's and 60's	12
60's and 70's	18

These figures also indicate that there are two periods during which learning interests fall off with particular rapidity. The first is between the forties and fifties, where the rate of decline increases by six percentage points, and the second occurs between

Table 9.3 Influence of Sex, Age, and Education on Interest in Learning (Per Cent Who Would Like To Learn More about Something)

Sex		
Men	70	(4,416)*
Women	72	(5,528)
Age		
20–29	83	(1,979)
30–39	81	(2,114)
40–49	76	(2,203)
50–59	65	(1,550)
60–69	53	(1,226)
70–79	35	(588)
Years of schooling		
0–4	43	(541)
5–7	54	(882)
8	59	(1,448)
9–11	71	(2,015)
12	78	(2,957)
13–15	85	(1,158)
16	85	(606)
More than 16	87	(292)

*All bases are weighted.

the sixties and seventies, where it accelerates by a similar factor. The particular significance of these results is that the two points where the effects of age on learning interests are most pronounced are during transitional periods which are quite meaningful in our culture. It is at just about fifty that one's children finish school and begin to leave home; it is just following the mid-sixties that the process of disengagement from the tasks and duties of adult life begins. In other words, the accelerated influence of age on learning interests at these two points is very understandable.

Another important finding is that up until the fifties there is surprisingly little drop-off of learning interest; in fact, the rates are only 7 per cent higher among persons in their twenties than among those in their forties. Moreover, it is only after seventy that less than half say they would like to know more about something.

Table 9.3 shows an equally dramatic differentiation of learning interests across the formal education continuum, and the incidence of learning interests more than doubles between the lowest educational bracket and the highest. It is somewhat more difficult to isolate points of especially marked change from this series of percentages, however, since unlike the age continuum shown in Table 9.3, the educational categories used here do not represent equal units of time. Nonetheless, the figures do suggest that a rather pronounced jump of interest occurs at the break between grade school and high school (between eight years and nine–eleven years of schooling) and that the peak interest level is achieved pretty much with entrance into college. Although people in the highest educational grouping do display the highest level of interest, the differences between the three college-educated groupings are quite minor.

Since both age and education have such an overwhelming influence on learning interests, the next step is to try to evaluate their independent and joint effects. When one looks at these characteristics singly on a cross-sectional sample taken from the current American population, one must be continually aware that the real comparison made is between younger and better educated and older and less well educated people. Table 9.4, therefore, cross-classifies persons by both age and education to show the combined influence of these factors on dispositions to learn. In this table, grouping by age and education has been changed to preserve adequate case bases.

The results of this table confirm (at least in part) our earlier interpretations of when it is in the life cycle that the impact of age takes its greatest toll from the ranks of potential adult learners. When education is controlled, the differences between the two younger groups are again quite minimal: over these years learning interests do fall off by 8 per cent among the college educated, but they decline only 1 per cent among high-school educated, and actually increase by some 3 per cent among those with only a grade-school education.

Between the two older groups, however, the rates of decrease are much more pronounced: they are 20, 18, and 22 per cent, respectively, among the college, high-school, and grade-school groups. At all educational levels, then, the effect of age on learning interests occurs in the later rather than in the earlier decades of adult life.

Interpretations of the relative effects of age and education can also be made from this table. If we first look at just the two younger age groups, we find that being in a higher educational category has a much more powerful influence on learning interests than does being in the younger age category. Thus "middle-aged" persons who have been to college are 8 per cent more likely to have a learning interest than are "younger" persons who have only been to high school; and "middle-aged" persons who have been to high school are 14 per cent more likely to want to learn more than are "younger" persons who never

Table 9.4 Age, Education, and Interest in Learning (Per Cent Who Have Something They Would Like To Learn More About)

Educational Level	Under 30	30 – 49	50 and Over
College	96 (584)*	88 (996)	68 (496)
High school	80 (1,376)	79 (2,406)	61 (1,154)
Grade school	65 (136)	68 (904)	46 (1,820)

*All bases are weighted.

reached high school. Up until the age of fifty, then, it is evident that formal education makes more difference in learning interests than does age.

This relative influence is completely reversed when we compare the two older groups. Here age clearly has the greater impact. Being under fifty and high-school educated rather than over fifty and college educated makes one 11 per cent more likely to want to learn; being under fifty and grade-school educated rather than over fifty and high-school educated makes one 7 per cent more likely to want to learn more. Indeed, the table also indicates that persons aged thirty to forty-nine who have never been beyond grade school are just as likely to want to learn more as are persons over fifty who have been to college.

In general, we can conclude that both age and education have important effects on aspirations to learn. The results indicate also that the main impact of age is found in the later decades of adult life, and that the impact of education, consequently, is relatively greater during the younger years of adult life.

THE ORIGINS OF LEARNING INTERESTS

The strong relationship between learning interests and formal education immediately leads us to inquire whether there is any causal connection between school achievement and disposition toward continued learning. From the evidence so far, of course, it is not at all clear whether this disposition develops as a consequence of educational experiences, or whether it emerges in response to outside influences, which in turn also propel one to higher levels of school attainment. It might very well be, for example, that parental stress on the value of learning is the most important influence affecting both how far one goes in school and whether or not one holds a favorable disposition toward continued learning during adult life.

Some evidence of the role of earlier life experiences in this regard can be reconstructed from other data collected in the study: In one section of the interview respondents were asked about the educational attainment of each parent, and also about the extent to which their parents had urged them to do well in school.

Let us first look at the influence of parents' education. Table 9.5 shows that parents' education does indeed relate both with how far one went in school and with the extent to which one maintains a favorable disposition toward learning in adult life. The first row shows that if the parents completed high school, the chances are about eight in ten that the respondent himself did so; where the parents did not complete high school, however, the chances that the respondent did so are reduced to approximately five in ten.

This particular finding is hardly new or revealing for, as Lipset and Bendix (1960) point out, it has been widely documented in the literature on social mobility that one's educational chances are greatly improved when one enjoys a more favorable social class position to begin with.

From the second row of the table, however, we also note that whether or not one's father or mother completed high school is also related to learning interests. The parental influence is not as strong here as in relation to years of schooling completed, but the percentage differences are at least substantial enough to encourage us to examine the question further. So far, of course, we still cannot say that parents' education has any effect at all which is independent of one's own educational attainment.

This issue is quickly resolved in Table 9.6, however. Here the

Table 9.5 Years of Schooling and Interest in Learning Something New, by Parents' Educational Attainment

Educational Level and Learning Interests	Father's Education		Mother's Education	
	Completed High School or More	Did Not Complete High School	Completed High School or More	Did Not Complete High School
Educational level (per cent who themselves completed high school or more)	79 (1,606)*	51 (6,223)	82 (1,941)	47 (6,197)
Learning interests (per cent who are interested in learning something new)	83 (1,599)	72 (6,236)	84 (1,948)	70 (6,202)

*All bases are weighted.

Table 9.6 Interest in Learning More, by Parents' Education, Respondent's Education, and Sex (Per Cent Who Would Like to Learn More about Something)

Respondent's Sex and Educational Level	Father's Education		
	Completed High School or More	Did Not Complete High School	Percentage Difference
Men (sons)			
Completed high school or more	85 (508)*	79 (1,486)	+ 6
Did not complete high school	73 (128)	62 (1,344)	+11
Women (daughters)			
Completed high school or more	87 (747)	82 (1,662)	+ 5
Did not complete high school	66 (200)	62 (1,695)	+ 4
	Mother's Education		
	Completed High School or More	Did Not Complete High School	Percentage Difference
Men (sons)			
Completed high school or more	84 (722)	77 (1,313)	+ 7
Did not complete high school	79 (188)	63 (1,329)	+16
Women (daughters)			
Completed high school or more	87 (854)	81 (1,594)	+ 6
Did not complete high school	70 (162)	62 (1,907)	+ 8

*All bases are weighted.

percentage differences in the third column indicate that regardless of whether one completed high school, the fact that one's father or mother did so increases the likelihood of a favorable disposition toward learning. This is found in all eight test conditions.

Table 9.6 also allows us to make a rough comparison of the relative impact of one's own education and the educational level attained by one's parents. For example, an over-all index of parental influence can be produced by averaging the eight percentage differences in the third column of the table, and this can then be compared with a similar measure of the effects of one's own education obtained by averaging the differences (not shown in the table) between persons whose parents are in the same educational categories, but who themselves differ in having completed or not completed high school.

These impact measures reveal an average difference of just under eight percentage points which can be attributed to the influence of parents' education and a difference of just under sixteen points attributable to one's own educational attainment. Thus both the parents' and the respondent's education have independent effects on learning dispositions, but the impact of one's own education is approximately twice as powerful as that which stems from having well-educated parents. Taken together, however, the two factors produce an average of about twenty-four percentage points of spread in the incidence of these interests. This is a quite impressive difference to obtain from fourfold tables of this type.

Table 9.6 also suggests that some types of parent-child relationships have stronger effects than others on these learning dispositions. From figures in the heart of the table, for example, the following tendencies may be noted.

1. The influence of parents' education is about the same on sons as on daughters except in one situation: among respondents who did not complete high school themselves but who had parents who did, more sons than daughters report an interest in learning new things. Their rates of interest are 7 per cent higher comparing on father's education and 9 per cent higher comparing on mother's education.

2. The impact of a father's education is in most situations about the same as that of a mother's, but once again, a discrepancy occurs where the father or mother completed high school but the son or daughter did not. In these situations, the influence of the mother's education appears to be slightly stronger than that of the father's, by six percentage points among sons and four percentage points among daughters.

These two tendencies suggest that the effect of parents' education is of considerable importance in situations where parents went further in school than did their children. The influence is particularly strong where it is the mother's education which is higher than the son's. On this latter comparison, in fact, sons who did not complete high school but whose mothers did are 2 per cent more likely to be interested in learning than are sons who completed high school but whose mothers did not.

Another way to consider these same results is to rearrange the data to answer the following question: Of the total percentage spread produced by the two factors, how much is contibuted by the respondent's education and how much by the parent's? We have already noted that for all relationships combined, about one-third of the total percentage spread was a function of the parents' education and two-thirds a function of the respondent's. What we are asking now, in effect, is whether this relation differs across the various parent-child comparisons. That it does so is demonstrated in Table 9.7. These measures, which are abstracted from the percentages of Table 9.6, show that a consid-

Table 9.7 Relative Contribution of Parent's Education and Respondent's Education to Total Differences in Learning Interests

Proportion of Total Percentage Spread Contributed By	Type of Parent-Child Comparison				
	Mother and Son (Per Cent)	Father and Son (Per Cent)	Mother and Daughter (Per Cent)	Father and Daughter (Per Cent)	Average for all Relationships (Per Cent)
Parent's education	55	37	28	18	34
Respondent's education	45	63	72	82	66

erable variation exists in the extent to which the total educational effects are split up between the respondent and his parents. They show (once again) that the influence of mother's education on sons is slightly stronger than that of the son's own education, and that, in decreasing importance, the other parent-child relationships rank as follows: fathers and sons; mothers and daughters; fathers and daughters. The main finding here, however, is simply that the impact of parental education on dispositions toward continuing learning does vary markedly, depending on the sexes of the parent and child involved.

A second indicator of background influence was obtained from the following question:

[QUESTION 43] How important was it to each of your parents that you studied hard and got good grades – was it very important, slightly important or rather unimportant? How about your father? How about your mother?

Answers to these questions represent a somewhat more direct measure of parental concern over education success, and in the analysis which follows responses of "very important" will be taken to imply a positive influence toward the learning process itself.

Whether these influences affect learning interests in adult life is examined in Table 9.8. This table takes the same format as Table 9.6 and can therefore be examined in a similar fashion. The main finding of the table is quite apparent: the importance parents give academic achievement does make a considerable difference in learning interests in later life – but only among sons and daughters who do not attain a very substantial level of formal schooling. The contrast between those who do and do not complete high school is particularly striking here.

An evaluation of the relative effects of years of schooling and parental influences can be derived (as it was from Table 9.6) by again isolating the proportion of the total percentage spread produced by each separate influence. When extracted from Table 9.8, the relevant measures are as shown in Table 9.9. Here, a pattern emerges which is similar, though not as pro-

Table 9.8 Interest in Learning More, by Importance Placed on School Achievement by Parents, Respondent's Education, and Sex (Per Cent Who Would Like To Learn More about Something)

Importance to Respondent's Father of Getting Good Grades in School			
Respondent's Sex and Educational Level	Very Important	Slightly Important or Rather Unimportant	Percentage Difference
Men (sons)			
Completed high school or more	80 (1,220)*	76 (748)	+ 4
Did not complete high school	66 (1,057)	57 (718)	+ 9
Women (daughters)			
Completed high school or more	83 (1,611)	80 (839)	+ 3
Did not complete high school	66 (1,366)	53 (1,013)	+13

Importance to Respondent's Mother of Getting Good Grades in School			
Respondent's Sex and Educational Level	Very Important	Slightly Important or Rather Unimportant	Percentage Difference
Men (sons)			
Completed high school or more	80 (1,439)	74 (669)	+ 6
Did not complete high school	68 (1,228)	50 (573)	+18
Women (daughters)			
Completed high school or more	82 (1,824)	83 (727)	− 1
Did not complete high school	70 (1,564)	47 (935)	+23

*All bases are weighted.

nounced, as that extracted from Table 9.6. The figures show that parents' concerns with academic achievement have a relatively stronger effect on sons than on daughters, and in addition, that the influence of mothers is stronger than that of fathers.

A review of these findings leads us to the conclusion that one of the important consequences of a formal education is the development of a general receptivity to continued learning during adult life. This receptivity or eagerness to learn can also be awakened during early family experiences, and in most cases where this does emerge early it leads to a fairly substantial level of formal school achievement. In some cases, however, even a favorable home environment is not enough to propel a student through high school, and it is in these cases of attenuated schooling that early family influences can play an important role in keeping alive a favorable disposition toward learning.

Parental influences with respect to learning seem to have somewhat stronger effects on sons than on daughters, the influence of mothers being somewhat more powerful than that of fathers. Corroborative findings of other studies have indicated that parents tend to value academic achievement more highly for their sons than for their daughters,[1] and that in our society gen-

[1]James S. Coleman, for example, notes that an "overwhelming majority of parents . . . [want] their sons to be brilliant students while a smaller majority . . . [want] their daughters to be outstanding as brilliant students" (1961, pp. 33–34).

Table 9.9 Relative Contribution of Respondent's Education and Parents' Concerns with Academic Achievement to Total Differences of Interest in Learning New Things

Proportion of Total Percentage Spread Contributed By	Type of Parent-Child Comparison				
	Mother and Son (Per Cent)	Mother and Daughter (Per Cent)	Father and Son (Per Cent)	Father and Daughter (Per Cent)	Average for all Relationships (Per Cent)
Parents' concern with academic success	40	31	28	27	32
Respondent's education	60	69	72	73	68

erally, women place greater importance than men on the value of high educational attainment.[2] In view of these tendencies, it is not too surprising to find that sons who fail to achieve the academic expectations held for them by their mothers should be the most likely of all to maintain a learning interest in later life.

THE PERSISTENCE OF LEARNING INTERESTS IN ADULT LIFE

A thorough investigation of learning interests should deal not only with their emergence and growth, but also with their maturation and decline. Indeed, in a study of the total adult population, the decline rather than the development of these dispositions is most evident, and, as noted in Table 9.3, a continuous drop-off in the incidence of learning interests occurs after the twenties. (In investigations of learning and aging, the declining capacity to absorb new information or acquire new skills in later life is usually of primary concern. That older people are also less motivated to learn is usually not emphasized so strongly. It should be clearly understood that in the present discussion our concern is with the motivation to learn rather than with the ability or capacity to learn.)

Throughout this section we approach learning interests on the premise that they are part of a more general psychological state which in everyday terminology could be described as optimism or pessimism. It is our main assumption, in short, that learning interests are tied in closely with more general feelings about both the present and the future. The present study contains a considerable amount of information with which to explore this assumption.

Our first concern in this regard is with occupational role and with the responses to that part of the interview which dealt with work. The following question was asked of all persons in the labor force.

[QUESTION 57] Would you say that you have gone about as far as you can go in your present line of work, or that you can probably go quite a bit further?

[2]From the analysis of a 1947 NORC survey, Hyman found that women in all age and social class brackets emphasized the value of education more than did their male counterparts (1953, p. 431).

Of those who answered this question, 48 per cent said they thought they could go further and 52 per cent said they had gone about as far as they could.

Of more direct interest to us, however, is that the answers to this question overlapped quite markedly the answers to our question about learning interests. Table 9.10 shows that among men optimistic about future job prospects 85 per cent were also interested in learning, while among those pessimistic about chances for advancement only 63 per cent revealed a learning interest.

This relationship is examined in more detail in Table 9.11, where men in the labor force are classified on three characteristics: age, level of formal schooling, and occupational outlook. This table confirms the hypothesis that prospects for advancement have a strong influence on learning dispositions, since the percentage differences in the third column are of considerable magnitude. The discrepancies, moreover, are larger among the older men than among the younger and are larger among the poorly educated than among the better educated. Among men over forty-five who failed to complete high school, in fact, the difference of thirty-one percentage points represents a substantial correlation ($Q = +.60$) between feelings of occupational optimism and interest in learning new things. Particularly among older and less well-educated men, then, a receptivity to learning is tied up quite intimately with whether or not one sees one's occupational future as promising.

Table 9.10 Interest in Learning and Occupational Outlook among Men in the Labor Force

Learning Interest	Feel They Can Go Further in Their Present Line of Work (Per Cent)	Feel They Have Gone as Far as They Can Go in Their Work (Per Cent)	Strength of Association (Q)
Per cent who are interested in learning something new	85 (1,997)*	63 (1,723)	+.54

*All bases are weighted.

The general importance of occupational outlook can be noted by the fact that its influence intercepts the effects both of age and education. Thus older and less well-educated men, who are optimistic, are just as likely to want to learn as are younger and better-educated men, who find themselves in an occupational dead end (78 per cent compared with 77 per cent, respectively). And while one is much more likely to be optimistic about occupational advancement if one is young and well educated, it is nonetheless true that it is one's perceived job chances and not simply such characteristics as age or education which keep a desire to learn kindled.

Additional evidence on this same theme is contained in Tables 9.12 and 9.13, which show respectively the influence of future economic prospects and residential expectations on dispositions toward continued learning. These tables include men and women who are classified both by age and education. Table 9.12 deals with the answers to the following question:

[QUESTION 59] Thinking ahead to five years from now, would you estimate that your family income will be higher, about the same, or lower than it is now?

Table 9.11 Influence of Prospects for Job Advancement on Wanting To Learn More, by Age and Education (Per Cent Who Would Like To Learn More about Something)

Age and Educational Level	Can Go Further on Their Jobs (Per Cent)	Have Gone as Far as They Can (Per Cent)	Percentage Difference
Men under 45			
High school graduates			
or more	87 (1,011)*	77 (414)	+10
Did not graduate			
from high school	85 (414)	70 (392)	+15
Men 45 and over			
High school graduates			
or more	84 (278)	63 (342)	+21
Did not graduate			
from high school	78 (294)	47 (575)	+31

*All bases are weighted.

In response to this question, some 53 per cent thought it would be higher, 36 per cent said "about the same," and the remaining 11 per cent who answered the question said "lower." In Table 9.12 the respondents are divided into those expecting a higher income and those expecting the same or a lower income.

The figures in the third column indicate that among all four age and education groupings, persons more optimistic about their economic circumstances are also more likely to be interested in learning. This relationship is more pronounced among persons over forty-five than among those under forty-five and is particularly pronounced among those older adults who did not go very far in school.

Table 9.13 isolates a slightly different factor—expectations of residential mobility over the following five-year period.[3] The results indicate that favorable learning dispositions are also related to expectations about residential change. And again, the relationships are stronger among older adults than among younger.

[3] In this table we have classified respondents in terms of their answers to the following question: "As far as you know, do you expect to be living at this address five years from now, or do you expect to move within that period?" In answer to this, 31 per cent expected to move, 62 per cent expected to stay, and 6 per cent didn't know.

Table 9.12 Interest in Learning More, by Future Economic Prospects, Age, and Education (Per Cent Who Would Like To Learn More about Something)

Age and Educational Level	Expect a Higher Income in Five Years	Do Not Expect a Higher Income in Five Years	Percentage Difference
Under 45			
Completed high school or more	88 (2,688)*	79 (626)	+ 9
Did not complete high school	78 (1,091)	72 (784)	+ 6
45 and over			
Completed high school or more	78 (597)	66 (924)	+12
Did not complete high school	72 (554)	49 (2,075)	+23

*All bases are weighted.

In combination these three sets of data suggest that favorable dispositions toward learning may be part of a more general set of feelings reflecting optimism or pessimism about the future. In addition, since people who expect to move were also found to be more interested in learning, we might infer that another component of this general state is readiness to change.

A link between readiness to learn and readiness to change has a certain amount of natural plausibility, too, since the learning process itself is certainly one which involves considerable changes for the individual. In any event, what is of particular significance in these results is the general finding that the influence of the aging process on interest in learning may be noticeably affected by general psychological outlook. When optimism about life and readiness to change fade, then so too does desire to learn.

ADDITIONAL CORRELATES OF LEARNING INTEREST

One other question investigated in this section is whether interpersonal contacts affected learning interests. Although respondents were not asked to recall any specific instances, they were asked if any of their relatives, friends, or acquaintances

Table 9.13 Interest in Learning More by Residential Expectations in Five Years, Age, and Education (Per Cent Who Would Like To Learn More about Something)

Age and Educational Level	Expect to Move within Five Years	Expect To Be Living at Same Address in Five Years	Percentage Difference
Under 45			
Completed high school or more	90 (1,615)*	82 (1,597)	+ 8
Did not complete high school	78 (773)	73 (1,074)	+ 5
45 and over			
Completed high school or more	84 (236)	70 (1,248)	+14
Did not complete high school	62 (424)	50 (2,250)	+12

*All bases are weighted.

had taken an adult education course during the previous year or so. Just over one-third of the sample (36 per cent) did know one or more such persons; 21 per cent mentioned a relative, 15 per cent a friend, and 4 per cent an acquaintance. Moreover, persons who did know a recent participant were considerably more likely to express an interest in learning something new themselves. Table 9.14, for example, shows rates of learning interest of 86 and 63 per cent for these two groupings, and these differences produced a Q coefficient of $+.57$ between the two factors in question.

Even though this association is apparent, its implications are not, and there are at least five ways in which the result can be reasonably interpreted. The most appealing sociological explanation, of course, is that knowing people who take courses stimulates one's own interest in learning. But the direction of cause and effect here could just as easily be the other way around, and it could be that having learning interests leads people to cultivate social contacts with adult learners. Still another possibility is that the two factors are not linked in any causal fashion at all, but are correlated with each other only because each is independently associated with a third factor. For example, higher education might lead people both to expand their learning horizons and to have more frequent social contacts with others who also take part in educational activities. Or similarly, in communities where adult education facilities abound, both learning interests and contacts with adult students could be positively affected. Finally, a fifth possibility is that the

Table 9.14 Relation between Learning Interests and Contacts with Recent Adult Education Participants

Learning Interest	Relative	Friend	Acquaintance	Anyone	No One
Per cent who would like to learn more about something	86 (2,082)*	88 (1,488)	86 (439)	86 (3,535)	63 (6,261)
				$Q = +.57$	

*Bases are weighted.

association is strictly a perceptual phenomenon. In other words, it might very well be that people who have an interest in learning are more aware of the learning pursuits of other people in their environment, and for this reason are more likely to know whether any of their relatives, friends, or acquaintances had been involved in these activities. If this were true, they might also be expected to report these contacts more frequently.

Although we cannot really determine which of these interpretations is most valid, we can at least make sure that the relationship exists independently of the influence of other factors already known to be associated with the presence of learning interests. Table 9.15 re-examines this finding in relation to "predictors" of learning interest discovered earlier and another factor, the individual's own recent experiences with adult education

Table 9.15   Interest in Learning More, by Knowing Someone Who Took an Adult Education Course Recently, Personal Experience in Adult Education Courses Recently, and Score on Predictors Index (Per Cent Who Would Like To Learn More about Something)

Score on Predictor Index	Know Someone Who Took a Course Recently	Don't Know Anyone Who Took a Course Recently	Percentage Difference
	Persons Who Took an Adult Education Course in Previous Two Years		
None	63 (54)*	73 (67)	−10
One	87 (164)	76 (111)	+11
Two	89 (260)	90 (254)	− 1
Three	91 (506)	93 (275)	− 2
Four	99 (233)	88 (99)	+11
	Persons Who Had Not Taken an Adult Education Course in Previous Two Years		
None	63 (368)	40 (1,677)	+23
One	81 (559)	62 (1,520)	+19
Two	84 (571)	67 (1,233)	+17
Three	93 (677)	73 (831)	+20
Four	97 (190)	84 (212)	+13

*All bases are weighted.

courses. The "predictor index" shown in this table was built by allocating one point each to persons who (*a*) were young; (*b*) were well-educated; (*c*) had well-educated parents; and (*d*) were optimistic about their future economic prospects.

Table 9.15 contains two important findings. First, it shows that knowing a recent participant had little effect on the learning interests of persons who themselves had been recent participants, but had a substantial impact on the interests of those without these experiences. Second, the table shows that recent experiences with adult education also function as an independent "predictor" of the disposition to learn new things—at least among those who said they did not know anyone else who had been involved in these activities recently.

Together these results suggest that either taking courses or having social contacts with people who do increases the likelihood that people will be favorably disposed toward continued learning. And while we cannot specify the direction of cause and effect at work in these findings, we can nonetheless conclude that a functional relationship does exist between social environment and learning interests.

What can we conclude about the incidence of favorable dispositions toward continued learning? One way to sum up the

Table 9.16 Combined Influence of Six Predictors on Interest in Learning More

Number of Predictors	Per Cent Who Would Like to Learn More about Something	
None	40	(1,677)*
One	63	(1,955)
Two	72	(1,957)
Three	80	(1,820)
Four	91	(1,424)
Five	92	(795)
Six	99	(233)

*All bases are weighted.

chapter is to assess the combined impact of the various correlates of learning interests by revising the index of predictors so
that it takes into account both recent adult education experiences and social contacts with recent participants. Table 9.16
accordingly shows the incidence of basic interest among persons
with different numbers of the six factors found to be related with
these dispositions. The table indicates the following: among
those who (*a*) are under forty-five; (*b*) have a high-school education or more; (*c*) have at least one parent who completed high
school; (*d*) are optimistic about their income in five years; (*e*)
know someone who took an adult education course during the
previous two years; and (*f*) took an adult education course
themselves during the previous two years, virtually everyone
could be said to have at least some desire for further participation.

Conversely, among persons possessing none of these attri-
butes, three in five could be said to be without even the slightest
interest in continuing education. The factors which have been
examined in this chapter, in short, account in considerable
measure for the presence or absence of a disposition which we
have assumed is of critical importance to membership in the
potential audience for continuing education.

10

Potential Audiences for Programs of Adult Learning II. From Interest to Action

Up to this point in the analysis we have assumed, at least implicitly, that anyone who acknowledged an interest in knowing more about some subject or skill could be considered a potential participant for some adult learning program. While this assumption can be defended if one is willing to accept a broad enough definition of the concept of a "potential" audience for adult studies, the mere existence of a desire to learn new things cannot be realistically viewed as a disposition with sufficient strength to actually propel an individual into registration in some course. Indeed, it should be perfectly obvious that people could want to know more about something and yet at the same time be completely repulsed by the thought of ever pursuing systematic studies in relation to their interests.

At this point in the analysis, then, we adopt a somewhat more realistic definition of a "potential audience" by screening out from those with learning interests only those who show some readiness to engage in systematic study as well. The new group with which we are concerned here consists of all those with learning interests who, in addition, responded positively to the following questions:

[QUESTION 17-K] Have you thought recently that you might like to enroll in some other type of adult education course?

[QUESTION 17-L] Have you ever thought you might like to enroll in an adult education course of some type?[1]

Three segments of the population can now be differentiated: persons interested in learning who have also thought about taking courses, those whose learning interests have not been converted into thoughts of formal courses, and those simply not interested in learning anything new at all.

In the previous chapter approximately seven adults in ten were found to express some interest in learning, and we now see in Table 10.1 that of these some 44 per cent had thought about taking a course while 26 per cent had not. This suggests that just under one-half of the total adult population (an aggregate of perhaps 50 million persons)[2] might be seriously considered as potential participants in adult education.

The remainder of this chapter is divided into five sections, dealing with the following topics: an examination of the types of people most likely to think about taking courses to satisfy their learning interests; a description of the types of subject matter people would like to learn more about and take courses in; an evaluation of how much people actually know about the educational facilities available to them; an analysis of people's feelings about different methods of learning new subject matter; and finally, an investigation of the barriers which prevent potential participants from actually becoming involved in systematic studies.

WHO THINKS ABOUT TAKING COURSES?

The first section of this chapter describes the type of people most likely to consider taking courses; Table 10.2, accordingly, indicates the rates at which men and women in different age and educational categories had thought about formal adult education courses in relation to their learning interests.

Preliminary inspection shows that all three of these background factors had at least some effect: younger persons were more likely than older ones to consider the possibility of organ-

[1]The first phrasing of this question was directed at persons who had taken some previous course; the second at those who had not.

[2]Total adult population, 114 million (44.4 per cent = 50,620,000).

ized study, better-educated persons were more likely to do so than those with less formal schooling, and women were more likely to do so than men. Of the three results, the first two are not surprising and are quite in keeping with earlier findings which indicated that younger and better-educated adults were much more likely to have taken a course during the previous year. It is somewhat more surprising, however, to learn that women were more likely than men to think about taking courses. This represents a quite new finding, in fact, since on the indices examined up to now, men and women showed almost identical responses: 21 per cent of men and 19 per cent of women had engaged in organized studies during the previous year (see Chart 5.1), and 70 per cent of men compared with 72 per cent of women had said they would like to know more about some subject or skill (see Table 9.3). In the conversion of learning interests into thoughts about taking courses, however, the over-all rates (which are not shown in Table 10.2) turned out to be 58 per cent for men and 67 per cent for women. This difference is hardly startling in its magnitude, but it is considerably wider than might have been expected from our earlier results. It suggests, moreover, that while men and women may be about equally disposed toward learning per se, women are more likely than men to think about participating in organized studies. Moreover, the finding that slightly fewer women than men actually do end up taking courses over the period of a year does not necessarily negate this interpretation, for that could proba-

---

Table 10.1 Interest in Learning and Thoughts about Taking Adult Education Courses

Interested in learning and have thought of taking a course	44.4%
Interested in learning but have not thought of taking a course	26.0
Not interested in learning anything	29.6
Total	100.0%
Total who answered	9,551
Incomplete information	413
Total sample (weighted)	9,964

bly be explained by the fact that men on the whole have access to considerably more educational resources than do women. For example, many more men than women have an opportunity to receive on-the-job training, and the relatively greater restrictions which women experience during the childbearing period have already been found to result in a sharp depression in their rates of educational participation during these particular years (see Table 5.3).

That men and women do indeed differ in their dispositions regarding educational participation was corroborated by addi-

Table 10.2 Translation of Learning Interests into Thoughts about Courses, by Sex, Age, and Education (Per Cent of Those Who Would Like To Learn More about Something Who Had Thought of Taking Adult Education Courses)

Age and Educational Level	Men	Women
Under 45		
Completed high school or more	69 (1,187)*	76 (1,551)
Did not complete high school	62 (584)	73 (756)
45 and over		
Completed high school or more	48 (458)	63 (596)
Did not complete high school	45 (607)	48 (833)

*All bases are weighted.

Table 10.3 Attitudes of Women and Men toward Selected Spare-Time Activities (Per Cent Who Said This Would Be a "Very Interesting" Way To Spend Spare Time)

Activity	Women	Men	Percentage Difference
Attend adult education classes	44 (5,429)*	31 (4,365)	+13
Take a course in some subject not related to your work or occupation	38 (5,386)	27 (4,364)	+11
Attend lectures or talks on current events in this part of the country	34 (5,394)	31 (4,360)	+ 3
Attend lectures or talks on current events in the world and nation	32 (5,449)	30 (4,399)	+ 2
Take a course in some subject related to your work or occupation	45 (5,355)	51 (4,326)	− 6

*All bases are weighted.

tional evidence. At one point in the interview respondents were asked to rate each of seventeen different "spare-time activities" along a scale which ranged from "very interesting" to "very boring" (see Question 9 in the interview schedule). Five of these seventeen items referred to activities of an educational or quasi-educational nature, and one of the five made specific reference to "adult education classes." The ratings respondents assigned to these five activities are summarized in Table 10.3, which shows the proportions who endorsed each as "very interesting." The most important column in this table is that which indicates the differences between men and women. These figures show that women reacted more favorably than men to four of the five activities listed. Only two of these differences are of a meaningful size, however, and the largest discrepancy of all is that found on the item "attend adult education classes" — which was endorsed as "very interesting" by 44 per cent of all women compared with 31 per cent of all men.

Upon closer scrutiny, it may also be noted that this first item is the only one of the five which describes educational participation without any reference whatsoever to subject matter. All the others make some mention of the type of content involved, although for the second item this could consist of anything not directly connected with one's employment. The significance of all this, of course, is that on all items except the first, and possibly the second, respondents could have reacted either to the activity aspect or to the content of the subject matter involved. Since the items on which the widest sex-linked differences are found are the two where the content is the most vague, there is at least some slight suggestion that women may be relatively more activity oriented than men — at least as far as educational pursuits are concerned. With regard to the two public affairs items, moreover, one might be tempted to argue further that since this general topic probably holds more intrinsic appeal for men than for women, the women who rated these items favorably may have done so more frequently because "lectures or talks" were mentioned, while men may have reacted relatively more often to the content. There is no real basis for accepting this interpretation, of course, since it is not possible to analyze people's reactions to these separate elements. The relative importance of content and form for members of the two sexes is at least clear in the reactions to the second and fifth items in the table: here it is rather evident that men had more favorable reactions to the fifth item because of its occupational context.

The most important finding in Table 10.3 is that men and women do appear to differ in their reactions to the general concept of "adult education classes." There is evidence, too, that the meaning of this term may be predominantly feminine in its denotative as well as connotative aspects. At another point in the interview respondents were asked a series of questions about what they thought typical adult education participants were probably like. The first of these questions was the following:

[QUESTION 26-A] Here is a different type of question. From your own experience or from what you have heard, what types of people would you guess most often attend adult education classes — would you say women or men?

In asking this question there was no expectation that respondents would — or even could — know the "correct" answer. The reason it was asked, rather, was to try to find out what people thought typical adult education participants were like. Indeed, it would be difficult to determine what the "correct" answer to this question really was. In the household screening interviews from the first phase of our inquiry, for example, a total of 2,076 adults were located who had received instruction during the previous year by attending classes. Of these participants 48 per cent were men and 52 per cent were women (see Table 4.4). However, in the sample as a whole only 47 per cent of the enumerated adults were men, and this would indicate that while a majority of the participants who attended classes may have been women, the rates at which men and women attended were virtually identical. Thus neither answer to Question 26-A could be considered to be the "right" one, and, technically speaking, the most correct answer would be to say that men and women attend about equally often. Thus we might expect the distribution of answers to this question to show approximately equal numbers of persons answering in favor of each sex.

This, however, did not turn out to be true; as Table 10.4

shows, of those who chose either sex, substantially more respondents answered "women" than "men" (52 per cent compared with 26 per cent). Only one respondent in six said he thought each sex attended equally often, and 6 per cent could not hazard even a guess.

Interestingly, Table 10.4 also shows that these impressions are held with about the same frequency by both women and men. The only variation between the sexes was that respondents were slightly more likely to identify "typical participants" with their own sex.

These responses suggest a fairly widely held impression that adult education classes are engaged in primarily by women. Thus in both its cognitive and evaluative elements, the meaning of the term "adult education classes" seems connected with feminine rather than masculine behavior. It is difficult to say what the effect of this might be on the motivation of men (or women) to participate; however, if one were willing to infer that taking adult education courses is widely perceived as a feminine thing to do, then one should also be willing to conclude that men would be more likely than women to say, "Adult education classes are not for me."

Table 10.4 Impressions of the Typical Adult Education Participant, by Sex

[Question 26-A] From your own experience or from what you have heard, what types of people would you guess more often attend adult education classes—would you say women or men?

Answer	Men (Per Cent)	Women (Per Cent)	Total (Per Cent)
Women	50	54	52
Men	28	24	26
They attend equally often	16	16	16
Don't know	6	6	6
Total	100	100	100
Base	4,344	5,319	9,663
No information	90	211	301
Total (weighted)	4,434	5,530	9,964

As a concluding note to this section we shall explore briefly the relation between one's perception of an adult education participant and one's own motivation to be one. In Table 10.5 men and women are classified according to their "level of readiness" to engage in educational activities. The "high readiness" category is made up of persons who earlier were classified as members of the potential audience — that is, persons interested in learning something who had thought about taking a course; the "medium" category consists of those who acknowledged an interest in learning but who had not thought about taking a course; and those in the "low" category are persons who did not identify any subject or skill about which they wanted to know more.

These figures show that the way one characterizes adult education participants does in part reflect one's own feelings about learning and course taking. The proportions who classified the typical participant as a member of their own sex drop from 33 to 28 to 20 per cent among men, and from 61 to 54 to 42 per cent among women as we read across the columns of high, medium, and low participation readiness. The disidentification ratio summarizes this tendency in another way; it shows the extent to which respondents excluded rather than included their own sex in their respónses to our question.[3] Clearly adults who are less interested in learning are more likely to disidentify with adult education participants.

These results suggest that some respondents probably did answer this question by projecting their own feelings about learning and course taking. On the other hand, even men with a high readiness to participate were more likely to identify the typical participant as a woman rather than a man, and this suggests that a stereotype does exist that enrollment in educational classes is more a feminine than a masculine thing to do. The

[3]The measure consists of the total number of persons who identified the typical participant with the opposite sex, divided by the total who identified "him" either as a member of their own sex or who said both sexes attend equally often. Thus among men with "low" participation readiness, 1.30 disidentified for every one who identified; among comparable women, only .47 disidentified for every one who identified.

Table 10.5 Impressions of the Typical Adult Education Participant, by Sex and Participation Readiness

Most People Who Attend Adult Education Classes Are	Participation Readiness					
	Men			Women		
	High (Per Cent)	Medium (Per Cent)	Low (Per Cent)	High (Per Cent)	Medium (Per Cent)	Low (Per Cent)
Women	49	51	51	61	54	42
Men	33	28	20	21	25	28
They attend equally often	14	15	19	15	15	18
Don't know	3	6	10	3	5	13
Total	99	100	100	100	99	101
Base (weighted)	1,687	1,205	1,323	2,554	1,276	1,553
Disidentification ratio	1.02	1.17	1.30	.28	.36	.47

more prominent element in the responses, in other words, would appear to be cognitive rather than affective.

THE CONTENT OF LEARNING INTERESTS
AND COURSE-TAKING INTENTIONS

In Chapter 9, people's learning interests were analyzed in terms of general dispositions toward the acquisition of new knowledge, information, or skills rather than in terms of the kinds of things about which people were interested in knowing more. In this next section, however, we examine the content of people's learning interests and of the courses they consider taking. Both sets of data are shown in Table 10.6.

The most important finding in this table is a rather curious one—the topics people most frequently want to know more about are not the ones most often mentioned when they think about taking courses. The list of learning interests is topped by subjects and skills in home and family life, while in terms of

Table 10.6 What People Want To Learn More about and Take Courses In

Category	Per Cent Who Would Like To Learn More about This Subject		Per Cent Who Had Thought about Taking a Course in This	
Any subject		71		50
White-collar vocational skills	17		21	
Regular school subjects	14		15	
Blue-collar vocational skills	14		8	
Hobbies and recreation	16		7	
Home and family life	23		7	
Personal development	8		4	
Religion, morals, and ethics	3		1	
Current events and public affairs	5		1	
Agriculture	2		*	
Miscellaneous other	1		*	
None or don't know		29		50
Total		100		100
Base		9,945		9,571
No information		19		393
Total sample (weighted)		9,964		9,964

*Less than 1 per cent.

course taking this category ranked well down on the list. In fact, while some 23 per cent said they wanted to know more in this area, only 7 per cent had ever considered taking a course in it.

Another way in which responses to these two questions differed was in the range of subject matter mentioned with any frequency. Altogether, interest was expressed in learning more about five different subject fields: family life, both white- and blue-collar vocational skills, hobbies and recreation, and regular school subjects. Thoughts about course taking, however, were fairly restricted to two fields, white-collar vocational subjects and academic topics.

Table 10.6 also shows that while considerably more respondents acknowledged learning interests than had thought of taking courses (71 compared with 50 per cent), both the academic and white-collar occupational fields were mentioned more often in connection with course taking than as areas in which people wanted to expand their knowledge or competence.

More generally, then, there appear to be rather widespread discrepancies in the extent to which different types of substantive interests become channeled into thoughts about courses. Course taking is evidently considered more appropriate to some learning interests than others.

Table 10.7 isolates a more direct measure of this tendency: it

Table 10.7 Extent to Which Different Learning Interests Become Channeled into Thoughts about Taking Courses

Type of Subject Matter	Total Persons Who Said They Would Like to Know More about This (Weighted)	Proportion of These Persons Who Thought of Taking a Course in This Field
White-collar vocational skills	1,735	.50
Regular school subjects	1,372	.41
Blue-collar vocational skills	1,409	.33
Home and family life	2,334	.22
Hobbies and recreation	1,575	.22
Personal development	747	.16
Current events and public affairs	543	.08
Religion	333	.07
Agriculture	182	.07
Miscellaneous other	86	.13

shows, for each category of subject, the proportion of persons who converted their interests into intentions about taking formal action. These figures indicate a remarkable variance. One-half of those who wanted to learn more about some white-collar occupational subject had thought about taking a course in that area, and substantial minorities of those interested in academic subjects or blue-collar vocational skills had also considered doing so. On the other hand, religion, public affairs, and agriculture do not appear to be associated with course taking. In each of these fewer than one person in ten had thought of taking an adult education course to satisfy these interests.

In general the subjects most likely to be thought of in terms of course taking are regular school subjects and vocational subjects other than agricultural. These fields represent the areas of adult learning more traditionally organized around the "course" format, and in this light the results have a ring of plausibility about them. But it is revealing, nonetheless, that formal instruction turns out to be so infrequently associated with many subjects about which people want to know more.

KNOWLEDGE OF FACILITIES FOR ADULT EDUCATION

One rather obvious determinant of a person's ability to channel a learning interest into action is that of appropriate instructional facilities in his environment. A crucial question at this point in the inquiry, then, is whether or not people are aware of the places to go in their community to satisfy a learning interest.

This is an extremely complex question. Knowing about the existence of appropriate educational facilities involves collecting information about communities rather than individuals, and the way to obtain this information is to survey the institutions in a community rather than its population. From our national survey of adults, in other words, it is really not possible to say very much at all about available facilities. In the third phase of our inquiry educational facilities were inventoried in four middle-sized cities, but our national study collected information only from interviews with randomly selected adults, and there is therefore no meaningful way for us to judge the adequacy of facilities for adult instruction at the various sampling points where respondents were interviewed. In most of the urban areas suitable facilities for adult instruction exist; but it would be risky to make any such assumptions for small towns or rural areas, or even for the suburban fringes surrounding major metropolitan centers.

Although we do not have any adequate basis for assessing the correctness of their information, we can at least try to determine what kinds of people, among those living in similar geographical environs, know and do not know of places which offer instruction to adults.

The information examined in this section is derived from the following two questions:

[QUESTION 11] If an adult living here wanted to take some lessons in how to speak a foreign language, are there any places nearby where he or she might get instruction of this type?

[QUESTION 16] Do you know of any places around here or nearby where people no longer in school can attend classes or receive instruction in subjects other than foreign languages?

First let us consider the overall distribution of response on these questions. Table 10.8 indicates that just over one-half of the respondents thought they knew of at least one place where adults in their community could go to receive instruction. One-third did not know whether or not any such facilities were available, and about one person in seven or eight claimed that such resources definitely did not exist where he lived. Almost as many persons knew of places offering foreign language instruction as were aware of resources for any other type of subject (52 and 55 per cent, respectively).

What types of institutions do people mention when asked about facilities for adult learning? Table 10.8 indicates that most thought either of a high school or of a college or university. On both questions, in fact, the only other facilities mentioned by more than one respondent in twenty were vocational or business schools and community institutions such as the YMCA, libraries, or museums (by 8 and 7 per cent, respectively, in answer to the second question).

For the most part, then, people think of the regular school system when they think of instructional facilities for adults. This is interesting since in the first phase of this study it was found that approximately two adults in three who had received instruction during the previous year had received it outside of the regular school system (Chap. 3, "Sponsorship of Studies"). The bulk of that instruction was in institutions such as businesses or churches, however, where individuals would have had to establish prior connections in order to come into contact with their instructional offerings. It is understandable, then, that these more private types of instructional facilities would not be mentioned very frequently in connection with foreign-language instruction or general community facilities for adult learning.

Table 10.8 suggests that one adult in three simply does not have any knowledge of the educational resources for adults in his community. While from one point of view this might be considered a discouraging lack of awareness in the general public, studies of public knowledge on practically any social

Table 10.8 Knowledge of Adult Education Facilities in Community

Type of Facility	Foreign Language Instruction (Per Cent)		Any Other Instruction (Per Cent)	
Know of some places where adults can study		52		55
High schools	28		34	
College or university	27		25	
Vocational or business school	2		8	
College or university extension	5		7	
Community institutions	4		7	
Elementary schools	*		2	
Private schools	4		1	
All other facilities	6		1	
Say there are no such places		15		12
Don't know of any such places		33		33
Total		100		100
Base		9,958		9,956
No information		6		8
Total (weighted)		9,964		9,964

*Less than 1 per cent.

event, issue, or resource invariably uncover a sizeable number of poorly informed people.[4] Since these frequently constitute from one-fifth to one-third of the whole adult population, the present result is by no means an unexpected one.[5]

For our purposes, it is perhaps more meaningful to ask about levels of awareness of educational facilities among those groups likely to use these resources. Table 10.9 demonstrates that information levels are indeed considerably higher among persons who are ready to participate. The proportion aware of at least one resource increased from 36 to 56 to 65 per cent, respectively, across the conditions of "low," "medium," and "high" par-

[4]Hyman and Sheatsley (1947) have noted that a fairly large segment of the general public could be described as "chronic know-nothings" with respect to virtually all spheres of social information. They remark that "there is something about the uninformed which makes them harder to reach [in information campaigns] no matter what the level or nature of the information" (pp. 412–23).

[5]Ignorance of adult education facilities may nonetheless be more extensive than ignorance of certain other types of community resources. For example, on a study of medical practices (NORC Survey No. 367) people were asked the following: "If someone around here got sick and didn't have any money to pay, is there any place he could go that would take care of him?" In answer, 68 per cent said "yes," 13 per cent "no," and only 19 per cent didn't know. And on another NORC survey (Survey No. SRS 160, June, 1963) respondents were asked if they had heard or read anything about their Better Business Bureau: 47 per cent had heard of the Bureau and were able to give correct information about its activities, 26 per cent claimed to have heard of it but could not identify its functions, and 27 per cent had never heard of it.

Table 10.9   Knowledge of Adult Education Facilities, by Readiness To Participate

Knowledge of Facilities*	Level of Participation Readiness		
	High (Per Cent)	Medium (Per Cent)	Low (Per Cent)
Know of places to study	65	56	36
Don't know of places to study	24	34	48
Say no such places exist	11	10	16
Total	100	100	100
Base (weighted)	4,213	2,478	2,847

*Other than for foreign-language instruction.

ticipation readiness, while across the same categories rates of uninformedness were cut in half—from 48 to 34 to 24 per cent. It is clear that people who have more reason to know about these things are more likely to know about them: at the same time, however, even among the potential participants one in four did not know.

One question obviously relevant to the present discussion is whether those who live in different kinds of communities are differentially aware of instruction facilities. To answer this we must take into account the individual characteristics which affect knowing or not knowing about existing facilities. From what we already know about who participates in adult education (and levels of public information in general) we expect persons of high socio-economic circumstances to know considerably more about adult education resources than persons of low socio-economic status. Therefore to isolate the influence of place of residence, it is necessary at the very least to make comparisons among persons in the same general economic brackets.

In Table 10.10, therefore, respondents are classified both by the size of community in which they live and by their socio-economic status. The table then reports the proportion who said they knew of at least one place nearby where an adult could go to receive instruction in some subject or skill.

While this table reveals vast discrepancies based on socio-economic status, it also shows that within the same social strata there are differences in levels of awareness which are a function of community size. The combination of these two factors produces a tremendous range in levels of awareness: among respondents of high socio-economic status living in middle-sized cities (50,000–2,000,000), as many as 85 per cent knew of at least one place where adults could receive instruction, whereas the comparable figure for persons of low socio-economic status in small towns or rural areas was 19 per cent. This suggests that knowledge of educational facilities is most widespread in middle-sized cities and least so in small towns or rural areas. In the middle-sized urban areas, central-city residents show a consistently higher level of awareness than do the suburban dwellers. This discrepancy is particularly noticeable among persons in the

Table 10.10 Knowledge of Adult Education Facilities, by Socio-Economic Level and Type of Community (Per Cent Who Know of Some Place Where an Adult Could Receive Instruction*)

Socio-Economic Level	Cities 2,000,000 or Over		Cities 50,000 – 2,000,000		Cities 10,000 – 50,000	Small Towns and Rural Areas
	Central City	Suburbs	Central City	Suburbs		
High	78 (376)†	79 (451)	85 (556)	81 (722)	79 (395)	52 (418)
Medium	60 (325)	58 (324)	70 (676)	62 (567)	60 (493)	46 (634)
Low	40 (360)	41 (225)	54 (723)	41 (471)	27 (572)	19 (1,338)

*Other than foreign-language instruction.
†Bases are weighted.

low socio-economic stratum, where it is 13 per cent. A comparable urban-suburban difference is not found at all among residents of the largest urban areas, however.

The most striking differences in the whole table are those related directly to socio-economic status. Persons of high socio-economic status who live even in small towns or rural areas are more likely to know of educational facilities than are persons of low socio-economic status living in most types of urban settings.

To sum up, the results indicate that there are substantial differences in the extent to which people living in cities of differing size know of the existence of facilities for adult instruction. This probably reflects a real difference in the availability of resources in different places, but the nature of our evidence allows us to do no more than speculate about that possibility.

METHODS OF LEARNING NEW SUBJECT MATTER

Although familiarity with local resources represents one important indicator of a person's capacity to convert a learning interest into action, formal instructional facilities by no means exhaust the appropriate sources to which one might turn. We have already seen that adults utilize a wide range of home-study techniques, and access to these does not depend upon knowledge of the instructional facilities available in one's community.

To derive a more general perspective on alertness to opportunities for learning, we asked our respondents what they would do if faced with the specific problem of acquiring facility in a completely new subject.

[QUESTION 13] Suppose you had a chance to travel to a foreign country and you decided that before you left you'd try to learn to speak the language of that country. How do you think you would probably go about learning it?

Our first step in analyzing the answers to this question was to classify people according to whether they would seek instruction of some sort or would try to acquire the knowledge on their

own. Table 10.11 shows that two-thirds (68 per cent) said they
would seek instruction while just over one-quarter (27 per cent)
said they would try to teach themselves.

Upon closer examination it is evident that most of those who
said they would look for instruction did not have very definite
ideas of exactly what they would do. Thirty-nine per cent made
only a general reference to "lessons" or "schools" and did not
identify any specific facility or resource to which they would
turn. The remaining persons in this category (29 per cent of the
sample) did identify a more specific channel: 15 per cent referred to a private teacher or tutor, 12 per cent mentioned a
local college or university, 7 per cent named a local high school,
3 per cent thought of a private school of languages, and another 3
per cent said they would take a home-study course from a correspondence school.

The most striking feature about these data is that altogether
less than one respondent in five indicated he or she would turn
to the regular school system to develop proficiency in a foreign
language. Since language courses usually abound in high-school

---

Table 10.11 How People Would Go about Learning a
Foreign Language

[Question 13] Suppose you had a chance to travel to a foreign country and you
decided that before you left you'd try to learn to speak the language of that country.
How do you think you would probably go about learning it?

Would seek instruction		68%
Private teacher or tutor	15%	
College or university	12	
Secondary school	7	
Private school of languages	3	
Correspondence school	3	
Vague reference to "school" or "lessons"	39	
Would try to teach themselves		27
Recordings or tapes	15	
Other home-study methods	16%	
All other methods		9
Don't know or uncodeable answer		15
Total		119%*
Base (weighted)		9,964

*Does not total 100 per cent because some persons mentioned more than one method.

and college curricula, and since many more adults than this knew of the availability of such courses, we might have expected high schools and colleges to be mentioned much more frequently than they were. A comparison of the figures in Tables 10.8 and 10.11 is quite revealing on this point: although 28 per cent knew language courses in local high schools, only 7 per cent would consider these channels themselves; and while 27 per cent knew of relevant courses in a local college or university (plus an additional 5 per cent who mentioned extension departments), only 12 per cent said they would probably take one themselves. It is clear that substantially more adults are aware of foreign-language instruction in the regular school system than would be willing to use it. This seems particularly true about facilities in the secondary-school system.

Just why these imbalances should be so marked is not altogether clear from the present data. The results suggest, however, that many adults may view the regular school system as an inappropriate source for the acquisition of skills which must be put to immediate use.

Among the 27 per cent who said they would try to learn the language on their own, 15 per cent made specific mention of instructional recordings or tapes, while 16 per cent talked of other methods of self-teaching.[6] It is notable that many more thought of some method of self-instruction than thought of taking a course in either a high school or a college. But it is equally notable, perhaps, that very few adults would go about learning a foreign language other than through either formal or informal studies: altogether, only 9 per cent talked of such methods as cultivating foreign-speaking friends, living with a foreign-speaking family, or spending time in a foreign-language community.

Finally, 15 per cent of the sample appeared to have no idea whatsoever of how to go about learning a foreign language and failed to make even vague references to either instruction, independent study, or other methods.

Awareness of how to go about learning a foreign language,

[6]Therefore, 4 per cent mentioned both recordings or tapes and some other method of individual study.

Volunteers for Learning

as one might readily suspect, differs among persons located in different echelons of the social hierarchy. This is clearly evident in Table 10.12, which shows how persons in three socioeconomic brackets would go about acquiring foreign-language skills. The most striking figures here are those which indicate the absence of knowledge of what to do. In the high socio-economic category, only 2 per cent could not think of any way to learn a foreign language, but this was the situation for 12 per cent in the middle socio-economic category and for as many as 27 per cent of the respondents of low socio-economic status. Thus a rather substantial proportion of persons of lower socio-economic background would be unprepared to take any kind of action at all if they ever found themselves requiring facility in a new language.

Adults in higher socio-economic positions were more likely to mention both formal and informal methods of learning a language, and, in addition, were more likely to identify specific resources in their environment to which they would turn. Among respondents of lower socio-economic status, for example, most who said they would seek instruction made only vague references to a "school" or to "lessons" (38 of 59 per cent), while in the high socio-economic grouping, a majority of the instruction seekers (40 of 77 per cent) named some specific resource that they would use. This result merely re-emphasizes

Table 10.12 How Adults Would Go about Learning a Foreign Language, by Socio-Economic Status (Per Cent Who Mentioned Each Method)

Type of Activity	High SES		Medium SES		Low SES	
Seek instruction		77		70		59
Specific source mentioned	40		30		21	
Vague reference to "school"	37		40		38	
Try to teach themselves		40		27		17
Other method		10		10		6
Don't know or uncodeable answer		2		12		27
Total		129*		119*		109*
Base (weighted)		2,950		3,054		3,735

*Does not total 100 per cent because some persons mentioned more than one method.

that persons in higher socio-economic brackets are more knowledgeable about the educational facilities available in their environment.

Another tendency (somewhat hidden in the figures of Table 10.12) is that methods of self-instruction made up a larger proportion of the total methods mentioned by persons of high socio-economic background than of those identified by persons further down the socio-economic ladder. In all socio-economic positions more people said they would look for instruction than would try to teach themselves, but the gap between these modes of solution is seen to close at the higher socio-economic levels. Techniques of self-instruction made up 21 per cent of all methods identified by persons of low socio-economic status, 25 per cent of those mentioned by persons located in the middle socio-economic grouping, and 31 per cent of those identified by persons of high socio-economic status. The people in higher educational and income brackets, then, are not only more likely to think of something to do in the first place, but are also relatively more likely to think about undertaking a learning task independently.

Although these responses suggest that persons in higher socio-economic brackets show more initiative in solving a hypothetical learning problem, we cannot conclude that people of high socio-economic status are necessarily most likely to prefer informal learning contexts. It is quite possible, for instance, that these persons mentioned individual study methods more often simply because they were very much more aware of the existence of these approaches. We are suggesting, in short, that persons of high and low socio-economic status differ more in their knowledge about methods of independent study than in their information about school classes or lessons with private instructors.

At the same time, there is probably good reason to think that persons low in socio-economic status are more favorably oriented than those of high socio-economic status to the more informal methods of learning. Since persons of low socio-economic status have for the most part had very abbreviated experiences in the school system we might expect them to be considerably more wary about engaging in formal learning activities.

This idea prompted us to collect more specific information about people's preferences for different learning methods. For example, the respondents were first asked to choose from among five specific ways of receiving foreign language instruction.

[QUESTION 14] Of the five methods listed on this card, which one would you prefer if you were learning to speak a foreign language?
  a) Attend regular classes in some sort of school
  b) Find a private teacher and take individual lessons
  c) Follow lessons given over television
  d) Take correspondence lessons by mail
  e) Buy a book or some recordings and study it on my own

In answer to this question, 46 per cent chose to attend classes, 36 per cent preferred private lessons, and only 17 per cent thought one of the home study methods would be preferable (see Table 10.13).

Although our primary interest here is in whether preferences for different learning situations vary among persons of different socio-economic levels, there is also reason to suspect that these orientations may vary by age and sex. Table 10.14, accordingly, examines the effect of all three of these factors simultaneously.

First, there are no consistent differences between men and

Table 10.13 Preferred Methods for Learning a Foreign Language

[Question 14] Of the five methods listed on this card, which one would you prefer if you were learning to speak a foreign language?

Attend regular classes in some sort of school	46%
Find a private teacher and take individual lessons	36
Buy a book or some recordings and study it on my own	12
Follow lessons given on television	3
Take correspondence lessons by mail	2
Total	99%
Base	9,542
Don't know	218
Wouldn't matter	133
No answer	71
Total (weighted)	9,964

women with regard to preferred learning situations. In the middle and high socio-economic positions, men were slightly more likely to choose home-study methods, but this tendency is not found among respondents of low socio-economic status.

Substantial differences may be attributed to the influence of age, however. Older persons were much less likely to select the formal classroom for learning and were more likely to mention private instruction and home-study techniques. These differences are found in each of the six conditions where age comparisons can be made.

With respect to socio-economic position, a quite interesting pattern of results may be noted. Persons in the middle socio-

---

Table 10.14 Preferred Context for Receiving Foreign-Language Instruction, by Sex, Age, and Socio-Economic Status (Per Cent Who Preferred Different Learning Contexts)

Method of Study	Men					
	Under 45			45 and Over		
	Low SES	Medium SES	High SES	Low SES	Medium SES	High SES
Regular classes	49	57	55	35	39	37
Private lessons	35	27	29	42	37	44
Home-study	15	16	17	23	24	19
Total	99	100	101	100	100	100
Base	566*	828	943	891	461	497
	Women					
	Under 45			45 and Over		
	Low SES	Medium SES	High SES	Low SES	Medium SES	High SES
Regular classes	48	55	52	34	44	43
Private lessons	36	31	38	39	39	41
Home-study	16	14	10	26	17	15
Total	100	100	100	99	100	99
Base	746	1,094	999	1,233	548	478

*All bases are weighted.

economic category were the most likely to select the classroom for foreign language instruction, and persons low in socio-economic status were least likely to do so. These tendencies were not pronounced, but they were found in each of the four test cases.

How can these results be interpreted? With preference patterns of this type, one is faced with the problem of deciding whether an observed difference can be attributed to the positive valence of one alternative or to the negative valence of another. Here, for example, it is unclear whether we should conclude that persons of middle socio-economic status are more favorably disposed than others to formal classroom settings for learning, or that there are really no differences at all in preferences for this form of instruction and the observed discrepancies are a function of the fact that persons of middle socio-economic status are less attracted than others to the more informal study methods listed. There is no adequate way to resolve this dilemma, although the evidence would be consistent with the interpretation that persons of lower socio-economic status indeed feel a certain reluctance to expose themselves to formal learning situations.

A second set of reactions to different learning contexts was elicited from another question placed much later in the interview. In this second question respondents chose from between just two alternatives: classes at some type of school and home-study lessons by correspondence. This question avoided mention of any specific subject matter.

[QUESTION 25] Suppose that a course was being offered on some topic that you were really interested in, and you could study it either by attending classes one evening a week at a nearby school, or by means of home-study lessons which would be mailed to your home once a week. If you had decided to enroll in the course, which of these two methods of study would you prefer—the classes at school, or the lessons mailed to you at home?

From the population as a whole this question elicited a response pattern heavily favoring attendance at classes: 79 per cent chose the classroom while only 21 per cent favored home study. In relation to the background factors of age, sex, and socio-economic status, however, differences were found which were quite similar to those on the earlier question. Thus Table 10.15 shows that younger persons were quite a bit more likely than older persons to choose the classroom, and the differences between men and women in these preferences are again found to be inconsistent. There is an interesting pattern underlying these sex-linked differences, however. In both age groupings, women of high socio-economic status were more likely to choose the school setting than were their male counterparts, but in the low socio-economic category this tendency was exactly reversed and more men than women selected the more structured setting.

The most relevant comparisons in the table, however, are those relating to socio-economic position. In each of the four groups, persons in the higher socio-economic positions were more likely to select the formal over the informal learning situation. However, the percentage spreads attributable to socio-economic position are considerably more pronounced among women than among men (19 and 27 per cent compared with 6 and 11 per cent in the younger and older age-groups, respective-

---

Table 10.15 Preferences for Formal Methods of Study, by Sex, Age, and Socio-Economic Status

[Question 25] Suppose that a course was being offered on some topic that you were really interested in, and you could study it either by attending classes one evening a week at a nearby school, or by means of home-study lessons which would be mailed to your home once a week. If you had decided to enroll in the course, which of these two methods of study would you prefer — the classes at school, or the lessons mailed to you at home?

	Per Cent Who Would Prefer To Attend Classes at School			
SES	Men		Women	
	Under 45	45 and Over	Under 45	45 and Over
High	90 (934)*	76 (487)	94 (985)	83 (466)
Medium	85 (796)	74 (417)	81 (1,072)	82 (499)
Low	84 (543)	65 (783)	75 (704)	56 (1,094)

*All bases are weighted.

ly), and they are also slightly wider among older than younger persons (by 5 and 8 per cent, respectively, among men and women).

To sum up, both age and socio-economic status can be said to have a considerable influence on people's attitudes toward methods of learning. Older adults and adults of lower socio-economic status are considerably less likely to prefer the classroom for learning, and the lack of interest in this method is particularly pronounced among older women of low socio-economic status.

BARRIERS TO PARTICIPATION

To conclude this chapter we will explore briefly some of the reasons why people who are interested in learning and ready to take courses do not actually do it more frequently.

To obtain information on barriers to participation, respondents were shown ten different statements which were described as "some of the reasons people have for not attending adult education courses" (see Question 20, Appendix 2). Each respondent was then asked whether or not the reason would apply to his own situation.

In Table 10.16 the rates at which each of these statements was accepted as applicable are shown for two different aggregates: for the sample at large and for the 44 per cent of the sample previously identified as persons with "high participation readiness." Two main types of barriers to participation may be identified in the list of statements: influences more or less external to the individual or at least beyond the individual's control and those based on personal attitude or disposition toward participation.

Three statements (the first, second, and fourth in Table 10.16) clearly refer to environmental constraints; being economically restricted, not having free time, or being unable to get away from home and family responsibilities in the evening are all obstacles which might prevent one from enrolling in a course even if one were quite highly motivated to do so.

The third item on the list — being too tired at night to go out to classes — is also of this same general quality; although it is not an external barrier in the same sense that the others are, it nonetheless is a consequence of daytime work and therefore not subject to very much personal control.

One additional statement—that there are no adult education resources available—is also primarily an environmental constraint. While some persons simply would be unaware of existing facilities, this barrier is still quite independent of feelings about taking courses. Together, these five items seem to characterize external situational barriers to enrollment.

Four other statements (the sixth, eighth, ninth, and tenth in Table 10.16) reflect personal attitudes toward participation. Disidentifying oneself with "studying types," feeling too old to learn new things, feeling too mature to go to adult education classes, or feeling one can learn all one needs to know without going to classes all represent dispositional states which might very well cause a person to shy away from enrollment in a course even if all the situational factors were favorable.

The remaining item—not having heard of interesting courses—is more difficult to assess in these terms. Since one might select this statement either because of a narrow range of learning interests, or because of sparse course offerings, it is not

Table 10.16 Reasons for Not Attending Adult Education Classes among Persons with High Participation Readiness and Total Sample (Per Cent Who Said That Reason Would Apply to Them)

Reasons	Persons With High Participation Readiness	Total Sample	Percentage Difference
Couldn't afford it	43 (4,140)*	48 (9,640)	− 5
Too busy	39 (4,187)	48 (9,693)	− 9
Too tired at night	37 (4,150)	45 (9,693)	− 8
Hard to get out of house at night	31 (4,204)	35 (9,755)	− 4
Don't know of available courses	30 (4,162)	35 (9,518)	− 5
Not the "studying type"	20 (4,164)	34 (9,611)	−14
Courses don't sound interesting	11 (4,066)	18 (9,136)	− 7
Feel too old to learn	8 (4,190)	23 (9,772)	−15
Would feel childish	4 (4,195)	12 (9,644)	− 8
Don't need classes	4 (4,205)	12 (9,666)	− 8

*All bases are weighted.

clear whether this condition is more representative of an environmental or of a personal constraint.

In Table 10.16 we find that in both the sample at large and among persons with acknowledged interests in learning and course taking the most frequently identified constraints are all situational rather than motivational. Moreover, all the barriers (and in particular the environmentally generated ones) were identified almost as often by the potential participants as by the adult population at large. The rank ordering of statements, in fact, is virtually identical in the two listings: the only inversion is that feeling too old to learn was ranked seventh by the total sample and eighth among potential participants.

The main blocks to participation in both groups are financial considerations, busy schedules, and the lack of physical energy at the end of the day. Each of these constraints was acknowledged by approximately two potential participants in five, while just under one-third of this group selected the two remaining "external" blocks—being tied up with family responsibilities or not knowing anywhere to go for instruction.

In comparison, none of the dispositional blocks was selected with nearly this frequency. Although 20 per cent of potential participants did say they were really not "studying types," only 8 per cent felt too old to learn new things and only 4 per cent felt either childish about attending classes or that they did not need formal instruction to learn what they wanted to know.

These results constitute only what could reasonably have been expected. Since persons with "high participation readiness" were originally classified as being favorably oriented toward educational pursuits, we could not expect them to identify with dispositional blocks more frequently than with situational ones.

A much more meaningful approach to the question of barriers to participation is to examine whether specific barriers have differential relevance to persons in different life cycle or social status positions. Accordingly, Table 10.17 isolates the rates at which potential participants in different sex, age, and socioeconomic categories found each of the ten statements applicable to their own situations. Because of the complexity of this table, we shall discuss its contents in two stages, first focusing on how responses to individual statements were related to each of the three background characteristics in the table and then summarizing the overall effect of situational and dispositional barriers on various types of individuals.

The main discrepancies in Table 10.17 are the following:

1. *Sex.* — On the average, women were 22 per cent more likely than men to feel housebound and 8 per cent more likely to feel they would not have the physical energy to go out to classes at night. There were no consistent and sizeable differences between men and women on any of the other statements, however.

2. *Age.* — Substantial age differences in response rates may be noted on three statements. Younger adults were, on the average, 14 per cent more likely to name financial considerations as a barrier,[7] while older persons, as might be expected, were much more likely to feel too old to learn new things (by 16 per cent on

[7]This discrepancy is not found between older and younger women of high socio-economic status, but it was sizeable in the other five age comparisons.

Table 10.17 Reasons Potential Participants Do Not Attend Adult Education Classes, by Sex, Age, and Socio-Economic Status (Per Cent Who Said Each Reason Would Apply)

Reasons	Men					
	Under 45			45 and Over		
	Low SES	Medium SES	High SES	Low SES	Medium SES	High SES
Couldn't afford it	79 (249)*	45 (418)	23 (478)	63 (184)	19 (127)	11 (161)
Too busy	30 (248)	47 (420)	42 (491)	27 (184)	44 (143)	38 (162)
Too tired at night	37 (234)	34 (426)	27 (486)	34 (194)	33 (138)	31 (156)
Hard to get out of house at night	21 (249)	11 (425)	10 (488)	17 (190)	23 (144)	16 (162)
Don't know of available courses	48 (233)	28 (427)	20 (488)	48 (185)	45 (139)	22 (162)
Not the "studying type"	23 (249)	21 (424)	9 (476)	30 (184)	48 (143)	11 (161)
Courses don't sound interesting	16 (227)	15 (420)	8 (475)	23 (190)	8 (118)	16 (162)
Feel too old to learn	4 (249)	5 (426)	1 (488)	38 (190)	13 (134)	14 (162)
Would feel childish	2 (244)	1 (428)	† (488)	23 (190)	4 (140)	4 (161)
Don't need classes	3 (238)	5 (428)	3 (488)	8 (190)	4 (145)	14 (161)

*All bases are weighted.
†Less than 1 per cent.

(Table 10.17 continued)

Table 10.17 *Continued*

Reasons	Women					
	Under 45			45 and Over		
	Low SES	Medium SES	High SES	Low SES	Medium SES	High SES
Couldn't afford it	74 (376)*	53 (642)	19 (659)	66 (290)	34 (206)	19 (236)
Too busy	31 (377)	40 (641)	42 (659)	34 (306)	27 (212)	48 (236)
Too tired at night	44 (358)	37 (636)	38 (652)	40 (306)	42 (212)	41 (236)
Hard to get out of house at night	40 (364)	49 (653)	44 (645)	37 (306)	36 (206)	26 (242)
Don't know of available courses	48 (376)	28 (642)	14 (648)	57 (295)	16 (212)	18 (242)
Not the "studying type"	31 (365)	19 (648)	13 (658)	26 (289)	13 (212)	27 (242)
Courses don't sound interesting	12 (360)	8 (631)	† (646)	15 (290)	11 (212)	7 (237)
Feel too old to learn	8 (362)	2 (648)	† (659)	27 (290)	11 (212)	10 (230)
Would feel childish	6 (371)	0 (648)	0 (659)	25 (295)	3 (212)	3 (242)
Don't need classes	2 (377)	4 (654)	1 (660)	8 (301)	† (212)	3 (237)
		(652)	(659)	(306)	(207)	(242)

*All bases are weighted.
†Less than 1 per cent.

the average) and to feel that it would be childish to go out to classes at night (by 10 per cent on the average).

Interestingly, however, age differences on these two latter statements were much more pronounced among respondents of low socio-economic status. Among men in this category, for example, feeling "too old to learn" was endorsed 34 per cent more often by those forty-five and over than by those under forty-five, while in the middle and high socio-economic groups the comparable differences were only 8 and 13 per cent, respectively. Among women, the equivalent discrepancies were 19, 9, and 10 per cent. With regard to feeling childish about attendance at classes the age differences by socio-economic status were of a similar order: they were 21, 3, and 4 per cent among the men and 19, 3, and 3 per cent among the women.

Apparently the influence of aging on disposition toward learning is much stronger in the lower socio-economic groups. In fact, quite substantial proportions of older persons of lower socio-economic status seem psychologically disposed to leave learning to the young. Even among the potential participants as many as 38 per cent of the men and 27 per cent of the women who were older and of low socio-economic status felt "too old to learn," while 23 per cent of these men and 25 per cent of the women said they would feel childish attending adult education classes.

3. *Socio-economic status.* — Other relationships between socio-economic position and barriers to participation are also evident in Table 10.17. Although socio-economic position is seen to affect selection rates on seven of the ten statements, there was only one, financial constraints, where the influence describes a linear pattern across all three socio-economic categories. The relation of socio-economic status to this particular barrier, however, is very strong: persons of low socio-economic status identified it 33 per cent more often than did persons of medium socio-economic status, and those in the latter category 20 per cent more often than those of high socio-economic position. It is most significant that large majorities of potential participants of low socio-economic status did say that lack of money prevented their enrollment in educational courses (79 per cent of younger men, 74 per cent of younger women, 63 per cent of older men, and 66 per cent of older women).

Four other consistent relationships may be noted in the comparisons of pairs of socio-economic categories.

1. Persons of low socio-economic status were much more likely than those of either middle or high socio-economic status to say they did not think any facilities for instruction existed in their community. Persons in the low category were, on the average, 21 per cent more likely to identify this barrier than were those in the medium, and they were 32 per cent more likely to do so than those in the high category.

2. Persons of high socio-economic status were more likely than those of low socio-economic status to say they were too busy to enroll in an educational course (by 12 per cent on the average).

3. Persons of middle socio-economic status were slightly but consistently more likely than those of high socio-economic status to say they would have difficulty in getting away from home during the evening (by 6 per cent on the average).

4. Respondents of low socio-economic status were an average of 7 per cent more likely than those of high socio-economic status to have not heard of any courses interesting enough to lure them into enrollment.

SUMMARY

Table 10.17 shows clearly that some barriers are more relevant to women than to men, that some have differential relevance to younger persons and older persons, and that a rather

Table 10.18 Total Number of Barriers Identified by Potential Participants, by Sex, Age, and Socio-Economic Status

a. External or Situational Barriers (Average Number of Barriers Per Person, Out of Five)

SES	Men		Women	
	Under 45	45 and Over	Under 45	45 and Over
Low	2.15	1.89	2.37	2.34
Medium	1.65	1.64	2.07	1.55
High	1.22	1.18	1.57	1.52

b. Internal or Dispositional Barriers (Average Number of Barriers Per Person, Out of Four)

SES	Men		Women	
	Under 45	45 and Over	Under 45	45 and Over
Low	.32	.99	.47	.86
Medium	.32	.70	.25	.27
High	.13	.43	.14	.43

c. Total Barriers (Average Number of Barriers Per Person, Out of Ten)

SES	Men		Women	
	Under 45	45 and Over	Under 45	45 and Over
Low	2.63	3.11	2.96	3.35
Medium	2.32	2.41	2.40	1.93
High	1.43	1.77	1.78	2.02

large number have a differential effect on potential participants at various levels of the social hierarchy.

Altogether, then, just how difficult is it for different kinds of people to engage in organized learning pursuits? To provide a summary answer to this question, Table 10.18 shows the average number of different "dispositional," "situational," and "total" hurdles mentioned in different sex, age, and socio-economic categories. These figures suggest a number of general conclusions concerning the kinds of problems different people face when they think about converting their interests into action.

Although older people identified more barriers than younger people, the "personal" and "environmental" constraints appear to have differential relevance to people of different ages. First, younger adults named slightly more situational hurdles than did older people, and although none of these age differences is particularly large, all six comparisons show higher figures for persons under forty-five than for those forty-five or older (see Table 10.18a). Older adults, on the other hand, were quite a bit more likely than the younger to select the dispositional items represented in the list of statements. Thus it would appear that younger potential participants have few personal qualms about enrolling in courses, but would have to cope with a substantial number of environmental obstacles in order to participate. Older persons, on the other hand, are relatively freer from situational obstacles, but are more likely (than younger persons) to feel held back by personal considerations.

On the whole the women identified more situational constraints to participation than the men did, although they were no more likely than men to identify the "dispositional" constraints. In five of six comparisons, however, women selected the larger number of "external" hurdles, and, as a result of these differences, the average number of "total barriers" was higher for women than for men — again in five cases out of six.

Finally, the results clearly show that persons of lower socioeconomic circumstances face both kinds of obstacles more frequently than do persons situated more favorably on the socio-economic continuum.

11

National Audiences of Educational Television

Although radio and television habits are among the more carefully charted of American behaviors, until recently there has been little reliable information concerning the audiences for educational television. This situation persisted mainly because the broadcast-measurement organizations which service the radio and television industries have never paid much attention to audiences for the more specialized broadcast media such as FM or shortwave radio, or either VHF or UHF non-commercial television stations.[1]

With the recent appearance of a detailed study of the audiences of nine educational television stations in different regions of the country, for the first time (Schramm, Lyle, and Pool, 1963), statistics have become available on the size, composition, exposure habits, and reactions of a number of different types of educational television audiences. Because of the inquiry's research design, however, no firm national estimates of educa-

[1] VHF and UHF are abbreviations for the terms "very high frequency" and "ultrahigh frequency" and refer to the wavelengths on which television stations transmit their signals. The VHF broadcasting band consists of the twelve channels (2–13) which most television stations operating in this country now use. The UHF band includes a much larger number of channels, but at the time of this study very few households were equipped with television sets which could pick up UHF signals.

tional television viewing could be made: although national projections were made from the results from the nine stations, no claims were made by the authors about the confidence which could be placed in the derived figures. From the evidence available, however, the authors concluded that by spring, 1962, educational television was probably attracting between 4.5 and 7 million "regular" viewers and between 8 and 13 million "occasional" viewers (Schramm, Lyle, and Pool, 1963, p. 57).

One of the most striking findings in the first phase of the present study was the very minimal use made by adults of television for formal instruction. Although nearly 25 million adults were estimated to have been active in one or another form of learning during the previous year, only 290,000 had followed a course of instruction on either commercial or non-commercial television, and only 1.5 per cent of all adult education courses reported had been studied by television. These findings led us to conclude that by the summer of 1962 television had not made a very significant impact in the field of formal instruction for adults.

The statuses of "course viewer" and "educational television viewer," of course, are quite distinct, and the fact that audiences for formal television courses are thin in no way measures the more general influence of educational television in the United States. Indeed, while most educational television stations do program some systematic instruction, formal courses make up only a tiny fraction of their overall program. In the Schramm study, in fact, it was reported that most adults who watched educational television did not seek formal courses, but were interested rather in programs which were only informally educational. These same authors also noted that the course viewers in their study probably included substantial numbers of persons who had followed a systematic presentation on some topic, but not a formal course as such (Schramm, Lyle, and Poole, 1963, p. 108). In the main, then, our earlier figures concerning the numbers of course viewers during 1961–62 seem highly plausible estimates.

In the second phase of our study a limited amount of information was also collected on people's knowledge and use of educational television stations. Since this information was obtained from a representative sample of the adult population and was collected within a few months of the field work for the Schramm study, the results provide useful supplementary information to that in *The People Look at Educational Television*. In a national sample survey, of course, one must frame questions which are meaningful to persons living in all regions of the country, and for this reason no specific information was sought concerning particular stations or programs. Moreover, since only small numbers of people were interviewed at any one sampling point, the present results do not lend themselves very readily to the task of estimating audiences for educational television stations in particular cities. On the other hand, precise national estimates can be made both of levels of public awareness and frequency of exposure to existing educational television stations. It is the express purpose of this chapter to report these results.

Information on people's more general uses of educational television was collected through the following steps. Respondents were asked whether or not there was an educational television station in their area. Those who said there was were then asked to identify the station by its call letters, channel number, and city or town. They were next asked whether they had ever viewed programs on that station, and if they had, they were asked how frequently they did so.

In processing these responses, we first differentiated persons who had correctly and incorrectly identified a television station by checking the answers against a list of the sixty-three educational television stations which were in operation at the time of the survey. Persons able to name either the call letters or the channel number and city of an existing station were considered knowledgeable about existing educational television facilities. Estimates of viewing frequency were subsequently restricted to those persons who had successfully identified a bona fide noncommercial educational television station.

Altogether the NORC national sample contains seventy-five "primary sampling units" – the major geographical locations within which interviews are taken.[2] Sixteen were in cities served by VHF educational stations at the time of the survey, and five others were in cities served by UHF educational television stations (Table 11.1, nn. 1 and 2). In addition, several other sampling points represent the areas of the country in which signals from educational television stations in nearby cities could be picked up. For example, a number of respondents in the Gary, Indiana, sampling point reported they had watched programs on Station WTTW from Chicago.

Table 11.1 shows the findings on people's awareness of educational television stations and gives figures both for the sample as a whole and for persons living in three types of areas—cities served by VHF educational television stations, those served by UHF channels only, and all other sampling points across the country. From these data one can both appraise levels of public awareness of educational television where such facilities are known to exist and evaluate separately the total number of adults in the country who, in 1962, knew of the existence of these facilities in their area.

In VHF educational television cities, a substantial majority of

[2]Some further comments should probably be made concerning the use of a national probability sample for purposes of measuring exposure to educational television stations, since this question was raised a number of times when our original estimates of course viewers were released. Because a national sample is designed to represent the total population of the country rather than just the population which can receive educational television signals, the sampling points at which interviews were taken did not include all the areas of the country in which educational television signals can be received, nor were they restricted to just those areas where there are educational television stations. While the national sample survey may not be the most efficient way to study audiences of educational television (since little useful information could be obtained from interviewing persons living several hundred miles from such a station) the method is certainly legitimate for purposes of producing unbiased estimates of national exposure to educational television. The essential feature of the probability sample is that every household in the country has the same initial chance of being selected in the sample. Households in educational television areas would therefore turn up in the sample in direct proportion to their incidence in the country at large. The sixty-three educational television stations in existence in 1962 were well dispersed geographically, and there is no reason to believe that the distributions of population and of educational television stations were so different as to introduce a bias on that score. The type of sample used in this study, therefore, allows us to make unbiased estimates of the number of adults who know of and have been exposed to educational television stations.

adults were aware of these facilities: in these sixteen centers, 76 per cent successfully identified the station while another 3 per cent reported there was a station but they were unable to name it. In UHF cities, on the other hand, only one-third of the local residents (34 per cent) were able to identify the station correctly, while another 10 per cent said there was such a station but could give no further information about it.

We would expect VHF stations to be better known than UHF ones, but such high levels of station recognition are surprising. This seems particularly true of the UHF cities. For example, although no detailed statistics on UHF receivers are available, it is unlikely that as many as one-third of the total households in Detroit, Philadelphia, Washington, Atlanta, and Buffalo in 1962 were equipped with UHF receiving sets.[3]

[3]Only 9 per cent of the total television sets both manufactured and purchased in the United States during 1962 were UHF-equipped sets (Electronic Industries Association, "Television Set Activity Report, 1962").

Table 11.1 Public Awareness of Educational Television Stations (Expressed in Per Cent)

[Question 29] Is there an educational television station in this area?

Response	Cities Served by VHF ETV Stations*	Cities Served by UHF ETV Only†	All Other Areas	Total Sample
Yes, and correctly identified an existing ETV station	76	34	14	27
Yes, but incorrectly identified commercial station as ETV	4	12	14	12
Yes, but unable to identify the ETV station	3	10	4	5
No	6	21	44	35
Don't know	11	22	24	21
Total	100	99	100	100
Base (weighted)	1,933	740	7,230	9,903
No information	3	0	58	61
Total cases	1,936	740	7,288	9,964

*Interviews were completed in 16 different cities served by VHF ETV stations. These figures therefore represent a combined index of awareness of the following stations: WGBH-TV, Boston; WQED, Pittsburgh; WTTW, Chicago: KETA, St. Louis; KQED, San Francisco; WMVS-TV, Milwaukee; KTCA-TV, Minneapolis; WJCT, Jacksonville; WEDU, Tampa; WBIQ, Birmingham; WKNO-TV, Memphis; KERA-TV, Dallas; KUHT, Houston; KAET, Phoenix (Tempe); KUED-TV, Salt Lake City; and KCTS-TV, Seattle.

†There were five cities in the NORC sample served only by UHF ETV stations at the time of the survey. These were: WTVS, Detroit; WNED-TV Buffalo; WETA-TV, Washington, D.C.; WHYY-TV, Philadelphia; and WETV, Atlanta.

Moreover, three adults in four in VHF educational television cities could name the local educational station, indicating widespread public knowledge of these facilities.

In the summer of 1962, just over one adult in four (27 per cent) knew of an existing educational television station. It is difficult to assess just what rate of overall awareness this figure represents, however, since we cannot estimate with any accuracy the proportion of households in the country which were at that time located within the range of an operating educational television station. However, if we were to assume that all those who correctly identified a station lived within its broadcasting range, we could conclude that at least 27 per cent of the population resided in an educational television area in June, 1962. The true proportion is likely to be slightly higher than this, of course, since it would be reasonable to assume that more adults would have access to educational television and yet be unaware of it than would know of it but not have access to it. In any event, based on an estimated population of 114 million adults as of June 1, 1962, we could estimate from Table 11.1 that roughly 30 million American adults knew of educational television facilities at the time this survey was conducted.

Finally, Table 11.1 provides some indication of the extent to which the term "educational television station" is misunderstood by adults. One adult in eight (12 per cent) said there was an educational station in his area, but, when pressed for further information, named a commercial station.

To what extent do adults use the educational television stations available to them? To derive meaningful measures, claims about viewing were counted only among those persons who were able to identify successfully a bona fide station, on the assumption that any exposure reported by other persons in all likelihood referred to informational programing on commercial channels.

In classifying viewers, the same definitions are employed as were used in the Schramm study. Thus a "regular" viewer is defined as one who claimed to view educational television at least once a week; an "occasional" viewer is someone who had been exposed to a station at least once, but was not in the habit of viewing it as frequently as once a week; and the category of "non-viewer" includes all those who identified a station but had never viewed it plus those who could not identify a station at all.

The exposure frequencies based on these definitions are summarized in Table 11.2. In the sixteen VHF cities, 18 per cent claimed viewing educational television at least once a week; 35 per cent said occasionally; and 47 per cent had never watched the station. In the five UHF cities, 3 per cent viewed regularly, 9 per cent were occasional viewers, while the vast majority, 88 per cent, had never watched the station at all.

On the whole these results are very close to the figures presented for both VHF and UHF stations in *The People Look at Educational Television,* in particular those describing the stations in Boston (a VHF educational television city), and Columbus, Ohio (a UHF educational television city). For Boston, Schramm, Lyle, and Pool reported the distribution of regular, occasional, and non-viewers at 21, 31, and 48 per cent, respectively, while for Columbus they were 3, 11, and 86 per cent, respectively (Fig. 10, p. 48). These two sources of data on educational television audiences during 1962 thus show a high degree of correspondence, in spite of the fact that the methods

Table 11.2 Use of Educational Television in Areas Served by ETV Stations (Expressed in Per Cent)

Classification of Residents	Cities Served by VHF ETV Stations		Cities Served by UHF ETV Stations	
Regular viewers (view once a week or more)		18		3
Occasional viewers (view but less often than once a week)		35		9
Non-viewers (have never viewed educational television)		47		88
Aware of station, never viewed it	23		22	
Unaware of station	24		66	
Total		100		100
Base (weighted)		1,932		739
No information		4		1
Total		1,936		740

employed to collect the information in the two studies differed and there were differences in the populations studied.[4]

When these measures of educational television exposure are extended to the sample as a whole, 5.4 per cent of adults become classified as regular viewers, and some 10.7 per cent as occasional viewers. With the data converted to this form, it is now possible to make national estimates of exposure, and Table 11.3 indicates that there were 6,200,000 regular and 12,200,000 occasional viewers of educational television stations as of June, 1962. Altogether, about one American adult in six remembered watching an educational television station at least once.[5] These estimates clearly confirm that "viewers" and "course viewers"

[4]In the Schramm study the population investigated was adults residing in households containing both a television set and a listed telephone. The NORC figures, on the other hand, refer to the total adult population including persons residing both in non-television homes and in housing units without listed or unlisted telephones. In January, 1962, 90 per cent of all American households and 92 per cent in standard metropolitan statistical areas were equipped with television sets (U.S. Department of Commerce, 1963, Table 707, p. 523). In the 1960 census, 83.4 per cent of housing units in standard metropolitan areas had a telephone available (U.S. Department of Commerce, Bureau of the Census, 1960, Table 13, pp. 1–44).

[5]This only represents exposure to stations located in the areas where people resided at the time of this survey. Additional persons would probably have viewed educational television programs while traveling or while living at former places of residence.

Table 11.3 National Estimates of Exposure to
Educational Television Stations

Exposure	Per Cent	Estimated Number of Adults
Regular ETV viewer (views once a week or more)	5.4	6,200,000
Occasional ETV viewer (views, but less than once a week)	10.7	12,200,000
Non-viewer (has never viewed ETV)	83.9	95,600,000
Total	100.0	114,000,000*
Base (weighted)	9,870	
No information	94	
N	9,964	

*Estimated number of American adults as of June 1, 1962.

of educational television represent aggregates of widely divergent size. Adult audiences of educational television's more informal educational and informational offerings, therefore, are unquestionably larger than those attracted to formal courses of instruction.

12

The Perception
of Education
across the Social
Continuum

One of the most persistent findings emerging from this inquiry is that a great disparity exists in the involvement in continuing education of segments of the population situated at different levels of the social hierarchy. In the first phase of our investigation, rates of participation in educational pursuits were found to vary widely among groups with differing amounts of formal education, and, in the earlier chapters of this second section, many additional aspects of people's orientation to adult education were shown to be influenced either by formal education or by the combined impact of schooling and economic position. Better-educated persons — or those higher on the socio-economic continuum — were found to be not only more active in learning pursuits, but also more interested in learning new things, more ready to turn to formal courses to satisfy learning interests, and more knowledgeable about the existence of facilities for adult learning. In addition, they were found to prefer different methods of study and to have different reasons for taking courses when they did enroll and for not taking them when they did not.

In this next chapter additional evidence linking social position with educational behavior is explored in order to understand better why these discrepancies in behavior and outlook were as pronounced as they were. Our general point of departure in this analysis was the premise that education and learning themselves may be perceived and evaluated in radically different ways by persons on different rungs of the social ladder. The proposition that there are distinct middle-class and working-class orientations to education is hardly new, of course, and the social stratification literature abounds with studies which both substantiate and elaborate this point.

In this study we are especially concerned with spelling out how these social-class differences in perspective affect participation in programs of adult learning. It is our general assumption that if adult education is to be as successful in recruiting from the working classes as from the middle classes educators must fully recognize the way in which lower-class individuals regard education and learning.[1]

SOCIAL CLASS AND THE PERCEPTION OF EDUCATION

What are the principal social class differences in the perception of education? Here are the most relevant differences which have either been noted in earlier studies or which emerged in the present investigation.

1. The lower classes place less emphasis on the importance of high educational attainment, and aspire less often to a college education. These tendencies have been noted repeatedly in sociological writings, and they are particularly well documented with empirical support. Hyman (1953, p. 430), for example, in reviewing survey evidence concerning how much education people think is necessary to get along in the world and how important they feel a college education is for their children, concludes that "whatever measure of stratification is employed the lower groups emphasize college training much less."

In the present study, information of a somewhat similar nature was obtained when respondents were asked how far they themselves would like to go in school if they were starting over again (see Question 41, Appendix 2). This question taps a rather

[1]Terms such as "middle class," "lower class," and "working class" will be used from time to time in this chapter to differentiate various levels of the social hierarchy. The actual measures which are used here to determine social position, however, are in most cases formal education and level of family income. Strictly speaking, the concept of "social class" as employed in sociological literature is not directly equivalent to these particular indicators alone.

different type of educational evaluation, since it asks people to appraise how important high educational attainment would be in their own lives if they had a chance to re-enter the educational system. Nonetheless, quite revealing differences in aspiration levels were found when these responses were examined in relation to our indicators of social position. Table 12.1 classifies respondents by age, sex, level of formal schooling completed, and total family income, and shows the proportions in each category who said they would at least want to graduate from college.

The most clear-cut result in the table is that aspirations for high educational achievement are very strongly related to the level of schooling actually completed: in all possible comparisons the high-school educated aspired to college graduation more often than the grade-school educated did; and similarly, all college-educated groups did so more frequently than those who did not go beyond high school.

However, the comparisons based on the other status dimension—economic level—are not nearly so clear-cut, and the aspirations of those in higher income brackets exceeded those of

Table 12.1 Value Attached to High Educational Achievement, by Sex, Age, Years of Schooling, and Family Income (Per Cent Who Said They Would Like To Complete College or More if They Were Starting Over Again in School)

Education and Income	Men		Women	
	Under 45	45 and Over	Under 45	45 and Over
Grade school				
Under $5,000	55 (224)*	47 (624)	31 (206)	40 (860)
$5,000 and over	38 (126)	63 (277)	24 (126)	43 (289)
High school				
Under $5,000	66 (465)	74 (223)	39 (748)	63 (416)
$5,000 and over	71 (794)	77 (480)	53 (1,165)	63 (521)
College				
Under $5,000	94 (106)	† (73)	92 (98)	99 (100)
$5,000 and over	99 (654)	97 (226)	96 (500)	92 (222)

*All bases are weighted.
†Not reported because unweighted case base was only 19.

persons with lower incomes in only seven of eleven possible comparisons. The reversals on the income dimension are particularly evident among younger men and women with only a grade-school education: in these situations, for example, the higher-income men were 17 per cent less likely than their less well-educated counterparts to want to go through college; and the higher-income women were 7 per cent less likely than the lower-income women to want this much schooling.

For young adults without any high-school education at all, of course, an income in excess of $5,000 a year represents a fairly substantial level of economic success, and these particular results are very likely a reflection of the attitude, "How much better off would I be with a college education?" It is interesting, however, that income level and aspirations to college education are positively correlated among poorly educated men and women over forty-five, and the reversal in this relationship is particularly noticeable among men.

The generalization that lower-class people place less value on formal education can probably be better expressed by the statement that it is persons without much formal schooling themselves who devalue high educational achievement. As between the economic and educational components of social class position, in any event, the more important influence by far is that of level of schooling.

Although our main focus in Table 12.1 is on the influence of the socio-economic indicators, this table also contains two other results of considerable interest. If we ignore comparisons among persons who went to college — since virtually all these respondents indicated they would "do it over again" — the table shows that across all eight comparisons men aspired to college graduation more often than women did, and in seven of eight comparisons older persons indicated higher aspirations than younger.

One curious aspect of the first of these results is that on most measures of educational evaluation, women are usually found to place a higher premium on the value of education. In the results reviewed by Hyman (1953, p. 431), for example, women in all age and social class groupings were found to emphasize more often the value of high attainment in school.

The explanation for these discrepancies is quite straightforward: even though women are in many ways more favorably oriented than men toward educational achievement, men go farther in school than women do on the average, and indeed, the much greater involvement of men in the world of work places them under considerably greater pressure to achieve a more substantial formal education.

To sum up, personal aspirations to high educational attainment appear to emerge in direct response to one's own successes in the educational sphere. Regrets over not having ever gone to college, however, seem to become more widespread as people grow older and probably develop with particular rapidity among men at about the time they realize they have gone as far as they will ever go in their occupations. On the whole, graduation from college is seen as important by more men than women.

2. "The average deprived person is interested in education in terms of how useful and practical it can be to him. . . . There is practically no interest in knowledge for its own sake; quite the contrary, a pragmatic anti-intellectualism prevails" (Riessman, 1962, pp. 12 – 13).

In the present study two groups of feelings were examined which bear directly on this general proposition: preferences for educational experiences which have an immediate reward as opposed to those which do not, and feelings of alienation from non-utilitarian educational experiences.

At one point in the interview, respondents were asked a sequence of questions on the types of subject matter they thought would be most appropriate for a hypothetical education course being planned by a local television station (see Questions 30 and 31, Appendix 2). After making specific recommendations as to content, the respondents were asked to choose between three general themes for the course: "practical skills for everyday living," "general knowledge about the world we live in," and "interests and hobbies for spare-time use."

Table 12.2 reports the first-choice mentions for each of these themes and classifies respondents by sex, age, and socio-economic position. The table reveals pronounced differences in the choices made by persons in different socio-economic posi-

Table 12.2 Course Preferences, by Sex, Age, and Socio-Economic Status (Per Cent Who Would Prefer Each Theme for the Subject of an Educational Course on Television)

Men

Course Theme	Under 45			45 and Over		
	SES Low	SES Medium	SES High	SES Low	SES Medium	SES High
Practical skills for everyday living	55	47	38	62	55	39
General knowledge about the world we live in	35	43	53	27	32	50
Interest and hobbies for spare-time use	9	10	9	11	13	11
Total	99	100	100	100	100	100
Base (weighted)	577	828	936	907	468	488

Women

Course Theme	Under 45			45 and Over		
	SES Low	SES Medium	SES High	SES Low	SES Medium	SES High
Practical skills for everyday living	55	48	38	50	46	23
General knowledge about the world we live in	36	38	51	30	36	58
Interests and hobbies for spare-time use	9	14	11	19	19	19
Total	100	100	100	99	101	100
Base (weighted)	736	1,097	975	1,283	575	483

tions: persons of low socio-economic status favored the practical skills by 22 per cent on the average; persons of middle status also selected this theme most often, but by an average plurality of only 12 per cent; and respondents of high status were 18 per cent more likely to choose the course dealing with general knowledge than the one teaching practical skills. As one scans the socio-economic continuum from low to high, in other words, one finds that the dominant orientation to education changes from an emphasis on usable knowledge to one placing much greater stress on knowledge as having value in its own right.

Table 12.2 also indicates that preferences for subject matter pertaining to use of leisure were relatively stable across all socio-economic groupings. The only discrepancy in the selection of this item was that older persons (in particular, older women) chose it slightly more often than did younger persons.

More direct measures of anti-intellectualism were obtained from two attitudinal questions asked somewhat later in the interview. Both questions focused on the value of a college education: the first asked whether advanced schooling was worth the bother if it was not "put to use," the second asked whether women who plan careers benefit more from college than women who plan to marry (see Questions 50-B and 50-C, Appendix 2). Our interpretation of these reactions is that either a rejection of the first position or an acceptance of the second would reflect an underlying disposition that knowledge does not have value unless applied to some tangible goal, and that this in turn is one of the principal manifestations of anti-intellectualism.

Table 12.3 shows the rates at which each of these attitudes was endorsed, and the results once again reveal the presence of strong relationships along the socio-economic continuum. The influence of socio-economic position is particularly pronounced in relation to the attitude that a college education is not worth the bother if it is not to be put to use: persons of low socio-economic status agreed with this 38 per cent more frequently than those of high status (on the average), and the position actually represents majority opinion among respondents of low status. Among persons in the high socio-economic category, on the other hand, only about one-third of the men and one-quarter of the women endorsed this position.

The socio-economic discrepancies in part *b* of Table 12.3 are not nearly as wide as they are in part *a*, although women of low status were an average of 18 per cent more likely than women of high status to say that a college education is of less value to a woman if it is not to be used to develop a career.

In general these results provide clear support for Riessman's general proposition that a pragmatic anti-intellectualism pervades the lower-class view of education. The results of Table 12.3 also suggest that dispositions of anti-intellectualism are held somewhat more often by men than by women.

3. Although education is widely recognized as an appropriate channel for social mobility, the average lower-class person is less ready than the average middle-class person to engage in continuing education even if tangible economic rewards are at stake.

Table 12.3 Attitudes of Anti-Intellectualism, by Sex, Age, and Socio-Economic Status

a. Per cent who agreed that "a college education should be put to use; if you don't use it, why bother with it."

SES	Men		Women	
	Under 45	45 and Over	Under 45	45 and Over
Low	72 (572)*	72 (956)	60 (747)	69 (1,326)
Medium	59 (823)	57 (472)	54 (1,082)	45 (570)
High	34 (931)	38 (504)	24 (992)	26 (469)

b. Per cent who agreed that "a college education is less important for a woman who wants to get married right after leaving school than for a woman who plans to have a career."

SES	Men		Women	
	Under 45	45 and Over	Under 45	45 and Over
Low	77 (560)*	72 (934)	73 (734)	67 (1,304)
Medium	79 (827)	71 (468)	67 (1,108)	66 (570)
High	67 (938)	64 (505)	56 (994)	47 (486)

*All bases are weighted.

Quite apart from the differentials in the value attached to college training, some writers have noted a lower-class resistance to and suspicion of educational accomplishment of any sort. This mistrust of education, moreover, has been identified even among persons who realize that additional education can help one to elevate one's social position. In describing the feelings of British miners toward education, for example, Hoggart (1957, pp. 71–72) makes the following observation:

That minority who become conscious of their class-limitations and take up some educational activity—so as to "work for their class" or "improve themselves"—tend to be ambiguously regarded. The respect for the "scholar" (like the doctor and the parson) to some extent remains. . . . On the other hand, there is often a mistrust of "book learning." . . . Parents who refuse, as a few still do, to allow their children to take up scholarships are not always thinking of the fact that they would have to be fed and clothed for much longer; at the back is this vaguely formulated but strong doubt of the value of education.

In the present study, data on the extent to which respondents endorsed adult education participation for purposes of economic betterment were obtained from the following question:

[QUESTION 27] Here is an imaginary situation. Suppose that a man has a chance for a promotion on his job, but in order to qualify for it he would have to take a course at night school and be away from home three evenings a week for about six months. Although he could use the extra money, his family doesn't really need it, so he doesn't know whether he should spend this much time away from his family.

If you were asked your opinion, would you advise him to definitely take the course, to take the course only if he were sure of getting the promotion, or to not take the course at all?

In answer to this question, 71 per cent of the total sample had no hesitation at all about recommending enrollment in the course, while 20 per cent would recommend it only if the promotion was certain, and 8 per cent would advise not taking it at all.

Table 12.4 indicates, however, that even though a majority of adults in all social categories advised definitely in favor of the course, there were substantial differences in rates of endorsement among persons in different socio-economic positions. On the average, respondents of middle status were 9 per cent more likely than persons of low status to definitely endorse enrollment; and persons of high status were 11 per cent more likely than those of middle status to do so. These tendencies, then, quite possibly reflect the same types of reservations about which Hoggart wrote. Even with the possibility of tangible monetary

Table 12.4 Endorsement of Adult Studies as a Channel to Economic Betterment, by Sex, Age, and Socio-Economic Status (Per Cent Who Would Definitely Recommend Taking the Course, Would Recommend It with Qualifications, and Would Not Recommend It at All)

	Men					
Recommendation	Under 45			45 and Over		
	SES Low	SES Medium	SES High	SES Low	SES Medium	SES High
Definitely take the course	62	69	81	58	65	82
Take the course only if promotion is guaranteed	30	24	14	26	21	11
Don't take the course at all	8	7	6	15	14	6
Total	100	100	101	99	100	99
Base (weighted)	584	819	912	973	462	507
	Women					
	Under 45			45 and Over		
	SES Low	SES Medium	SES High	SES Low	SES Medium	SES High
Definitely take the course	69	77	85	59	72	79
Take the course only if promotion is guaranteed	27	17	10	25	23	18
Don't take the course at all	4	6	5	16	5	3
Total	100	100	100	100	100	100
Base (weighted)	735	1,092	970	1,290	574	467

reward, fairly sizeable minorities of adults of low status would seem to have at least some reluctance to turn to continuing education in order to "improve themselves."

On the other hand, these results do not necessarily imply that lower-class persons are any less aware of the consequences of education in relation to upward social mobility. Indeed, when our respondents were asked to select from a list of six factors the two which were most important "in helping a person get ahead the fastest," people of low status were no less likely than those of high to select "a good education" as one of the two factors. Table 12.5 reveals socio-economic variations on practically all other factors listed, but formal education was mentioned most frequently by persons in all social categories, and the rates of selection on this item were remarkably stable across the three socio-economic levels.

In other words, lower-class resistance to adult education experiences does not appear to stem from feelings that education cannot do anything for a person, nor from a belief that one does not need education to get ahead in the world. The feelings, rather, seem to be of a more diffuse nature and are undoubtedly a carry-over from feelings of alienation from school and education which develop during one's earliest contacts with the formal educational system. The emergence of an alienation from education among lower-class children has been cited repeatedly in the sociological literature. For example:

The lower-class individual is taught by his culture to be anxious about different social dangers. Whereas the middle-class child learns a socially adaptive fear of receiving poor grades in school, of being aggressive toward the teacher . . . the slum child learns to fear . . . being taken in by the teacher, of being a softie with her. To study homework seriously is literally a disgrace. Instead of boasting of good marks in school, one conceals them, if he receives any (Davis, 1951, p. 30).

Given an exposure to childhood influences even a fraction as forceful as these, it would be highly unrealistic to expect a complete reversal of disposition in adulthood.

Table 12.5 Views of How To Get Ahead the Fastest, by Sex, Age, and Socio-Economic Status (Per Cent Who Selected Each Factor as One of the Two Most Important Things To Do in Order To Get Ahead the Fastest)

	Men						Women						Total Sample
	Under 45			45 and Over			Under 45			45 and Over			
Factor	SES Low	SES Medium	SES High	SES Low	SES Medium	SES High	SES Low	SES Medium	SES High	SES Low	SES Medium	SES High	
A good education	69	66	67	69	73	66	77	78	76	68	68	72	71
Hard work	47	50	51	36	38	57	42	51	50	34	41	42	44
Personality	30	38	37	25	35	30	35	35	41	30	34	46	34
Brains	34	19	22	39	29	28	25	22	23	43	36	29	29
Know the right people	18	18	17	17	19	15	13	10	7	17	10	7	14
Good luck	2	5	6	.14	3	1	6	3	1	6	8	*	5
Total	200†	196†	200†	200†	197†	197†	198†	199†	198†	198†	197†	196†	197†
Base (weighted)	594	838	934	978	470	510	752	1,104	991	1,336	586	484	9,854

*Less than 1 per cent.

†Does not total 100 per cent because respondents were asked to select two factors.

4. The average lower-class person does not perceive education in terms of personal growth or self-realization, and this may explain why the lower classes are much less ready to turn to adult education for recreational purposes than they are for purposes of vocational advancement.

Earlier in this section some evidence was encountered which suggested that learning for recreation was more frequent in the middle classes than in the lower. Specifically, persons of high status who had taken adult education courses during the previous five years were found to be much more likely than their counterparts of low status to have done so in relation to spare-time interests (Chap. 8).

Several other measures of educational experiences and learning interests also reflect a lower-class de-emphasis on recreational learning. In Table 12.6, for example, profile measures are shown which allow us to compare the subjects different people mentioned on three separate measures—the content of courses studied at any time since leaving school, the subjects and skills people said they would like to know more about or would like to be able to do better, and the subjects they recommended for a new (hypothetical) television course being planned for their community.

These data reveal, almost without exception, that the gap in emphasis between vocational and recreational learning tends to close as one examines the socio-economic continuum from low to high. In other words, practically all conditions show that vocational subject matter was given a heavier emphasis by respondents of low status, and that mentions of recreational topics were relatively more frequent in the high socio-economic group. When respondents of high and low status are compared directly on the total number of recreational subjects mentioned, eleven of the twelve comparisons indicate a relatively heavier emphasis among persons of high status. These discrepancies are summarized in Table 12.7.

Although most of these figures turn out to be smaller than 10 per cent, they do confirm that both the learning interests and the educational experiences of lower-class persons reflect a lesser concern with recreational subject matter. Perhaps the most

Table 12.6 Nature of Experiences with and Orientation to Continuing Learning, by Sex, Age, and Socio-Economic Status

a. Content of Courses Taken at Any Time since Leaving School (Per Cent of Total Course Titles)

Subject Matter	Men under 45			Men 45 and Over		
	SES Low	SES Medium	SES High	SES Low	SES Medium	SES High
Vocational	64	60	52	74	71	54
Academic	17	13	22	5	7	17
Home and family life	2	1	2	*	4	1
Spare-time interests	7	7	9	4	5	10
Public affairs	*	2	2	4	1	2
All other	10	17	12	12	11	16
Total	100	100	99	99	99	100
Total course titles (weighted)	364	809	1,127	286	326	695

Subject Matter	Women under 45			Women 45 and Over		
	SES Low	SES Medium	SES High	SES Low	SES Medium	SES High
Vocational	41	44	34	39	41	37
Academic	16	7	13	5	10	18
Home and family life	15	15	14	25	11	10
Spare-time interests	10	16	20	14	17	20
Public affairs	4	1	5	*	2	2
All other	14	17	15	17	19	13
Total	100	100	101	100	100	100
Total course titles (weighted)	277	791	1,258	504	447	692

*Less than 1 per cent.

Table 12.6 Continued

b. Subjects Respondents Would Like To Know More About (Per Cent of Total Subjects Listed)

Subject Matter	Men under 45			Men 45 and Over			Women under 45			Women 45 and Over		
	SES Low	SES Medium	SES High	SES Low	SES Medium	SES High	SES Low	SES Medium	SES High	SES Low	SES Medium	SES High
Vocational	61	58	37	56	66	42	23	22	18	11	22	13
Academic	12	9	23	9	6	16	10	12	14	9	14	11
Home and family life	3	5	5	5	9	9	42	36	30	42	36	32
Spare-time interests	9	11	18	2	8	17	9	16	24	12	16	30
Public affairs	1	7	9	7	4	8	3	4	6	5	3	3
All other	14	11	7	21	8	7	14	10	7	21	8	10
Total	100	101	99	100	101	99	101	100	99	100	99	99
Total subject titles (weighted)	602	972	1,240	578	348	565	784	1,411	1,469	902	516	628

(Table 12.6 continued)

Table 12.6 Continued

c. Type of Subject Matter Recommended for ETV Course (Per Cent of Total Subjects Recommended)

Subject Matter	Men under 45			Men 45 and Over		
	SES Low	SES Medium	SES High	SES Low	SES Medium	SES High
Vocational	38	27	18	39	28	18
Academic	35	36	36	20	26	36
Home and family life	7	5	7	11	14	7
Spare-time interests	3	6	9	8	8	4
Public affairs	6	15	20	9	12	25
All other	11	11	9	13	12	10
Total	100	100	99	100	100	100
Total subjects recommended (weighted)	565	873	1,292	741	412	605

Subject Matter	Women under 45			Women 45 and Over		
	SES Low	SES Medium	SES High	SES Low	SES Medium	SES High
Vocational	21	15	9	15	10	11
Academic	28	32	36	23	31	30
Home and family life	23	23	17	31	19	15
Spare-time interests	7	10	10	7	17	16
Public affairs	7	10	20	8	13	19
All other	13	9	8	17	11	9
Total	99	99	100	101	101	100
Total subjects recommended (weighted)	769	1,252	1,301	1,064	587	599

surprising aspect of these summary measures, however, is that the strongest socio-economic influence is seen in relation to people's interests rather than their actions: on the average, persons of high status were 14 per cent more likely to emphasize learning for leisure when they talked about things they wanted to know more about, while the comparable figure for courses actually taken was only 6 per cent. An important difference between the lower and middle classes, of course, is their differential ability to pay for instruction, and because interest is free whereas most instruction is not, one might quite reasonably have expected just the opposite result. Yet the figures clearly indicate that the sharpest socio-economic differences with respect to recreational learning are that respondents of high status are much more likely to want to learn more in this area. This suggests that members of the lower classes infrequently associate formal learning with leisure-time interests. Indeed, one quite reasonable interpretation of these data is that "education" and "spare-time enjoyment" are concepts which convey quite opposite meanings to the average lower-class person, who might be much more likely to perceive both education and learning as things one is required to do, and not things one would choose on one's own. From this perspective, lower-class persons would not regard learning or education as related to use of leisure. While these feelings are undoubtedly a part of the generally pragmatic perspective from which the lower classes view education, they also seem to reflect a slightly different aspect of this disposition. These feelings, rather, seem more akin to what

Table 12.7 Per Cent by Which Mentions of Recreational Subject Matter Were More Frequent among High-Status Persons Than among Low

Experience	Men under 45	Men 45 and Over	Women under 45	Women 45 and Over
Previous courses taken	+2	+ 6	+10	+ 6
Current learning interests	+9	+15	+15	+18
Subjects recommended for a TV course	+6	− 4	+ 3	+ 9

Riessman (1962, p. 12) described when he observed that the deprived classes do not perceive education in terms of an "opportunity for the development of self-expression, self-realization, growth, or the like." It might very well be this perspective, in other words, which lies behind the lower-class underemphasis on recreational learning.

Two sets of information were collected in this study which pertain directly to this discussion. The first measured what people thought was the main value of a good education, while the second tapped people's images of the typical adult education participant.

When adults were asked, "What do you think is the main value of having a good education?" a number of rewards were identified. First, 86 per cent of the responses were in terms of how education helps a person get along in the world. Among this group, 45 per cent mentioned specifically that a good education helps a person enter a "respected" occupation or find a good job; 39 per cent mentioned economic or "style of life" benefits; and 38 per cent answered in more general terms by stressing the consequences of education in helping one "get ahead in the world," "gain respect," or "compete better in life." All these answers were concerned with the different ways that education helps one find a suitable place in society.

In comparison with these more instrumental rewards, 46 per cent of the respondents mentioned non-economic consequences of a good education, and 32 per cent said that a good education makes one a "better," "more responsible," "more informed," or "wiser" person. The well-educated individual, in other words, is seen as better simply for having gone farther in school. In this sense a good education has some intrinsic value all its own and is worthwhile quite apart from any occupational, economic, or social-status benefits it may also bring.

Next, about one respondent in seven (14 per cent) said that a good education teaches one to "get more out of life," or "enjoy life more," or have a "more satisfying life." These responses, too, were made without any specific reference to economic benefits.

Finally, a few persons (some 7 per cent of the sample) answered in terms of the effect of education on one's role as a parent or homemaker: you can "bring up children better" or "can help educate your children" were typical answers of this type.

These were the main kinds of benefits which adults associated with the value of a good education, and our chief concern at this point is to trace the saliency of these various meanings for people in different positions in the social hierarchy. The relevant data are presented in Table 12.8.

Table 12.8 shows that while socio-economic benefits were recognized by large numbers of respondents in all categories, the "non-instrumental" benefits were mentioned much more frequently by persons in the higher socio-economic positions. As a consequence, the gap in emphasis between the instrumental and non-instrumental functions of education is one which narrows rapidly as one scans the socio-economic continuum from low to high: moving up the ladder, for example, this gap decreases from 57 to 46 to 12 per cent among younger men; from 61 to 39 to 29 per cent among older men; from 66 to 37 to 13 per cent among younger women; and from 56 to 35 to 16 per cent among the older women. Thus, while practically all adults stress the importance of education for upward social mobility, only members of higher social classes feel that a good education is valuable for other reasons.

Table 12.8 also reveals interesting differences with regard to specific benefits. All categories of respondents of low status, for example, value education for occupational placement as their most frequent answer. In the middle socio-economic category, socio-economic rewards were again most frequently mentioned, but here two groups (the younger men and older women) answered most often in terms of monetary rewards, while the other two groups (the older men and younger women) mentioned the job-placement function most frequently. The benefits cited most frequently by persons of high status, however, were of a rather different quality. Here the younger men and women each answered most often in terms of the positive effects of education

Table 12.8 Perception of the Main Rewards of a Good Education, by Sex, Age, and Socio-Economic Status

[Question 47] What Do You Think Is the Main Value of a Good Education?

a. Men

Main Sphere of Reward	Under 45			45 and Over		
	SES Low (Per Cent)	SES Medium (Per Cent)	SES High (Per Cent)	SES Low (Per Cent)	SES Medium (Per Cent)	SES High (Per Cent)
Occupational, economic, or status benefits	89	89	79	85	87	86
Job or occupation	57	45	31	54	42	24
Monetary rewards	41	48	44	33	38	53
General	34	32	37	37	38	43
Non-socio-economic benefits	32	43	67	24	48	57
Makes one a better person	23	31	46	18	38	37
Enjoy life more	6	8	26	5	8	23
Home and family sphere	3	9	6	2	8	3
All other benefits	3	2	2	2	*	1
Don't know or uncodeable	3	2	1	9	4	2
Total	127†	136†	149†	120†	139†	146†
Base (weighted)	594	845	944	985	478	510

*Less than 1 per cent.
†Totals more than 100 per cent because some persons mentioned more than one type of benefit.

Table 12.8 Continued

b. Women

Main Sphere of Reward	Under 45			45 and Over		
	SES Low (Per Cent)	SES Medium (Per Cent)	SES High (Per Cent)	SES Low (Per Cent)	SES Medium (Per Cent)	SES High (Per Cent)
Occupational, economic, or status benefits	94	86	79	89	87	86
Job or occupation	65	48	37	52	43	35
Monetary rewards	36	35	33	36	46	39
General	29	41	40	37	45	52
Non-socio-economic benefits	28	49	66	33	52	70
Makes one a better person	18	33	46	22	41	39
Enjoy life more	5	11	22	9	17	42
Home and family sphere	9	13	12	5	6	6
All other benefits	1	1	2	1	3	*
Don't know or uncodeable	3	4	3	5	2	2
Total	126†	140†	150†	128†	144†	158†
Base (weighted)	758	1,110	999	1,382	586	486

*Less than 1 per cent.
†Totals more than 100 per cent because some persons mentioned more than one type of benefit.

for the individual himself. Among the older persons of high status, women stressed the benefits for one's general social position, while men most frequently mentioned economic rewards.

It is quite clear from these results that the meanings which are attached to the value of education vary markedly across different segments of the population. From the lower-class point of view, education is valuable mainly because it leads to occupational success and job security. This emphasis is also primary in the middle socio-economic groups, although the direct monetary consequences of a good education are also recognized. Finally, the wealthier and better educated third of the population—or at least the younger portion of this aggregate—tends to value education primarily for its own sake.

For our discussion of recreational learning, the most relevant results in Table 12.8 are those pertaining to the non-economic perspectives on education, and perhaps most specifically to that particular focus which relates education with the enjoyment of life. This view of the value of education is one which is heavily influenced by social class position. Virtually no respondents of low status said that a good education would help one get more out of life, but this response was made by substantial numbers of persons of high status—in fact, by over 40 per cent of the older women in this class. It may very well be the absence of just this attitude which lies behind the lower-class "underrepresentation" on spare-time learning interests. At least, the person who does associate education with the enrichment of his life should be much more ready to fit his recreational interests into the range of experiences for which learning activities would have some meaning.

Additional evidence about recreational learning was obtained from a quite different type of question. Around the middle of the interview the respondents were asked what they thought the people were probably like who frequently attended adult education classes (see Question 26-A–G). This question was of a quasi-projective nature, since there would be virtually no way for anyone to have accurate information about what adult education participants were really like. As indicated earlier, the purpose of the question was to try to tap any dominant imagery which might pervade popular thinking about participants. Although we are concerned here with only two of the seven dimensions covered by the question ("getting ahead in life" versus "enjoying life" and "being pretty satisfied with life" versus "being a little dissatisfied"), we shall present the results from all seven dimensions, both because the findings are of some substantive interest in themselves, and because a review of all seven will provide a better context for interpreting the dimensions of direct interest.

Chart 12.1 shows the responses of persons in different sex, age, and socio-economic categories. The bars in these charts are secondary measures which represent the percentage differences between choices of the most frequently mentioned characteristic and its alternative.[2] Although this mode of presentation deviates from the more conventional style, it does serve to accentuate both the direction and dominance of imagery attached to the dimension in question. The right-hand column of figures in the charts indicates the proportion of respondents who were able to make a substantive selection on that dimension.

In interpreting these data there is some question about what size percentage difference could be said to represent "dominant imagery" on a given characteristic. On the criterion of statistical significance, any percentage difference of 18 per cent or more in these charts would have less than five chances in one hundred of

[2]To calculate these scores, all responses were first percentaged, including those on which no choices at all were made between the alternatives presented. Next, the smaller substantive response was subtracted from the larger, and the resulting scores thus reflect the degree to which the one "image" was dominant over its alternative.

For example, on the male-female dimension rated by younger men in the low socio-economic category, 49 per cent answered "a woman," 26 per cent said "a man," and 26 per cent either said that both sexes attend adult education classes equally often or could not answer the question at all. The dominant imagery here, then, is feminine, and by a plurality of 23 per cent (49 minus 26 per cent). Thus the top bar in part *a* of Chart 12.1 shows a value of 23 per cent on the female side of the center line.

By including non-choices in the original percentaging, this method makes the assumption that any person who did not choose between one of the two alternatives would have a fifty-fifty chance of falling into either substantive category if he were in fact forced to choose one or the other.

	Direction and Strength of Image	Per Cent Who Chose on This Dimension

A. Sex. The People Who Most Often Attend Adult Education Classes Are

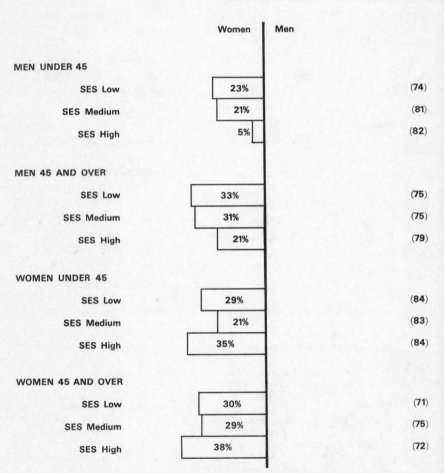

Chart 12.1 Dominant Images of the Typical Adult Education Participant, by Sex, Age, and Socio-Economic Status

Direction and Strength of Image	Per Cent Who Chose on This Dimension

B. Age. Those Who Attend Adult Education Classes Most Often Are

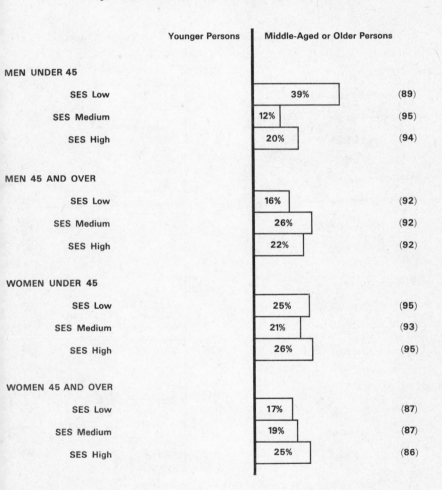

	Younger Persons	Middle-Aged or Older Persons

MEN UNDER 45

SES Low	39%	(89)
SES Medium	12%	(95)
SES High	20%	(94)

MEN 45 AND OVER

SES Low	16%	(92)
SES Medium	26%	(92)
SES High	22%	(92)

WOMEN UNDER 45

SES Low	25%	(95)
SES Medium	21%	(93)
SES High	26%	(95)

WOMEN 45 AND OVER

SES Low	17%	(87)
SES Medium	19%	(87)
SES High	25%	(86)

Chart 12.1   *Continued*   *(Chart 12.1   continued)*

Direction and Strength of Image	Per Cent Who Chose on This Dimension

C. Education. Those Who Attend Adult Education Classes Most Often Are People Who

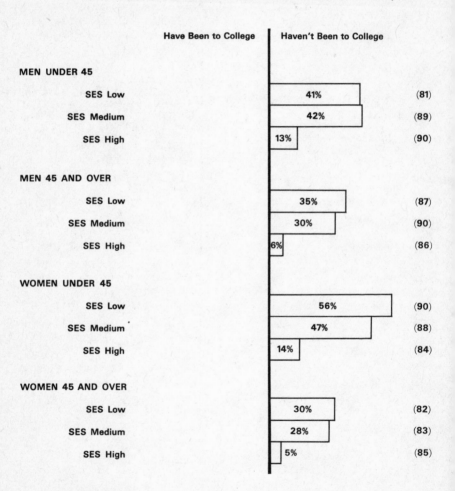

	Have Been to College	Haven't Been to College	
MEN UNDER 45			
SES Low		41%	(81)
SES Medium		42%	(89)
SES High		13%	(90)
MEN 45 AND OVER			
SES Low		35%	(87)
SES Medium		30%	(90)
SES High		6%	(86)
WOMEN UNDER 45			
SES Low		56%	(90)
SES Medium		47%	(88)
SES High		14%	(84)
WOMEN 45 AND OVER			
SES Low		30%	(82)
SES Medium		28%	(83)
SES High		5%	(85)

Chart 12.1 *Continued*

Direction and Strength of Image	Per Cent Who Chose on This Dimension

D. Type of Knowledge Sought. Those Who Attend Adult Education Classes Most Often Are People Who Want to Learn

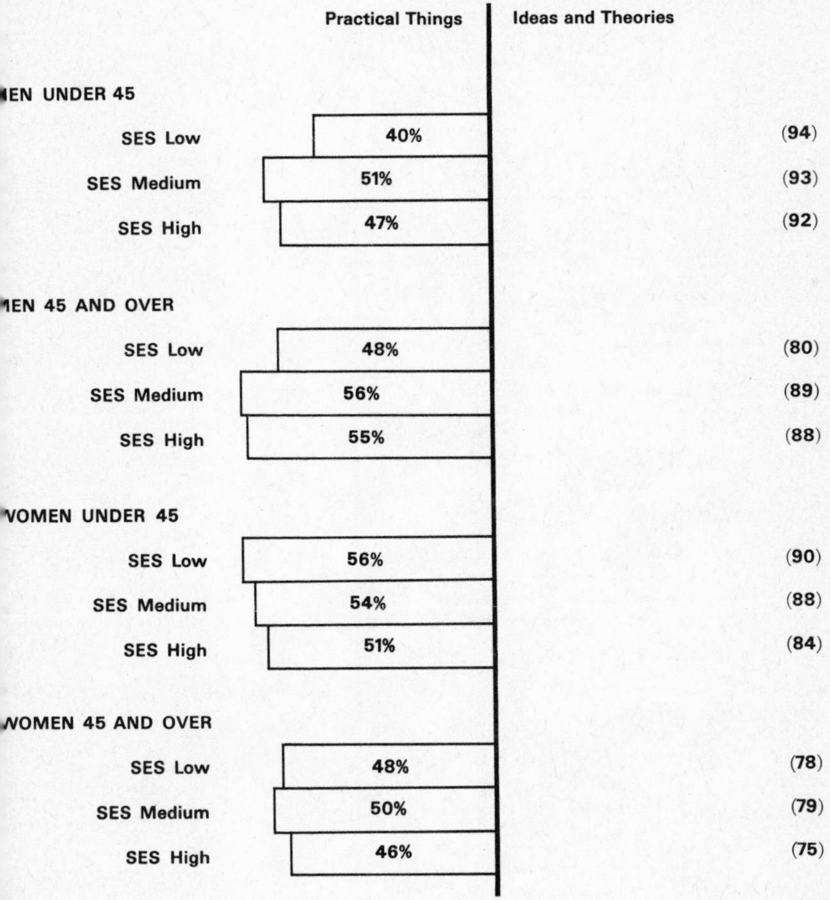

	Practical Things	Ideas and Theories	
MEN UNDER 45			
SES Low	40%		(94)
SES Medium	51%		(93)
SES High	47%		(92)
MEN 45 AND OVER			
SES Low	48%		(80)
SES Medium	56%		(89)
SES High	55%		(88)
WOMEN UNDER 45			
SES Low	56%		(90)
SES Medium	54%		(88)
SES High	51%		(84)
WOMEN 45 AND OVER			
SES Low	48%		(78)
SES Medium	50%		(79)
SES High	46%		(75)

Chart 12.1 *Continued*   *(Chart 12.1 continued)*

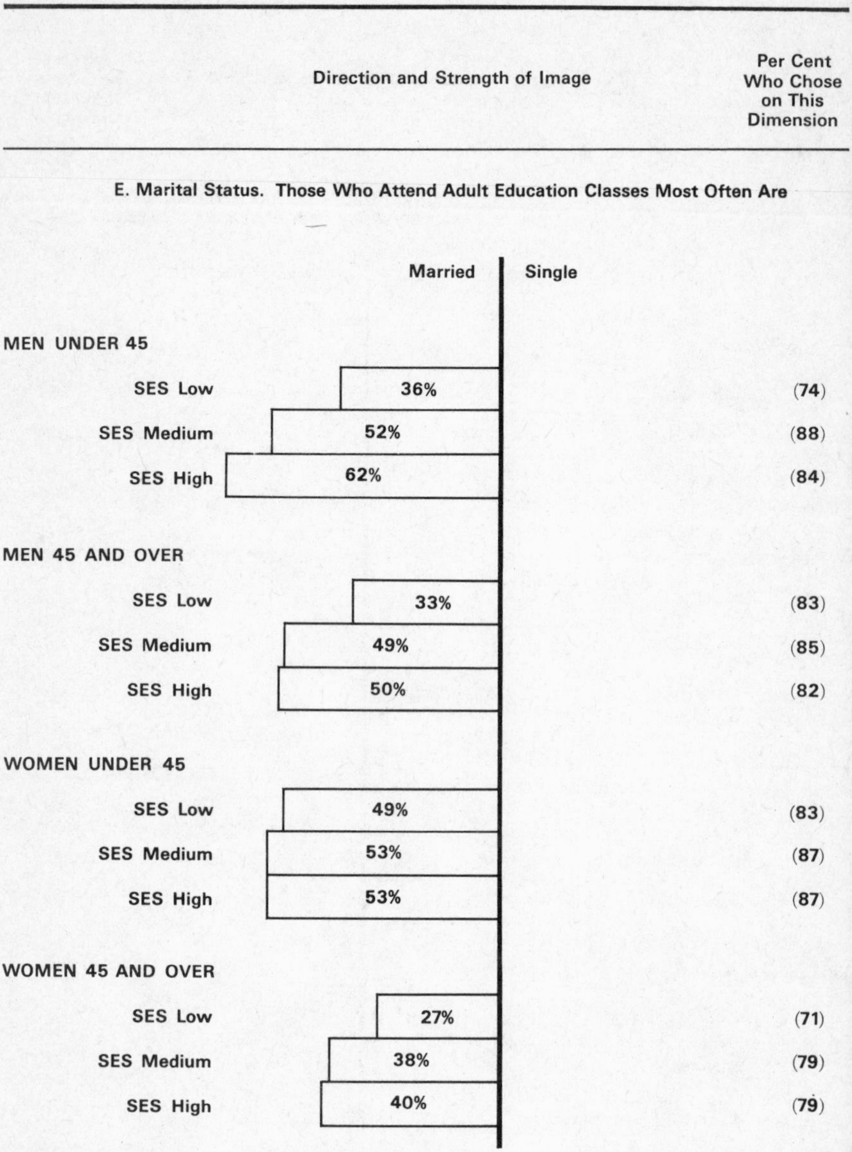

	Direction and Strength of Image	Per Cent Who Chose on This Dimension

E. Marital Status. Those Who Attend Adult Education Classes Most Often Are

| | Married | Single | |

MEN UNDER 45

SES Low	36%	(74)
SES Medium	52%	(88)
SES High	62%	(84)

MEN 45 AND OVER

SES Low	33%	(83)
SES Medium	49%	(85)
SES High	50%	(82)

WOMEN UNDER 45

SES Low	49%	(83)
SES Medium	53%	(87)
SES High	53%	(87)

WOMEN 45 AND OVER

SES Low	27%	(71)
SES Medium	38%	(79)
SES High	40%	(79)

Chart 12.1   *Continued*

Direction and Strength of Image	Per Cent Who Chose on This Dimension

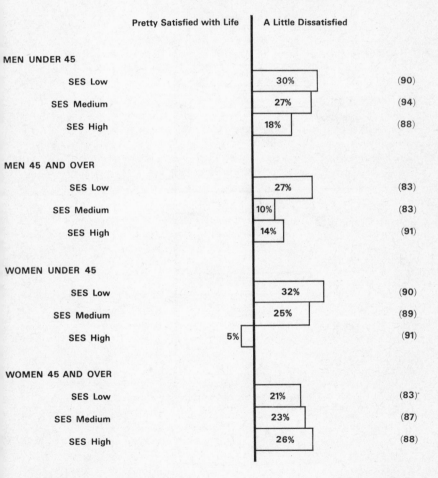

F. Satisfaction with Life. Those Who Attend Adult Education Classes
Most Often Are People Who Are

Pretty Satisfied with Life | A Little Dissatisfied

MEN UNDER 45

SES Low — 30% — (90)
SES Medium — 27% — (94)
SES High — 18% — (88)

MEN 45 AND OVER

SES Low — 27% — (83)
SES Medium — 10% — (83)
SES High — 14% — (91)

WOMEN UNDER 45

SES Low — 32% — (90)
SES Medium — 25% — (89)
SES High — 5% — (91)

WOMEN 45 AND OVER

SES Low — 21% — (83)
SES Medium — 23% — (87)
SES High — 26% — (88)

Chart 12.1 *Continued*   *(Chart 12.1 continued)*

Direction and Strength of Image	Per Cent Who Chose on This Dimension

G. Main Goal in Life. Those Who Attend Adult Education Classes Most Often Are People Whose Main Goal Is To

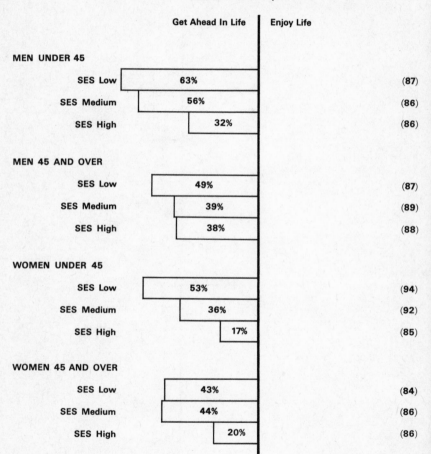

Get Ahead In Life | Enjoy Life

MEN UNDER 45
SES Low — 63% (87)
SES Medium — 56% (86)
SES High — 32% (86)

MEN 45 AND OVER
SES Low — 49% (87)
SES Medium — 39% (89)
SES High — 38% (88)

WOMEN UNDER 45
SES Low — 53% (94)
SES Medium — 36% (92)
SES High — 17% (85)

WOMEN 45 AND OVER
SES Low — 43% (84)
SES Medium — 44% (86)
SES High — 20% (86)

Chart 12.1 *Continued*

having been produced by sampling fluctuations, and in many categories differences much smaller than this would be "significant" at the .95 level of confidence.[3] However, strict statistical significance may not be the most crucial criterion for interpreting these results. The more important question, rather, is whether there is a meaningful consensus in the answers of various categories of people. To satisfy this criterion, an arbitrary decision was made to interpret all discrepancies of 25 per cent or over as representing a "high level of consensus" on a given dimension. On this criterion the following interpretations can be made of the results in Chart 12.1.

Sex. — As has been noted earlier, the typical adult education participant is more often seen as a woman than as a man. This imagery was consistent in direction for all twelve groups of raters, although only seven of the twelve groups display a high level of consensus.

Age. — All categories of respondents rated the typical participant as "middle-aged" or "older" more frequently than as "younger." High consensus was found among only five of twelve groups, however.

Formal education. — All twelve groups of respondents described the typical participant more often as someone who had not been to college than as someone who had, and among eight of the twelve groups this imagery could be described as "dominant." Interestingly, however, the four groups of persons high in socio-economic status all displayed considerably less agreement on this view, although in no case did an actual majority identify the typical participant as someone with a college education.

Type of knowledge sought. — The respondents were asked whether people who attended adult education classes more often sought "practical" knowledge or were more often interested in

[3]The smallest unweighted case base in any one category here was 123, among older men in the middle socio-economic category. For an expected value of P = .5 on a sample of this size, one standard error would be 4.5 per cent, and a percentage difference of 18 per cent would therefore be significant at the 2σ level. In most other cells much smaller differences are statistically significant at this same level of confidence: for example, 399 younger men of high socio-economic status were interviewed, and a percentage difference of just 10 per cent would be significant at the 95 per cent level for this group.

new "ideas and theories," and on this dimension the dominant imagery by far was that practical interests override theoretical ones. All twelve groups of raters were in high agreement on this point.

Marital status. — Adult education programs are sometimes described (even by educators) as mating grounds for middle-class persons over age thirty, but this imagery would not appear to be very widespread among the general public. The typical adult education participant was viewed by all categories of respondents as more often married than single, and all twelve groups indicated high levels of agreement on this judgment. One interesting secondary finding, however, is that the respondents of high status were in more agreement on this point than were those of medium or low status. This may reflect a more general tendency for the lower classes to define learning activities as appropriate only when one is young and single. In other words, the idea that education is something which one might pursue throughout one's life is probably held less widely by the lower than by the middle classes.

Satisfaction with life. — The typical participant is more often seen as "a little dissatisfied" than "pretty satisfied" with life. However, only six of the twelve groups were in high agreement on this, and in one group, younger women of high status, a slight majority answered in the opposite direction.

The most interesting aspect of these results, however, is that the younger men and women in different socio-economic positions gave quite different answers to this part of the question. Both the low and middle socio-economic groups were in substantial agreement that the typical adult education participant is someone who is a little dissatisfied with his life, but this was not at all the case for respondents of high status: for example, among men under forty-five levels of consensus fell off from 30 to 27 to 18 per cent across the three socio-economic levels, and among younger women the corresponding figures were 32, 25, and −5 per cent. This indicates, then, that at least the younger members of the low socio-economic aggregate are less likely to associate adult education participation with the kinds of things one would do if one were satisfied with life. This again seems to reflect the dominant perspective from which the average lower-class person views education: learning and education, in short, are seen as channels to upward social mobility, but they are not regarded as activities which have any meaning at all if one is satisfied with one's position in life.

Main goals in life. — Finally, adult education participation is identified with "getting ahead in life" much more than with "enjoying life," ten groups out of twelve responding with a high level of agreement on this. However, it was again the respondents of low status who held this view most universally, and in the higher socio-economic groups, the level of consensus dropped off quite sharply. These findings go along with the results of the previous section, and generally confirm that lower-class persons are much more likely than others to perceive and evaluate educational participation from the point of view of instrumental rewards.

To sum up, the evidence reviewed in this section quite strongly supports the proposition that the lower classes do not view education in terms of self-realization and do not think of learning as an experience which is rewarding in its own right. The value of education, rather, is perceived strictly in terms of tangible gains, and learning pursuits are not associated with pleasurable life experiences. These underlying dispositions toward education are quite consistent with the vocational concentration of lower-class educational behavior.

SOCIAL CLASS AND THE PERCEPTION OF LEISURE

At the same time, there is a reasonably strong case for the contention that the lower social classes need instruction for recreational use the most. What little evidence is available suggests that the lower social classes now enjoy as much leisure as do persons in higher socio-economic positions,[4] that they have greater difficulty in finding things to do with their newly found

[4]One of the earliest empirical studies of use of leisure conducted during the thirties indicated that blue-collar workers enjoyed slightly fewer leisure hours than did either white-collar personnel or professionals and executives (see Lundberg *et al.,* 1934, Chap. 4). Since then, however, there have been uneven increases in leisure time, with blue-collar workers benefiting the most, and professionals and executives the least. In *The Changing American Market* (1955), for example, the editors of *Fortune* comment that "the time gains of recent years have gone first of all to factory workers, service employees, and others who . . . do not have the most leisure dollars."

free time, and that they are in general less enthusiastic about the prospects of having more.[5] Of course, the eventual automation of American industry will undoubtedly mean that American adults in general—and blue-collar workers in particular—will come to spend an even greater proportion of their lives away from their jobs.

These various tendencies pose a significant challenge to the field of continuing education. The dilemma is that the segment of the population which may soon have the greatest amount of free time at their disposal are on the one hand, the least ready to handle more, and on the other, the least likely to turn to educational pursuits as a way of expanding their interests.

In the present study, a considerable amount of information was collected concerning people's uses of and feelings about spare time, and in the main this evidence corroborates the point that the lower-class dissociation of learning and education from leisure-time pursuits is one which could produce quite serious consequences if carried over into the age of automation.

Table 12.9 reviews the findings from four direct questions dealing with the amounts of spare time people have and their feelings about having more. These results indicate the following:

Table 12.9a reveals that within three of four categories considerably more respondents of low rather than of medium or high status answered that they had a "great deal" of spare time, as opposed to "some" or "hardly any at all." These socioeconomic discrepancies are particularly strong among older respondents, especially older men.

In Table 12.9b lower-class respondents are seen to be less likely than others to say they would like to have more spare time than they already have. These discrepancies are not as pronounced as the ones in part *a* of the table, but in all four cases, more high- than low-status persons wished they had more free time. The differences were 11 per cent among younger men, 4

[5]For example, David Riesman (1958, p. 369) reports that an informal poll of a union local showed that while leaders were in favor of a shorter work week, rank-and-file union members were not: some of the latter, in fact, could think of nothing to do with an extra day except sleep.

per cent among younger women, 19 per cent among older men, and 15 per cent among older women.

Third, respondents of low status were considerably more likely to say they had difficulty in filling their spare time: a substantially larger proportion of low than of high-status persons said they "frequently" or "occasionally" found themselves with spare time they did not quite know what to do with (Table 12.9c). The impact of aging on use of spare time, moreover, appears to affect lower-class men much more than others. Three of the comparisons of the "under forty-five" and "forty-five and over" groups indicate very minimal differences on the measure in question, but among the men of low status the percentage indicating at least "occasional" uncommitted free time was 15 per cent higher in the older group.

Finally, Table 12.9d suggests that the prospect of a period of

---

Table 12.9 Selected Reactions to Use of Spare Time by Sex, Age, and Socio-Economic Status

a. Perceived Amount of Spare Time Available (Question 2) (Per Cent Who Say They Have a "Great Deal" of Spare Time)

SES	Men		Women	
	Under 45	45 and Over	Under 45	45 and Over
Low	14 (590)*	39 (985)	18 (758)	26 (1,364)
Medium	13 (845)	16 (478)	12 (1,104)	19 (586)
High	13 (943)	12 (510)	9 (993)	15 (485)

b. Reactions to Having More Spare Time (Question 3) (Per Cent Who Would Like To Have "More" Spare Time)

SES	Men		Women	
	Under 45	45 and Over	Under 45	45 and Over
Low	53 (584)	32 (967)	58 (752)	39 (1,348)
Medium	63 (840)	50 (479)	53 (1,093)	47 (585)
High	64 (943)	51 (511)	62 (998)	54 (486)

*All bases are weighted.   (Table 12.9   continued)

Table 12.9 *Continued*

c. Amount of Uncommitted Spare Time (Question 4) (Per Cent Who Say They "Frequently" or "Occasionally" Find Themselves with Spare Time They Don't Quite Know What To Do With)

SES	Men		Women	
	Under 45	45 and Over	Under 45	45 and Over
Low	25 (589)*	40 (978)	28 (758)	30 (1,365)
Medium	22 (845)	22 (479)	27 (1,110)	22 (587)
High	19 (944)	17 (505)	16 (998)	15 (480)

d. Reactions to a Hypothetical Forced Confinement (Question 8-D) (Per Cent Who Think a Month's Forced Confinement "Might Be Rather Pleasant")

SES	Men		Women	
	Under 45	45 and Over	Under 45	45 and Over
Low	20 (578)	15 (906)	37 (739)	26 (1,330)
Medium	19 (831)	27 (473)	24 (1,069)	31 (580)
High	25 (930)	31 (498)	41 (974)	37 (470)

*All bases are weighted.

free time is less appealing to persons of low than of high status. These reactions were extracted from the following question:

[QUESTION 8] Suppose you had to take a complete rest for a month. You wouldn't be sick at all and would be at home and free to move about, but you wouldn't be able to work, engage in much physical exercise, or take part in any social activities outside of your home. . . . Do you feel that an experience of this sort might be rather pleasant, or that on the whole it would be unpleasant?

The main socio-economic differences in reactions to this question are found among the older respondents, where considerably more high than low-status persons indicated they would look forward to a month's retreat from their usual routines. Older, low-status men were 16 per cent less likely to so indicate than their counterparts of high status, while the comparable figure for women was 11 per cent. All told, this question produced wide differences in the incidence of positive response among different categories of people: as many as 41 per cent of the women under forty-five of high status thought it would be "pleasant," compared with just 15 per cent of the older men of low status.

These data confirm that lower-class individuals are no more likely than persons at higher levels to feel deprived of spare time, are indeed more likely to find themselves with "time on their hands," are less likely to want more free time to themselves, and are more likely than others to view a month of time with "nothing to do" as a generally unpleasant prospect.

One final set of data on this general topic demonstrates even more clearly that persons of low socio-economic status are less prepared than others to cope with additional amounts of spare time. Just before respondents were asked whether they would find a forced confinement "pleasant" or "unpleasant" (Question 8-D) they were asked what they would probably do with their time during such a period. Table 12.10 presents the responses of persons in different sex, age, and socio-economic categories, and reveals important socio-economic differences not only in the content or style of spare-time use, but in the extent to which people were able to think of anything definite at all to do with a month of free time.

With regard to use of leisure, the results reflect the well-known social class differences in orientation to print versus audio-visual mass media. They also show that persons of high status most frequently mentioned hobbies and sedentary pastimes and musical or artistic activities; home handicrafts were named most frequently by medium-status men, but by high-status women; and the most frequent references to prayer or meditation were made by low-status persons.[6]

In this discussion, however, our primary interest is not in styles of leisure-time use, but in people's ability or inability to make any substantive uses of extra time. The most critical response categories in Table 12.10, then, are those where people

[6]For a much more elaborate review of social class differences in the content of leisure-time expenditure see R. Clyde White, 1955.

Table 12.10 What People Would Do with Their Time during a Forced Confinement, by Sex, Age, and Socio-Economic Status (Per Cent Who Mentioned Each Activity)

Activity	Men					
	Under 45			45 and Over		
	SES Low	SES Medium	SES High	SES Low	SES Medium	SES High
Read or study (other than Bible)	48	66	80	43	57	85
Watch TV or listen to radio	54	56	44	43	61	48
Relax and rest only	21	17	13	33	22	21
Sedentary hobbies and related pastimes	12	16	26	6	10	18
Home handicrafts	4	13	10	7	21	7
Music and arts	3	8	11	1	*	9
Visit friends	12	9	13	11	10	10
Meditate, pray, read Bible	6	4	1	5	3	1
Housework or household chores	13	13	10	6	6	6
Other	*	3	1	2	3	2
Don't know or no answer	7	2	2	10	7	2
Total	180†	207†	211†	167†	200†	209†
Base (weighted)	594	845	944	985	478	510

Activity	Women					
	Under 45			45 and Over		
	SES Low	SES Medium	SES High	SES Low	SES Medium	SES High
Read or study (other than Bible)	54	68	78	49	65	81
Watch TV or listen to radio	42	38	31	38	42	47
Relax and rest only	22	16	12	17	9	8
Sedentary hobbies and related pastimes	5	16	23	9	13	19
Home handicrafts	41	47	59	42	46	47
Music and arts	5	12	16	3	8	13
Visit friends	10	7	13	7	9	20
Meditate, pray, read Bible	3	2	1	8	*	5
Housework or household chores	13	14	13	9	8	9
Other	*	1	2	2	1	*
Don't know or no answer	3	2	1	7	7	1
Total	198†	223†	249†	191†	208†	250†
Base (weighted)	758	1,110	999	1,382	586	486

*Less than 1 per cent.
†Does not total 100 per cent because some persons gave more than one activity.

said that the only thing they would do would be to rest or relax, or that they simply would not know what to do at all.

Each of these responses was given most often by persons of low status and least often by those in high socio-economic positions. Because these answer categories are independent of any others, they can be combined, and when this is done the results in Table 12.11 emerge. These figures are revealing because of their absolute size and because of the relationships they indicate. They show that at least one-quarter of all lower-class respondents—and over 40 per cent of lower-class men—would have little idea about how to use extra time, except to relax, rest, or loaf. The proportions are considerably smaller in the middle and high socio-economic groups, although fairly substantial numbers of older men in all socio-economic brackets would probably be pressed to find things to do during such a period.

SUMMARY

The lower-class underemphasis on education for recreation cannot be said to result from the fact that the lower classes have no spare time, or from the fact that they are absorbed with a multitude of concrete leisure-time interests: members of the low socio-economic group very clearly have spare time on their hands, have less facility for filling their non-working hours, and have reservations about the prospects of having more free time. The results suggest that the imbalance comes from very basic social class differences in the definition of appropriate uses of education. Self-fulfilment or personal growth through continuing

Table 12.11 Per Cent Who Would Not Know What To Do With a Month's Forced Confinement, or Who Would Use It Only To "Rest or Relax"

Sex and Age	Low SES (Per Cent)	Medium SES (Per Cent)	High SES (Per Cent)
Men under 45	28	19	15
Men 45 and over	43	29	23
Women under 45	25	18	13
Women 45 and over	24	16	9

education—the central organizing premises of many programs of adult learning—are concepts which have no meaning at all to most lower-class individuals. And it is here, perhaps, that adult educators face their most critical challenge.

Continuing education has an obvious role to play in preparing American adults to handle more and more leisure time; yet, for a sizeable sector of the adult population, the virtues of continuing education can probably be understood and appreciated only in the language of tangible benefits, concrete rewards, and practical gains.

Part III

Community Facilities for the Instruction of Adults

Introduction
to
Part III

Up to this point our examination of the dynamics of adult participation in educational pursuits has dealt for the most part with the readiness of adults to recruit themselves into systematic learning experiences. In Part II, for example, we discussed the reasons people have for taking courses, the general nature of their learning interests, their perception of and attitudes toward adult education, and their beliefs about the importance of educational achievement. This analysis has concentrated heavily on how motivational factors work to propel adults toward formal and informal participation in learning endeavors.

These perspectives, however important they may be, isolate just part of the story. To gain a full appreciation of the educational behavior of adults it is necessary to proceed beyond considerations of individual dispositions and motives to an examination of external environmental influences as well. Quite apart from the question of individual motivation, for example, it is obviously crucial to assess the importance of community facilities for adult learning.

Just as individuals differ in their readiness to engage in continuing education, so too communities can be expected to vary, perhaps markedly, in the extent to which they provide attractive, appropriate, and accessible facilities. The influence of environmental factors of this sort has been neglected so far in this inquiry; it is to this question that we turn our attention in the next section.

In our original thinking about this phase of the investigation, two general questions were of primary concern to us: what ranges of instructional facilities are available to American adults in "typical" urban settings, and whether the presence of different types of facilities in a community has a perceptible effect on the educational behavior of its adults.

It was immediately apparent that an examination would have to be made of a rather large sample of American cities and towns to insure adequate coverage of the various types of adult education programs in different parts of the country. At the same time, however, it was possible to allocate only limited resources to this phase of our study, and therefore it was necessary to limit our inquiry drastically. Thus, rather than attempt what would have amounted to a necessarily superficial survey of American communities, we decided to use the intensive case study for our examination of resources.

Our general plan was to select about a dozen middle-sized American cities, similar in general demographic features, from which we could with the aid of knowledgeable informants choose for intensive study a pair of cities substantially different in the extent and types of educational resources available for local adults. Following this, our next step was to take detailed inventories of each city's resources by having field representatives systematically seek out and record information concerning all instructional programs offered during some predetermined period of time. This provided us with detailed descriptions of the instructional offerings in two cities and with a test case by which to appraise the impact of learning facilities on individual dispositions and behavior. Following the completion of these inventories, we interviewed representative samples in each of the two cities to find out how much adults really know about what is available to them in their own community and to measure the extent of environmental influences on individual motivation and behavior.

Part III deals with the results of the community facilities phase of our inquiry. Chapter 13 outlines the steps taken in the selection of communities for study, describes how the inventories were made in each city, and outlines how educational institutions and their offerings were defined and classified. Chapters 14 and 15 deal with the results of the inventories, the former with the varieties of institution and types of instruction, and the latter with a detailed institution-by-institution description of the course offerings in the cities eventually selected for intensive study. Following this, in Chapter 16 we marshal our evidence concerning the effects of differential resources on people's reactions to and involvement in continuing education.

Although most of the information to be reported in this part is straightforward and factual, we have nonetheless disguised the names of the cities studied and of the institutions, organizations, and individuals contacted. This is done to preserve the full anonymity guaranteed to everyone who supplied us with information.

13

General Design of the Community Facilities Studies

THE SELECTION OF COMMUNITIES FOR STUDY

Once the decision had been made to limit the scope of the facilities inventories to case studies of two middle-sized communities, the next problem was to establish criteria which would allow us to make a meaningful selection of cities. Our general goal was to find one city in which adult education resources were fairly plentiful and a second in which they were not. In addition, it was important that the cities be approximately the same size, located in the same region, and not too grossly dissimilar in such key demographic features as main types of industry, racial composition, and median family income. For both financial and methodological reasons, we also decided that the selection would have to be made from among cities in the 100,000–300,000 population range in the Middle West.

Information of two types was required for making an objective selection: census data regarding the demographic composition of different cities, and information from which some sort of initial appraisal could be made concerning the variety of available adult education facilities. Our first step was to enumerate all the standard metropolitan statistical areas in the North Central region which in 1960 had urbanized populations of between 100,000 and 300,000. This yielded us an initial listing of twenty-four cities. Next, in order to confine the study to relatively independent urban populations and to avoid the problem of having cities in which adults might easily commute to some nearby center to attend classes of one sort or another, we decided to omit all cities located within a fifty-mile radius of some other standard metropolitan area. On this criterion, eight cities were eliminated from the list, leaving us with a total of sixteen geographically independent centers from which to make a final selection.

The next task was to obtain some preliminary idea of the range of educational facilities available to adults in each of these centers, and the plan which seemed most feasible here was to try to secure this information from local residents connected with the field of adult instruction. Rather than travel to each of these sixteen centers, however, we decided to try to obtain this information by a short questionnaire which was mailed to selected informants in each city. We enlisted the cooperation of the Adult Education Association (AEA) and were able to secure a list of the names and addresses of all association members in the sixteen cities on our list. This enabled us to further narrow the range of cities to fourteen, there being no AEA members in the two smallest centers on our list.

At this point questionnaires were drafted in which three types of information were requested: data concerning the institutions and organizations active in the field of adult instruction, information on the general ranges of subject matter for which instructional facilities were available in the city, and information concerning the availability or non-availability of courses of instruction in a number of specific subject fields.[1] These forms were mailed to seventy-nine AEA members in the fourteen communities, and fifty of these were completed and returned to us. At least one form was returned from each city on the list, and in thirteen of the fourteen cities two or more people provided us with the information we had requested.

When these evaluations were examined, it quickly became apparent that our experts differed quite considerably in their familiarity with the educational resources in their communities, and some were able to provide a great deal more information

---

[1] A copy of this questionnaire is reproduced in Appendix 2 along with copies of all other data-collecting forms used in the community studies.

than others. What loomed as a far more serious problem, however, was that informants from the same cities sometimes disagreed about the institutions and groups which were active and inactive in adult instruction. In several cases these discrepancies were of considerable proportion—for example, in one city where our first informant identified twenty-two of twenty-seven institutions and organizations as active and none as inactive, while a second reported twelve to be active and ten to be inactive.

Faced with differences of this magnitude, it was evident that our preliminary information on community resources was of unknown validity, and while that supplied by some of our judges was undoubtedly accurate and comprehensive, we had no way of being certain whose evaluations were the more correct. For purposes of selecting two communities, in any event, we were forced to conclude that we were still not much better off than when we started.

To cope with this dilemma, we decided to enlarge the scope of the inventory-taking phase of the study and to collect information on facilities in four cities rather than in just two. On this basis, then, the final selection of cities for the comparative study could be postponed until further results were available.

The next step was to re-examine the information supplied us by the local judges for the purpose of choosing two cities which apparently were well supplied with facilities and two others which apparently were not. The ratings supplied by the AEA members were summarized and a tentative ranking of cities produced (Table 13.1). The cities are ordered from high to low on a measure which averages each city's rank order position on the three separate measures reported in the main columns of the table—that is, (*1*) the mean number of institutions and groups (out of twenty-seven reported as active); (*2*) the mean number of subject areas (out of nine in which a "large number" of courses were reported as available); and (*3*) the mean number of specific course titles (out of thirty-six reported as offered somewhere in the city during the previous year).

Although no illusions can be entertained about the accuracy of these rankings, we nonetheless reasoned that if two centers were selected from near the top of the list and two more from

Table 13.1 Summary of Information on Community Resources Provided by Local Judges

City	Urbanized Population (1960)	Number of Judges Reporting	Mean Number of Institutions and Organizations Identified as Active (of 27)	Rank	Mean Number of Course Types Available in Large Numbers (of 9)	Rank	Mean Number of Specific Course Titles Estimated as Available (of 36)	Rank	Combined Rank Order
A	290,000	1	23.0	1	7.0	2.5	25.0	1.5	1
B	180,000	2	21.0	2	7.0	2.5	24.5	3	2*
C	170,000	4	17.0	9.5	8.0	1	25.0	1.5	3*
D	160,000	7	19.7	3	6.7	4.5	20.9	5	4
E	180,000	2	18.0	6.5	6.5	6	21.0	4	5
F	140,000	6	19.5	4	6.0	7.5	18.6	8	6
G	220,000	3	14.0	13	6.7	4.5	20.0	6	7*
H	170,000	6	16.8	11	6.0	7.5	19.0	7	8
I	110,000	2	18.5	5	4.0	12	15.5	12	9
J	140,000	3	17.0	9.5	4.7	11	16.7	9	10*
K	240,000	4	15.8	12	5.0	9.5	16.2	10	11
L	120,000	3	17.7	8	3.7	13	11.0	13	12
M	120,000	5	13.4	14	5.0	9.5	15.8	11	13.5
N	290,000	2	18.0	6.5	2.5	14	7.5	14	13.5

*Selected for study.

near the bottom, we would probably maximize our chances of concluding with a pair of communities with substantially different numbers of available resources. Cities B and C were therefore selected on the assumption that one would probably turn out to be relatively well equipped with resources, and Cities G and J on the assumption that at least one of these would contain fewer resources than either City B or City C. Although other centers might have been chosen from the very bottom of the listing, Cities G and J obviously provided the best matching with B or C in terms of the population criterion.

Our general suspicions of the validity of the initial information about the cities proved to be highly justified on the basis of the results of the inventories. Although City J did indeed turn out to have the fewest facilities of the four, our expectations concerning the others did not turn out quite as anticipated. City G was found to contain the most plentiful resources in absolute numbers, with Cities B and C ranking second and third, respectively. In retrospect, then, it is clear that our plan to base the final selection of communities on data provided by local informants turned out to be a rather serious strategic error.

The four cities selected for the inventories were assigned the study names of Peters, Brewer, St. Stevens, and Earltown. As indicated in Table 13.2, St. Stevens was the largest of the four,

Table 13.2 Comparison of Demographic Characteristics of Cities Selected for Facilities Inventories*

Characteristic	Peters	Brewer	St. Stevens	Earltown	U.S. Average
Population	180,000	170,000	220,000	140,000	–
Median family income	$6,390	$6,830	$6,615	$5,300	$5,660
Median years of schooling (persons 25 and older)	10.8	12.2	11.2	10.2	10.6
Per cent employed in manufacturing	36	47	41	31	27
Per cent employed in white-collar occupations	44	42	44	43	41
Per cent unemployed	4.2	4.1	4.4	6.2	5.1
Per cent non-white	5.7	4.7	6.9	6.6	11.4
Per cent foreign born	2.4	6.1	4.9	0.6	5.4

*Source: 1960 U.S. census.

with a 1960 urbanized population of approximately 220,000; Peters and Brewer were second and third with populations of 180,000 and 170,000, respectively, while Earltown was the smallest with 140,000 people. All four cities were located in two adjacent midwestern states, two in each state.

In other demographic features Peters, Brewer, and St. Stevens were all considerably above the United States median family income of $5,660, while Earltown, in a less prosperous region of the Middle West, had a median family income of $5,300 ($360 below the average). These income differentials are also reflected in other socio-economic features of the four cities, and in particular by the median years of schooling completed by adults over twenty-five and the percentage of unemployed in the labor force. On both these indicators, Brewer, Peters, and St. Stevens were somewhat better off than the United States average while Earltown was somewhat worse off. In general, then, three of our cities could be characterized as prosperous, with the fourth considerably less so.

The extent of industrial activity in our cities differed quite markedly; in Brewer, for example, 47 per cent of the labor force was engaged in manufacturing, as compared with the 41 per cent in St. Stevens, 36 per cent in Peters, and 31 per cent in Earltown. On the other hand, the communities were almost identical in the proportion of the labor force in white-collar occupations; all four cities fell between 42 and 44 per cent on this index.

Finally, in terms of racial and ethnic composition, the cities had quite similar proportions of non-whites in their populations, all four being considerably below the United States average of 11.4 per cent. With regard to proportion of foreign-born, on the other hand, Brewer was slightly above the national average with 6.1 per cent, St. Stevens was slightly under at 4.9 per cent, and Peters and Earltown were much lower, with 2.4 per cent and 0.6 per cent, respectively.

INVENTORY PROCEDURES

The first step in making the inventories was to establish contacts and recruit field personnel in each city. Fortunately, NORC had resident field supervisors in both St. Stevens and

Brewer. In Earltown and Peters, however, new field representatives had to be hired and trained.

The first contacts made in each city were with the AEA members to whom questionnaires had been sent during our preliminary survey; they put us in touch with the directors of adult programs in local colleges and high schools, with whom a series of initial interviews were arranged in November, 1962. The task of tracking down detailed information on an institution-by-institution basis was turned over to the field representatives, and a set of systematic procedures was established for the completion of the inventories, which were to include an exhaustive enumeration of all instructional programs for adults offered during the autumn semester of that year—that is, between September 1 and December 31, 1962.

As in the first phase of our study, educational activities were defined very broadly and were delimited on the basis of two identifying criteria. The first criterion was that an activity have as its main purpose the transmission of some type of knowledge, information, or skill. The second was that the activity had to involve some form of instruction, although here again no restrictions were made in the form such instruction might take. We were interested in an institutional inventory rather than a behavioral one, and we were not faced with the additional task of enumerating independent self-instruction.

Within this broad framework, the principal task was to contact all institutions and organizations in the four cities and to find out which had offered educational programs to adults during the four months with which we were concerned.

Three main classes of institutions and organizations were identified, each having a somewhat longer list of sub-types.

1. *Educational institutions.*—Within this category, five sub-types were further identified.

    a) Publicly supported colleges and universities
    b) Privately supported colleges and universities
    c) Publicly supported secondary schools
    d) Privately supported secondary schools
    e) Profit-making or proprietary schools

The following information was obtained from these institutions: a list of all courses for adults (credit and non-credit) which had been offered during the fall semester of 1962, an estimate of the total adult enrollment in these classes, and a separate enumeration of all educational activities which did not involve regular classroom instruction. This latter category included all public lectures, concerts, workshops, conferences, or seminars which had been specifically organized for the local adult public during fall, 1962. Field workers were instructed to prepare complete lists of these activities, to designate the dates on which they had been held, and where possible to secure attendance figures.

College and secondary-school information was most typically collected from printed course catalogues. Since these catalogues often listed many more classes than actually met, however, it was necessary to edit them very carefully with the directors of the adult programs. In most cases, enrollment figures were obtained separately for each class which met.

Proprietary school information was usually obtained by telephone from the directors of the schools. In practically all cases this information was offered freely, although on occasion enrollment statistics were withheld. One problem encountered in this connection was that age is not given on the enrollment records in many proprietary schools. Most business colleges, technical schools, and driving schools, for example, instruct youths as well as adults, and music and dancing schools also offer classes for children. The standard approach to this problem was to ask for information only about courses designed for adults, but at the same time we did not insist on a rigid age criterion when counting adult enrollments. Unlike the behavioral inventory, the survey of facilities was not restricted to those resources used exclusively by persons old enough to vote. Our general conception of an adult education resource, rather, embraced the complete range of facilities available to and used by persons no longer enrolled full-time in the regular school system.

2. *Other community institutions.* — The organizations in this class were involved in a wide range of social functions.

a) Government agencies
b) Private businesses and companies
c) YMCA's and related community centers
d) Churches and synagogues
e) Hospitals and other medical centers
f) Libraries, museums, and art centers

Since different procedures were employed in obtaining information from these varied institutions, we shall discuss each one independently.

a) Government agencies.   As with proprietary schools, government agencies in each city were first identified from local telephone directories. Eleven branches of government — municipal, county, state, and federal — were included in the survey. At city and county levels, initial contacts were made with information officers or other functionaries who routinely dealt with public requests for information. In other cases, however, it was necessary to contact each government department individually.

Field workers were instructed to differentiate between two main types of educational activity within these agencies: efforts to teach or instruct the public and training courses provided for employees. The former category covered an extremely wide range of activities, including police and fire department training programs in security skills, civil defense, traffic regulations, or safety skills; park district programs in recreational topics and skills; state and federal programs of vocational training or retraining; Co-operative Extension agricultural programs; and Internal Revenue Service seminars for local professional and business groups. Information was also recorded on all lecture tours of government agencies and all formal speaking engagements made to local groups by government officials. Data on information campaigns conducted through the dissemination of pamphlets or news releases, on the other hand, were not collected as part of the inventory.

With respect to employee training programs, two general criteria were established which applied to courses sponsored either by public agencies or by private companies. First, only programs which involved instruction for a minimum period of five working days or thirty-five hours were classified as bona fide training programs. Second, and more important, the period had to be devoted exclusively to training, in the sense that employees could not be engaged as productive workers while the instruction was being received. Under this latter criterion, then, on-the-job training in the traditional sense of learning while doing was not classified as formal training for purposes of the inventory.

In addition to courses provided by employers themselves, information was also collected on tuition reimbursement programs in which employers subsidized the enrollment of their workers in courses at other institutions.

b) Business and industry.   The local Chambers of Commerce provided printed directories which listed all companies in each city plus additional information concerning their size and functions. From initial inquiries we learned that very few small businesses were engaged in employee training as we had defined it; therefore we decided to limit this part of the investigation to companies which employed a minimum average of fifty workers. Information on both independent training courses and tuition reimbursement programs was subsequently obtained for each company of this size or larger.

c) YMCA's and related community centers.   Catalogues of course offerings at YMCA's and YWCA's were reviewed with adult education directors so that classes which had actually met could be differentiated from those which failed to attract the minimum enrollment required. Data from these institutions were collected in a routine manner.

d) Churches and synagogues.   Because of the large numbers involved, a one-third sample of churches and synagogues was drawn from an alphabetized listing of the religious institutions in each city. Attempts were then made to contact either the clergymen or other church officers in each of the selected institutions, and information was requested concerning instructional programs of either a religious or secular nature which had been provided for adults during the period covered by the inventory.

In recording this information care was taken to distinguish

between activities sponsored by the church as a whole and those conducted under the auspices of clubs, organizations, and associations representing some special segment of the congregation. To clarify the issue of sponsorship, only those programs organized by the clergy, the church executive, or the congregation as a whole are classified here as church sponsored; those organized by special sub-groups in the church are classified within the religious sub-category of the voluntary organizations and associations—the third major group of educational sponsors identified for purposes of the inventory.

e) Hospitals. For hospitals, nursing schools, and other medical centers, information was obtained concerning any courses of instruction available either to the general public or as in-service training to employees. However, regular curricular offerings to student nurses or medical students or interns were not covered by the inventory.

f) Libraries, museums, and art centers. Finally, contacts were made with the public libraries in each city and (where existing) with appropriate officials in museums and art institutes.

3. *Voluntary organizations and associations.*—Although the activities of these groups could hardly be considered as community facilities in the same sense as the instruction offered in schools and other public institutions, it was nonetheless reasonable to assume that many of these groups probably did sponsor activities whose central purpose was to provide members with new knowledge, information, or skills. Our expectations were that most of these activities would be of the more short-lived variety, such as study groups, discussion groups, and presentations by guest speakers or lecturers. It seemed clear that we would require a rather special set of definitions and specifications to carry out a meaningful appraisal of the educational activities of voluntary organizations. Accordingly, lectures, talks, and speeches were counted only when a minimum of four presentations had been made on the same topic or subject; and similarly, study groups and discussion groups were included only if four or more sessions had been devoted to the same general problem area during the period under study. As with other phases of the inventory, however, the most important criterion governing

inclusion rested on the principal functions of an activity; programs which were primarily social or recreational in nature were
not counted in the survey even though the acquisition of
knowledge, information, or skill might certainly have been a
consequence.

Finally, to restrict the inventory to the more prominent community organizations, the decision was made to record only
those activities which reached a total audience of twenty or
more adults.

Directories of local clubs and organizations were obtained
from the Chamber of Commerce in each city, and since these
lists turned out to be quite lengthy, a one-third sample of organizations was selected for each city. Presiding officers in these
groups were then contacted by telephone. Three types of data
were collected for each group: a statement of the general goals
of the organization as formally defined, an estimate of the total
membership of the group, and a full description of all group
activities during the fall of 1962 which (*a*) were essentially
educational in nature and (*b*) involved a minimum audience of
twenty adults.

One problem encountered very early in the inventory concerned the overlapping sponsorship of programs of instruction.
In high-school and university extension courses, for example, a
local manufacturer might guarantee the minimum number of
students necessary to hire an instructor, while the local high
school or university provided classroom space. Field workers
were instructed to keep running notes on such situations, and
these notes were then checked carefully to make sure that the
same activities were not recorded twice in the survey. As a
general rule of thumb, the "main sponsor" was judged to be the
institution which provided the physical setting for the instruction.

In summary, then, this chapter has outlined the main steps
taken in selecting cities for study and in rounding up information
on their adult education facilities. Regardless of the formal field
procedures established, the ultimate success of an investigation
of this type rests heavily on the ingenuity of field workers in

tracking down relevant leads and on the willingness and ability of local functionaries to provide detailed information about their programs. Moreover, even though careful checks were made to fill in the more obvious gaps in our results, it is always possible that some facility or resource was overlooked. There were a few situations, too, in which for various reasons the information obtained was not of uniform quality in all four cities studied; these discrepancies, however, occurred mainly in connection with the more informal instructional programs where no printed announcements, catalogues, or attendance records were available. On the whole, however, except for the fact that some institutions were sampled rather than completely enumerated, the results can for all practical purposes be presented as an exhaustive enumeration of the educational facilities available to adults in four middle-sized cities during fall, 1962.

14

Adult
Education Facilities
in the
Middle-Sized City
I. An Overview

The next two chapters are devoted to the findings of the facilities inventories. In this chapter we sketch a general overview of the institutions and organizations and the general areas of instruction in all four cities. Following this, Chapter 15 presents a much more detailed analysis of the educational facilities in Peters and St. Stevens—the two cities in which personal interviews were subsequently conducted with samples of the adult public.

Our survey in this chapter covers three rather general topics: the range of institutions and organizations actively engaged in providing educational programs for adults, the fields of subject matter with which different institutions and organizations concern themselves, and the variation between cities in these patterns of involvement.

THE SPONSORSHIP OF ADULT EDUCATION
Our first task is to describe the general pattern of adult education sponsorship in the middle-sized city, and in this initial section we deal with the question of which institutions and organizations were active and inactive in this field.

Table 14.1 indicates the number of cities out of four in which institutions and organizations of specific types were found to

Table 14.1 Programs of Adult Education in Four Midwestern Cities, September—December, 1962 (Number of Cities Out of Four in Which Some Type of Adult Instruction Was Found)

Type of Institution or Organization	Academic	Vocational			Hobbies and Recreation	Home and Family Life	Personal Development	Religion	Public Affairs	Other
		White Collar	Blue Collar	Agri-cultural						
Educational institutions										
Public colleges, universities	1	3			1	1	1	1	1	
Private colleges, universities	4	3	4		4		3	2	3	1
Public secondary schools	4	4	4	1	4	4	3	1	2	2
Private secondary schools	1	1						1		
Proprietary schools	2	4	3		4	2	3			4
Other community institutions										
Government agencies		4	4	3	3	2	1		3	3
Business and industry	1	4	4				3			1
YMCA's, etc.	1				3	3	3			
Churches, synagogues	2				1	1	2	4	2	1
Hospitals		3	4			1				
Libraries, museums, etc.	2				2					
Voluntary organizations										
Service groups										
Medical or welfare groups		1	1			1	1			1
Civic and political							1			
Business and professional		4				1			3	
Labor unions										
Cultural and educational	1				2		1			
Fraternal and social							1			
Veterans						1				
Hobby and recreational					3		1			
Religious						1		4		1

provide at least some kind of instruction in different fields of learning. The table classifies subject matter in the ten categories employed in earlier sections of the monograph, and it also differentiates institutions and organizations by major class and sub-type. Voluntary organizations and associations are subdivided here into ten categories reflecting the broad functions of each group. Although this mode of presentation necessarily obscures quite substantial differences in the scope of involvement of different institutions, it does allow us to make an initial appraisal of the kinds of programs most typically present and absent in the four cities we studied.

First of all, a great many cells in the table are empty, indicating that we found no instruction of that type in any of the cities. Practically all these blanks, moreover, show that the institution or organization in question was indeed inactive, rather than non-existent. There is one important exception, however; neither Earltown nor Peters had a publicly supported college or university.[1] More generally, however, a blank cell can be interpreted to mean that in each city at least one institution or organization of that type was contacted and found to be inactive in adult instruction.

A second general scanning of Table 14.1 reveals that nine different types of institutions or organizations had provided instruction in one or more subject areas in all four cities. These were as follows:

1. *Private Colleges and Universities* — active in all four cities in providing academic and recreational courses;

2. *Public High Schools* — typically active in five different fields: both white- and blue-collar vocational areas; academic; recreational; and home and family life;

3. *Proprietary Schools* — active in the white-collar vocational area, recreational field; and "miscellaneous other" category (typically schools of driver training);

4. *Government Agencies* — active in the two main vocational spheres;

[1]During the period covered by our inventory one of the state universities conducted a small number of extension courses in Peters, but these were housed in rented quarters and were not available to the general public.

5. *Business and Industry*—providing training programs in both the white- and blue-collar occupational areas in each community;

6. *Churches and Synagogues*—active in providing religious instruction to adults;

7. *Hospitals*—active in the blue-collar vocational areas (typically in-service training courses for hospital orderlies or nurses' aides);

8. *Business and Professional Associations*—typically active in sponsoring educational programs in the white-collar vocational area (and usually in the business spheres); and finally,

9. *Religious Organizations and Associations*—active in religious instruction.

These, then, represent the most typical patterns of institutional involvement in adult education. Most of these same sponsors provided educational programs in other subject fields as well, but over and above these nine, there were only three others which offered instruction in some specific subject area in as many as three of the four cities: these were public colleges or universities in the white-collar vocational field, YMCA's in recreation, home life, and personal development, and hobby clubs. All in all, just a little over one-half of the twenty-one types of institutions and associations contacted in the study were typically found to be involved in educating adults.

One general indicator of over-all involvement is provided by the total number of entries recorded for each type of sponsor across all four cities. Each type of institution or organization could be active in as many as ten different subject fields in up to four different cities, thus indicating a maximum of forty situations in which instruction might be provided. These scores represent a very broad kind of involvement index—one which combines the variety of subject matter offered with the number of institutions of each type in the different cities.

When the institutions and organizations are ranked on these scores, the most extensive involvement in adult instruction is clearly found in the public secondary schools, where at least some type of course coverage was provided in twenty-eight out of forty possible conditions—an average of seven subject fields out of ten in each city (see Table 14.2). Three other classes of sponsor (government agencies, proprietary schools, and private colleges and universities) are also characterized by a fairly extensive involvement, with courses available in one-half or more of the total possible situations. It is revealing, moreover, that government agencies of one type or another offered more broadly based programs of instruction for adults than did four of five types of educational institutions listed.

Tables 14.1 and 14.2 also indicate the types of institutions relatively inactive in adult education. For example, we find (*a*) that private secondary schools sponsored an adult program in only one city out of the four; (*b*) that libraries, museums, or art centers offered only minimal facilities for adult instruction and were completely inactive in two of the four cities; and (*c*) that among labor unions no instructional programs at all were found

Table 14.2 Scope of Involvement in Adult Education of 21 Types of Institutions and Organizations

Rank	Class*	Type of Institution or Organization	Total Number of Subject Areas in Which Instruction Was Offered in Four Cities (Maximum Possible, 40)
1	I	Public secondary schools	28
2	II	Government agencies	23
3	I	Proprietary schools	22
4	I	Private colleges and universities	20
5	II	Business and industry	13
6	II	Churches and synagogues	13
7	II	YMCA's and related community centers	10
8	I	Public colleges and universities	9
9	II	Hospitals	8
10	III	Business and professional associations	8
11	III	Hobby and recreation groups	5
12	III	Religious organizations and associations	5
13	II	Libraries, museums, and art centers	4
14	III	Medical and welfare associations	4
15	I	Private secondary schools	3
16	III	Educational and cultural associations	3
17	III	Community service organizations	2
18	III	Fraternal and social organizations	1
19	III	Civic and political organizations	0
20	III	Labor unions	0
21	III	Veterans' organizations	0

*I = Educational institutions; II = other community institutions; III = voluntary organizations and associations.

which fitted our criteria for inclusion in the inventory. On the other hand, the absence or virtual absence of formal educational programs in most of the voluntary organizations is just about what we might have anticipated.

Altogether, some 181 instructional programs were recorded in the inventory, and less than one-half of these (45 per cent) were sponsored by bona fide educational institutions. As many as 39 per cent were in other community institutions, while 15 per cent were sponsored by voluntary organizations and associations. Thus more than one-half of the adult education resources located were in institutions and organizations whose primary functions were not educational. This is not at all inconsistent with our earlier findings (Table 3.14) concerning the institutions which adults most often attend when they take courses, however, and the finding that more adults take courses outside schools than within them would seem to reflect the simple fact that more educational programs exist outside of the regular educational institutions. These results indicate nothing about the relative scope of different educational programs, of course, but they do reveal a surprisingly wide range of non-academic locations in which adults can acquire new information, knowledge, or skills.

Table 14.1 also contains information on the range of sponsors in different subject fields. For example, when the entries in Table 14.1 are summed along the columns instead of across the rows the resulting figures provide a measure of the number of different institutional settings in which instruction was available.

There are two meaningful measures: the overall sum of resource locations for each subject field and the subtotals for the three main classes of sponsors. Both sets of figures are presented in Table 14.3.

As in the previous tables in this section, the figures in Table 14.3 do not give the number of physical locations in which instruction was provided, but rather the number of different types of sponsors of adult instruction. In other words, religious instruction might be available in any one of one hundred or more churches in each city, and on-the-job training in thirty or forty companies, but Table 14.3 reports these different locations

Table 14.3 Number of Institutional Settings in Four Cities for Studies of Different Types of Subject Matter

Subject Category	Total Number of Institutional Settings (Maximum Possible, 84)	Main Types of Community Organizations		
		Educational Institutions (Maximum, 20)	Other Community Institutions (Maximum, 24)	Voluntary Organizations (Maximum, 40)
Vocational: white collar	31	15	11	5
Hobbies and recreation	27	13	9	5
Personal development	23	10	9	4
Vocational: blue collar	20	7	12	1
Academic	19	12	6	3
Home and family life	17	7	7	3
Public affairs	14	6	5	3
Miscellaneous other	14	7	5	2
Religion	12	4	4	4
Vocational: agriculture	4	1	3	0

as just one source. Individuals usually belong to just one church or synagogue and are usually employed by just one company, so in this sense the figures are not entirely misleading indicators of the range of sponsors to which a given individual might direct himself for more education.

In any event, Table 14.3 does indicate the fields of subject matter offered by both the widest and narrowest range of sponsors. It shows that the largest number of facilities were available in white-collar vocational education, recreational learning, and personal development subjects. And, from the lower end of the continuum, facilities are seen to be most sparsely distributed in agricultural education, religious instruction, and current events and public affairs. The fact that our inventories were restricted to urban centers probably explains the paucity of institutional involvement in agricultural instruction.

More generally, these results are again consistent with our earlier findings concerning the subject areas in which adults most frequently study; it will be recalled that vocational and recreational studies constituted approximately one-half of all courses taken by American adults over the period of a year, with vocational studies the most frequent by a considerable margin.

Next, the right-hand columns of Table 14.3 provide information on two additional questions: the main areas of instruction offered by different classes of sponsors; and the community setting in which instruction in different subject fields was most typically found. Focusing first on the involvement of different sponsors, the results indicate (*a*) that educational institutions were most typically active in white-collar vocational skills, recreational courses, and academic education, in that order; (*b*) that other community institutions were most typically involved in vocational education for white- and blue-collar occupations; and (*c*) that voluntary organizations and associations showed no predominant emphasis on any particular subject field.

The most important finding is the differential emphasis of schools and other community institutions in vocational education. For example, when the figures on vocational programs are extracted from Table 14.3, they are found to be distributed quite differently within the two main classes of community institutions.

Program	Regular Schools (Per Cent)	Other Community Institutions (Per Cent)
White-collar	65	42
Blue-collar	30	46
Agriculture	4	12
Total	99	100
N	23	26

In the public, private, and proprietary schools there are considerably more vocational education programs in professional, technical, business and clerical fields than in blue-collar fields; in the non-academic institutions, on the other hand, there is more balance between these two main occupational sectors.

Finally, Table 14.3 can also be examined for the sponsorship patterns most typical of different categories of subject matter, that is, the extent to which different types of instruction are available within or outside of formal educational institutions. When appropriate measures are extracted, the pattern shown in Table 14.4 emerges. There is considerable variation in the spon-

Table 14.4 Proportion of Educational Programs Located within Regular Educational Institutions

	Per Cent	Number of Programs
Academic subjects	63	(19)
Miscellaneous other	50	(14)
Hobbies and recreation	48	(27)
White-collar vocational skills	48	(31)
Personal development	43	(23)
Current events and public affairs	43	(14)
Home and family life	41	(17)
Blue-collar vocational skills	35	(20)
Religion	33	(12)
Agriculture	25	(4)
All programs	45	(181)

sorship of different categories of instruction. First, it is clear that the only area typically sponsored by formal schools is academic education. On the other hand, three fields (blue-collar vocational training, agricultural education, and religious instruction) are typically sponsored outside of regular schools; most other categories were just about as likely as not to be found outside a bona fide educational institution.

In sum, these initial results have pointed to a number of salient features concerning the organization of adult education within middle-sized communities. Instructional resources were found to be most plentiful in vocational training, forming some 30 per cent (55 of 181) of the independently organized programs of instruction enumerated in the four cities. The principal finding, however, is that adult instruction is by no means the exclusive concern of official educational institutions, but rather is spread quite widely throughout the whole social organization of the community. Educational institutions do play a dominant role in academic instruction, but they seem to face heavy competition for the adult student in areas of learning not traditionally defined as belonging to the academic institution.

VARIATION FROM CITY TO CITY

Before moving ahead to a more detailed review of the course content offered in different institutions, we shall briefly consider the variation among the four cities in the patterns of available facilities. Here we are concerned with which institutions or organizations provided programs of instruction as well as the forms the programs took. Five main classes of programs are distinguished.

1. The course. This covers all programs of instruction where there was a set body of knowledge or skill to be mastered by the student, and where an instructor or teacher was present to guide the progress of the student.

2. The lecture series. The most important feature of the lecture series, as defined here, is that there was no set curriculum that the student was expected to master, and no attempt on the part of the speaker or lecturer to evaluate the progress of the student or to test how much was learned. This form is typically employed for the transmission of information rather than of knowledge or skill.

3. The study group or discussion group category embraces all educational activities generated by participants themselves where no paid functionaries were present who could be termed instructors, teachers, lecturers, or speakers.

4. Employee training. This is actually a special type of "course," used in all situations where employees received job-related instruction on the premises of their employers.

5. Sponsorship. This covered educational activities for which organizations either reimbursed their members or employees for tuition expenses incurred at an educational institution or provided funds directly to a school or college so that a course of instruction could be offered.

As was mentioned in the previous chapter, a number of minimum standards governed the recording of lectures, discussion groups, and employee training: a series of lectures or a study group was recorded only if four or more sessions were devoted to the same topic over the four-month period of the inventory; employee training programs were counted only if a minimum of one week or thirty-five hours was devoted to the exclusive function of job training. Finally, the educational programs of voluntary organizations and associations were included only if they reached a minimum audience of twenty adults.

Classified in these terms the facilities found in each city are described in Table 14.5. The entires in the table represent the principal forms of instruction employed: "C" for courses; "D" for discussion or study groups; "E" for employee training; "L" for a lecture series; and "S" for program sponsorship or tuition reimbursement. Although this mode of presentation produces an extremely complex form from which to evaluate community differences, it nonetheless provides the reader with a comprehensive summary of the ranges of sponsors, types of subject matter, and forms of instruction found in each city.

Although some readers may wish to ponder over the contents of these tables at considerable length, our purpose now is to evaluate the extent to which the four cities varied in available facilities. To make such comparisons we must extract summary

Table 14.5 Main Types of Adult Education Facilities in Four Midwestern Cities

a. Brewer (Population 170,000)

Type of Institution or Organization	Academic	Vocational			Hobbies and Recreation	Home and Family Life	Personal Development	Religion	Public Affairs	Other
		White Collar	Blue Collar	Agri-cultural						
Educational institutions										
Public colleges, universities		C–L*								
Private colleges, universities	C	C	C		C		C		C	C
Public secondary schools	C	C	C	C	C	C	C		C	C
Private secondary schools										
Proprietary schools	C	C			C	C	C			C
Other community institutions										
Government agencies	S	S	E	C					L	C–L
Business and industry		E	E				S			E
YMCA's, etc.					C	C	C			
Churches, synagogues			E					C–D		
Hospitals	C–D	C–E								
Libraries, museums, etc.	C–D									
Voluntary organizations										
Service groups										
Medical or welfare groups			C							
Civic and political										
Business and professional		L							C–L	
Labor unions										
Cultural and educational					C					
Fraternal and social							D			
Veterans										
Hobby and recreational										
Religious						D		D		

*Legend: C-regular classes or courses of instruction; D-discussion groups or study groups; E-employee training program; L-lectures, speeches or demonstrations; S-sponsorship of educational programs conducted elsewhere.

(Table 14.5 continued)

Table 14.5 Continued

b. Earltown (Population 140,000)

Type of Institution or Organization	Academic	Vocational			Hobbies and Recreation	Home and Family Life	Personal Development	Religion	Public Affairs	Other
		White Collar	Blue Collar	Agri-cultural						
Educational institutions										
Public colleges, universities	C*	C								
Private colleges, universities	C	C	C		C	C	C	C		
Public secondary schools		C	C		C	C	C			
Private secondary schools										C
Proprietary schools	C	C	C		C	C				
Other community institutions										
Government agencies		E–S	E	C–L		D	D		L	
Business and industry		E	E				E			
YMCA's, etc.										
Churches, synagogues								C		
Hospitals			E							
Libraries, museums, etc.					C					
Voluntary organizations										
Service groups										
Medical or welfare groups										
Civic and political										
Business and professional		L				L				
Labor unions										
Cultural and educational					D					
Fraternal and social										
Veterans										
Hobby and recreational					C					
Religious								D		C

*Legend: C=regular classes or courses of instruction; D=discussion groups or study groups; E=employee training program; L=lectures, speeches or demonstrations; S=sponsorship of educational programs conducted elsewhere.

Table 14.5 Continued

c. Peters (Population 180,000)

Type of Institution or Organization	Academic	Vocational			Hobbies and Recreation	Home and Family Life	Personal Development	Religion	Public Affairs	Other
		White Collar	Blue Collar	Agricultural						
Educational institutions										
Public colleges, universities		C*								
Private colleges, universities	C	C-L			C				L	C
Public secondary schools	C	C	C		C	C	C			C
Private secondary schools		C	C		C					
Proprietary schools		C			C		C			C
Other community institutions										
Government agencies		C-E	E		C				C	C
Business and industry		E-S	E-S							
YMCA's, etc.	C				C	C	C			
Churches, synagogues	D				C	C	C	C-D	C	C
Hospitals		E	C-E							
Libraries, museums, etc.	D									
Voluntary organizations										
Service groups						C	C			
Medical or welfare groups		L								
Civic and political							C			
Business and professional		C-D							L	
Labor unions										
Cultural and educational	C									
Fraternal and social										
Veterans										
Hobby and recreational					C					
Religious								C-D		

*Legend: C-regular classes or courses of instruction; D-discussion groups or study groups; E-employee training program; L-lectures, speeches or demonstrations; S-sponsorship of educational programs conducted elsewhere.

(Table 14.5 continued)

Table 14.5 Continued

d. St. Stevens (Population 220,000)

Type of Institution or Organization	Academic	Vocational			Hobbies and Recreation	Home and Family Life	Personal Development	Religion	Public Affairs	Other
		White Collar	Blue Collar	Agri-cultural						
Educational institutions										
Public colleges, universities	C–L*	C–L			C	C–L	C	L	L	
Private colleges, universities	C–L				C	C	C	C–L	L	
Public secondary schools	C	C	C		C	C	C	C		
Private secondary schools	C	C	C		C		C			
Proprietary schools		C	C		C		C			C
Other community institutions										
Government agencies		C–E	C–E	C–D		C				C
Business and industry		E–S	E–S				E			
YMCA's, etc.					C	C	C			
Churches, synagogues	D					D		C–D	D	
Hospitals		C–E	C–E		C	C				
Libraries, museums, etc.					C					
Voluntary organizations										
Service groups										
Medical or welfare groups										L
Civic and political										
Business and professional		C							C	
Labor unions										
Cultural and educational										
Fraternal and social										
Veterans										
Hobby and recreational					C		C			
Religious								D		

*Legend: C–regular classes or courses of instruction; D–discussion groups or study groups; E–employee training program; L–lectures, speeches or demonstrations; S–sponsorship of educational programs conducted elsewhere.

measures from Table 14.5. Even though these data reveal nothing about the scope of different programs, they allow us to compare cities in terms of the number of different institutional settings in which specific types of instruction were available.

For the first comparison let us examine the total number of entries recorded for each city as a rough general index of the overall diversity of available programs of instruction. In making these comparisons the considerable differences in size among the cities must be taken into account, with St. Stevens, the largest, being approximately one and one-half times larger than Earltown, the smallest.[2] Because of this, standardized indices of the number of different programs available per 100,000 population are also computed for this general analysis.

When the total number of entries are summed for each city, the pattern in Table 14.6 emerges. In absolute numbers these figures indicate a considerable range in the available facilities in the four communities, with fifty-two separate educational programs available in St. Stevens, compared with only thirty-four in Earltown. Yet on a per capita basis, the standardized measures on the right indicate very little variation at all among the four cities, and approximately twenty-five different types of educational programs were found in each city for each 100,000 persons in its population. These results suggest that while our four cities did indeed differ considerably in the diversity of facilities available, these discrepancies appear to be explained largely by

[2]Their populations were 220,000 and 140,000, respectively.

Table 14.6 Educational Facilities Available in Four Communities

City	Total Entries (Maximum, 210)	Number of Different Types of Programs per 100,000 Population
St. Stevens (220,000)	52	23.6
Peters (180,000)	48	26.7
Brewer (170,000)	46	27.1
Earltown (140,000)	34	24.3

the fact that in larger cities sponsorship of adult instruction is more widely spread through the social structure of the community. In larger cities there are more places to study more things, but there are also more people to share the additional facilities; because of this it is unclear whether we can interpret the absolute differences as indicating that one city was really better stocked with resources than another. Certainly in terms of the range of resource-types available on a per capita basis, our four cities turned out to be very similar indeed.

When similar comparisons are made within the three main institutional categories, moreover, the results again show the communities to be more alike than unlike in terms of available resources. These results are presented in Table 14.7, first in absolute numbers, then in the standardized measures. Here again, there are quite substantial differences in the actual numbers of different types of programs, with St. Stevens having considerably more resources in its educational institutions, and St. Stevens and Peters together having the largest number in the other community institutions. However, when these figures are weighted by the size of the community, the comparative advantages of these cities tend to disappear, particularly so in the case of instructional programs in schools.

Table 14.7 Ranges of Adult Education Programs in Different Classes of Institutions, by City

City	Total Number of Different Programs Located In		
	Educational Institutions	Other Community Institutions	Voluntary Organizations and Associations
St. Stevens	26	20	6
Peters	19	20	9
Brewer	21	18	7
Earltown	16	12	6
	Number of Programs Per 100,000 Population		
St. Stevens	11.8	9.1	2.7
Peters	10.6	11.1	5.0
Brewer	12.4	10.6	4.1
Earltown	11.4	8.6	4.3

Table 14.7 does indicate one community difference of some interest, however, in distribution of facilities within each city. Peters has the lowest per capita resource rate in the regular schools, but the highest in the other two categories — a feature which is accented more sharply when the allocation of resources within each community is examined in percentage form (Table 14.8). From these figures it is quite clear that a relatively greater proportion of the adult education resources in Peters were outside of the regular educational institutions, and that the patterns for each of the other cities were much more similar. Peters was the only community of the four, moreover, which had more facilities in the "other" institutions category than in the regular schools (20 compared with 19).

These results suggest further that one important way in which the communities differed was in the proportion of their total adult education resources available to the general public as opposed to private sectors of the community. To examine this tendency more precisely, all of the entries in Table 14.5 were reclassified according to whether the instruction was available to the general adult public or only to persons connected with some organization or company. All programs were considered to be public except the following three types: (*a*) educational activities of private organizations and associations; (*b*) all instruction sponsored by churches and synagogues; and (*c*) all programs of employee training or program sponsorship, regardless of where they were located.

When the resources in each community were classified on this basis the following results emerged.

Type of Program	St. Stevens	Brewer	Earltown	Peters
Per cent available to the general public	69 (65)	63 (52)	61 (36)	54 (56)

The cities did indeed differ in terms of the public-private pattern of their adult education resources. In St. Stevens a substantial majority of all programs were available to the general public, while in Peters almost half were organized privately.

Two final summary measures were next extracted from the entries in Table 14.5, the first allowing us to make comparisons on the ranges of instruction offered by the same institutions in different cities, and the second focusing on the number of different locations in which specific types of subject matter could be studied in each city. These measures are derived from the row and column totals for each city in Table 14.5 and are presented, respectively, in Tables 14.9 and 14.10.

Looking first at Table 14.9, the following community differences may be noted.

1. St. Stevens had by far the most extensive adult education program located in a public college or university, and in addition was the only city with any program at all in the private secondary school sector.

2. Public secondary schools varied considerably in their subject coverage, and ranged from five fields in Earltown to nine in Brewer.

3. In Brewer, companies and businesses sponsored or provided instruction in five different subject fields—a range somewhat wider than in the other cities.

4. In Earltown, no educational programs were available in the YMCA's.

5. The churches and synagogues in Peters and St. Stevens were involved in a considerably wider range of subjects than those in other cities.

In addition, the figures in the last three rows of Table 14.9 indicate (*a*) that in each city over one-half of the twenty-one different classes of sponsors provided instruction in at least one

Table 14.8 Per Cent of Community Resources Located in Different Institutional Sectors

Category	Peters (N = 48)	Brewer (N = 46)	Earltown (N = 34)	St. Stevens (N = 52)
Educational institutions	40	46	47	50
Other community institutions	42	39	35	38
Voluntary organizations	19	15	18	12
Total	101	100	100	100

field of subject matter; (*b*) that in Peters and St. Stevens well over one-half were active in two or more subject fields; but (*c*) that it was only in St. Stevens that a substantial number provided instruction in three or more fields of subject matter. In that city, however, ten different types of sponsors – including all categories of educational institutions and all "other" community institutions except libraries and museums – were active in as many as three different fields of instruction.

Finally, let us compare cities on the number of different places

Table 14.9 Range of Instruction Provided by Different Adult Education Sponsors in Different Cities (Number of Subject Areas Out of Ten in Which Instruction Was Available)

Type of Institution or Organization	Brewer	Earltown	Peters	St. Stevens
Educational institutions				
Public colleges, universities	1	0	1	7
Private colleges, universities	5	5	5	5
Public secondary schools	9	5	8	6
Private secondary schools	0	0	0	3
Proprietary schools	6	6	5	5
Other community institutions				
Government agencies	6	6	5	6
Business and industry	5	3	2	3
YMCA's and related community centers	3	0	4	3
Churches and synagogues	1	1	6	4
Hospitals	2	1	2	3
Libraries, museums and art centers	1	1	1	1
Voluntary organizations				
Service groups	0	0	2	0
Medical or welfare groups	1	0	2	1
Civic and political groups	0	0	0	0
Business and professional	2	2	2	2
Labor unions	0	0	0	0
Cultural and educational	1	1	1	0
Fraternal and social	1	0	0	0
Veterans' organizations	0	0	0	0
Hobby and recreational	0	2	1	2
Religious organizations	2	1	1	1
Per cent of total institutions and organizations active at all	71	57	76	71
Per cent active in more than one subject field	43	33	52	57
Per cent active in more than two subject fields	29	24	29	48

where particular types of subject matter could be studied. From Table 14.10 we note that Peters had the largest number of sponsors in four fields (academic, white-collar vocational, public affairs, and "other"), St. Stevens in four others (hobbies and recreation, home and family life, personal development, and religion), Brewer in one (agriculture), and Earltown in none. The most extensive coverage for any one subject area was in Peters, with nine different places for instruction in white-collar vocational subjects. Peters was also the only city which lacked instructional resources for a given subject field: this was agriculture, an understandable deficiency in an urban area of 180,000 people.

The most notable differences between cities occur in public affairs education and instruction in the personal development field; for the former category, places for instruction ranged from a high of five in Peters to a low of one in Earltown, and for the latter the range was seven in St. Stevens to three, again in Earltown. Five other subject fields varied by as much as three settings; hobbies and agriculture varied by two, and only blue-collar vocational education did not vary at all in the number of instructional settings. In each of the four cities five places were found where blue-collar vocational training was available.

On the basis of these results a number of tentative conclusions can be offered concerning the nature and organization of adult education resources in the middle-sized city.

1. In most cities the sponsorship of adult education programs appears to be about evenly split between regular schools and other sectors of the community. There was some but not a great deal of variation along this dimension.

2. At least one-half of the educational programs in each community were available to the public at large as opposed to private groups of individuals, but considerable variation between the cities was also found.

3. Cities of this size have at least one setting where instruction can be received in each main field of subject matter, with the only exception being agricultural education. Facilities are most plentiful for white-collar vocational training and recreational learning.

Table 14.10 Range of Locations in Which Instruction Was Available, by City and Subject (Number of Institutions Out of 21 in Which Instruction Was Available)

| City | Academic | Vocational | | | Hobbies and Recreations | Home and Family Life | Personal Development | Religion | Public Affairs | Other |
		White Collar	Blue Collar	Agriculture						
St. Stevens	5	8	5	1	8	6	7	5	4	3
Peters	6	9	5	0	7	3	6	2	5	5
Brewer	5	8	5	2	6	4	6	2	4	4
Earltown	3	6	5	1	6	4	3	3	1	2

4. Larger cities offer more places where adults can study and a wider variety of subject matter. On a per capita basis, however, adult education resources were found to be very evenly distributed across the four cities we studied.

5. The greatest variation among cities was found in facilities for public affairs and personal development instruction. The least variation was in blue-collar vocational training programs.

15

Adult
Education Facilities
in the
Middle-Sized City
II. A Detailed Enumeration
of Resources

At this point we turn to a much more detailed appraisal of the programs offered in two of our four cities. The cities finally selected for intensive study were Peters and St. Stevens—a selection based not so much on differences in the number of resources as on the differences in the scope and emphasis of the programs they offered. We have already noted that these two cities differed markedly in their facilities available to the general public, but there was a second, even more striking way in which their resources differed.

When we came to examine the activities offered by different institutions, we found that there were many more adults enrolled in college-level adult education courses in Peters than in St. Stevens; conversely, rates of enrollment in secondary-school adult education courses were very much higher in St. Stevens than in Peters. These enrollment statistics are presented in Table 15.1, where it may be quickly noted that the differences are most substantial.

Even though these figures represent total registrations rather than the number of different individuals enrolled, they nonetheless suggest quite strongly that in the regular school system adult education resources in Peters were heavily concentrated at the college and university level, while in St. Stevens they were piled up almost as heavily within the secondary school sector. Moreover, on a per capita basis there were almost three times more college-level registrations in Peters as in St. Stevens, and better than three times as many secondary school enrollments in St. Stevens. On the basis of these discrepancies rather than of any differences in the overall number of facilities, we made our final decision to select Peters and St. Stevens for the intensive case study. These cities were the largest of the four originally chosen, and with urbanized populations of roughly 180,000 and 220,000 similar enough in size to allow a meaningful comparative study to be made.

As detailed a description as possible of the actual content of instructional offerings found in each of these two cities is presented in this chapter. Resources are reported by institutions so that intercity comparisons may be highlighted at each point in the discussion. We first focus on the adult education activities of educational institutions, then on those found in other community institutions and in voluntary organizations and associations.

Table 15.1 Enrollments in Regular School System Adult Education Programs in Peters and St. Stevens, September – December, 1962

Sector	Peters		St. Stevens	
	Number	Per Cent	Number	Per Cent
	Total Enrollments			
Colleges and universities	3,305	80	1,363	28
Secondary schools	850	20	3,561	72
Total	4,155	100	4,924	100
	Rates of Enrollment per 100,000 Population			
Colleges and universities	183.6		62.0	
Secondary schools	47.2		161.9	
Total	230.8		223.8	

FACILITIES IN EDUCATIONAL INSTITUTIONS

1. *Colleges and Universities*

An exhaustive listing of all college-level courses for adults in Peters and St. Stevens during fall, 1962, is presented in Table 15.2, with the number of students enrolled in each course. A glance at this table indicates that two institutions of higher learning provided courses for adults in St. Stevens compared with just one in Peters. Actually two universities were giving adult instruction in Peters at the time of our inventory, but only one of these offered any kind of organized curriculum. The second, an extension division of the state university, conducted five short courses during fall, 1962, but since it had no premises of its own these programs had to be housed in borrowed quarters and were offered on an ad hoc basis. Peters University provided facilities for one of these courses (a short course on the economics of tool engineering); two others, also in industrial engineering, were housed by a local manufacturer; and two short courses in restaurant management were held in space provided by the municipal government. The total enrollment in these programs was eighty-three persons.

For all practical purposes, however, the university-level adult educational facilities in Peters consisted of those offered at Peters University, a private non-sectarian university with a daytime undergraduate enrollment of approximately 4,000 students. The adult education facilities at Peters University were housed in an evening college, which, during fall, 1962, attracted some 1,075 adult students with a total of 3,305 course registrations.

St. Stevens, by comparison, had four different colleges and universities, but only two of these—a two-year extension center of the state university (here named State Extension) and a small coeducational religious college (Charles College here)—provided programs of instruction for adults. The other two, a nationally famous private men's university and a small women's college, offered no formal courses specifically designed for the adult population of the community.

We have already reported that there were many more course

Table 15.2 Lists of Adult Classes Which Met in St. Stevens and Peters Colleges and Universities, Fall, 1962

Subject Category	St. Stevens		Peters
	State Extension (Total Enrollments, 855)	Charles College (Total Enrollments, 508)	Peters University Evening College (Total Enrollments, 3,305)
Academic	Spanish (3)* 92 French 44 Review English 43 Review mathematics 35 Russian 21 German 21 Literary writing 10 Vertebrate fossils 8	American history 78 Education psychology 56 Language arts 62 Sociology 37 American economy 11	Psychology (5) 312 Mathematics (12) 240 History (2) 178 English (4) 146 Physics (4) 140 Economics (5) 90 Political science (2) 76 Astronomy 47 Chemistry (3) 30 Russian (2) 21 Geography 21 Philosophy 21 Spanish 17 Great Books 10
Vocational: technical	Medical technology 39 Air science 37	None	Mechanical engineering (5) 90 Industrial engineering (2) 76 Electronics (3) 41 Electrical engineering (3) 40 Technical drawing (2) 40 Civil engineering (2) 34 Industrial processes (3) 27 Technical mathematics 24 Blueprint reading 9 Engineers refresher 4

*Number in parentheses indicates number of courses if more than one.

Table 15.2 Continued

Subject Category	State Extension (Total Enrollments, 855)	Charles College (Total Enrollments, 508)	Peters University Evening College (Total Enrollments, 3,305)
Vocational: education	None	Education (3) 88	Education (28) 533
Vocational: business	Real estate (2) 65 Insurance (3) 57 Business management 39 Systems and data 30 Marketing 23 Purchasing 20 Small business mgmt. 19 Production and inventory 18 Business writing 17 Credit and collection 16 Business economics 13 Taxes 10	None	Accounting (8) 183 General business (6) 163 Marketing (5) 77 Business administration (5) 56
Vocational: clerical	Secretarial training 21	None	Business correspondence 25 Typing 22 Secretarial refresher 5
Vocational: other	None	None	Nursing (4) 50 Speech therapy (3) 22 Machine shop 11
Hobbies and recreation: fine arts	Music appreciation 15 Acting 3 Art 3	Survey of fine arts 103	Music (5) 132 Art (12) 91
Hobbies and recreation: Other	Photography 11	None	Leather and metal crafts 19
Home and family life	Marriage and family 7	None	Interior decorating 34
Personal development	Speed reading 50 Vocabulary building 40 Critical thinking 21 Self-expression 7	Public speaking 21	Speech (4) 51 Speaking and word power 14 Reading skills clinic 11
Religion	None	Old Testament 52	Religions of the world 35
Public affairs	None	None	International affairs (2) 37

enrollments in colleges and universities in Peters than in St. Stevens, and the course listings in Table 15.2 reveal, in addition, that local residents in Peters had considerably more college-level courses to choose from than did the residents of St. Stevens. In comparison with 158 different courses available at Peters University, State Extension and Charles College in St. Stevens together offered just forty-eight. Of thirty-seven at State Extension, fifteen were in business and ten were in first- or second-year academic subjects; the eleven offered at Charles College included five in academic subjects and three in education.

Obviously, college-level adult education resources were much greater in Peters than in St. Stevens in all fields, but particularly in technical subjects, academic instruction, and teacher training. The comparisons are indicated in Table 15.3, which shows the total number of college courses of each type offered in the two cities.

Instructional activities other than classes, however, were available more frequently in St. Stevens than in Peters. The involvement of Peters University in non-classroom adult education was quite minimal at the time of our inquiry, and the only additional programs offered were two series of lectures — one on East Asia and the other on space age communications.

In St. Stevens, on the other hand, three of the four colleges and universities offered some kind of educational program over and above regular classroom courses. State Extension was the

Table 15.3 Total College Courses Offered in Peters and St. Stevens

Subject matter	Peters	St. Stevens	Difference
Academic subjects	44	15	29
Vocational: education	28	3	25
Vocational: technical	23	2	21
Hobbies and recreation	18	5	13
Vocational: other	11	1	10
Vocational: business	24	15	9
Personal development	6	5	1
All other	4	2	2

most active of the three, and through either full or partial sponsorship had a total of eight different lecture series under way during fall, 1962. Three of these were on religious themes, while others were in literary criticism, international economics, psychology, principles of investment, and interior decorating. During the same period, Charles College, in conjunction with a local service group, conducted one series of five lectures under the general title of "The World around Us" and finally, the private women's college in St. Stevens sponsored two lecture series — one entitled "Christian Culture," the other "Theories of Love."

The only adult education activity reported for Midwest University (the largest educational institution in the city) was a modern problems discussion group consisting of eight adults and one faculty member.

2. *Secondary Schools*

Table 15.4 presents a complete listing of course titles offered in the city and suburban secondary schools of the two cities. As is evident both from the total enrollment figures and the number of courses listed, secondary-school adult education was much more highly developed in St. Stevens than in Peters. Ninety-nine different classes were given in the St. Stevens public high schools during fall, 1962, while eight others met in the city's Catholic high school and in the suburban schools surrounding the city. In Peters, by comparison, only thirty classes met in the city high schools and another nineteen in suburban schools. These totals also indicate that the secondary-school offerings in St. Stevens were much more highly centralized within the city schools than in Peters; 97 per cent of courses available in St. Stevens met in high schools within the city, compared with 61 per cent in Peters.[1]

Unlike the community differences at the college level, St. Stevens offered more at the secondary-school level in just three areas: academic education, white-collar technical courses, and

---

[1]These differences do not simply reflect a grossly different city-suburban population ratio for the two cities. The 1960 census indicated that 60 per cent of the urbanized population in St. Stevens was located within the central city, while the comparable figure for Peters was 57 per cent.

Table 15.4 Lists of Adult Classes Which Met in St. Stevens and Peters City and Suburban Secondary Schools, Fall, 1962

Subject Category	St. Stevens			Peters	
	City High Schools (Public) (Enrollment, 3,276)	City High Schools (Private) (Enrollment, 225)	Suburban High Schools (Enrollment, 60)	City High Schools (Public) (Enrollment, 450)	Suburban High Schools (Enrollment, 400)
Academic	English (10)* Speech (2) Math (8) Biology Chemistry Physics (2) Statics and dynamics American government Economics International relations Sociology History (3) French (2) German (2) Spanish (2) Russian	Child Psychology	None	English American literature Mathematics (2)	Conversational French
Vocational: white collar Technical	Metallurgy Drafting Technical reports Industrial processes Hydraulics Tool design Electronics (4) Machine design Descriptive geometry Surveying	None	None	Electronics	None
Business and clerical	Typing (2) Shorthand (2) Bookkeeping Business arithmetic (2) Business law Office practice (2) Distributive education	None	Typing	Typing Shorthand (4) Bookkeeping Office practice	Typing (2) Shorthand (2) Bookkeeping Business machines

Table 15.4 Continued

Other	None	Principles of education	None	Traffic management (2)	None
Vocational: blue collar	Auto mechanics (8) Machine shop (5) Practical nursing Electricity Electric motors Television (3) Welding (2) Foreman training Plan reading (2)	None	Machine shop	Woodshop Carpenter's mathematics Blueprints Estimating Welding Sheet metal (2) Decorating Plumbing (2)	Welding Electricity
Hobbies and recreation	Oil painting	None	None	Ceramics	Contract bridge Dancing (2) Watercolor painting
Home and family life	Home economics (4) Sewing (2) Tailoring	None	Sewing	Clothing Tailoring	Sewing Tailoring Interior decorating
Personal development	Basic English (3) Health	None	None	Basic English Eighth-grade curriculum	Reducing Reading improvement
Religion	None	Religion (2) Church history	None	None	None
Current events and public affairs	None	None	None	Civics	None
Other	None	None	None	None	Driver training

blue-collar vocational training. These differences are pinpointed in Table 15.5. The principal difference between the two cities results from the combination of an abundant academic curriculum in St. Stevens and an almost complete absence of academic instruction in Peters; forty academic courses were available in the former city compared with just five in the latter. Both cities offered a sizeable number of courses in the blue-collar field, but extensive training programs in auto mechanics and television repairs in St. Stevens resulted in an overall advantage for that city. In the technical area, moreover, thirteen courses met in St. Stevens compared with just one electronics course in Peters.

These three fields of instruction, then, account for practically all differences in the secondary-school adult education facilities in the two cities. The figures indicate a much more even balance within the other categories, with Peters enjoying a modest advantage in the field of recreational instruction.

One of the more interesting findings to have emerged thus far is that the adult education functions of universities and secondary schools in the two cities appeared to be quite reversed, particularly with regard to the academic and technical subjects. In technical education, for example, Peters offered twenty-three courses at the university level and only one in the high schools,

Table 15.5 Total Secondary-School Courses for Adults in Peters and St. Stevens

Subject Field	St. Stevens	Peters	Difference
Academic subjects	40	5	+35
Vocational: blue collar	25	12	+13
Vocational: technical	13	1	+12
Home and family life	8	5	+ 3
Religion	3	0	+ 3
Personal development	4	4	0
Vocational: business	12	13	− 1
Vocational: other	1	2	− 1
Public affairs	0	1	− 1
Hobbies and recreation	1	5	− 4
All other	0	1	− 1
Total	107	49	+58

while in St. Stevens thirteen were offered in the secondary schools and just two in the colleges and universities. Moreover, in Peters most of the instruction in this field was available only as part of the degree program in engineering at the Peters University Evening College. None of the resources listed for St. Stevens, on the other hand, carried any credit toward an academic degree.[2] Clearly, the task of providing technical instruction to the adult population was handled quite differently in each community.

Quite apart from the intercity comparisons, Table 15.4 reveals a number of interesting features concerning the general nature of secondary-school adult education. Of these, the following are particularly relevant.

a) Secondary schools appear to be almost completely inactive in instruction in public affairs. Only one course was offered in the two cities, and that was a regular high-school civics course.

b) All high schools except the Catholic had typing classes for adults, and in addition most offered shorthand and sewing. These seem to be staple courses in a secondary-school adult education curriculum.

c) It is quite evident that private secondary schools are relatively inactive in adult education. The main focus of the one program which we did find was on religious education.

d) Rather surprisingly, the high schools in our two cities were found to provide only a modicum of instruction in the recreational field. Although five classes of this type met in Peters during the period of our inventory, only one was offered in St. Stevens. When compared with the overall incidence of adult studies in this area, the category is clearly underrepresented in the secondary-school curricula.

In relation to this last point, some interesting differences emerge when the courses in city high schools are compared with

[2]It should be pointed out, however, that Midwest University in St. Stevens also contained an engineering school, and that a number of employers in the area had enrolled their engineers in the graduate program there. Since these facilities were part of the regular engineering department of the university, however, they were not enumerated in the inventory as facilities organized primarily for the adult community.

those in suburban schools. Although there were no suburban facilities to speak of in St. Stevens, a meaningful comparison was possible along this dimension in Peters. To obtain a more comprehensive picture of the orientation of adult programs in these two settings, however, we decided to examine all courses listed in the school catalogues rather than just those which were actually given during the period of our inquiry. This task proved to be quite revealing in itself, for it turned out that there were many more courses scheduled than were actually given. Of ninety-two courses listed for the city high schools, thirty actually met; and of fifty-seven listed for the suburban schools, only nineteen were taught. Thus about two-thirds of the total courses scheduled failed to attract the necessary registration—indicating a quite significant mortality rate in these programs.

The results of our content analysis of catalogues are presented in Table 15.6, where substantial differences may be noted between the two settings. In the city schools, 84 per cent of the courses offered were either academic or vocational, while the comparable figure for the suburban schools was as low as 32 per cent. Blue-collar vocational courses, moreover, were virtually nonexistent in suburban curricula, but represented some 26 per cent of the courses offered in the city schools. The main courses

Table 15.6 Comparison of Subject Matter Offered Adults in Suburban and City Secondary Schools: Peters, Fall, 1962 (Per Cent of Total Classes Offered)

Subject Category	City High Schools	Suburban High Schools
Academic	40	11
White collar: vocational	18	16
Blue collar: vocational	26	5
Hobbies and recreation	2	26
Home and family life	9	26
Personal development	3	11
Public affairs	1	2
All other	–	4
Total	99	101
Total courses listed	92	57

in the suburban programs, rather, were in recreation and home and family life — categories which made up over one-half of the suburban classes but only 11 per cent of those offered in the city schools.

This result reflects a tendency noted in the first section of the study, that at least among the better-educated segments of the population, rates of study in the recreational field were substantially higher among suburban than among urban dwellers (see Table 5.13). Whether this reflects a genuinely higher demand or the fact that suburban populations simply enroll in the courses which are most available to them is, of course, a moot point. In any event, it seems clear that the suburban high schools in Peters placed a much stronger emphasis on this field of instruction than the city schools did.

3. *Proprietary Schools*

Next, our inventory found fifty-two profit-making schools in which instructional programs of one type or another were offered to adults. St. Stevens had thirty-one of these schools, ten more than Peters. The large majority of these schools provided instruction in recreational skills or vocational training, and in terms of these broad functions the schools were distributed as follows in our two cities:

Area of Instruction	St. Stevens	Peters
Hobbies and recreation	19*	11
Vocational education	8	8
Other	5*	2
Total schools	31	21

*One of the schools provided instruction both in dancing and in foreign languages.

The main difference between the two cities was in the number of schools teaching recreational skills. Each city had eight vocational schools, while other types of instruction were offered at five locations in St. Stevens and at two in Peters.

Beginning with St. Stevens, the thirty-one proprietary schools included the following:

a) Recreational
   (1) Nine music schools with a total adult enrollment of 256 students.
   (2) Eight dancing schools with a combined enrollment of 360 adults. Four of these schools also offered instruction in body conditioning and physical fitness (to about thirty adults); one also offered classes in music (to twenty-five or thirty adults); and one combined dancing instruction with courses in foreign languages (to about thirty-five adults).
   (3) One flying school which gave instruction to about sixty or seventy adults during the period of our inventory.
   (4) One art school with twenty-five adult students.
b) Vocational education
   (1) Three hairdressing schools reporting a total enrollment of 215 students.
   (2) One IBM school with seventy-two registered students.
   (3) Two commercial and business colleges: one quite large, reporting 273 students registered in accounting, secretarial, typing, shorthand, and comptometer classes; and one much smaller school which would divulge information neither about its enrollment nor its course offerings.
   (4) One industrial electronics school with 120 registered adults, offering a seventy-five-week course in radio and television maintenance and repair, automatic timing devices, and so on.
   (5) One tool and die design school, offering courses in industrial mathematics, mechanical drawing, tool design, and die design. No enrollment figures were provided.
c) Other proprietary schools
   (1) One school of physical fitness and exercising with nineteen students.
   (2) Two driving schools with approximately 250 students.
   (3) One Dale Carnegie Institute which reported from thirty to thirty-five students during the period covered in our survey.

The twenty-one proprietary schools in Peters consisted of the following:

a) Recreational
   (1) Five dancing schools, most of which restricted their instruction to ballroom dancing. Three of the five provided us with enrollment figures, which totaled 190 adults.

(2) Four music schools, of which three reported enrollments totaling 800. It was not clear, however, whether all these enrollees were adults.

(3) One school of judo and karate, with forty students.

(4) One riding academy, offering a four-week riding course to a class of thirty.

b) Vocational education

(1) Three hairdressing colleges, reporting a total enrollment of 160 aspirant hairdressers.

(2) One barber college with forty-two enrolled trainees.

(3) One "charm and career" school for women, reporting 250 enrollees.

(4) One school of practical nursing with forty-four enrolled students.

(5) One technical college offering extensive training in the field of industrial electronics. Total enrollment was 260.

(6) One college of business and commerce which offered diplomas in the following fields: accounting and auditing; promotion and selling; management assistance; junior accounting; executive secretarial; receptionists; clerical and business machines; speedwriting; shorthand; IBM keypunching; and calculating machines. The school reported an annual day-school enrollment of 410, an evening school enrollment of 375, and an enrollment of 160 in a special division for real estate agents.

c) Other proprietary schools

(1) One driver-training school with an enrollment of 160.

(2) One school of public speaking and "leadership," offering both classes and individual instruction in the areas of human relations, public speaking, and salesmanship. No enrollment figures were made available to us.

These profiles thus indicate a very similar range of proprietary schools in each city, with music and dancing schools in plentiful supply, and at least one business college, technical college, hairdressing school, and driving school available in each city. These six fields of instruction pretty well characterize the educational activities of profit-making schools, since they account for forty of the fifty-two schools located in the two cities.

Because the figures on adult registrations in these schools were in some cases withheld and in others simply estimated by the proprietors, it is impossible to derive an accurate figure on the total adult enrollment in these schools during the period of our inventory. For some schools the statistics can be assumed to be quite accurate, and for others at least rough estimates can be made with some degree of confidence. The totals in Table 15.7, in any event, can probably be reported as at least not grossly inaccurate.

In sum, then, the known and estimated adult enrollments in proprietary schools totaled to 1,744 in Peters and to 1,713 in St. Stevens. Taking into account that some schools are not included here and that some of the other figures may be inflated by the inclusion of children and teen-agers, we can probably conclude that somewhere in the vicinity of 2,000 adults in each city attended classes at profit-making schools during the period of our inventory. Even if these totals are only roughly correct, they indicate that proprietary schools represent an extremely important segment of the educational resources used by adults in these cities. Indeed, if accurate, they suggest that in Peters more adults attended profit-making schools than attended secondary schools and that in St. Stevens more took courses in these schools than did so in the colleges and universities.

FACILITIES IN OTHER COMMUNITY INSTITUTIONS

1. *Government Agencies*

When government agencies were surveyed, a large number of activities were reported which would not be classified as system-

Table 15.7 Total Adult Enrollment in 52 Proprietary Schools

Type of School	St. Stevens	Peters
Music schools	256	Unknown
Dancing schools	360	About 300
Other recreational instruction	About 90	70
Hairdressing or barbering schools	215	204
Commercial and business colleges	About 300	About 450
Technical schools and colleges	192	260
Other vocational schools	Unknown	About 300
Driving schools	250	160
All other	About 50	Unknown
Total known or estimated	1,713	1,744

atic programs of instruction according to the criteria set up for our inventory. First, officials from agencies or departments representing all levels of government gave frequent speeches, talks, or lectures to various groups in the community, and while these programs were sometimes organized as information campaigns by the agencies themselves, most often they took the form of *ad hoc* presentations initiated at the request of some local organization, interest group, or radio or television station.

A second way in which public agencies were involved in adult education was through financial support: grants to educational institutions to allow programs to be set up or administered, and direct financial assistance to individuals to enable them to enroll in vocational training classes. The most extensive of these endeavors during the period of our survey was that of the State Employment Service in St. Stevens, which was in charge of administering funds available under federal manpower retraining legislation. Enrollees for these programs were selected by the Employment Service and then entered vocational programs in the city's high schools. During the period of the inventory, 110 men had been recruited into training programs in mechanical drafting, clerical skills, auto mechanics, and service station work.

The other programs of this type were as follows. In both cities the State Rehabilitation Office provided tuition support for handicapped adults to enter vocational programs in the local schools. At the time of the survey, ninety-eight persons in Peters and seventy-eight in St. Stevens had received assistance under this plan. In St. Stevens, the County Public Health Department sponsored classes for expectant parents, which were conducted in local hospitals. St. Stevens also had a Federal Apprenticeship Training Bureau which coordinated the various apprenticeship programs in local industries. During the period covered by our survey 268 men were enrolled in programs in construction work, graphic arts, metal work, maintenance work, and auto mechanics.

Another type of educational activity which did not quite fall within the limits of our inventory was that of agricultural extension workers. Co-operative Extension offices were located in both St. Stevens and Peters, however, and agricultural agents conducted numerous meetings and demonstrations for farm groups in surrounding rural areas during the period of our study.

The two categories of instruction which met the criteria of our inventory best were programs of in-service or employee training for government workers, and formal courses of instruction offered to the general public or to specialized groups not employed by the government. Our findings on these activities are listed in Tables 15.8 and 15.9.

Table 15.8 indicates that during the period of our inventory ten different government branches, agencies, or departments in St. Stevens and five in Peters provided training of one type or another to their employees or personnel.[3] These programs were found at all levels of government—federal, state, county, township, and municipal.

Although no enrollment statistics were made available to us, the largest of these programs in terms of the number of adults reached were undoubtedly those offered within various branches of the armed services. In St. Stevens the reserve units of the army, navy, air force, and marine corps—and the national guard as well—all reported that courses had been given in the military and technical fields relevant to service occupations.

Within other branches of government, the most extensive activities were those provided by the municipal police and fire departments and the county welfare and public health departments. During the period covered by our survey, several hundred men in each center received training in protection and security, although the bulk of this instruction was given to volunteer firemen in the small municipalities surrounding the two cities.

Six agencies in St. Stevens and four in Peters also provided programs of instruction directly to the public. As indicated by Table 15.9, the largest of these was a program of arts and crafts instruction sponsored by the city recreation department in Peters. These classes were conducted in a municipal recreation center, and nine hundred persons were estimated to have been

[3]In Peters no information was obtained from the armed forces units there, but these branches would in all likelihood have offered a range of training courses similar to those found in St. Stevens.

in attendance during fall, 1962. A similar program, which included films and lectures as well, was organized for senior citizens by the recreation department in St. Stevens.

The state and county health and civil defense authorities also offered courses of instruction to various publics in each city. The activities of the former consisted of public health courses

Table 15.8 In-Service and Employee Training Programs Sponsored by Government Agencies and Departments in Peters and St. Stevens, Fall, 1962

Level of Government	Agency or Department	Content of Instruction and Number of Employees or Personnel Involved	
		St. Stevens	Peters
Federal	Armed forces (reserves)	Service school Cooking school Communications Mechanical school Surveying school Air force job specialties Officer career courses Command and general staff (no figures)	No information available
	Selective service	Letter writing (3)	None
	Social Security Administration	Management training (3) Claims (19) Stenography (8)	None
	Internal Revenue	Tax law Public relations Accounting (no figures)	None
State and county	Police	Security training (no figures)	None
	County airport	Safety and rescue procedures (15)	None
	Welfare	Public welfare (40)	Social service work (15)
	Public Health	Sanitation (20)	Public Health (75)
City and township	Fire	Firefighting (350) Officer training (no figures) Radioactive monitoring (426)	Firefighting (330)
	Police	Police work (no figures) Training course for school-crossing guards (55)	Police work (30)
	City hall	None	Correspondence course in municipal gov't (10)

aimed at special groups connected either with the health professions or with the administration and maintenance of public institutions, while those of the latter were aimed at the public at large and covered the first-aid field. Curiously, it was the Peters Fire Department which conducted a course under the title of "Civil Defense."

Finally, three additional programs were recorded in St. Stevens for which there were no equivalent offerings in Peters. First, the St. Stevens police department sponsored a continuing program of driver education, with one section devoted to retraining drivers convicted of serious traffic violations and another for training driving instructors. In addition, the County Welfare Department offered several classes in home management and child care to female relief recipients. And finally,

Table 15.9 Formal Courses of Instruction Offered to the General Public or to Groups Other Than Government Employees, by Government Agencies: Peters and St. Stevens, Fall, 1962

Level of Government	Agency or Department	Content of Instruction and Number of Persons Enrolled	
		St. Stevens	Peters
Federal	–	None	None
State and county	Soil Conservation Agency	Soil conservation (177)	None
	Public Welfare	Cooking and sewing (40) Child care (40) Household management (25)	None
	Civil Defense	Medical self-help (358)	First aid (31)
	Health	Home nursing (8) Nursing home administration (20) Training course for school custodians (100) Safety (25)	Public health for nurses (57)
City and township	Recreation	Crafts for senior citizens (40)	Arts and crafts (900)
	Fire	None	Civil defense (22)
	Police	Driver improvement (300) Training course for driving instructors (35)	None

during the late fall of 1962, a program of instruction on soil conservation was offered to several farm groups by the County Soil and Water Conservation officials.

2. *Business and Industry*

For the survey of business and industry, all companies that employed fifty or more persons were contacted and information was obtained concerning any training programs or other educational courses offered by the company to its employees. A total of 134 companies were contacted in the two cities—68 in St. Stevens and 66 in Peters—and the incidence of educational programs among them is reported in Table 15.10.

These results indicate that companies were involved in two ways in the education of their employees: through training programs of their own and by providing tuition reimbursement for enrollment in courses at educational institutions, the latter being more prevalent.

About one employer in four in each city had offered support of this type during fall, 1962. These reimbursement plans varied considerably from company to company, however: some offered

Table 15.10 Involvement of Business and Industry in Employee Education, by City

Type of Involvement	St. Stevens (Per Cent)		Peters (Per Cent)	
Own training program, or tuition reimbursement to employees		35		30
Tuition reimbursement	24		27	
Own training program	19		14	
Inactive		65		70
Total		100		100
Total companies with 50 or more employees		68		66
Number of employees who received tuition reimbursement (September–December, 1962)		292		451
Number of enrollments in company-sponsored training programs (September–December, 1962)		2,930		490

higher rates of support for credit than for non-credit courses, and others based the amount of reimbursement on the academic performance of the employee. One St. Stevens manufacturer, for example, allowed 90 per cent reimbursement for a grade of A, 65 per cent for B, 40 per cent for C, and none at all for a grade of D or lower. Under most of these programs, the courses chosen had to be related to the employee's current or aspired position within the company, although this was not a universal mandate. In any event, during the period of our inventory 292 employees in St. Stevens and 451 in Peters took advantage of company-sponsored tuition reimbursement programs.

The most direct mode of involvement, of course, is for a company itself to take over the functions of training its employees, and programs of this type were located in 19 per cent of the companies in St. Stevens and in 14 per cent of those in Peters. The figures again are not grossly dissimilar, but the presence of extremely active programs in two St. Stevens industries resulted in a sizeable difference between the cities in the overall enrollment figures for these programs. In St. Stevens, there were nearly three thousand compared with fewer than five hundred in Peters, and, even though these figures represent total registrations rather than the number of different workers involved, they suggest that many more workers in St. Stevens than in Peters had benefited from company training programs. In Peters, of course, considerably more workers had received instruction under tuition sponsorship plans, and these two findings in combination reveal a somewhat different pattern of industrial involvement in the two cities. The most likely explanation for this difference relates to the nature of resources for technical and business studies available at the university level in each city. In particular, the presence of strong engineering and business programs in the Evening College of Peters University and the absence of such programs in St. Stevens suggests that university adult education facilities were better suited to the needs of business and industry in the former city than in the latter. More generally, this suggests that when local colleges and universities do provide full adult programs in the business and technical fields there is less need for private companies themselves to enter the field of employee training.

Table 15.10 shows that about one employer in three was engaged in one or other (or both) of these two types of programs, and that the general incidence of these programs was about the same in each city—35 per cent in St. Stevens and 30 per cent in Peters.

One additional finding of considerable interest is that larger companies are much more likely than smaller ones to provide educational benefits for their employees. The evidence for this is contained in Table 15.11, where the 134 companies have been divided into four categories based on the number of workers employed. Here, extremely large differences appear, with the incidence of activity ranging from 19 per cent among companies hiring no more than 100 employees to 75 per cent among those who employ 500 or more. Moreover, quite similar trends may be noted for both reimbursement plans and training programs: for the former the incidence ranges from about one company in seven to better than six in ten; and for the latter from fewer than one in ten to exactly 50 per cent. These results indicate quite clearly that very few small businesses provide any kind of educational benefits for their employees, and that one's chances of

Table 15.11 Involvement of Business and Industry in Employee Education, by Size of Company

Activity	Number of Employees			
	51 – 100 (Per Cent)	101 – 250 (Per Cent)	251 – 500 (Per Cent)	Over 500 (Per Cent)
Conduct own training programs or provide tuition reimbursement to employees	19	21	44	75
Tuition reimbursement	13	15	33	62
Own training program	8	5	22	50
Inactive	81	79	56	25
Total	100	100	100	100
Base (number of companies)	53	39	18	24

access to company-sponsored educational programs are much higher in a large organization than in a small one.

Two of the larger employers in the St. Stevens area offer interesting illustrations of the extremely varied range of some employee training programs. The first of these was the program of an electrical equipment manufacturer who operated two plants in the St. Stevens area and employed over 6,000 workers in the two operations. During the period of our inventory this company sponsored fifteen different educational programs for a combined enrollment of 1,657. These activities are shown in Table 15.12.

The second example comes from a manufacturer of automotive equipment which conducted courses not only for its 2,000 St. Stevens employees but for the dealers and servicemen handling the company's products as well. This company reported 1,231 enrollments for seven fields of study (Table 15.13).

Table 15.12 Employee Training Program of One St. Stevens Manufacturer (Electrical Equipment)

Course	Number of Employees Involved
6-week computer course	345
40-hour supervisory training course	309
10-hour communications course	302
Training course for foremen	185
An office personnel training course	135
Reimbursement of 85 per cent of tuition fees of engineers engaged in graduate studies at Midwest University	130
20-hour orientation course for new employees	62
14-hour speech course	48
16-hour conference leadership course	40
24-hour course in product testing	28
24-hour course in quality control	28
20-hour pre-supervisory training course	15
8-hour course in report writing	12
2-week retraining course for hourly workers displaced from their jobs	12
6-month junior engineer's training program	6

3. *YMCA's and Related Institutions*

In both Peters and St. Stevens special educational programs for adults were found in the YMCA's. Table 15.14 confirms that these institutions were indeed active in each city, and that in Peters courses of instruction were available in the YWCA as well. Four categories of subject matter are represented in these listings, with courses in the recreational, home life, and personal development areas available in both cities, and instruction in foreign languages (classified in the academic category) available only in Peters. All in all, over 900 course enrollments were reported for Peters, and, compared with the 224 reported for St. Stevens, this implies a considerably more extensive adult program in the former city than in the latter.

Twenty-five course titles are listed in Table 15.14; of these ten (42 per cent) are in recreation and eight (33 per cent) are in home and family life. A much more revealing indicator of the relative scope of these programs, however, is that 81 per cent of the total enrollments in all three institutions were in just three types of courses: swimming classes (40 per cent), dancing classes (26 per cent), and contract bridge lessons (16 per cent). The YMCA's contribution to adult education, therefore, can be said to be primarily in the general field of recreational skills.

4. *Churches and Synagogues*

In order to survey the religious institutions in each city, a

---

Table 15.13 Employee Training Program of One St. Stevens Manufacturer (Automotive Equipment)

Course	Number of Employees Involved
72-hour supervisory training course	418
72-hour pre-supervisory training program	300
Technical training course for dealers and servicing agents	243
16-hour product-testing course	180
24-hour course in industrial electronics	50
36-hour course in industrial hydraulics	30
Sales training course	10

Table 15.14 Adult Education Programs in YMCA's and YWCA's, Peters and St. Stevens, Fall, 1962

Category of Instruction	Peters, YMCA (Total Enrollment, 287)		Peters, YWCA (Total Enrollment, 618)		St. Stevens, YMCA (Total Enrollment, 224)	
Academic subjects	French (2)*	17	Conversational Spanish	8	None	
	German	8				
Hobbies and recreation	Bridge (2)	68	Bridge (3)	68	Bridge	44
	Dancing (5)	151	Dancing (4)	102	Dancing	38
	Painting (3)	31	Swimming and exercising (18)	387†	Swimming (4)	60
	Photography	6				
Home and family life	Investments	6	Millinery	8	Furniture upholstering	28
			Sewing (2)	16	Investments	9
			Christmas crafts	16		
			Interior decorating	7		
			Auto mechanics for women	6		
Personal development	None		Swimming and exercising (18)	387†	Body building	15
					Judo	15
					Reducing	15

*Number in parentheses indicates number of courses if more than one.
†Cross-classified.

one-third sample of the churches and synagogues was selected and attempts were then made to contact either the clergy or church officers in each of these institutions. Information was subsequently obtained from eighty of eighty-three churches selected in St. Stevens and from forty-nine of fifty-nine selected in Peters, with completion rates of 96 per cent and 83 per cent, respectively.

From the results of this survey, it is possible to identify three ways in which churches and synagogues provide formal religious instruction to the adult members of their congregations.

a) Special classes or discussion groups to instruct converts or prospective church members in the basic teachings and doctrines of the church.

b) Study or discussion groups led by clergymen or church elders designed to help adults increase their knowledge of the history and teachings of the church.

c) Special programs for the training of Sunday school teachers, church missionaries, and other church functionaries.

Although it was not always clear whether the educational activities reported by church representatives were genuinely distinct from the regular religious services and social functions of the church, it would appear that at least a majority of the religious institutions in each city did offer at least one of these forms of instruction: over 90 per cent in St. Stevens and a minimum of 60 per cent in Peters reported activities that would probably fit into one or another of these categories.

In addition to these activities, some 12 per cent of the churches in Peters and 8 per cent in St. Stevens reported instructional activities in subject matter other than religion. In Peters, the following activities were reported by six different churches: an anti-communism class to thirty adults (Protestant Sectarian); a literary study group with fifteen members (Congregational); music instruction on wind instruments to eighteen adults (Salvation Army); an adult choir class in which basic musical training was provided to twenty-four adults (Church of God); a program of public speaking classes to sixty adults

(Catholic); and a first-aid class to seven adults (Seventh Day Adventists).

In St. Stevens, four different types of non-religious instructional programs were located—again in six different churches or temples: three literary groups involving some ninety-five adults (Unitarian, Methodist, and Jewish); two world-affairs study groups (total membership undetermined) (Unitarian and Jewish); two family life study groups involving seventy adults (Nazarene and Catholic) and one class in family living to thirty adults (Nazarene); a social problems study group (membership undetermined) (Methodist).

5. *Hospitals*

Although neither city had a medical school, there were three schools of nursing in Peters and two nursing schools and a school of medical technology in St. Stevens. In addition to these facilities, the local hospitals in both cities also provided in-service training for hospital orderlies and nurses' aides and classes in practical nursing.

In St. Stevens only, in-service training for hospital administrators, ward clerks, and x-ray technicians and classes for expectant parents (co-sponsored with the County Health Department) were available. The only educational programs of hospitals open to the general public were training classes in practical nursing, which were available in both cities, and parenthood classes, available in St. Stevens only.

6. *Libraries, Museums, and Art Centers*

In St. Stevens the libraries and museums were completely inactive in adult education, although the public library occasionally made its facilities available to study groups of one type or another. However, St. Stevens did have a well-organized community art school which was supported in part from tax dollars and in part from student tuitions. During the period covered by the inventory this school conducted ten different classes in drawing, painting, sculpture, and art appreciation, and had a total enrollment of 302 adults.

In Peters the only educational program offered in any institution of this type was a Great Books discussion group of fifteen members which met in the public library.

VOLUNTARY ORGANIZATIONS AND ASSOCIATIONS

Very few educational programs which met the minimum requirements set up for this section of the inventory were found in the voluntary organizations and associations in either city. Although guest speakers and lecturers are standard fare at the regular meetings of organizations of this type, these programs are typically *ad hoc* presentations, with the subject matter shifting from meeting to meeting. On occasion, of course, examples were found of private groups that had organized lecture programs or study groups which went on for more than one or two sessions, or had provided systematic programs of instruction, either for their members or for some outside group. It is only these more enduring types of instructional and informational programs which will be discussed in the following section of the report. As was indicated earlier, the educational programs of voluntary organizations and associations were recorded only if a minimum of four meetings or sessions were devoted to the same topic, and if the program reached a total audience of at least twenty adults.

By taking a one-third sample of the voluntary organizations and associations in each city, information was obtained from a total of 153 groups in Peters and 142 in St. Stevens. Of these, Table 15.15 shows that 12 per cent in Peters and 7 per cent in St. Stevens were engaged in one or another type of educational activity which satisfied the minimum recording standards. Although these rates of activity are low, they nonetheless represent a sizeable difference between the two communities.

Upon closer scrutiny it turned out that while most of the educational activities conducted by voluntary groups were for the members of the organization itself, six of the twenty-nine programs in the two cities (21 per cent) were organized for the benefit of some other group in the community. At least to a limited extent, then, voluntary organizations can be said to function as producers as well as consumers of adult education facilities.

Quite surprisingly, only three lecture programs were found which met the minimum standards, illustrating the fleeting nature of these programs in voluntary organizations. Well over one-half of the organizations and associations contacted reported that speakers or lecturers had addressed their group during fall, 1962, but only three of these programs consisted of as many as four presentations on the same general topic offered to a minimum audience of twenty adults. By comparison, seven situations were found in which a program of formal instruction had been presented to members of the organization.

A brief description of the content of these different programs concludes the inventory. Though the list of programs is not exhaustive, it does illustrate the range of studies which were undertaken by private groups in the two cities. The programs were as follows.

Study groups (Peters seven, St. Stevens six). — Twelve of the thirteen study groups were in religious organizations and associations, and all of these were concerned with religious studies of one type or another. There were six in each city. The only other study group found in either city consisted of a group of Peters physicians who met once a month to discuss medical problem cases.

Courses of instruction for group members (Peters six, St.

Table 15.15 Incidence of Instructional Programs in Voluntary Organizations and Associations, Peters and St. Stevens, Fall, 1962

Classification	Peters (Per Cent)		St. Stevens (Per Cent)	
Active in one or more programs of instruction		12		7
Study groups	5		4	
Formal programs of instruction for members	4		1	
Lectures for members	1		1	
Programs of instruction for outside groups	3		1	
Inactive except for occasional speakers or *ad hoc* study groups		88		93
Total		100		100
Total groups contacted		153		142

Stevens one). — Seven different organizations were found which offered courses of instruction.

a) Two music clubs in Peters, which sponsored singing classes for their members.
b) An amateur art group, which hired instructors for drawing and painting classes (Peters).
c) A science academy, which sponsored seminars and classes in different fields of physical science (Peters).
d) A 4-H club, which conducted training classes for group leaders (Peters).
e) A scouting association, which provided classes for scout leaders (Peters).
f) A sportsmen's club, which offered physical fitness classes and instruction in various athletic recreations (St. Stevens).

Organized programs for outside groups (Peters four, St. Stevens two). — The organizations which offered instructional facilities to outside groups or to the public at large were as follows.

a) 4-H clubs conducting homemaking classes (Peters).
b) A businessmen's club, which offered instruction for new brokers and real estate agents (Peters).
c) The mental health associations, which in both cities sponsored workshops for professionals in the mental health field and in St. Stevens offered lectures on mental health to the general public.
d) A health association, which offered classes in nutrition and weight control and public health forums to the public at large (Peters).
e) A professional engineers association, which sponsored a refresher course for persons who had been previously employed in engineering. This course was conducted at a local high school, but instructors were supplied by the association (St. Stevens).

Lecture series (Peters two, St. Stevens one). — All three organizations which sponsored lecture programs were business groups, and all three offered public affairs topics. In both cities programs were offered on "The Nature of Communism" and "Action Politics," and in Peters a "Civil Defense and Home Survival" series was presented as well.

SUMMARY

The following generalizations can be made regarding the nature and abundance of resources for adult education in the two cities selected for this case study.

1. Although the regular school system attracted approximately the same number of adult registrations in each city,[4] the distribution of these resources differed radically in the two communities. Many more college courses were available in Peters than St. Stevens, particularly in academic instruction, teacher training, and engineering. Adult residents in St. Stevens, on the other hand, had a much wider selection of secondary school courses to choose from, particularly in the academic and technical fields and in vocational courses for blue-collar occupations.

2. Although St. Stevens had ten more proprietary schools than Peters, the range of instructional fare in these schools was much the same in the two cities. Both had a number of dancing, music, and hairdressing schools; each housed a major technical college; and each had one large business and commercial college. Although enrollment statistics were incomplete, approximately two thousand adults in each city attended these schools during fall, 1962.

3. Government agencies were found to be active in adult education in four different ways: through the lectures and speaking engagements of public officials, through programs of financial support offered either as grants to educational institutions or as scholarships to individuals, through training programs for civil servants and members of the armed forces, and through courses for groups in the community at large. Although enrollment statistics on in-service training programs sponsored by government were generally inadequate, the agencies which offered courses to the general public had combined enrollments of 1,168 in St. Stevens and 1,010 in Peters. On the basis of these figures it is clear that government agencies made a quite significant contribution to the overall adult education resources in the two communities.

4. Because of the presence of two very extensive company

---

[4]These totaled 4,924 in St. Stevens and 4,238 in Peters. On a per capita basis these represent registration rates of 224 and 235 per 100,000, respectively.

training programs in St. Stevens, considerably more workers in that city than in Peters had been enrolled in employer-sponsored courses during the period of the inventory. In Peters, on the other hand, more workers had received benefits under company-run tuition reimbursement programs, and the most plausible interpretation for this reversal of emphasis is that the presence of well-developed engineering and business administration programs at the Evening College in Peters somewhat obviated the necessity of direct involvement in employee training on the part of private industries in Peters.

Employee training programs were found much more frequently in large companies than in small ones, and while this was hardly unexpected, it is quite revealing that large corporations were also much more likely to provide tuition support for the continuing education of their workers.

5. Although the YMCA's had instructional programs in both cities, considerably more adults were attracted to these classes in Peters than in St. Stevens (905 compared with 224 total enrollments). A majority of these courses were in hobbies and recreation, with the main emphasis on three fields: swimming lessons, dancing classes, and instruction in contract bridge.

6. Although the information obtained from churches was not of uniform quality, it is safe to conclude that a majority of the religious institutions in each city provided some type of religious instruction for adults. Much smaller proportions of churches (some 8 per cent of those contacted in St. Stevens and 12 per cent in Peters) reported educational programs in other fields of subject matter.

7. Hospitals were only minimally active in education, although in both cities in-service training courses were available to medical technicians and hospital service workers, and courses in practical nursing were offered to the general public.

8. One major educational resource available in St. Stevens, but not in Peters, was a community art center. Facilities for art instruction in Peters, on the other hand, were available at the university and the YMCA. Interestingly, no formal adult programs were sponsored by the public libraries in either city.

9. The educational activities of voluntary organizations and

associations were found to be relatively sparse in both cities. Although most of these groups did schedule speakers or lecturers for their meetings, very few of these programs had sufficient continuity to be meaningfully classified as formal programs of instruction. Thus only 12 per cent of the organizations in Peters and 7 per cent in St. Stevens sponsored or conducted activities which survived the minimum recording criteria for the inventory.

In conclusion it is clear that in the two cities described in this chapter the provision of educational facilities for adults was shared among a sizeable number of community institutions: in both cities the high schools, colleges, proprietary schools, government agencies, private businesses, and YMCA's made substantial contributions to the overall educational resources of the community. Residents of St. Stevens had more resources in the secondary schools and private industry and, unlike their counterparts in Peters, had access to a community art school. Adult residents in Peters, on the other hand, had a much wider range of university-level courses to choose from, and the YMCA programs in that city were somewhat better developed as well. All in all, the educational facilities in these cities could be described as more similar than dissimilar, and the most important question for the final section of the study therefore is what the consequences are of having the principal adult education resources of the community organized within different levels of the regular school system.

16

Knowledge of
and Reactions to
Existing Educational
Facilities

The final chapter in this section is concerned with the general question of how adults perceive, evaluate, and use the educational resources in their local communities. There are two main issues on which the analysis is centered: the extent to which adults are aware of the educational resources available in their local environment and the extent to which differences in the availability of facilities have any detectable effect on the attitudes and behavior of adults living in different communities.

As soon as the results of the inventories had been examined, it became apparent that Peters and St. Stevens offered a unique opportunity for a comparative study of cities which differed markedly in resources at different levels of the regular school system. In deciding on these two cities for the follow-up study, moreover, our attention was deflected away from the general problem of the effects of gross community differences in the overall supply of resources and was focused rather on the question of the relative impact of having the principal resources concentrated in an evening college or in the public high schools. The most plausible hypothesis in this connection was that an extensive high-school program would be better suited to the learning needs of the less well-educated in the population, while conversely, a relative abundance of facilities at the college level would be more important for the educational interests of persons who had gone farther in their formal schooling. One possible outcome of the differential distribution of facilities in Peters and St. Stevens, in other words, was that among high-school graduates, rates of interest and participation in educational pursuits might be found to be higher in Peters, while among those who had not finished high school exactly the opposite tendency would be expected.

To carry out this phase of the study, random samples of households were selected from the urbanized areas of the two cities, and personal interviews were then conducted with persons between the ages of twenty-one and sixty-five. Interviews were obtained from 281 of 335 adults sampled in St. Stevens and from 265 of 320 in Peters, with completion rates of 84 and 83 per cent, respectively.

Although the interview schedule for this phase of the study covered an extremely wide range of topics (see Appendix 2), only those results having a direct bearing on the substantive concerns of the present chapter will be reported here. These are the results which pertain to people's knowledge of facilities for study, their preferences for different institutional settings for study, their prior experiences with continuing education, and their readiness to become involved in formal learning activities.

KNOWLEDGE OF FACILITIES FOR LEARNING

In Chapter 10 we reported that 52 per cent of the national sample of adults said they knew of some place in the community where adults could receive instruction in a foreign language, while 55 per cent said they knew of places where other types of subjects could be studied. Since there was no way in the national survey to test the correctness of the answers given to these questions, however, it was not possible to represent these findings as more than claims to information. In the community studies, on the other hand, it was possible to check the answers people gave to these questions against the information obtained from the inventories, and for this reason the present data provide a much more valid measure of the extent to which adults are aware of the different educational resources in their community.

As an overall measure of awareness, respondents were first asked the following question:

[QUESTION 18] Do you know of any places in or around (CITY) where people no longer in school can attend classes or receive instruction in any subject at all?

The answers of both high-school graduates and non-graduates on this question are reported in Table 16.1. These indicate that in Peters and St. Stevens considerably more adults were able to name at least one active institution than was the case in the nation as a whole: among those who had not completed high school, almost two in three named at least one institution correctly; among those who had completed at least twelve years of schooling, 85 per cent in St. Stevens and 89 per cent in Peters made at least one correct identification. These levels are roughly equivalent to the proportions of persons of high and middle socio-economic status in cities between fifty thousand and two million who claimed to know of at least one adult education facility (see Table 10.10).

For the cities as a whole, weighted estimates[1] indicated that some 77 per cent of the adults in St. Stevens and 79 per cent in Peters correctly identified at least one adult education resource. In cities known to contain numerous adult education facilities, then, we could conclude that over three-quarters of the adult population were aware of at least one of these facilities.

The more interesting findings in Table 16.1 pertain to the types of institutions named by residents in each city. First, as in the national survey, the institutions which most often came to mind in this connection were the colleges and high schools. Among high-school graduates these facilities were identified by approximately two persons in three, and in spite of the differential scope of involvement of these institutions in the two cities, secondary schools were mentioned slightly more often by the Peters group, and colleges and universities just as frequently by those in the St. Stevens sample.

---

[1]Because the samples yielded disproportionate numbers of high-school graduates in the two cities (a discrepancy which was not indicated by the 1960 census figures for the two cities), most of the results to be discussed in this chapter will be reported separately for persons who did and did not complete high school. In cases where single estimates are made for the cities as a whole, they are weighted to contain the same proportion of high-school graduates as was found in the combined samples for both cities.

Table 16.1 Awareness of Facilities for Adult Instruction, by Education and City (Per Cent Who Named Each Institution)

Active Institutions Named	Less Than 12 Years of School		12 Years of School or More	
	St. Stevens	Peters	St. Stevens	Peters
Named one or more resources correctly	65	64	85	89
City or suburban high school	56	40	64	70
College or university	23	39	71	70
YMCA or YWCA	20	11	24	35
Local business college	7	23	17	26
Other proprietary schools	2	5	7	5
Miscellaneous other	14	15	27	28
Did not name any institution	35	36	15	11
Total	100	100	100	100
Base	127	100	152	164

Among the non-high-school graduates, however, sizeable discrepancies in awareness may be noted: some 16 per cent more non-graduates in St. Stevens than in Peters mentioned secondary-school facilities, while in Peters a similar plurality mentioned college and university facilities. Moreover, in St. Stevens non-high-school graduates were much more likely to name secondary schools than universities (56 per cent compared with 23 per cent) while among the comparable group in Peters, rates of identification of these two facilities were almost identical (40 and 39 per cent).

These results suggest that a differential availability of facilities can produce substantial differences of awareness in one segment of the public but not in others. A majority of high-school graduates in both cities were aware of both high-school and college facilities, and their awareness did not appear to depend very much on whether facilities were plentiful or scarce. Among non-graduates, on the other hand, levels of awareness fluctuated in direct response to the scope of various offerings: where a program was more highly developed, persons in the lower educational bracket were much more likely to be aware of it.

Two other community differences may also be noted in Table 16.1. First, private business colleges seem much better known in Peters than in St. Stevens, since much higher proportions in both educational categories identified these as available facilities. Business colleges, moreover, were the only proprietary schools mentioned by any significant portion of the population: fewer than 10 per cent in either city mentioned all other profit-making schools put together.

A second difference between the communities, and a quite interesting one, was that while YMCA programs were better known to non-high-school graduates in St. Stevens than in Peters (20 per cent compared with 11 per cent), they were mentioned by high-school graduates considerably more often in Peters than St. Stevens (35 compared with 24 per cent). Since the course offerings at these institutions were much the same in both cities, there is no readily apparent explanation for this difference. The results seem to suggest, however, that these institutions aimed their programs at quite different audiences in the two cities.

Apart from these institutions, no other educational facilities were mentioned by as many as one person in ten. When adults in these two cities thought about facilities for learning, then, they thought almost exclusively of four types of institutions: secondary schools, colleges and universities, private colleges, and YMCA's. They tended not to think of government agencies, local industries, churches and synagogues, proprietary schools other than business colleges, voluntary organizations, or other community institutions as places one might go to receive instruction.

As might be anticipated, high-school graduates were not only more likely to name at least one learning facility, but were aware of a much wider range of resources than their less well-educated neighbors. Table 16.2 shows that approximately one-third of the secondary-school graduates in each city were able to name four or more local resources, while only about one-tenth of the non-graduates were able to name that many. High-school graduates identified an average of just under three different facilities, while non-graduates named less than one and one-half, on the average.

Next, respondents were asked if they knew of any places in the community where instruction was available in each of thirteen specific subjects (see Question 19). These were selected to represent all major subject categories, and included the following:

Category	Subject Title
Academic	Elementary mathematics
	Advanced mathematics
Vocational: white collar	How to manage a business
	Typing and shorthand
Vocational: blue collar	Auto mechanics
Hobbies and recreation	Dancing lessons
	Swimming lessons
	Music appreciation
Home and family skills	Cooking or homemaking
Personal development	Public speaking
	Speed reading
Religion	Different religions of the world
Public affairs	Politics and government

Although some instruction was available in practically all these fields around the time our respondents were interviewed, some facilities were more plentiful in one city than in the other, and there were a number of other cases where the instruction was offered at different institutions in the two cities. Classes in typing and shorthand, business management, dancing, and swimming were plentiful in both cities, and similarly, public speaking, speed reading, and music appreciation, although less plentiful, were nonetheless available in both cities. Courses in mathematics, on the other hand, were offered primarily at the university level in Peters, but at the secondary-school level in St. Stevens. For example, in Peters there were twelve mathematics courses recorded at Peters University, compared with just two in the secondary schools; in St. Stevens, only one was recorded in the colleges and universities, compared with eight in the secondary schools. Facilities for adult studies in home economics and government were somewhat more plentiful in St. Stevens than in Peters, while in comparative religion the only instruction recorded in either city was a course at Peters University. The most striking difference in available resources among the subjects listed here, however, was in auto mechanics. During the period of our inventory, an extensive training program in this field was available in St. Stevens, and although similar training had been offered in the Peters high schools at times in the past,

Table 16.2 Number of Different Adult Education Facilities Identified, by Number of Years of Education and by City

Number of Facilities Identified	Cumulative Percentages			
	Less Than 12 Years		12 Years or More	
	St. Stevens (N = 127)	Peters (N = 100)	St. Stevens (N = 152)	Peters (N = 164)
Four or more	7	10	33	38
Three or more	18	30	55	62
Two or more	45	42	77	78
One or more	65	64	85	89
Mean number identified	1.42	1.48	2.93	2.94

there was no such instruction during the 1962–63 school year.

The responses which people gave to these questions were examined to determine the subjects for which adults are more and less likely to identify facilities, to find out whether rates of awareness among specific subgroups in the population differed between the two cities, and to determine the institutions most frequently associated with certain selected subjects from the listing.

Table 16.3 shows the proportion of adults in each city who named one or more local institutions in connection with each of the thirteen subjects.[2] Here, subjects are ordered according to the frequency with which facilities were named by the St. Stevens respondents, although with only minor inversions the same

[2]These answers have not been classified according to whether they were "correct" or "incorrect" in terms of the specific course offerings listed in the inventories. Rather, they indicate only that a person said he had heard about such instruction, and was then able to name a specific local institution where the instruction had been offered. The general problem with scoring the answers according to the findings of the inventory in question is that the instruction in question may very well have been offered at periods other than those covered by our facilities survey. Later in this section, however, some attempt will be made to appraise the validity of the sources people identified.

Table 16.3 Awareness of Facilities for Studies of Specific Subjects, by City (Per Cent Who Named One or More Institutions for Each Subject)*

Subject	St. Stevens (N = 279)	Peters (N = 264)	Difference
Swimming	89	84	+ 5
Typing and shorthand	80	81	− 1
Dancing lessons	70	78	− 8
Advanced mathematics	70	66	+ 4
Elementary mathematics	66	53	+13
Public speaking	59	68	− 9
How to manage a business	56	64	− 8
Politics and government	54	49	+ 5
Cooking or homemaking	53	47	+ 6
Auto mechanics	47	35	+12
Music appreciation	47	44	+ 3
Speed reading	39	47	− 8
Different religions of the world	30	33	− 3

*Estimates based on samples matched on proportion of high-school graduates.

ranking describes the answers given by the Peters sample as well.[3] The figures are seen to range from highs of 89 and 84 per cent for swimming instruction to lows of 30 and 33 per cent for instruction in comparative religion. Facilities for instruction in typing and shorthand, and dancing were familiar to about three-quarters of the adults in each city, and at least one-half identified some facility in connection with a majority of the subjects listed. However, learning facilities for auto mechanics, music appreciation, speed reading, and comparative religion were unfamiliar to more than one-half of the respondents in each city, and in Peters, in addition, fewer than one-half could name institutions offering courses in cooking and homemaking or in politics and government.

The overall differences between the cities are shown in the third column of the table, where it may be noted that only two subjects were characterized by discrepancies of ten or more percentage points:[4] 13 per cent more persons in St. Stevens than in Peters identified resources for studying elementary mathematics, and 12 per cent more knew where to go for training in auto mechanics. Both these differences can be quite readily interpreted on the basis of the known facilities in each city; the advantages of St. Stevens in connection with mathematics instruction in the secondary schools and in training in auto mechanics have already been pointed out.

In general, these results indicate quite clearly that awareness of instructional facilities varies tremendously across different fields of subject matter. Large majorities of adults in both communities knew where to go to learn how to swim, dance, or type, but fewer than one-half knew where an adult could learn to be an auto mechanic, attend music appreciation classes, take a speed reading course, or study comparative religion.

Table 16.4 re-examines these same results by comparing levels of awareness among aggregates with differing amounts of formal education. In this table responses are presented separately for persons who did and did not complete high school, and

---

[3]The rank-order correlation between the two listings is .93.

[4]For samples of this size any percentage difference of ten or larger would be statistically significant at the two sigma level.

Table 16.4 Awareness of Facilities for Studies of Specific Subjects, by Educational Attainment and City (Per Cent Who Named One or More Institutions for Each Subject)

a. Persons with Less Than Twelve Years of Formal Schooling

Subject	St. Stevens (N = 127)	Peters (N = 100)	Difference
Elementary mathematics	58	41	+17
Auto mechanics	39	23	+16
Advanced mathematics	56	46	+10
Music appreciation	36	26	+10
Politics and government	35	26	+ 9
Swimming	84	78	+ 6
Different religions of the world	20	14	+ 6
Cooking and homemaking	41	36	+ 5
How to manage a business	43	42	+ 1
Typing and shorthand	72	72	0
Speed reading	25	32	− 7
Dancing lessons	62	71	− 9
Public speaking	38	51	−13
Sum of discrepancies			+51

b. Persons with Twelve or More Years of Schooling

Subject	St. Stevens (N = 152)	Peters (N = 164)	Difference
Elementary mathematics	72	62	+10
Auto mechanics	52	44	+ 8
Cooking and homemaking	62	55	+ 7
Swimming	92	88	+ 4
Politics and government	68	66	+ 2
Advanced mathematics	80	80	0
Music appreciation	55	56	− 1
Typing and shorthand	85	88	− 3
Public speaking	74	80	− 6
Different religions of the world	38	46	− 8
Dancing lessons	75	83	− 8
Speed reading	49	58	− 9
How to manage a business	65	79	−14
Sum of discrepancies			−18

within these subgroups the subjects are ordered according to the sizes of the discrepancies between cities. Looking first at the non-graduates, part *a* shows that St. Stevens respondents were considerably more likely than their Peters counterparts to name facilities for studying mathematics (both elementary and advanced), auto mechanics, and music appreciation, while the Peters sample showed a dominance of ten or more points only in their awareness of resources for instruction in public speaking. Moreover, the third column of part *a* shows a total of nine positive signs compared with just three negative ones; when summed these work out to a sizeable advantage in favor of the St. Stevens group. By comparison, however, part *b* indicates no such overall advantage favoring the St. Stevens high-school graduates: here the third column contains just five positive signs compared with seven negative ones, and what net advantage exists at all is seen to favor the respondents in Peters.

On the basis of these findings, we may conclude that non-high-school graduates in St. Stevens were on the whole better informed about adult education facilities than their Peters counterparts, and that a slight tendency in the opposite direction characterized persons who had completed high school. This is an interesting result, and one which might very well reflect the fact that the main facilities for adult instruction were housed in different educational institutions in the two communities. The results, in short, would be quite consistent with the general proposition that educational facilities are more likely to come to the attention of persons with little formal education when they are organized at the secondary-school level, and more likely to be known to the better-educated when they are offered in a local college or university.

A somewhat different way to approach these same data was to ask what the relative effects of a better formal education actually were on people's awareness of the adult education facilities in these two kinds of settings. In other words, just how much more knowledgeable about resources were high-school graduates than non-graduates, and to what extent did these discrepancies vary between the two cities studied? While evidence pertaining to both these questions could be extracted from Table 16.4, more direct indicators of these tendencies are produced when correlation coefficients between formal schooling and knowledge of resources are computed for each different field of study in each city. These results are presented in Table 16.5.

The first and most apparent finding is that irrespective of city or subject matter, the better educated were more likely than the less well educated to name facilities. All values in Table 16.5 are positive, and the lowest (for auto mechanics in St. Stevens) is +.27, a statistically significant Q value.[5]

Some of these values, moreover, are extremely high, with six falling above .60 and three others above .50. Thus, in nine of the twenty-six conditions examined here, a prediction of whether a person was aware or unaware of facilities would be improved by at least one-half if it were known whether or not he had graduated from high school. At the same time, these relatively high coefficients are all found in subject areas which would not have much meaning or relevance in the lives of persons who had not completed a high-school education: they are found in the more

[5]The appropriate test of statistical significance for Q involves a conversion to chi-square, which in the case of awareness of instruction for auto mechanics in St. Stevens works out to a value of 5.35. With one degree of freedom, the probability that this result occurred by chance factors alone is less than .025.

Table 16.5 Relation between Formal Education and Awareness of Facilities for Different Studies, by City (Q Coefficients between Having 12 or More Years of Schooling and Naming One or More Facilities for Instruction)

Subject	St. Stevens	Peters	Discrepancy
Public speaking	.65	.58	+.07
Cooking and homemaking	.41	.37	+.04
Swimming	.37	.37	.00
Speed reading	.48	.49	−.01
Dancing lessons	.29	.33	−.04
Typing and shorthand	.38	.47	−.09
Politics and government	.60	.69	−.09
Elementary mathematics	.30	.41	−.11
Advanced mathematics	.52	.65	−.13
Auto mechanics	.27	.45	−.18
Music appreciation	.37	.57	−.20
Different religions of the world	.43	.68	−.25
How to manage a business	.42	.68	−.26

intellectual subject areas on the list (comparative religion, music appreciation, and politics and government), in advanced technical studies (advanced mathematics), and in training for organizational leadership (business management and public speaking). In subjects relatively more meaningful to the lower- or lower-middle-class way of life (such as dancing, auto mechanics, or cooking and homemaking), on the other hand, the coefficients tend to be considerably lower. Thus, while the influence of formal schooling on awareness of resources is strong, it is most pronounced in areas where it would be expected to be, so the results are highly plausible.

The most pertinent findings in the present discussion, however, are those in the third column of Table 16.5, which indicate the relative sizes of the correlations in the two cities. Here a very clear pattern emerges: ten of the thirteen coefficients were higher in Peters than in St. Stevens, and only two were lower. The incidence of positive and negative signs, in other words, is clearly in imbalance, indicating that the influence of formal schooling on awareness of resources was much stronger in Peters — a city in which adult education programs were predominantly on the university level — than in St. Stevens, where these courses were relatively abundant in the high schools and relatively scarce in the colleges and universities.

These findings add only a slightly different perspective to our earlier results, but they do suggest that a concentration of adult facilities in institutions of higher learning widens the differences in awareness of the better and more poorly educated segments of the population, while a concentration in the secondary schools tends to narrow this difference. More important, perhaps, the results suggest once again that if the same programs of instruction are offered in different educational institutions, they will come to the attention of different segments of the adult public at quite different rates.

This latter tendency was quite clearly evident when a further examination was made of the facilities named in connection with different types of subject matter. There is little need to report all these data, but Table 16.6 shows the resources correctly identified for four subjects in which instruction was in plentiful supply

Table 16.6 Types of Facilities Identified for Selected Subjects, by Formal Schooling and City (Per Cent Who Correctly Named Different Resources)

Subjects	Less Than 12 Years			12 Years or More		
	St. Stevens (N = 127)	Peters (N = 100)	Difference	St. Stevens (N = 152)	Peters (N = 164)	Difference
Typing and shorthand						
Secondary school	52	21	+31	57	38	+19
Local business college	17	44	−27	37	52	−15
College or university	17	17	Nil	17	16	+ 1
How to manage a business						
Secondary school	16	3	+13	14	10	+ 4
College or university	9	21	−12	25	37	−12
Local business college	3	15	−12	9	17	− 8
Elementary mathematics						
Secondary school	50	20	+30	51	36	+15
College or university	9	17	− 8	28	22	+ 6
Advanced mathematics						
Secondary school	41	15	+26	32	18	+14
College or university	17	31	−14	53	62	− 9

in both cities: typing and shorthand, business management, and elementary and advanced mathematics. Perhaps the most interesting results here are those concerning typing and shorthand instruction, since in both cities courses in these skills were offered in the colleges, the high schools, and the private business schools as well. Table 16.6, however, shows extremely large differences in the rates at which these institutions were named in the two cities: among persons with less than twelve years of schooling, 52 per cent in St. Stevens, compared with 21 per cent in Peters, named a secondary school, while among high-school graduates the comparable figures were 57 and 38 per cent, respectively. In Peters, 27 per cent more non-graduates and 15 per cent more graduates than in St. Stevens associated private business or colleges with typing and shorthand. Colleges and universities were named much less frequently, although (rather surprisingly) by equal proportions in both cities. Thus, even though typing and shorthand instruction was available in all three settings in both cities, the institutions in St. Stevens which most frequently came to mind were the secondary schools, while in Peters they were the private business colleges.

The other three sections of Table 16.6 again indicate the greater propensity of St. Stevens residents to name secondary-school facilities; in addition, they show a similar tendency in Peters to associate the university with resources for adult instruction. For courses in business management, for example, the Peters groups named a university 12 per cent more often than the St. Stevens groups did, and they were also more likely to think of private business colleges in this connection. St. Stevens residents, on the other hand, were again more likely to mention high schools as places to study business management. There is a similar tendency when the facilities for mathematics are named: for elementary mathematics, one-half of the St. Stevens respondents correctly identified a local high school; although high schools were most frequently mentioned by the Peters sample as well, they were named far less often than in St. Stevens. Advanced mathematics show a similar pattern; more persons in St. Stevens than in Peters named a high school, while more in the latter city named a university.

The evidence presented in this section suggests a number of conclusions. First, it is quite obvious that public awareness of educational facilities for adults varies markedly with the subject matter. Large majorities of adults are aware of facilities for learning skills such as swimming, dancing, or typing, while considerably fewer than one-half know of places to study subjects such as auto mechanics or speed reading, or more esoteric topics, such as comparative religion.

Second, it was clear from the evidence that information about adult education facilities is unequally distributed throughout the adult public. Persons who have been to school longer are much more knowledgeable about these facilities than are those with less education, and although this difference was greatest in professional, technical, or managerial subjects, it was nonetheless sharply evident too in those fields of learning which would be of genuine interest and importance to lower- and lower-middle-class respondents.

Third, evidence was also found to support the general proposition that the educational offerings of different institutions come to the attention of quite different segments of the population. Persons without much formal schooling were more likely to know about facilities in the secondary schools than those in other institutions; high-school graduates were much better informed than their less well-educated neighbors about instruction in the local universities.

Finally, a halo effect was found to surround the institutions most active in adult education in each city. In fields of study where courses were available in a number of different community settings, adults were much more likely to be aware of the facilities in the dominant institution than of those in less prominent locations. For most fields of instruction, in short, St. Stevens respondents thought first of the secondary schools, while adults in Peters tended to name the local university.

PREFERRED SETTINGS IN WHICH TO RECEIVE INSTRUCTION
Somewhat later in the interview, respondents were asked about the types of institutions they would prefer to attend, if they decided to take courses in a number of different subjects

(see Question 30). Since this topic is of some substantive interest in its own right and was not discussed very thoroughly in Part II, we shall interrupt our main theme with a brief discussion of the study settings most often preferred for different types of subject matter, and the ones most attractive to different groups in the population. Our principal aim is to assess whether the differential involvement in adult education of the Peters and St. Stevens high schools and universities had any influence on the relative attractiveness of these two learning settings in the two cities.

To measure reactions along this dimension, people were asked to choose from a list of five different institutions the ones they would prefer to attend for instruction in each of six different subjects. The choices were: a college or university, a local high school, a church, a YMCA or community center, and a private school. One of these places was to be selected for courses in (*a*) politics and government; (*b*) music appreciation; (*c*) speed reading; (*d*) different religions of the world; (*e*) "a course related to the line of work you're in – or to some line of work you're interested in"; and (*f*) depending on the sex of the respondent, a course in either "how to do your own home improvements" or in cooking or homemaking.

Table 16.7 combines the two samples and reports the setting selected for each of the six subjects. Two tendencies appear: quite different settings were chosen in connection with different subjects, and while for some subjects one particular setting was a predominant choice, for others preferences tended to be distributed over more than one setting. As anticipated, churches were chosen by a clear majority of adults for instruction in comparative religion, and, similarly, many more persons selected the university setting than any other for courses in politics and government and for courses related to their vocational fields. For the other three subjects, the dominant choices tended to be divided between two settings: for speed reading, they were about evenly split between universities and secondary schools; for music appreciation, between universities and private music schools; and for home and family life skills, between high schools and YMCA's or community centers.

Table 16.7 Preferred Settings for Studies of Different Subjects (Per Cent of Combined Sample Who Selected Each Type of Institution)

Institution	Subject Matter					
	Politics and Government	One's Own Line of Work	Speed Reading	Music Appreciation	Comparative Religion	Home-Life Skills
College or university	51	48	42	36	26	15
High school	24	24	39	18	4	44
Church	8	2	1	5	60	1
YMCA	12	9	3	10	7	30
Private school	5	17	15	32	2	9
Total	100	100	100	101	99	99
Base	503	447	481	486	498	464

The figures also indicate that for all subject fields except comparative religion, more adults chose to study within the regular school system than outside of it. There were quite substantial differences, however; the choice of colleges and secondary schools ranged from highs of 81, 75, and 72 per cent for instruction in speed reading, politics and government, and vocational studies to lows of 59, 54, and 30 per cent for courses in home and family skills, music appreciation, and comparative religion.

While these findings are hardly startling, they do confirm that people tend to prefer different settings for studies of different types; that in most cases people would rather study in a university or high school than in a private school, YMCA, or church; and that levels of agreement about the best settings for adult studies vary quite markedly from subject to subject.

Next, to compare the preferences of different population aggregates, Table 16.8 shows the combined responses on all six fields of subject matter for persons in different sex, age, and educational groups. In this table there are four conditions in which to compare the preferences of high-school graduates and non-graduates, of men and women, and of older and younger adults, and for each of these comparisons the percentage differences in response patterns is averaged over the four. Although the resulting measures indicate only relative discrepancies rather than absolute ones, they do highlight the spots of balance and imbalance in the overall preference patterns of different groups.

First let us compare the response patterns in the two educational categories. Here the values of the averaged percentage differences were as follows—with the positive signs indicating that an institution was selected relatively more frequently by persons in the higher bracket.

Colleges and universities	+21
YMCA's and community centers	+ 3
Churches	− 4
Private schools	− 8
Secondary schools	−12

Table 16.8 Preferred Settings for Study, by Sex, Age, and Education (Per Cent of Total Selections for Six Fields of Subject Matter)

Institution	Men				Women			
	Under 45		45 or Over		Under 45		45 or Over	
	Less Than 12 Years	12 Years or More	Less Than 12 Years	12 Years or More	Less Than 12 Years	12 Years or More	Less Than 12 Years	12 Years or More
College or university	31	48	30	56	19	40	21	42
High school	33	17	26	19	36	23	36	22
Church	14	10	16	10	15	13	17	12
YMCA	4	12	8	9	16	14	10	14
Private school	18	13	20	7	15	10	16	9
Total	100	100	100	101	101	100	100	99
Base	203	526	267	205	288	688	379	316

These figures indicate that high-school graduates were, on the average, 21 per cent more likely than non-graduates to select a college or university as the preferred setting for study, and were 12 and 8 per cent less likely to choose secondary schools or private schools. In interpreting this result, it is not clear whether the primary emphasis should be that high-school graduates overchose the university setting, that they underchose high schools and private schools, that non-graduates underchose institutions of higher learning, or that they overchose secondary and proprietary schools. The discrepancies indicate major differences in the preferred study settings of the two groups, however, and the most plausible interpretation is that as people graduate from high school they shift their educational orientation away from the secondary school to the college or university.

Next, let us examine the comparisons based on sex, which are computed to indicate the relative choices of men over those of women.

Colleges and universities	+11
Private schools	+ 2
Churches	− 2
YMCA's and community centers	− 5
Secondary schools	− 6

Although these results are equally vulnerable to a number of competing explanations, they seem to show that the university setting is much more important to men than to women, and that the other differences mainly reflect the greater tendency of men to choose this setting. The basis for this interpretation is that, on the whole, university training has more prestige than that gotten from other institutions, and that this consideration would be differentially important to men because of their concern with occupational success.

The final set of comparisons is based on age and indicates the relative preferences of older adults. These values worked out as follows:

Colleges and universities   + 3
Churches   + 1
YMCA's and community centers − 1
Private schools   − 1
Secondary schools   − 2

There are no differences here which suggest that younger and older adults prefer different settings for formal learning pursuits.

The main conclusions which can be drawn from the results of Table 16.8 are (*a*) that high-school graduates are much more likely than non-graduates to prefer the college or university as a setting for adult studies, and much less likely to want to study in secondary schools; (*b*) that a university setting for instruction is also more important to men than it is to women; and (*c*) that age does not seem to alter people's orientations toward one or another institutional setting.

At this point we return to the central theme in this chapter and make comparisons between the two cities of preferences for different study settings. Here our main interest is in the extent to which preferences for universities and secondary schools differed between the two cities, and, since sex and formal schooling were found to influence preferences on this dimension, the community comparisons are presented in Table 16.9 with both of these factors controlled. This table again sums the responses across the six subject fields examined and in this sense represents a measure of general orientation toward study settings rather than choices connected with any particular field of subject matter.

To what extent did the institutional orientations in St. Stevens differ from those in Peters? The first task is to determine whether the profiles were indeed different, and this in turn requires statistical comparisons between the response distributions for the four pairs of subgroups. Accordingly, chi-square goodness-of-fit tests were conducted on each pair of response distributions; these results are reported in Table 16.10. In three cases the overall preferences were not significantly different between the cities, while in the fourth case they were. Thus, residents in the two cities had much the same general orientation to the five different institutional settings, although among men

Table 16.9 Preferred Settings for Study, by Sex, Education, and City (Per Cent of Total Selections for Six Fields of Subject Matter)

Institution	Men				Women			
	Less Than 12 Years		12 Years or More		Less Than 12 Years		12 Years or More	
	St. Stevens	Peters	St. Stevens	Peters	St. Stevens	Peters	St. Stevens	Peters
College or university	27	34	47	53	18	23	41	40
High school	34	22	21	15	35	37	22	23
Church	15	15	8	11	17	15	12	13
YMCA	6	7	10	12	13	12	13	16
Private school	18	21	15	9	18	13	12	8
Total	100	99	101	100	101	100	100	100
Base	267	203	344	387	384	283	497	507

who had completed high school, the preference patterns could indeed be said to be different.

Next the overall chi-square values were subdivided into three component elements: the amount contributed by differences in preferences for universities and secondary schools, the differences in preferences among the other three institutions, and differences in the selection of institutions in and out of the regular school system. When these results were computed, they indicated that the overall chi-square values tended to obscure important differences in preferences for specific institutions. The second part of the table ("Partitioned Chi-Square") reveals that among both groups of men relative preferences for universities and secondary schools were significantly different between the two cities. Both these differences, moreover, were in the direction indicating that more of the Peters men selected the university setting while more in St. Stevens preferred the secondary-school context: the findings are therefore consistent with the relative prominence of these two institutions in the two cities.

When the overall chi-squares are partitioned, they also indicate that men who had completed high school differed in their preferences for the three institutions outside the regular school system. This finding is somewhat more difficult to interpret, although it is evident from Table 16.9 that most of the discrep-

Table 16.10 Overall and Partitioned Chi-Square Values on Preferences for Different Study Settings between Cities, by Sex and Education

Measures	Men		Women	
	Less Than 12 Years	12 Years or More	Less Than 12 Years	12 Years or More
Over all chi-square (d.f. = 4)	8.2 (n.s.)	12.9 (P < .02)	5.4 (n.s.)	6.2 (n.s.)
Partitioned chi-square Within regular school system (d.f. = 1)	6.6 (P = .01)	5.1 (P < .025)	.9 (n.s.)	.4 (n.s.)
Within other institutions (d.f. = 2)	.4 (n.s.)	7.7 (P < .025)	1.1 (n.s.)	5.8 (n.s.)
Between regular school system and other institutions (d.f. = 1)	1.2 (n.s.)	.1 (n.s.)	3.4 (n.s.)	.002 (n.s.)

ancy here was contributed by a greater tendency on the part of St. Stevens men to name private schools as the preferred study setting.

Quite interestingly, none of the comparisons among women yielded statistically significant results, indicating that women in both cities were just about as likely to choose a university as a high school, a church as a YMCA or private school, and a setting within the regular school system as outside of it. More generally, none of the comparisons between the two main classes of institution yielded significant results; this in turn suggests that differences in the overall organization of adult education resources in the two cities did not move differential proportions of adults either toward or away from the regular school system.

The most important findings to emerge from the inter-city comparisons are that men in the two cities were differentially attracted to the universities and secondary schools and that no similar tendency could be detected among women. At a more general level this suggests that the prominence of an educational institution does make a difference to men, but is of little or no importance to women — a finding again consistent with the interpretation that because of relatively stronger concerns with occupational mobility, it is more important to men than to women to attend educational institutions which are regarded as prestigeful.

DIFFERENTIAL EXPOSURE TO CONTINUING EDUCATION

The next section of this chapter deals with the question of whether differences in the nature of the resources had any effect on the educational behavior of adults in the two cities. Since the secondary schools in St. Stevens were much more active than those in Peters, and since college facilities were more abundant in Peters, we expected that more non-high-school graduates in St. Stevens than in Peters would have been exposed to adult education courses at some time in their lives, while a reverse tendency would be found among graduates.

Next, assuming an inverse functional relationship between the availability of appropriate institutional resources and the need to engage in independent education, we expected that rates of independent study among non-graduates would be higher in

Peters than in St. Stevens, while among graduates they would again be the reverse.

Evidence on both of these points is presented in Table 16.11, which shows rates of involvement in both formal courses and independent studies of the two main educational groups in each city.[6] We see that the results do not support our expectations, since both educational groups in St. Stevens have higher overall rates of exposure to formal adult education courses. Indeed, the fact that 14 per cent more high-school graduates in St. Stevens than in Peters had at some time taken a course represents a rather sharp negation of the predicted trend. On the other hand, the rates of independent study offer at least minimal support for the general hypothesis; among the non-graduates the rates are slightly higher in Peters than in St. Stevens, while among the graduates the St. Stevens sample shows the higher overall incidence of activity.

Thus the results presented in Table 16.11 support one part of our general hypothesis, but not the other. Spelled out in greater detail, the rationale for the specific hypotheses developed above is the general premise (*a*) that secondary schools and universities are differentially appropriate and attractive to different segments of the adult population, and (*b*) as a consequence, when communities differ in the extent to which they offer facilities of these types, the differences should be reflected in the educational behavior of different sectors of the population. To be more specific, it was reasoned that the most appropriate and attractive study setting for persons who had not gone very far in school would be the secondary school, on the argument that the instruction offered in these institutions would be most closely in keeping with the levels of formal learning already achieved by this segment of the population. Thus where secondary-school adult education programs are plentiful, we would expect non-high-school graduates to engage in formal study to a greater extent and in independent study to a lesser extent. Where secondary-school facilities are weak, on the other hand, the antici-

---

[6]These results are derived from the answers to Questions 22 and 29 in the interview. The questions were phrased to be identical with those asked in the national survey.

Table 16.11 Exposure to Adult Education Experiences, by Education and City

Activities	Less Than 12 Years of School			12 or More Years of School		
	St. Stevens	Peters	Difference	St. Stevens	Peters	Difference
Formal courses (per cent who have ever taken an adult education course)	53 (127)	42 (100)	+11	80 (148)	66 (164)	+14
Independent study (per cent who have ever engaged in independent study)	41 (127)	44 (100)	− 3	60 (152)	49 (164)	+11

pated effect would be just the opposite: non-graduates should be less likely to enroll in formal courses and more likely to use independent study.

For this much of the general rationale, then, the results in Table 16.11 provide at least modest support, but the expectations regarding the behavior of the better-educated sectors of the population are not supported by the data. The university would appear to be the most attractive setting for continuing education for high-school graduates; therefore we expected that persons in cities well-stocked with resources at the university level would show a relatively stronger tendency to enroll in courses and a lesser propensity to pursue learning on their own. The evidence in Table 16.11 does not support this general interpretation, however, and, if anything, suggests that a concentration of resources at the university level lowers the probability of involvement by high-school graduates, in both formal and informal learning.

One other possibility is that the university may not represent the most attractive study setting to persons who graduated from high school but never attended college, and since our high-school-graduate category contained persons both with and without prior college experiences, our next step was to re-examine the results within these smaller subgroups. Accordingly, persons in the higher educational bracket were subdivided into three types: those who had completed high school but never gone further, those who had begun college but never finished, and those who had completed a full four years of college. When the rates of experience with formal and informal adult studies are examined for these particular groups, then, a quite revealing pattern emerges. Table 16.12*a* indicates clearly that persons with no college or some college were much more likely to have taken courses if they lived in St. Stevens, but that the difference is completely erased—and even slightly reversed—among the university graduates. These findings suggest that our original expectations concerning the effect of the availability of adult education resources on better-educated adults are to a certain extent supported, but only among persons at the very top of the educational continuum.

Table 16.12 Nature of Adult Education Experiences, by Formal Schooling and City

Years of Schooling	Per Cent Who Have Ever Taken an Adult Education Course (a)			Per Cent Who Have Ever Engaged in Independent Study (b)			Proportion of Formal Course Enrollments among Total Activities (c)		
	St. Stevens	Peters	Difference	St. Stevens	Peters	Difference	St. Stevens	Peters	Difference
Less than 12 years	53 (127)	42 (100)	+11	41 (127)	44 (100)	− 3	56 (119)	49 (86)	+ 7
12 years	73 (94)	54 (96)	+19	51 (94)	44 (96)	+ 7	59 (117)	55 (94)	+ 4
13–15 years	89 (28)	70 (40)	+19	72 (29)	52 (40)	+20	54 (46)	57 (49)	− 3
16 years or more	89 (28)	97 (29)	− 8	81 (31)	59 (29)	+22	50 (50)	62 (45)	−12

In addition, however, the intercity comparisons of rates of independent study now show a continually increasing discrepancy in the hypothesized direction as one moves upward on the educational scale. We are apt to find relatively higher rates of independent study in the better-educated group in the city with fewer university-level adult education facilities. This part of the general hypothesis, then, is supported rather strongly.

Finally, the interaction of both of these trends is summarized in Table 16.12c through measures which represent the tendency for each group to undertake learning in formal courses rather than by independent study.[7] Here again, the most critical column is that showing the differences between cities. If they are consistent with the interpretation that the overall educational resources in St. Stevens met the learning needs of persons with little formal schooling, while those in Peters were better geared to the interests of the better-educated, the values in this column should shift in a negative direction in the progressively higher educational groups. The results indicate precisely this pattern and therefore constitute quite substantial support for our general hypothesis.

Our findings tend to confirm the hypothesis that the manner in which adult education resources are organized within a community does affect the educational behavior of different groups of adults. Although based on findings from just two cities, the results suggest that if adult programs are organized in the secondary schools rather than universities, there will be higher rates of post-school educational experiences in all sectors of the population except college graduates. An extensive adult program at the secondary-school level, in short, should attract a wider range of adults than an equally extensive program in a local university.

Finally, there was evidence that a functional relationship may indeed exist between the types of resources available and the rates at which different groups in the population become involved in independent education. Persons who live where edu-

---

[7]The measures represent the number of persons in each category who had taken a formal course over the combined number who had either taken a course or engaged in independent study.

cational resources are available in institutions consistent with the level of their own educational attainment are more likely (if they engage in adult studies at all) to turn to an institution for their instruction than to undertake learning ventures on their own.

DISPOSITIONS TOWARD CONTINUING EDUCATION

In this final section we examine the attitudes of people in each city toward participation in formal learning pursuits. Our main purpose here is to determine whether the results on rates of study can be extended to the dispositional level as well. Two kinds of data are examined here as indicators of people's readiness to engage in learning pursuits. The first deals with the extent to which people identified different barriers to taking courses, while the second compares the proportions of persons in each city who indicated they either currently or at some time in the past had considered taking an adult education course.

From the answers given to Question 26 we can see the extent to which respondents in the two cities mentioned different barriers which had prevented them from enrolling in educational courses. These responses are reported in two ways in Table 16.13 so as to allow comparisons both on individual reasons and on scores which combine the responses to various items. As in our earlier treatment of similar data from the national survey, the items are grouped into those barriers resulting from environment or life-cycle position and those which more closely reflect personal feelings concerning participation in formal learning situations.

Turning first to the individual items, the most notable finding in Table 16.13 is that there was only one comparison out of a total of sixteen in which a substantial difference was found between the two cities, this being in the number of non-high-school graduates who felt they could not afford to enroll in a course.[8] Non-graduates in Peters were 16 per cent more likely than those in St. Stevens to give economic circumstances as a reason for

[8]This was the only comparison among the sixteen which yielded a statistically significant difference. A test of differences between proportions here produced a Z value of 2.4, which would have a chance expectancy of less than .02.

Table 16.13 Perceived Barriers to Participation in Adult Education Courses, by Education and City (Per Cent Who Thought Each Reason Would Apply to Them)

Reasons	Less Than 12 Years			12 Years or More		
	St. Stevens	Peters	Difference	St. Stevens	Peters	Difference
a Situational factors						
Couldn't afford it (E)	51 (120)	67 (100)	−16	32 (154)	39 (165)	−7
Usually too tired at night (B)	44 (124)	48 (99)	− 4	32 (153)	36 (165)	−4
Too busy (H)	43 (123)	41 (99)	+ 2	46 (153)	51 (164)	−5
Don't know of available facilities (A)	22 (116)	23 (96)	− 1	9 (152)	10 (164)	−1
Scores on index of situational readiness						
$\overline{X}$	2.28	2.16		2.78	2.62	
s^2	1.65	1.13		1.02	1.03	
t		.74 (n.s.)			1.36 (n.s.)	
b Dispositional factors						
Not the studying type (D)	38 (122)	42 (98)	− 4	21 (151)	27 (164)	− 6
Feel too old to learn (F)	28 (123)	27 (100)	+ 1	5 (154)	8 (162)	− 3
Would feel like a stranger (G)	24 (123)	27 (96)	− 3	10 (154)	7 (165)	+3
Would feel childish (C)	9 (123)	15 (98)	− 6	1 (153)	4 (165)	− 3
Scores on index of dispositional readiness						
$\overline{X}$	2.91	2.83		3.61	3.52	
s^2	1.58	1.49		.41	.59	
t		.48 (n.s.)			1.12 (n.s.)	

non-participation, and a similar, though not statistically significant, difference may be noted among the graduates, too, on this item.[9] Since the relative economic circumstances of respondents in these two cities could not explain these discrepancies,[10] the most likely interpretation is that they reflect the very real differences in the costs of instruction in the most prominent adult education centers in each community. Enrollment at Peters University involved a tuition outlay of between $60 and $90 per course, whereas tuition costs in the St. Stevens secondary schools were, on the average, only a small fraction of this amount.

The most important finding in Table 16.13 is that on fifteen of sixteen comparisons no significant differences were found between the residents of the two cities. Moreover, when indices of "situational" and "dispositional" readiness were built from these various items, no significant differences were found between these distributions, either. In carrying out this further analysis, it was reasoned that a rejection of the various dispositional barriers would constitute some kind of measure of a person's psychological readiness to engage in adult studies, and, consequently, two "readiness" indices were constructed out of the items in parts *a* and *b* of Table 16.13 by assigning one point to each response which rejected the applicability of a statement. This produced two "readiness" scales with scores ranging between 0 and 4; when the means on these scales were compared in each of the four cases where intercity comparisons were possible, it was found that sampling variability could have produced all the differences. Interestingly, however, in all four comparisons higher mean values were found among the St. Stevens respondents, but none was sufficiently higher to challenge the hypothesis that they were produced by chance factors alone.

The results suggest that the organization of adult education facilities in a community, while making a considerable difference in the rates at which different groups accumulate experience

[9]$Z = 1.3$; $P = .194$.

[10]Median family incomes were actually quite a bit higher among the Peters respondents than those in St. Stevens. Among non-high-school graduates they were $5,500 and $5,104, respectively, and among graduates, $7,815 compared with $6,888.

with continuing education, had little effect on people's attitudes about participation. At least, when given the opportunity to disidentify as persons who would engage in adult studies, neither the non-graduates in Peters nor the graduates in St. Stevens were any more likely than their counterparts in the other city to show a relatively higher incidence of disidentification — which would be expected if the organizational differences between the communities affected people's attitudes in the same manner as their behavior. To the extent that the negation of the four items classed as dispositional barriers together represent a valid index of readiness to take courses,[11] the results can certainly be interpreted as evidence that the kinds of community effects found in the previous section of the chapter do not extend to psychological readiness to engage in adult education.

Since respondents were asked not only whether they had ever taken a course, but in addition whether they had ever considered taking one (Question 22-J and 22-K), intercity comparisons can be made on a number of additional measures which represent different stages in the general process of becoming enrolled in educational courses. These are the stages of (a) "interest arousal," as reflected by the number of adults in each city who had ever considered taking an adult education course; (b) the "implementation" stage, measured in terms of the rates at which people converted their intentions into behavior; and (c) the process of "interest retention," defined as the extent to which persons once having taken a course renewed their interest and decided to take additional courses. Each of these measures represents a general behavioral tendency which might be expected to vary depending on the nature and scope of adult education facilities in a community. The findings on each of these measures are reported in Table 16.14.

[11]The index is only a modestly good predictor of whether or not a person has ever taken an adult education course. The correlations (gamma) between scores on the dispositional index and having ever taken a course were .46 among the St. Stevens sample but only .24 in Peters. On the other hand, the index is a relatively strong predictor of whether people have even considered taking courses, and the gamma values with these intentions (as measured by Questions 22-J or 22-K) were .52 in St. Stevens and .63 in Peters. This indicates that the index has some validity as a general measure of people's dispositions concerning participation.

Table 16.14 Intercity Comparisons of Three Processes of Adult Education Participation, by Education

Process	Less Than 12 Years			12 Years or More		
	St. Stevens	Peters	Difference	St. Stevens	Peters	Difference
Interest arousal (Per cent who had either taken an adult education course or had thought about taking one)	74 (127)	73 (100)	+ 1	91 (150)	92 (165)	– 1
Implementation (Per cent who had actually taken a course among those who had ever thought of taking one)	71 (94)	58 (73)	+13	87 (137)	72 (151)	+15
Interest retention (Per cent who would like to take another course among those who had taken one)	48 (67)	50 (42)	– 2	63 (119)	63 (108)	Nil

From the first row of the table it is clear that earlier findings concerning differences in enrollment rates in the two cities cannot be interpreted merely as a reflection of underlying differences in the extent to which residents of the two communities had ever been interested in taking courses. Indeed, when persons who had thought about taking a course were added to those who had actually done so, virtually identical results emerged for residents of the two cities. These findings suggest that differences in the nature of facilities in the two cities did not matter at the level of interest arousal.

Similarly, the figures in the last row of the table reveal almost identical rates of "interest retention," suggesting that the kinds of learning experiences encountered by participants in the two cities did not affect the rates at which they thought about taking additional courses. Roughly one-half of the non-graduates in each city and just under two-thirds of the graduates had recently thought about taking an additional adult education course.

Where the cities do differ, however, is at the intermediary level, where for both educational groups the "implementation" rates are considerably higher in St. Stevens than in Peters. Among non-graduates who had ever thought about taking a course, 71 per cent in St. Stevens compared with 58 per cent in Peters had actually taken one; among graduates the comparable rates were 87 and 72 per cent, respectively.[12] In effect, then, the non-graduates in St. Stevens were just about as likely as the graduates in Peters to convert their intentions into actions, which is rather striking evidence of where the real differences between these cities actually lay. The findings lend further support to the general conclusion that the manner in which adult education facilities are organized in a community affects the rates at which adults will enroll in courses, but does not affect the extent to which they develop favorable dispositions toward continuing education.

[12]The percentage difference between non-graduates does not quite reach the .95 level of confidence ($Z = 1.8$; $P = .072$), but that between the two groups of graduates does ($Z = 3.1$; $P < .01$).

SUMMARY

This brings us to the conclusion of the section of the study concerned with the nature of community facilities for adult instruction. This chapter has attempted to assess the effect of different types of educational facilities on people's behavior and attitudes regarding continuing education. A comparative analysis was made of the effects of living in a community where the chief facilities for adult instruction were in an evening college of the local private university, as opposed to one where the most comprehensive facilities were offered in the city's secondary schools.

The general premise which guided this analysis was that persons with little formal schooling would have their learning needs better served by programs offered at the level of the secondary school, while persons who had gone farther in their formal education would find the instructional offerings of a college or university more appropriate for their adult education. It was on the basis of this assumption that specific hypotheses were formulated concerning intercity differences in people's awareness of resources, experiences with continuing education, and dispositions toward becoming involved in formal educational pursuits.

On the whole, the results of the analysis support the general conclusion that when instructional resources for adults are organized at different levels of the regular school system, their impact is quite different for different segments of the adult population. There was some evidence that persons with little formal schooling were more aware of the educational resources available to them if they lived in the city with the more extensive secondary-school program, and conversely, that persons who had gone farther in school knew more about available resources if they lived in the city with university facilities. With respect to preferred settings for study, the results confirmed that secondary schools are on the whole more attractive than universities to persons who have not finished high school, while the converse is true of persons who go farther in their education. At the same time, however, it was also found that at least among men, the relative prominence of an institution also has some bearing on the question of the preferred context for receiving instruction.

The most interesting and important findings to emerge from the analysis were those concerning the effect of community facilities on rates of study and on people's feelings about becoming involved in continuing education. Considerably more persons in the city dominated by the secondary schools rather than the university had at some time been enrolled in a course, and this difference in exposure was found among all categories of adults except college graduates. However, no similar difference was found in people's feelings about becoming enrolled in courses, nor in their intentions concerning enrollment. Upon closer scrutiny, it turned out that the rate at which persons who intended to study went on to convert their intentions into actions was considerably more pronounced in the city served primarily by a secondary-school adult education program.

The most plausible explanation for these varying tendencies is that the resources in St. Stevens were, on the whole, accessible to a much larger proportion of local adults than were those in Peters. Quite apart from the question of how appropriate the facilities were to the needs and interests of adults in these cities, there can be little doubt that the lower costs of instruction in the St. Stevens secondary schools, as compared with the Evening College at Peters University, meant that the most comprehensive resources of the community were more accessible in St. Stevens. While this is not necessarily true of high-school and college facilities in all cities, the general implication is that when instructional facilities are indeed made more accessible, the net result is a much deeper penetration into what was earlier termed the "potential audience" for programs of adult instruction. The effect of adult education programs is seen less in recruitment of new adults into the "potential audience" than in a greater likelihood that persons with defined learning interests will convert these interests into concrete actions.

Part IV

The Education of the Late Adolescent

Introduction
to
Part IV

In the first three sections of this monograph, major attention was given to the incidence, content, and determinants of those educational experiences which occur among adults after the termination of full-time schooling. Parodoxical though it may seem, a special national sample of adolescents and very young adults (many of them full-time students) was also interviewed in the course of NORC's program of research.

At the beginning of this inquiry it was anticipated that the audience reached by adult education was not necessarily restricted to adults. It was also understood that this audience was not restricted to persons who had completely terminated their experience in the regular school system. Obviously there is a point in time when, for many students, participation in the formal and informal systems is characterized by overlap, patterns of discontinuity, and shifts from one system to the other. Therefore, a special study was undertaken to cast some light on the supplementary school experiences of persons at or near this moment of transition.[1] Part IV reports on that inquiry.

NORC's research into adult education sought to provide a national base line assessment of this behavior and to yield a broad point of reference for researchers who have, in the past, typically reported on samples which were small, specific to single areas, and limited to partial segments of the adult student population. In large measure this aim has been realized, but not without producing a rather anomalous situation in the process.

[1] The term "supplementary education" is more appropriate for this age group than "adult education." It will be used throughout this section to refer to participation of persons aged seventeen – twenty-four in learning endeavors outside the formal graded school system.

A significant part of our present knowledge of the school experiences of younger persons is also based on small samples which are again specific to single areas and limited to segments of the student (or dropout) population. If one accepts the "reasonable" assumption that adult participation in learning can be linked to earlier school experiences, then one also accepts an important limitation upon our ability to explain this behavior. For while we now have our base-line assessment of adult education, the literature has yet to offer a comparable base line for the education of younger persons[2] and, inevitably, it provides little transit for those who are anxious to shuttle between these points.

Any study which aims to fill this gap (at least in part) necessarily involves a number of emphases. Our analysis responds to these problems in the following fashion: initially an attempt is made to specify rates of remaining in school and returning to school (among persons aged seventeen – twenty-four) at each age and level of the formal educational process (Chap. 17). Next we discuss some correlates of successful adjustment to high school and consider the effect of such adjustment on current school-going plans in the graded school system. Special notice is taken of those persons who have chosen to return to the regular system after an absence of at least one year (Chap. 18). Our focus then shifts to the expectations that persons aged seventeen – twenty-four express concerning their adult working lives and the interplay between these career goals and their adjustment to school (Chap. 19). In the next chapter the question of supplementary education is considered, and patterns of early behavior in this area are initially outlined and then discussed in light of the regular school adjustments these youngsters have made, their eventual career expectations, etc. (Chap. 20). The chapter concludes with a background comparison of decisions to seek further training in either the formal or informal school systems.

[2]The Project Talent series of researches will, upon their completion, constitute an important corrective to this situation (see Flanagan *et al.*, 1960, 1962, 1963, for early reports in this series).

17

The Impact
of Selected Social
Variables
on Late
Adolescents

GRADES OF SCHOOL COMPLETED AND IMMEDIATE SCHOOL PLANS

This section of the report offers an analysis of the participation of young persons in supplementary education. The 813 cases available for analysis represent a weighted probability sample of the non-institutionalized population of the United States aged seventeen – twenty-four (the exact nature of the sample is described in Appendix 1). Although we shall presently discuss the nature of secondary school experiences, in this chapter we are primarily concerned with the problem of staying in school at each age and phase of the educational process and the social correlates of remaining in and returning to school.

NORC sampled a sequence of eight consecutive ages which can be grouped by two-year age intervals. The current educational attainment of these young persons is shown in Table 17.1. In general, the percentage distributions show an expected gradient (i.e., attainment is correlated with age) but the third column of the table ("13 – 15 Grades") also suggests a recent increase in rates of college attendance.

Additionally, the two-year grouping highlights the increasing number of younger persons currently available for schooling. The relative size of the case bases in the final column of the table vividly reflects the "baby boom" of recent decades and underlines the timeliness of our present attempt to come to terms with the educational experiences of this generation, and of those who are immediately preceding them through school.[1]

We can open our discussion of remaining in school by considering the number of persons who were actually attending school between September, 1961, and summer, 1962 ("last year"), and the number planning to attend between September, 1962, and spring, 1963 ("this year"). These figures appear in Table 17.2.

[1]Comparing the figures in Table 17.1 to estimates available from census reports, it is apparent that the NORC statistics tend to overestimate school attainment at the twelfth-grade level, particularly among younger respondents. A thorough examination of this imbalance uncovered these two sources of bias. First, the definition of school attendance employed in the NORC survey equated progress toward certificates of school completion with progress toward regular degrees. NORC thus includes, for example, attendance at schools where one might receive a certificate of proficiency in hairdressing or accounting. The Bureau of the Census, less concerned with the shadow area between "regular" and "irregular" educational endeavors, instructs its interviewers to record only that portion of school attendance which is directed toward the receipt of conventional diplomas and degrees (cf. U.S. Bureau of the Census, 1963, p. 4). The more generous NORC definition thus yields a more generous estimate of educational attainment. Second, even when differences in type of school attended are taken into account, there is in the NORC sample a slight but perceptible overrepresentation of better-educated persons among respondents below the age of twenty. Apparently this difference is a function of sampling error. It is not strong enough to cause serious concern.

Table 17.1 Grades of School Completed, by Age

Age	Grades of School Completed				Total	
	11 Grades or Less (Per Cent)	12 Grades (Per Cent)	13 – 15 Grades (Per Cent)	16 Grades or More (Per Cent)	Per Cent	N
17 – 18	52	43	5	0	100	239
19 – 20	25	47	25	2	99	198
21 – 22	28	47	19	6	100	189
23 – 24	26	49	13	12	100	179

N	805
NA on age	1
NA on grades	7
Total N	813

In the first column of the table ("In School Last Year"), we observe a distinct gradient in the pattern of responses. From a high of 86 per cent within the seventeen–eighteen age group, the proportion recently attending school drops by roughly one-half with each two-year increment in age. According to the second column ("Will Be in School This Year"), a similar gradient describes the percentage planning to attend school during the academic year following the date of interview. In this case the figures range from 66 per cent (among the seventeen–eighteen age group) to 13 per cent (among the twenty-three–twenty-four age group).

Examining both columns together we can draw the obvious conclusion that exposure to formal schooling varies inversely with age. Yet if we observe the difference between the percentage recently in school and the percentage planning to be there in the immediate future, we are also provided with a rough measure of the net loss of students that the schools experience over time. We are then confronted with a much less obvious finding: within the later age categories there is no net loss at all; the proportions of those recently attending and those planning to attend are virtually identical. Thus, although it is true that a high proportion of early adolescents attend school, it is also true that a substantial proportion leave school during these same years. Note that our comments are restricted to within-group (or age-cohort) comparisons. There is considerable loss between the two older categories, but this is smaller than the rate which occurs in earlier years.

Our data invite emphasis upon a transitional aspect of expo-

Table 17.2 Percentage in School Last Year and Percentage Planning To Be in School This Year, by Age

Age	In School Last Year	Will Be in School This Year
17–18	86 (238)	66 (240)
19–20	43 (200)	31 (200)
21–22	25 (192)	25 (192)
23–24	12 (179)	13 (180)

sure to school—a view of educational experiences which takes explicit notice of rates of movement into and out of classrooms during adolescence and early adulthood. We can approach this matter directly by combining our major points of reference (attendance last year and this year) into a fourfold classification of immediate school plans and examining the distribution of respondents within these categories according to their current ages. The data appear in Table 17.3, and the reader is encouraged to refer to the table as we discuss its categories and content.

Under the heading "Staying In" we have placed all respondents who were attending school last year and who expect to continue their education without interruption. These stay-ins diminish over the years, dropping from 64 per cent to 7 per cent between seventeen and twenty-four. Persons departing from school are those youngsters recently in school who anticipate at least a one-year absence, and the second column of Table 17.3 indicates that this category of dropouts, especially large in the early years of adolescence, also decreases over time. Youngsters staying out of school are those whose absence covers both points of our time scale (last year—this year). Within the parameters of our classification, these are our long-term absentees. Not surprisingly, their numbers steadily increase with age. The final category contains those youngsters planning to return to the

Table 17.3 Immediate School Plans, by Age

Age	Immediate School Plans				Total	
	Staying In (Per Cent)	Departing (Per Cent)	Staying Out (Per Cent)	Returning (Per Cent)	Per Cent	N
17–18	64	22	12	2	100	238
19–20	26	17	52	5	100	200
21–22	19	6	68	7	100	192
23–24	7	6	82	6	101	179

N	809
NA on plans	3
NA on age	1
Total N	813

regular school system after at least a one-year absence. Persons returning to school form a category of special interest both to those concerned with the retention rates of schools (especially, but not exclusively, high schools) and to adult educators. Such individuals (returnees) deserve more attention than we can give them here; let us only observe that re-entry increases during late adolescence and early adulthood. Above we noted that within the later age categories the proportions recently attending school and those planning to attend are virtually identical. Now we see why. Within the twenty-one–twenty-two and twenty-three–twenty-four age cohorts, the percentage returning and dropping out are roughly the same. There is within-cohort stability; the only loss that occurs is a function of inter-cohort differences.

These data can be recomputed and expressed as rates. The rate of remaining among persons aged seventeen–eighteen, for example, is not the percentage remaining of all persons aged seventeen–eighteen who were in school last year. The rate of departing is this figure subtracted from 100.

By the same logic, the actual rate of returning within this age category is the number returning after an absence of at least one year divided by the total number of persons aged seventeen–eighteen who did not attend school during the previous academic year (returnees plus stay-outs). The rate of staying out would then be this figure subtracted from 100. Table 17.4 indicates rates of remaining and returning for the appropriate age categories.

Rates of remaining are highest among the seventeen–eighteen and twenty-one–twenty-two age group, but there is no obvious

Table 17.4 Rates of Remaining and Returning, by Age

Rates	Age			
	17–18 (Per Cent)	19–20 (Per Cent)	21–22 (Per Cent)	23–24 (Per Cent)
Staying in	75 (205)	61 (86)	75 (48)	55 (22)
Returning	12 (33)	9 (114)	9 (144)	7 (157)

way of interpreting these differences without taking into account the level of educational attainment characteristic of each group. Since a majority (52 per cent) of the seventeen–eighteen age group have completed less than twelve grades of school, the rate at this age is presumably quite sensitive to decisions to continue secondary school education. Similarly, the number of high-school graduates not bound for college should act to depress the nineteen–twenty-year-old rate of remaining and the proportion of continuing college students should increase the figure for persons aged twenty-one–twenty-two.

Comparable problems arise when we consider rates of returning. The proportion returning among those out of school reaches 12 per cent at seventeen–eighteen and varies between 7 and 9 per cent thereafter. From additional data it can be determined that the actual number of returnees is greatest at twenty-one years of age, and the mean age of returning for the entire sample is also twenty-one (which, incidentally, makes the returnee about one year older than the typical respondent). The rate of returning is highest among younger persons, because the proportion of persons aged seventeen–eighteen who were out of school last year (and thus in a position to return) was the lowest among the four age-groups sampled. Also obscured by these figures is the fact that the typical returnee in this sample is a high-school graduate aiming at advanced training (after an absence from school of 2.4 years).

Thus these rates, which will concern us for the balance of this chapter, become meaningful only when they are specified by

Table 17.5 Rates of Remaining and Returning, by Grades of School Completed

Rates	Grades of School Completed			
	11 Grades or Less (Per Cent)	12 Grades (Per Cent)	13–15 Grades (Per Cent)	16 Grades or More (Per Cent)
Remaining	81 (115)	51 (138)	87 (87)	67 (21)
Returning	6 (159)	9 (235)	15 (34)	– (15)

educational attainment. Table 17.5, which presents the appropriate rates in these terms, offers a more coherent picture of the process of selective remaining and returning.

Prior to high-school graduation, 81 per cent of those in school elect to continue. Stated differently, this figure means that almost 20 per cent of the nation's high-school population (in the seventeen–twenty-four age range) leave school each year at some point prior to graduation. At the moment of graduation roughly one-half of the surviving students express plans to continue, and for those recently in college the rate of staying in climbs to 87 per cent. Among the handful of continuing college graduates and postgraduate and professional school students in the sample, about two-thirds of those recently attending are retained by the schools.

Rates of returning demonstrate a different pattern entirely. Where comparisons are possible, these rates are directly correlated with grades of school already completed. The pattern is quite similar to that reported for participants in adult education. At the moment, of course, we are concerned with persons returning to regular (credit-earning) school work, but the parallel is striking enough to suggest that similar factors may underlie both phenomena.

In the balance of this chapter we examine selected social correlates of educational attainment and rates of remaining and returning. Our purpose is twofold. First, we hope to gain some appreciation of the movement of students into and out of classrooms during the years of late adolescence and early adulthood. Second, we shall attempt to identify a number of variables associated with these shifts and we hope, in the process, to specify factors that will also prove illuminating as we address those problems reserved for the chapters to follow. Initially, let us consider the impact of sex and marital status on educational attainment and current rates of remaining in school and returning.

SEX AND MARITAL STATUS

The three sections of Table 17.6 provide data on the differential behavior of the sexes in this area. (Because of the small number of college graduates in the sample, the "16 Grades or More" category has been combined with those who have completed any post-secondary training at all.) According to Part *a*, girls are more likely to have completed high school than boys, but they are less likely to complete training at more advanced levels. Part *b*, which reflects the intentions of those recently in school at each level, suggests that at high-school graduation

Table 17.6 Educational Attainment, Rates of Remaining, and Rates of Returning, by Sex

a. Grades of School Completed by Sex

| Sex | Grades of School Completed | | | Total | |
	11 Grades or Less (Per Cent)	12 Grades (Per Cent)	13 Grades or More (Per Cent)	Per Cent	N
Men	36	41	23	100	361
Women	33	51	17	101	445

	N	806
	NA grades	7
	Total N	813

b. Rates of Remaining, by Grades Completed and Sex

| Sex | Grades of School Completed | | |
	11 Grades or Less (Per Cent)	12 Grades (Per Cent)	13 Grades or More (Per Cent)
Men	82 (67)	49 (68)	86 (64)
Women	79 (48)	53 (70)	79 (44)

c. Rates of Returning, by Grades Completed and Sex

| Sex | Grades of School Completed | | |
	11 Grades or Less (Per Cent)	12 Grades (Per Cent)	13 Grades or More (Per Cent)
Men	7 (62)	11 (81)	– (19)
Women	5 (97)	8 (154)	7 (30)

proportionately more girls than boys expect to continue their schooling. If actual performance (Part *a* of the table) is taken as a guide, it would seem that these intentions are often unfulfilled. Indeed, at the thirteenth grade level and beyond, even the expectations voiced by the females become congruent with patterns of previous performance.

Rates of returning show a slightly higher percentage of males at the two attainment levels which permit comparisons. Neither difference is substantial, and it appears that sex cannot be counted as an especially useful predictor of decisions to return to the regular school system.

Turning next to Table 17.7 and the question of marital status, we find patterns of attainment quite similar to those with sex. At the twelfth-grade level, persons who have been married enjoy a slight edge over those who have remained single, just as the girls enjoy a slight edge over the boys, but again the margin is reversed within the post-secondary category.

It is difficult to read much meaning into these numbers, for the proportions cited ignore the fact that persons aged seventeen–twenty-four have been exposed to the risk of marriage for varying lengths of time. Thus, for a seventeen-year-old female, the decision to marry may affect quite directly the amount of education she is to receive. A comparable decision for a twenty-four-year-old girl may be irrelevant to her academic career.

Much more meaningful are the attendance decisions reflected in parts *b* and *c* of the table. Part *b,* for example, presents the rates of remaining of single and married persons and allows a glimpse of the effect of current marital status on immediate school plans. The numbers tell an interesting story.

Among recent high-school graduates a margin of 42 per cent separates the plans to remain in school of single and married persons. One's initial temptation is to underline the disruptive impact of matrimony on continuing education. The temptation is short-lived, however, because the margin separating single and married persons beyond the high-school level drops sharply (to 19 per cent). Obviously, being married does not exactly help college students, but it seems to hurt them much less than those who are behind them in school. We shall return to this point; for the moment let us briefly observe that attainment and marital status do not generate comparable differences among those returning to school. Here we find the rate reaching its highest point among single persons who have completed twelve grades of school. Among married persons, the effect of educational attainment on plans to return is negligible.

Remaining in school, in any event, seems to be curiously

Table 17.7 Educational Attainment, Rates of Remaining, and Rates of Returning, by Marital Status

a. Grades of School Completed by Marital Status

| Marital Status | Grades of School Completed | | | Total | |
	11 Grades or Less (Per Cent)	12 Grades (Per Cent)	13 Grades or More (Per Cent)	Per Cent	N
Single	35	44	21	100	436
Married	33	49	18	100	370

N	806
NA on grades	7
Total N	813

b. Rates or Remaining by Grades Completed and Marital Status

| Marital Status | Grades of School Completed | | |
	11 Grades or Less (Per Cent)	12 Grades (Per Cent)	13 Grades or More (Per Cent)
Single	84 (105)	57 (118)	89 (78)
Married	– (10)	15 (20)	70 (30)

c. Rates of Returning by Grades Completed and Marital Status

| Marital Status | Grades of School Completed | | |
	11 Grades or Less (Per Cent)	12 Grades (Per Cent)	13 Grades or More (Per Cent)
Single	7 (46)	14 (73)	– (14)
Married	5 (113)	6 (157)	6 (35)

related to marital status. There is a strong possibility that sex is a factor in this finding for, as Table 17.8 suggests, married persons of high-school age are more often female. Thus at eighteen years of age, 19 per cent of the available females, but only 1 per cent of the available males are already married. Even by twenty-four only 10 per cent of the girls remain single but about 40 per cent of the young men have yet to marry. Does marriage affect school attendance differentially for the sexes? A partial answer is available in Table 17.9, where we can observe the per cent attending school last year by age, sex, and marital status.

For males alone we can make only a few reliable comparisons. Attendance drops sharply for single men as age increases. The most surprising comparisons are those between single and married men from twenty-one to twenty-four years of age. At these age levels the proportions recently in school are unaffected by marital status.

Among females, a completely different picture prevails. Attendance figures for single females do not decline with any regularity. In fact, 71 per cent of the girls who are still unmarried at age twenty-one – twenty-two have recently attended school. This figure is 64 per cent higher than that for the married girls and 40 per cent higher than the proportion of all boys at the same age. Yet the girls have by no means resigned themselves to academic spinsterhood. A glance at the case bases tells us

---

Table 17.8 Percentage Ever Married, by Age and Sex

Age	Sex	
	Men	Women
17–18	1 (122)	19 (118)
19–20	21 (91)	53 (109)
21–22	56 (82)	78 (110)
23–24	61 (70)	90 (110)
N		812
NA on age		1
Total N		813

that by twenty-three–twenty-four many of the previously single girls have found a mate and, presumably, turned from the blackboard to the bassinet. Finally, we note the sharp differential in recent attendance between all married males and married females. It could almost be said that matrimony is kind to the academic fortunes of men, but cruel to those of women.

Table 17.10 repeats the previous arrangement of categories directing attention to anticipated school attendance. In general, the previous trends reappear. It is especially interesting to note that while 45 per cent of the seventeen–eighteen-year-old married females were in school last year (Table 17.9), only 9 per cent plan to continue. Matrimony seems especially hard on the continuing education of younger girls. Once more, the behavior of married males beyond twenty draws our attention. At twenty-three–twenty-four the earlier pattern (Table 17.9) has weakened, but the plans of those aged twenty-one–twenty-two again imply that more married than unmarried men at this age plan to continue as students.

In summary, we can say that marital status seems to affect the school plans of the sexes quite differently. Single girls are avid

Table 17.9 Percentage in School Last Year, by Age, Sex, and Marital Status

Age	Sex			
	Men		Women	
	Marital Status			
	Single	Married	Single	Married
17–18	91 (121)	– (1)	90 (94)	45 (22)
19–20	58 (72)	– (19)	53 (51)	21 (58)
21–22	31 (36)	30 (46)	71 (24)	7 (86)
23–24	22 (27)	26 (43)	– (11)	2 (98)

N	809
NA on last year	3
NA on age	1
Total N	813

schoolgoers (but there quickly comes a time when single girls are hard to find). Married women are quick to abandon classrooms. Compared to the unattached girls, single men are likely to shun school, but at certain ages (their early twenties) the school attendance of married men easily matches that of their bachelor peers.

The differential in remaining in school among married persons of both sexes is readily evident from Table 17.11. Here we again

Table 17.10 Percentage Planning To Be in School This Year, by Age, Sex, and Marital Status

Age	Sex			
	Men		Women	
	Marital Status			
	Single	Married	Single	Married
17–18	73 (121)	– (1)	71 (96)	9 (22)
19–20	46 (72)	– (19)	39 (51)	14 (58)
21–22	28 (36)	39 (46)	58 (24)	8 (86)
23–24	19 (27)	12 (43)	– (11)	8 (99)

N	812
NA on age	1
Total N	813

Table 17.11 Rates of Remaining, by Grades of School Completed, Sex, and Marital Status

Sex	Grades of School Completed			
	Less Than Twelve		Twelve or More	
	Marital Status			
	Single (Per Cent)	Married (Per Cent)	Single (Per Cent)	Married (Per Cent)
Men	83 (63)	– (4)	68 (106)	62 (26)
Women	85 (42)	– (6)	71 (90)	33 (24)

present rates of remaining among persons recently attending school; controls are introduced for sex, educational attainment (the sample is dichotomized at the point of high-school graduation), and marital status.

The most substantial differences in the table are those between married girls (at the twelfth-grade level or beyond) on one hand, and single girls and married men on the other. Looking first at the differences between the sexes, we note that the rate of remaining for married girls is almost one-half the figure for married men. Compared to the figure for single girls at the same point in the educational process, it is slightly less than half. Stated differently, the rate of remaining in school for relatively well-educated young men who are also married is well above the comparable figure for married girls, and only slightly lower than that rate among men who have never married.

An astute gambler might wager that these school-going married males would more often (than single males) be attending school part time, be working while at school, and be taking vocationally oriented courses. He would be correct in every instance. Unfortunately, only sixteen such cases fell into our sample, and these particular characteristics, while they are surely suggestive, are not reliable, given the size of our sample.

COMMUNITY SIZE

Earlier sections of this monograph have emphasized the concentration of adult schooling in urban and suburban areas of the country. If the participation rates of adults can be used as a guide, we would expect to find higher attainment levels directly associated with size of home community for younger persons as well. Table 17.12*a* confirms this hunch: there is a distinct concentration of persons aged seventeen–twenty-four with more than a high-school education in large cities.

There is a good chance that migration patterns influence this skew—sending better-educated persons into the cities and surrounding suburbs, whatever the size of their actual community of origin. We have to examine current school-going decisions before accepting the favored position of city dwellers and suburbanites without important qualifications.

The size of our sample makes comparisons feasible only if we divide these cases into two groups: persons currently living in communities of at least 50,000 inhabitants, on one hand, and residents of less-populated places, on the other. Table 17.12*b* presents current rates of staying in school for these two groups, controlling, as before, for grades of school completed.

Table 17.12 Educational Attainment, Rates of Remaining, and Rates of Returning, by Community Size

a. Grades of Schooling Completed, by Community Size

Community Size	Grades of School Completed			Total	
	11 Grades or Less (Per Cent)	12 Grades (Per Cent)	13 Grades or More (Per Cent)	Per Cent	N
2,000,000 and more	27	43	30	100	178
50,000–2,000,000	34	49	17	100	313
10,000–50,000	43	41	16	100	135
Less than 10,000	34	49	17	100	180

N	806
NA on grades	7
Total N	813

b. Rates of Remaining, by Grades Completed and Community Size

Community Size	Grades of School Completed		
	11 Grades or Less (Per Cent)	12 Grades (Per Cent)	13 Grades or More (Per Cent)
50,000 and more	79 (66)	58 (83)	84 (75)
Less than 50,000	84 (49)	40 (55)	82 (33)

c. Rates of Returning, by Grades Completed and Community Size

Community Size	Grades of School Completed		
	11 Grades or Less (Per Cent)	12 Grades (Per Cent)	13 Grades or More (Per Cent)
50,000 and more	9 (90)	13 (146)	20 (30)
Less than 50,000	1 (69)	3 (89)	– (19)

According to the rates computed, urban residence has the greatest impact on the plans of persons who have just completed high school. A margin of 18 per cent separates the college-going plans of high-school graduates in the two types of communities. The other differences to be found are much smaller by comparison, but among the current high-school generation (those not yet graduated) the pattern is reversed. Persons living in larger communities may be more likely to attend college once out of high school, but they are also more likely to leave high school before the twelfth grade.

Part *c* of the table is also revealing. Returnees are disproportionately drawn from urban places, and among city dwellers, the

Table 17.13 Educational Attainment and Rates of Remaining and Returning, by Race

a. Grades of Schooling Completed, by Race

| Race | Grades of School Completed | | | Total | |
	11 Grades or Less (Per Cent)	12 Grades (Per Cent)	13 Grades or More (Per Cent)	Per Cent	N
White	32	48	21	101	687
Negro	51	37	12	100	110

N	797
NA on race*	10
NA on grades	6
Total N	813

b. Rates of Remaining and Returning, by Race

Race	In School Last Year: Rate of Remaining (Per Cent)	Not in School Last Year: Rate of Returning (Per Cent)
White	70 (314)	6 (375)
Negro	69 (42)	25 (69)

N	800
NA on race	10
NA on plans	3
Total N	813

*Includes Orientals.

rate of returning increases sharply as attainment increases. The parallel between these findings and those reported for school-going among adults is striking. In both cases urban residence counts as a distinct advantage.

RACE

Our sample contains 692 whites, 111 Negroes, and 10 members of smaller racial groups and unknowns. Therefore, we have enough cases to compare whites and Negroes in terms of school attainment and the by now familiar rates of remaining and returning. We do not have enough cases to control for attainment as we compute these rates, but the patterns generated are sufficiently intriguing to warrant the inclusion of Table 17.13 in this report.

From part *a* of the table we learn that whites typically advance much farther in school than Negroes. Only 32 per cent of the whites have not yet been graduated from high school, but 51 per cent of the Negroes fall into that category. Just about twice as many whites as Negroes have ever been exposed to college.

Once we have digested part *a* of the table, part *b* comes as something of a surprise. Looking first at rates of remaining among recent attenders, we find no difference between the races at all. Thus, while Negroes have been leaving school in proportionately greater numbers than whites, they are quite reluctant to tell interviewers that leaving school figures very heavily in their immediate plans. Among those who are currently out of school, the responses of Negroes are even more extreme. Out-of-school Negroes are four times more likely to insist that they will be attending school during the coming academic year. How deep do these "expectations" actually run? Patricia Sexton (1963) has argued that Negro career expectations "often reach into the Walter Mitty and Superman worlds of fantasy," an observation which seems quite congruent with the data reported above.

SOCIO-ECONOMIC STATUS

Our measure of social status in this section of the analysis derives from a quantitative index of social position recently developed by Duncan (1961). Taking the census list of 425 detailed occupations, Duncan assigned a score to each job; the score was a function of both the education attained and income received by all males so employed in the civilian labor force in 1950. The occupations were then regrouped according to decile rank, or the particular tenth of the labor force into which they fell on the basis of the assigned score. By dichotomizing this decile ranking it is possible to identify each of the 425 occupations scored by Duncan as being either above or below that point which divides Americans into the "highs" and "lows" of social status. A high socio-economic designation simply means that the occupation in question is a position which is typically held by a person who has more education and earns more money than the majority of his working countrymen. A selected list of occupations appears in Table 17.14. Each occupation cited is identified by its socio-economic designation for this chapter (high–low), its decile rank, and the original socio-economic index score assigned to it.

Each respondent was asked (Question 45-A), "What kind of work does your father do?" (Or, if deceased: "What was your father's main occupation during most of his lifetime?") The answers were coded by decile ranks, but to simplify presentation in Table 17.15, educational attainment and the appropriate rates are presented in terms of the high–low split described above.

Looking first at Table 17.15*a* we note the concentration of persons low in socio-economic status at the "eleven grades or less" level of attainment, and the disproportionate number of persons high in socio-economic status who have completed at least some college. Part *b* (rates of remaining) again underlines the favored position of high-status respondents at each phase of the educational process. Differences between the two positions reach their highest points at the level of high-school graduation (twelve grades) and exposure to college (thirteen grades or more). At these points a margin of about 25 per cent differentiates the immediate school plans of the two groups.

The advantage held by those of higher status does not reappear in part *c*, however. Returnees, especially among the college generation, more often tend to be low-status students. Stated differently, we can observe that 49 per cent of the total sample falls into the low socio-economic category, yet the category contains 54 per cent of all returnees. The difference is hardly dramatic, but it does indicate a slight bias toward those of more humble origin. This pattern may well be a function of the disproportionate number of Negroes found at the lower levels of the social ladder.

Table 17.14 Selected Occupations, by Socio-Economic Status, Decile Rank, and Socio-Economic Index

SES	Occupation	Decile	Socio-Economic Index
High	Doctor	10	92
	Manager, banking and finance	10	85
	Electrical engineer	10	84
	Real estate agent	9	62
	Secretary	9	61
	Sales clerk	8	47
	Electrician	8	44
	Policeman	8	40
	TV repairman	7	36
	Plumber	7	34
	Piano tuner	7	33
	Welder	6	25
	Bus driver	6	24
Low	Auto mechanic	5	19
	Bartender	5	19
	Operative (manufacturing)	4	17
	Cook	4	15
	Laborer (metal industry)	3	14
	Farm owner or tenant	3	14
	Elevator operator	2	10
	Taxi driver	2	10
	Janitor	2	9
	Construction laborer	2	7
	Porter	1	4

SUMMARY

Our initial glance at school behavior has centered on the experiences of persons aged seventeen – twenty-four in the "regular" school system. In particular, we have discussed the problems of educational attainment and rates of remaining in and returning to school.

Table 17.15 Educational Attainment, Rates of Remaining and Rates of Returning, by Socio-Economic Status

a. Grades of School Completed, by Socio-Economic Status

SES	Grades of School Completed			Total	
	11 Grades or Less (Per Cent)	12 Grades (Per Cent)	13 Grades or More (Per Cent)	Per Cent	N
High	25	51	24	100	387
Low	42	43	15	100	380

N	767
NA on SES	39
NA on grades	7
Total N	813

b. Rates of Remaining, by Grades Completed and Socio-Economic Status

SES	Grades of School Completed		
	11 Grades or Less (Per Cent)	12 Grades (Per Cent)	13 Grades or More (Per Cent)
High	87 (54)	63 (70)	90 (72)
Low	76 (55)	40 (63)	65 (31)

c. Rates of Returning, by Grades Completed and Socio-Economic Status

SES	Grades of School Completed		
	11 Grades or Less (Per Cent)	12 Grades (Per Cent)	13 Grades or More (Per Cent)
High	7 (42)	10 (125)	9 (22)
Low	6 (106)	10 (101)	17 (24)

The data initially presented suggested a perceptible increase in exposure to college among younger persons, although a slight sampling bias is in some measure responsible for this pattern. After a preliminary consideration of immediate school plans, it was noted that rates of remaining in school were highest among those who had not yet reached the conventional points of termination of schooling at the twelfth and sixteenth grades. Persons who had recently attended school, but who had not yet received either a high-school diploma or a college degree were most likely to expect to remain. Rates of remaining tended to drop after graduation from either high school or college. On the other hand, there appears to be a direct, although modest, correlation between educational attainment and the proportions returning to school after an absence of at least one year.[2]

These findings on attainment, staying in school, and returning were then re-examined and specified in terms of five social background variables: sex, marital status, community size, race, and socio-economic status. Concerning current educational attainment, we noted that females are more likely to have completed high school but less likely to have moved on to more advanced levels of training. At the twelfth-grade level persons who have been married also enjoy a slight edge over those who have remained single, but the margin is reversed at the postsecondary level of schooling. Clear advantages in attainment accrue to those who are urban residents, white, and relatively high in social status.

Rates of remaining proved to be easier to specify than the relative proportions planning to return to school after an absence of at least a year. Continuous exposure to school is particularly characteristic of single persons from seventeen to twenty-four, but married males who have completed twelve or more years of school are also quite likely to plan to continue. Urban residence becomes an advantage primarily at the level of high-school

[2]The general problem of the returnee in the regular school system has received only a modest amount of systematic research attention. Given the findings presented earlier in this report, it is apparent that a great deal of work must be done if we are ever to learn how to induce those most in need of academic and vocational retraining to return eventually to school (see Greene, 1962; Saleem and Miller, 1961).

graduation. A disproportionate number of city dwellers chose to continue into college immediately. On the other hand, the advantage of being high in status is reflected in the school-going decisions of persons at every level of educational attainment.

Concerning rates of returning to school, we were able to uncover few substantial differences. On the whole, decisions to return to the regular school system after an extended absence appear to be most characteristic of persons who have at least completed high school. Single persons plan to return more often than those who are married,[3] but there is little difference to report by sex. One of the strongest findings uncovered in this area is the direct correlation among city dwellers between school attainment and decisions to return. A returning rate of 20 per cent was reported for out-of-school urban respondents who had been exposed to at least some college. Interrupted schooling of this sort appears to be mainly characteristic of low-status respondents; a sizeable number of Negroes, for example, insist that they will soon return to school.

[3]On a percentage basis it should be noted that there is a disproportionate number of widowed, divorced, and separated persons among the returnees. Of all persons planning to return to school, 11 per cent have experienced a broken marriage of some type: on the other hand, only 2 per cent of the general sample have been widowed, divorced, or separated.

18

Adjustment to High School and Its Implications

The preceding chapter has given us an initial appreciation of the kinds of variables which constitute the social dimensions of remaining in school during adolescence and early adulthood. We have shown that staying in school, and, presumably, early adjustment are related to the same factors which influence educational attainment and have observable social correlates.

But this has not really been made explicit. From Table 17.15, for example, one might infer that persons of low socio-economic status adapt less successfully to school. We do not really know this, however. We have only observed that at every age they are less likely to remain in school than their peers of high status, and we then surmise that persons of low social position, in one sense or another, get along less well with their textbooks, teachers, and fellow students. Such inferences should and can be made explicit and testable.

What is called for is an index which embodies a number of strategic aspects of school adjustment. To be useful, the measure should be constructed so that it is sensitive to the school adaptation of the largest possible number of respondents. For example, an index reflecting high-school experiences would provide us with an especially appropriate measure, since 95 per cent of our sample is either now attending or has attended secondary school. An index of adjustment to high school might prove especially relevant because the latter half of these years represents, in effect, the first period of school attendance which is not obligatory under the general law of the land. Thus we turn to the questionnaire to seek out items that might reliably differentiate our sample into successful and unsuccessful adapters to high school.

AN INDEX OF ADJUSTMENT TO HIGH SCHOOL

We can arbitrarily separate high-school adjustment into two components, academic and social. However the relevance of each may be weighted by high-school students themselves, we shall weight them equally as we develop our index. Specifically, we have in mind a combination of responses to four items on the questionnaire, Questions 31(i), 32, 33, and 34. Let us review them in turn and consider their wording and the patterns of response which they elicited.

As a first attempt toward specifying adjustment to high school we may appropriately ask about the importance that each respondent attached to his academic grades when he was a student. This was done in Question 31 (i). The exact wording of the question and the distribution of answers appear in Table 18.1.

Table 18.1 Importance of Grades

[Question 31 (i)] When you think back over your high-school days, how important was it to you then (has it been to you) to study hard and get good grades? Would you say A, B, C, or D [on the flash card]?

        A. Extremely important
        B. Slightly important
        C. Not very important
        D. Couldn't have cared less

Distribution of Responses	N	Per Cent
Extremely important	357	44
Slightly important	296	36
Not very important	94	12
Couldn't have cared less	18	2
Don't know	1	*
No answer	10	1
Never attended high school	37	5
Total	813	100

*Less than 1 per cent.

Forty-four per cent of the sample felt that studying hard and getting good grades was extremely important. Two per cent "couldn't have cared less." We note with interest that thirty-seven persons (5 per cent of the sample) have never attended high school at all. As we present the components of our index, this group will be carried along at the bottom of each table.

Table 18.2 presents another item relevant to academic behavior — estimated rank in class. Thirty-five per cent of the respondents place themselves in the top third of their class. We should, perhaps, be grateful for the happy congruence between the number of persons who chose this description and the number to whom it could objectively apply. Young people seem especially reluctant to place themselves in the bottom third of their class: only 11 per cent felt that that was their place in the academic scheme of things. However, the two items, class rank and importance of grades, are, as one might suspect, positively related ($Q = +.57$) and apparently reflect related components of academic adjustment.

Concerning social adjustment, let us first consider a subjective measure of involvement in peer activities, the respondent's judgment of himself in relation to the "center" of things that go on in high school. The exact question and the answers, appear in Table 18.3. Apparently, there is little elbow room at the center of student activities (one-half of the sample say that they were "pretty close" to that spot). Another indication of the same type

---

Table 18.2 Estimated Rank in Class

[Question 32] At high school, were your grades more often in the upper third of your class, in the middle third, or in the lower third?

Distribution of Responses	N	Per Cent
Upper third	284	35
Middle third	391	48
Lower third	86	11
Don't know	2	*
No answer	13	2
Never attended high school	37	5
Total	813	101

*Less than 1 per cent.

of behavior is provided in Question 34-A. At this point in the interview those who reported membership in any clubs or teams at all were asked to specify the total number of groups to which they belonged.

Table 18.4 contains the relevant data. The 45 per cent claiming membership in three or more student groups contains a substantial number of persons who find themselves at the "center" of things in high school ($Q = +.71$), and we shall employ

---

Table 18.3 Involvement in Student Activities

[Question 33] How close were you to the center of the student activities that went on at your high school — were you pretty close to the center, a little on the outside, or completely outside of things?

Distribution of Responses	N	Per Cent
Pretty close to the center	404	50
A little on the outside	253	31
Completely outside of things	107	13
Don't know	6	1
No answer	6	1
Never attended high school	37	5
Total	813	101

Table 18.4 Club and Team Memberships

[Question 34] Did you belong to any clubs, organizations, or athletic teams in high school? [If Yes] [Question 34-A] Which ones? (Any others?)

Number of Memberships Reported	N	Per Cent
None	181	22 ⎫
One	99	12 ⎬ 50
Two	128	16 ⎭
Three	136	17 ⎫
Four	80	10 ⎪
Five	55	7 ⎬ 45
Six	45	5 ⎪
Seven or more	46	6 ⎭
No answer	6	1
Never attended high school	37	5
Total	813	101

both of these indicators in our more general index of adjustment.

Each of the following characteristics was assigned one point: (*1*) Describing grades and studying hard as "extremely important"; (*2*) self-placement in the top third of one's high-school class; (*3*) being "pretty close to the center" of student activities; and (*4*) reporting at least three club memberships.

As Table 18.5 indicates, scores range from zero to four, and respondents with a score of at least three are designated as "successful" adjusters to high school. For the moment we are concerned with the distribution of this top 29 per cent throughout the social structure. The 37 non-attenders (who have necessarily earned a score of zero) will be carried along with those who responded negatively to each of the four items scored.

CORRELATES OF SUCCESSFUL ADJUSTMENT

We return to the battery of variables which were introduced in Chapter 17 and around which we organized our discussion of immediate school plans. Of course, we are working toward an assessment of the influence of high-school adjustment on these very plans, and, having broadly sketched the social dimensions of school-going intentions, it is now appropriate to discuss actual school adjustment in comparable terms. Table 18.6 contains the relevant data in seven sections. Let us take them in the order presented.

Age.—We do not expect to find any systematic differences in adjustment to high school by age, for there are no obvious reasons why today's nineteen-year-olds, for example, should have

Table 18.5   Index of Adjustment to High School

Number of Indicators	N	Per Cent	Index Description
None	172*	21	Unsuccessful adjustment
One	204	25	Intermediate adjustment
Two	198	24	Intermediate adjustment
Three	149	18	Successful adjustment
Four	90	11	Successful adjustment
Total	813	99	

*Includes 37 persons who have never attended high school.

behaved much differently on this measure than today's twenty-two-year-olds when both were in secondary school. But we find, in part *a* of the table, that seventeen – eighteen-year-old persons describe their high-school adjustment in terms that are more positive than those used by older persons. Perhaps this is because they lack whatever perspective one develops toward these events as one matures. It is more likely that the difference can

Table 18.6 Per Cent Adjusting Successfully to High School, by Selected Social Variables

		a. Age		
	17 – 18	19 – 20	21 – 22	23 – 24
	33 (240)	26 (200)	30 (192)	28 (180)

N	812
NA on age	1
Total N	813

b. Sex	
Men	Women
22 (366)	35 (447)

Total N   813

c. Marital Status	
Single	Married
30 (439)	28 (374)

Total N   813

d. Sex and Marital Status			
Men		Women	
Single	Married	Single	Married
25 (257)	15 (109)	37 (182)	34 (265)

Total N   813

(Table 18.6 continued)

Table 18.6 *Continued*

e. Community Size			
2,000,000 and Over	50,000 – 2,000,000	10,000 – 50,000	Less Than 10,000
39 (180)	29 (315)	26 (135)	22 (183)

Total N   813

f. Socio-Economic Status	
Low	High
23 (381)	37 (392)

N   773
NA on SES   40
Total N   813

g. Race	
White	Negro
30 (692)	27 (111)

N   803
NA race*   10
Total N   813

*Includes Orientals.

be attributed to chance fluctuation, and in any event there are no ready explanations at hand for this difference.

Sex. — Contrary to what we might have inferred from earlier data, females are much more likely than males to adapt successfully to high school. This finding may not fit very neatly with their demonstrated readiness to marry earlier and leave school, but few teachers would question its validity. In the relevant literature females are consistently pictured as relatively cooperative and docile students, and that is the image which they project in part *b* of Table 18.6.

Marital status. — According to part *c* of the table, persons who are currently married have high-school experiences which are about as successful as the experiences of those who are single.

It should be interesting to consider sex and marital status simultaneously, to see if the lack of relationship between school adjustment and marital status applies to both girls and boys. These data appear in part *d* of the table.

Sex and marital status.—Twenty-five per cent of the single males have adjusted successfully to high school; the comparable figure for married males is a full ten points lower. This discrepancy is roughly three times greater for males than for females, and what it implies, essentially, is that girls who leave school to marry are not necessarily the less talented students. The brighter ones are leaving, too. This picture does not apply to young men, however, where marriage between seventeen and twenty-four is an adventure that seems to have little appeal to those who were wise and well behaved in secondary school.

Census estimates of median age at marriage have been close to age twenty for females since 1950 (cf. Taeuber and Taeuber, 1958, p. 154). Will the marriage—school adjustment pattern for girls hold if we consider only those married during or before their twentieth year? The data appear in Table 18.7 and once again there is little difference to report between the high-school adjustment of all females aged seventeen—twenty-four, on one hand and of those who marry rather early in life, on the other. A slight tendency toward early marriage is suggested among less successful high-school adapters, but these figures are far from comparable to the already noted differences which obtain among males.

Community size.—The pattern of school adjustment by size of home community reaffirms the previously noted advantages of urban residence. We find, in fact, a direct correlation between community size and successful high-school adjustment, yielding a percentage spread of 17 per cent between those residing in big

Table 18.7 Per Cent Adjusting Successfully to High School among All Women and Married Women 17–20 Years Old

All women	35	(447)
Married women 17–20 years old	32	(76)

cities and those living in rural communities. Once again urban residence counts as an advantage rather than a disability.

Socio-economic status. — The previous pattern of successful behavior among persons of high socio-economic status reasserts itself in part *f* of Table 18.6. Our measure of status yields a percentage spread of 14 per cent in favor of high-status persons.

Race. — Negroes adjust to high school somewhat less favorably than whites. The difference of three percentage points, however, is surprisingly slim.

We might usefully pause at this point to review patterns of adjustment to high school as they are reflected in Table 18.6. School adjustment is more favorable among females than males, and experiences are markedly less successful among those males who marry before age twenty-four. Urban residence is positively associated with school adjustment, and persons of high socio-economic status typically adjust much better than those of lower status.

The character of high-school adjustment should have important implications for later patterns of school attendance. We shall discuss several phases of this problem next.

CURRENT SCHOOL STATUS AND HIGH-SCHOOL ADJUSTMENT

By combining two pieces of information — grades of school completed and immediate school plans — we can generate a typology which reflects the current school status of the individual respondents surveyed. Table 18.8 contains this information under four general headings.

High-school dropouts. — By our definition a high-school dropout is a person without a secondary-school diploma who does not plan to be attending school in 1963. In all, 172 persons fit our definition. This figure includes the thirty-seven persons who have never attended high school at all; it also includes 114 other individuals who had abandoned school at least one year before they were interviewed, and another 21 cases who were planning to leave school for the first time at the moment they were interviewed.

High-school students.—We located 102 persons who were not yet graduated from high school and who intended to continue their studies during the coming year. We found that ninety-three had been enrolled in high school during 1962; 9 were returning to high school after an absence of at least one year.

High-school graduates.—From Table 18.8 we can also identify 281 persons who had terminated their schooling upon re-

---

Table 18.8 Current School Status (Grades Completed and Immediate School Plans)

---

172 High-School Dropouts
    37 never attended high school.
   114 departed from high school (without graduating) before 1962 and are staying out.
    21 attended high school in 1962 and are departing prior to graduation.

102 High-School Students
    93 attended high school in 1962 and will stay in.
     9 who once attended high school did not attend in 1962, but will return.

281 High-School Graduates
    68 attended high school in 1962, were graduates, and will stay out.
   213 were graduated from high school before 1962 and are staying out.

249 At Least Some College
    11 attended college in 1962 and are leaving.
    29 departed from college before 1962 and are staying out.
    70 were graduated from high school in 1962 and will enter college.
    22 were graduated from high school before 1962 and will enter college.
    76 attended college in 1962 and will stay in.
     5 who have some college, did not attend in 1962, but will return.
     7 attended college in 1962, were graduated, and are departing.
    13 were graduated from college before 1962 and are staying out.
    14 attended college in 1962, were graduated, and will stay in school.
     2 were graduated from college before 1962 and will return to school.

N	804
NA on school status	9
Total N	813

ceipt of a high-school diploma. This number includes 68 respondents who had just received their diplomas prior to the interviewing phase of this study. Another 213 persons were graduated at least one year before and had never returned to school.

At least some college.—The most heterogeneous category in Table 18.8 is the final one, which includes all individuals who have completed (or are immediately aiming toward) at least some schooling beyond the high-school level. There are forty persons who had sought college-level training, but who had not remained in school long enough to receive a degree. Eleven recent dropouts and twenty-nine long-term stayouts are in this group. Another portion of the final category contains all persons who have completed a high-school education and who will be attending school regularly during the approaching academic year. Also included are all college graduates. This is the way these groups break down: seventy-six persons are remaining in school at the college level; seventy high-school graduates are about to begin their higher education, as are twenty-two persons who left high school more than twelve months ago; fourteen recent college graduates are aiming at postgraduate training, as are two persons who have held degrees for more than twelve months. Five students are returning to college after interrupting their studies and, finally, the category also contains twenty persons who have already been graduated from college and who will not be in school next year.

Initially we can ask how high-school adjustment relates on one's movement through the regular school system. We can do this by characterizing each type of current status by the proportion adapting successfully to high school. According to Table 18.9, and also according to our particular definition of high-school adjustment, 30 per cent of those persons currently in high school can be described as successful adjusters.

Terminated high-school graduates are somewhat off the pace set by the current generation of secondary-school students. Note that only 10 per cent of the high-school dropouts can be described as successful adjusters. Since 37 of these persons were never in secondary school at all, it is appropriate to re-percentage this figure to a new base, that is, to consider only the 135 dropouts who have ever attended high school. Among this group, then, we find that 13 per cent adjusted successfully. Thus, whatever base is employed, we can safely characterize high-school dropouts as a group which reports a distinctly inferior academic and social adaptation to school. At the other extreme, we note that 50 per cent of the college group reports a successful adjustment. This is 20 per cent higher than the group currently attending high school and much higher than those who have terminated their schooling at any point prior to attendance at college. Taken together, these figures imply that the character of high-school adjustment is a decisive factor in remaining in school, and that it is especially strategic in shaping plans for college. The following section discusses this problem from another point of view.

RATES OF REMAINING AND RETURNING BY ADJUSTMENT TO HIGH SCHOOL

One method of assessing the impact of past adjustment upon school-going plans is to consider the rates of staying in school which occur among different types of adjusters at different points in the educational process. Table 18.10 sheds some light on this problem. In this table are rates of remaining among persons who last year attained one of three levels of schooling cited.

Table 18.9 Per Cent Adjusting Successfully to High School, by Current School Status

Current School Status		
High-school dropouts	10	(172)
High-school students	30	(102)
High-school graduates	23	(281)
At least some college	50	(249)
N	804	
NA	9	
Total N	813	

The first row of the table shows that 91 per cent of those successful students who were in high school the previous year (but who were not seniors) elected to continue their schooling. By comparison, we find a staying-in rate of 77 per cent among less successful adapters. The observed difference (14 per cent) can be taken as a measure of the advantage which successful adjusters enjoy relevant to continuous schooling at this level. Note that this advantage is especially pronounced among recent high-school graduates. Of the successful adapters 67 per cent are college bound, compared to 43 per cent of the less successful in their graduating class. From the third row of the table, we are led to draw the somewhat unexpected inference that high-school adjustment, however important it may be in determining who arrives in college, has no effect at all in determining who stays there, once admitted.

Is school adjustment also a decisive factor in determining who returns to school? A partial answer can be found in Table 18.11 and that answer seems to be a qualified "no."

We can make a complete comparison at only one grade level — the twelfth — but this is an opportunity not to be overlooked, given the already demonstrated impact of school adjustment on the plans to remain of high-school graduates. How, then, does adjustment influence plans to return to school?

According to Table 18.11, its influence is minimal. Successful adjusters have a slightly higher rate of returning to school at the

Table 18.10 Rates of Remaining for Those in School Last Year, by Adjustment to High School and Grade of School Attained Last Year

Grade Attained Last Year	Adjustment to High School		Observed Difference (Per Cent)
	Successful (Per Cent)	Less Successful (Per Cent)	
Grades 9–11	91 (32)	77 (79)	−14
Grade 12	67 (43)	43 (95)	−24
Grades 13–16	87 (47)	87 (40)	−

very grade level when most returnees do indeed return and where the impact of adjustment on plans to continue (i.e., of those recently in school) is highly significant.

We can underline this point by directing attention to Table 18.12, which indicates the proportions who have adjusted successfully to school according to the content of their immediate school plans (a measure introduced in Chap. 17).

Not surprisingly, 43 per cent of all stay-ins are or have been successful adjusters to high school. Note that the percentage for returnees is a full 14 points lower. Once we observe that our definition of successful adjustment automatically placed 29 per cent of all respondents in that category, it becomes apparent that returnees have adjusted no better than the typical respondent in this survey, even though they are primarily oriented toward college-level training. The mystery is deepened if we pause to recall their other characteristics. As noted in Chapter 17, they tend more often to be low in socio-economic status and/or Negroes, urban, generally single, but often victims of broken marriages, somewhat older than the average respondent, and they have typically been away from school for about two years.

Since we have no further information at hand and no very obvious way to explain the intended re-entry of these students, we can only return to these bare facts and attempt to reassess their significance in provoking the decision to go back to school. If, in addition, we consider that at least 281 other persons in the sample share a roughly comparable level of educational attain-

Table 18.11 Rates of Returning for Those Out of School Last Year, by Adjustment to High School and Highest Grade Attained

Highest Grade Attained	Adjustment to High School		Observed Difference (Per Cent)
	Successful (Per Cent)	Less Successful (Per Cent)	
Grades 9–11	– (15)	6 (103)	–
Grade 12	11 (56)	9 (179)	–2
Grades 13–16	10 (21)	– (13)	–

ment (high-school graduates) and decided not to return, then we have also underlined their truly minority status and the uniqueness of their educational plans. And now, how are we to explain these plans?

To begin with, we can say that these individuals, in contrast to their school-going peers, have experienced a measure of direct contact with the adult environment of the outside world. Can we assume that their decision to return to school was provoked by a certain disenchantment with this contact? That so many persons planning to return are from urban and deprived backgrounds may provide some clues. It may well be that for some persons participation in a life of full-time employment and other adult responsibilities becomes, for them, participation in an environment which cannot be mastered and which proves hostile and disappointing. We will never know how many of these persons actually carried out their stated intention to return. However, it is tempting to infer that for those who have encountered special disappointments in their years out of school, education may become a special symbol, an avenue of endeavor which, if it is successfully pursued, could provide the opportunity that is subjectively felt to be necessary for successful adjustment to one's adult environment.

We do not have to focus specifically upon Negroes, widows, and divorcees to entertain this hypothesis sensibly. All of these returnees are, by definition, persons with at least some direct

Table 18.12 Per Cent Adjusting Successfully to High School for the Total Sample, by Immediate School Plans

Immediate School Plans		
Total sample	29	(813)
Staying in	43	(254)
Departing	25	(108)
Staying out	22	(410)
Returning	29	(38)
N	810	
NA on plans	3	
Total N	813	

contact with life beyond the classroom. For some of them we can find special characteristics from which we infer that this life, in some sense, disappointed and perhaps threatened them. For many of the others, perhaps sheer contact was enough. There is always a certain distance to be traveled before a value or norm that individuals endorse becomes a rule in terms of which they actually behave. Thus we are all patriotic, at least to a point; yet not everyone volunteers for the Peace Corps. By the same token, it is obvious that education is "important," yet not everyone intends to return to school after leaving. Our hypothesis, briefly stated, is that for returnees education has become especially important, although we cannot always say why.

AN INDEX OF PRACTICALISM

We see the particular orientation of returnees toward education as especially stressing the "pay-off" value of further schooling. And this pay-off, or reward, is presumably defined in terms which highlight the practical consequences of school attendance rather than its more intrinsic rewards. An index was developed to verify these speculations and to guide the analysis at this point. There are at least three questionnaire items which might conceivably specify such an orientation.

[QUESTION 42(i)] How important is it to have a college education in order to get a good paying job around here? [Respondents were asked to choose an alternative from answers that ranged from "absolutely necessary" to "you're better off without it."]

[QUESTION 42(ii)] How important is it to have a college education in order to be respected and looked up to by most people around here? [Again, the answers ranged from "absolutely necessary" to "you're better off without it."]

[QUESTION 43] Which [factors] are most important in helping a person get ahead? [Six items were listed, each respondent was told to select the two most important. One of the items was: A good education.]

Table 18.13 presents the answers given to those three questions. From part *a* of the table we learn that 44 per cent of the

Table 18.13 The "Pay-off" Value of Education

a. Importance of College for a Job That Pays Well

[Question 42 (i)] How important is it to have a college education in order to get a good paying job around here — would you say A, B, C, or D [on the flash card]?

Distribution of Responses	N	Per Cent
Absolutely necessary	360	44
It helps but it isn't necessary	384	47
Doesn't matter one way or the other	51	6
You're better off without it	5	1
Don't know	8	1
No answer	5	1
Total	813	100

b. Importance of College To Being Respected

[Question 42 (ii)] How important is it to have a college education in order to be respected and looked up to by most people around here?

Distribution of Responses	N	Per Cent
Absolutely necessary	103	13
It helps but it isn't necessary	425	52
Doesn't matter one way or the other	274	34
You're better off without it	2	*
Don't know	7	1
No answer	2	*
Total	813	100

c. Important Factors in Getting Ahead

[Question 43] [Show flash card] Of the six things on the card, which two do you think are most important in helping a person get ahead?

Distribution of Responses	N	Per Cent
Brains	141	17
A good education	563	69
Good luck	28	3
Hard work	462	57
Know the right people	67	8
Personality	354	43
Don't know	2	*
No answer	2	*
Total	813	197†

*Less than 1 per cent.
†Totals more than 100 per cent because respondents were asked to give more than one answer.

entire sample felt that college was "absolutely necessary" for a job that paid well. Only 7 per cent felt that it did not matter or that they were better off without college. Apparently, the general relevance of college for occupational success is rather widely accepted. Part *b* of Table 18.13, on the other hand, suggests that a much smaller proportion viewed college as the sine qua non of social prestige. Only 13 per cent of the sample described college as "absolutely necessary" if one is to be respected and looked up to. The modal response was, "It helps but it isn't necessary," and another third saw it as irrelevant. From part *c* of the table, we learn that 69 per cent of all respondents found a good education important in getting ahead: hard work ranks second, followed by personality, brains, knowing the right people, and good luck.

Taken together, the responses to these three questions produced a rough ordering of respondents in terms of the practical component of their orientation toward education. One point each was thus assigned to the following answers: (*1*) Viewing college as "absolutely necessary" for a good paying job; (*2*) seeing college as "absolutely necessary" in order to be respected and looked up to by others; and (*3*) counting a good education as one of the most important factors in getting ahead.

The distribution of scores can be seen in Table 18.14. The sample can be dichotomized so that exactly 38 per cent of all respondents may be termed relatively "high" on practicalism; these are the persons who earned either two or three points in answering the three questions. For the purposes of this report designation "highly practical" (or "high on practicalism") will

Table 18.14 Index of Practicalism

Number of Indicators	N	Per Cent	Index Description
None	165	20	Low
One	331	41	Low
Two	256	31	High
Three	61	7	High
Total	813	99	

refer to a single conviction which these 317 persons are felt to share: a conviction that education has important consequences for the occupational and social contexts of their lives.

PRACTICALISM, ADJUSTMENT TO HIGH SCHOOL, AND IMMEDIATE SCHOOL PLANS

How does practicalism influence school plans? By turning to Table 18.15 we can begin to explore this question; the table indicates the proportion of the total sample ranking high on this measure and then describes the relative performance of respondents in each category of school plans.

A glance at the row of figures is enough to assure us that the index of practicalism aptly answers the problem that it was designed to meet: 68 per cent of all returnees are highly practical in their orientation to education. This figure is 29 per cent above the norm for the entire sample and 25 per cent above the comparable proportion among stay-ins. Returnees seem quite convinced that education is especially important, although their previous adjustment to school can often suggest the contrary.

We can nail this point down by considering school adjustment and practicalism simultaneously, and examining the rates of remaining and returning which occur within this more detailed matrix. Table 18.16 contains the relevant data.

The first row of Table 18.16—proportions expecting to attend school this year, under both conditions—yields a fairly regular

---

Table 18.15 Per Cent High on Practicalism for the Total Sample, by Immediate School Plans

Immediate School Plans		
Total sample	39	(813)
Staying in	43	(254)
Departing	37	(108)
Staying out	34	(410)
Returning	68	(38)
N	810	
NA on plans	3	
Total N	813	

gradient in intentions. High-school adjustment shows the greatest impact on these plans, but within each category of adjustment a highly practical attitude carries important weight. Scanning the second row of the table ("Rates of Remaining"), we find the impact of practicalism reappearing, but in a somewhat less definite fashion. The final line of the table shows us why: practicalism makes its important contribution to school-going intentions among returnees—those persons aiming at school who were not attending last year. For 15 per cent of the unsuccessful adjusters, a highly practical attitude toward education seems to be pushing them toward a behavior which would have been difficult to predict, given their previous performance at school.

SUMMARY

In this chapter an index of adjustment to high school was developed from a set of four relevant questionnaire items. This measure underlined the superior high-school performance of females, city dwellers, and persons high in social status. Males married before their twenty-fifth birthday were found to have performed rather poorly in high school, but this was not the case for married females.

Table 18.16 Per Cent Expecting To Attend School This Year and Rates of Remaining and Returning, by Adjustment to High School and Practicalism

Attendance and Relevant Rates	Adjustment to High School			
	Successful		Less Successful	
	Practicalism			
	High	Low	High	Low
Persons who expect to be attending school this year	57 (94)	46 (144)	37 (222)	26 (350)
Rate of remaining	84 (56)	77 (80)	67 (94)	62 (132)
Rate of returning	18 (38)	6 (64)	15 (128)	4 (218)

Secondary-school adjustment was seen to be quite highly correlated with current school status (those in college reported the highest levels of adjustment), and it proved to be especially important in influencing initial decisions to enter college among those who had been attending school continuously. On the other hand, persons whose educations had been interrupted and who had chosen to return to school after an absence of at least a year had not been particularly successful as students when they were in high school. These individuals — returnees — were found to place special emphasis on the practical consequences of schooling for occupational status and in the area of social deference. In a later chapter we shall examine the relationship between these variables and participation in supplementary education.

19

Career
Goals and
Patterns of Adjustment
to the
Regular School
System

This chapter is concerned with the interplay of school and work. We focus upon patterns of adjustment to "regular" schools and upon the relationship between such adjustment and the types of careers that youngsters expect to pursue. The role of "irregular" schools will concern us in the next chapter.

The terms "school" and "work" come together quite nicely. Their union has in fact provided a point of departure for a number of important contributions to the literatures of social stratification and the sociology of education.[1] While we are mindful of these contributions, it is also clear that the age range of our sample and the type of data at our disposal invite particular attention to areas of analysis which have not received a large amount of systematic attention to date. The material in this chapter is thus organized along the following lines.

1. Initially we examine the distribution of mobility goals within the late adolescent and young adult population. For the age range being considered, analysis of employment goals is, at least

[1]Cf. Rivera (1963), especially Chaps. 3 and 5, for an overview of this literature.

initially, more appropriate than consideration of current job placement. Many respondents are not employed at all (they are still students); those who are working are probably employed at the lowest-level job they will ever hold.

2. In the area of employment goals we can usefully compare eventual job expectations with status of origin and separate out those individuals who are especially ambitious, given their particular social backgrounds.

3. These relatively ambitious persons are then compared to their peers in terms of their behavior in the regular school system. It becomes apparent as this analysis unfolds that consideration of the mobility orientations of girls requires separate attention, and a distinct mode of analysis was evolved to relate their work goals to school adjustment.

4. Next, that sector of the sample currently working full time will be scrutinized to determine early adjustment to work among those aged seventeen — twenty-four, the sector's correlates, and in particular, its relationship to behavior in school.

MOBILITY GOALS AND SEX

In order to have available information that might specify the relationship between school experiences and anticipated social mobility, each respondent was asked a sequence of questions dealing with eventual work preferences and expectations. Question 46, which opens the sequence, asks: "Is there any particular line of work that you'd really like to get into eventually?" Those who acknowledged a specific job preference (75 per cent of the sample) were asked to identify and to describe it; next they were asked [Question 46-E(2)]: "What do you think you'll probably end up doing?" The answers given by males and females to this question appear in Table 19.1. The occupational classification employed in the table is that of the Bureau of the Census.

The three top categories specify the ways in which persons could legitimately choose not to cite a Census job title. They could have no preference at all, they could be unable to voice a concrete expectation, or (for girls) they could choose the role of homemaker. Combining these categories separately for each sex, we find that 31 per cent of all males and 46 per cent of all females managed to avoid identifying a particular occupational destination. In the sections to come we shall pay some attention to persons who chose this option; for the moment, let us consider the performance of those who were able to offer a concrete job expectation.

For each sex we find a major cluster of responses at the level of professional and technical personnel. The literature on occupational goals indicates that this pattern is not unusual. Below this level we find another concentration of males among craftsmen and foremen, and clusters of females among clerical workers and also among service workers.

These job choices were also coded in terms of socio-economic deciles (Table 17.14 is reproduced below as Table 19.2). Considering the mean decile rank of the expectations cited, males are aiming toward decile rank 7.8, females toward exactly the same point. Perhaps surprisingly, there is no difference in decile goal levels between the sexes.

Table 19.1   Occupational Expectations by Sex

Occupational Expectations (Census Classification)	Sex	
	Men (Per Cent)	Women (Per Cent)
No specific job preference	22	27
Don't know, expected employment	9	6
Expect to be a housewife	0	13
Professional, technical, and kindred workers	35	25
Farmers and farm managers	4	0
Managers, officials, and proprietors	7	1
Clerical and kindred workers	1	13
Sales workers	*	*
Craftsmen, foremen, and kindred workers	14	*
Operatives and kindred workers	5	3
Private household and service workers	1	12
Farm laborers and foremen	*	*
Laborers, except farm and mine	1	*
Total per cent	99	100
Total N	366	447

*Less than 1 per cent.

It should be emphasized, however, that these decile ranks were derived from the social characteristics of the male labor force. This means, for example, that male secretaries are responsible for placing that category of worker in decile rank 9. As Table 19.1 indicates, clerical work of this sort is rather frequently chosen by females. According to the Report of the President's Commission on the Status of Women (1963, p. 37), there is no necessary correspondence between the job titles of

Table 19.2 Selected Occupations, by Socio-Economic Status, Decile Rank, and Socio-Economic Index

SES	Occupation	Decile	Socio-Economic Index
High	Doctor	10	92
	Manager, banking and finance	10	85
	Electrical engineer	10	84
	Real estate agent	9	62
	Secretary	9	61
	Sales clerk	8	47
	Electrician	8	44
	Policeman	8	40
	TV repairman	7	36
	Plumber	7	34
	Piano tuner	7	33
	Welder	6	25
	Bus driver	6	24
Low	Auto mechanic	5	19
	Bartender	5	19
	Operative (manufacturing)	4	17
	Cook	4	15
	Laborer (metal industry)	3	14
	Farm owner or tenant	3	14
	Elevator operator	2	10
	Taxi driver	2	10
	Janitor	2	9
	Construction laborer	2	7
	Porter	1	4

men and women and the salary that each sex receives. The report notes that "lower pay rates for women doing the same work as men are not uncommon."

The simple fact is that there is no easy way of specifying the relevance of the decile scale for the job choices of females, therefore any quantitative analysis of occupational goals which utilizes the decile scale (as in the section below) would be well advised to restrict its scope to males. This restriction becomes more palatable if we refer again to Table 19.1 and remind ourselves that almost one-half of the females in our sample chose not to offer a specific job title when they were asked about their employment plans. Apparently, there are major differences between the sexes in their orientations toward the world of work. We shall re-examine this problem in a later section.

The literature on mobility goals is notable for its dependence upon rather small and regionally specific samples. While our major concern in this area is to describe the relationship between expected mobility and the use that is made of different types of educational institutions, we can usefully introduce this problem by describing, in a general fashion, the current social location of those who aim for high-level jobs.

The five sections of Table 19.3 provide a useful point of departure. Each section specifies (for males) the proportion expecting to attend at least some college, in terms of the particular control introduced, the percentage of male respondents voicing a specific job preference, and the mean decile rank of the expected occupations offered by all males in the relevant categories.

Scanning the first row of part *a* of the table, we find a sharp drop in college intentions among males aged twenty-three – twenty-four. The pattern repeats itself in the figures below, where we find the smallest proportion of those with specific job preferences in that same age category. Again, when we consider the mean decile rank of those jobs cited as "expected," we find a gradient which emphasizes the relative modesty of the mobility goals of those who are most mature.

According to these figures, extreme ambition would seem to be a prerogative of the very young. The relevant literature has mentioned the gradual salience of "reality factors" for the mobility goals of youth. The implication is that a youngster's expectations concerning a career are initially high, but are often revised as he comes to experience and appreciate the dimensions of post-adolescent life. The behavior of those aged

Table 19.3 Performance on Mobility Variables among Men, by Selected Social Variables

Mobility Variables	a. Age			
	17 – 18	19 – 20	21 – 22	23 – 24
Per cent expecting at least some college	51 (120)	51 (88)	47 (82)	29 (69)
Per cent with a specific job preference	83 (122)	77 (91)	83 (82)	68 (69)
Occupational expectations (mean decile rank)	8.1 (93)	7.9 (60)	7.7 (63)	7.2 (38)
	b. Marital Status			
	Single	Married		
Per cent expecting at least some college	53 (251)	30 (103)		
Per cent with a specific job preference	79 (256)	78 (105)		
Occupational expectations (mean decile rank)	8.1 (186)	7.2 (66)		
	c. Community Size			
	2,000,000 and Over	50,000 – 2,000,000	10,000 – 50,000	Less Than 10,000
Per cent expecting at least some college	53 (70)	47 (133)	38 (73)	46 (82)
Per cent with a specific job preference	85 (71)	82 (135)	78 (74)	69 (85)
Occupational expectations (mean decile rank)	8.3 (56)	8.1 (95)	7.2 (52)	7.5 (52)

Table 19.3 *Continued*

Mobility Variables	d. Race	
	White	Negro
Per cent expecting at least some college	46 (317)	46 (39)
Per cent with a specific job preference	78 (324)	85 (39)
Occupational expectations (mean decile rank)	7.9 (224)	7.2 (29)
	e. Socio-Economic Status	
	High	Low
Per cent expecting at least some college	58 (171)	32 (170)
Per cent with a specific job preference	82 (176)	75 (172)
Occupational expectations (mean decile rank)	8.5 (129)	7.1 (114)

twenty-three – twenty-four in this sample adds a measure of empirical support for such contentions.

Most surprising, perhaps, is the fact that the specificity of work goals is lowest among the oldest respondents. There also seems to be some movement toward uncertainty as one travels beyond the point where high status looms as a possibility.

In part *b* of the table we find that educational and occupational goals are quite responsive to marital status. Specific job preferences appear to be unaffected by the presence or absence of a mate. The observed differences in the first and the third rows of part *b* might be attributed, at least in part, to the ages of single and married men (see Table 17.8), but even when age is controlled, we can report a slight tendency for single males to report higher goals.

Part *c* of Table 19.3 suggests that college expectations, specificity of job preference, and high occupational goals are especially characteristic of big-city males. Urban residence seems to elevate mobility goals in much the same fashion as it affected educational attainment and adjustment to school.

Once again (in part *d*) we find Negroes demonstrating a tendency to match whites in their stated intentions. According to these figures, there is little to separate the races in terms of educational or occupational goals. Since this question has already provoked a sizeable literature, we shall only note the congruence of our findings with published reports on this subject, admit that a ready explanation for the extreme mobility goals of Negroes is not yet available, and move on to part *e* of the table.

The final section points to a rather sizeable difference in the goals of high- and low-status males. A gap of 26 per cent separates the college-going intentions of these two groups, and the observed difference in level of expected occupation is the largest to be observed in any of the categories yet compared. Socioeconomic status seems to be a major influence upon the mobility goals of males. Given the literature to date (and common sense) this finding rings true. We shall consider it again in the following section.

MALES: AN INDEX OF ANTICIPATED MOBILITY

Our discussion of the distribution of ambition may have been informative, but it is seriously incomplete. What we did was to locate "pockets" of commitment to relatively high status. This is only one-half the story. We did not specify the status background of the persons inhabiting these "pockets," and the analysis as it now stands implies that we have accepted (for example) the assumption that all married persons aged seventeen – twenty-four had fathers who were equal in status to fathers of seventeen – twenty-four year-old bachelors.

The question raised by this example has to do with relative versus absolute mobility. This is the issue: can we treat without difference the son of a doctor and the son of a cook, when both announce that they expect to be doctors?

Clearly, we cannot. Sons of cooks log much more social mileage on the road to an M.D. than sons of doctors. And, although Table 19.2 passes over this point in silence (with the exceptions of parts *d* and *e*), it is obvious that any close look at "ambition" has to take into account the socio-economic origin of the person expressing a desire to be "up there."

There is another complication. A glance at Table 19.2, and a bit of mulling over it, teaches us one more lesson. If the cook's son chooses to be a plumber, and if the plumber's son chooses to be a doctor, then they have both chosen to move the same amount of social distance—exactly three notches up the scale. Who is more ambitious?

Our feeling is that both are equally ambitious, and should be treated as such. It thus becomes necessary to refine our notion of expected mobility, so that we can identify those who are mobile, relative to their peers, at each level of the social ladder. Table 19.4 provides the necessary framework for a resolution of this problem.

Table 19.4 Anticipated Mobility among Men, by Status of Origin (Socio-Economic Decile Rank)

Expected Shift (in Deciles)	Socio-Economic Decile Rank (Men)				
	1 – 2	3 – 4	5 – 6	7 – 8	9 – 10
Up nine	2				
Up eight	13				
Up seven	4	12			
Up six	3	12			
Up five	2	1	6		
Up four	4	3	10		
Up three	3	2	5	6	
Up two	1	4	9	14	
Up one	2	8	1	6	16
No shift	2	13	5	9	28
Down one	0	1	4	4	5
Down two		1	1	5	5
Down three		0	0	3	1
Down four			1	0	3
Down five			0	0	1
Down six				0	0
Down seven				0	1
Down eight					2
Down nine					0
N	36	57	42	47	62
Median (rounded)	Up seven	Up four	Up three	Up one	No shift

Along the horizontal axis of the table, all males able to identify their father's line of work are grouped in terms of the decile
level of his occupation. Intervals of two deciles are employed to
maintain adequate case bases. The vertical margin of the table
indicates the difference (in deciles) between status of origin
—father's job—and the level of the job each male respondent
eventually expects to hold. The concentration of cases at the top
of each column of figures suggests that many persons aim to move
as far as it is possible for them to go, given their point of origin.
These clusters suggest that the most appropriate measure of
typical shifts within status categories would be a median. Thus
at the base of each column a rounded median is presented,
indicating the level of expected mobility typical of the five socio-
economic groupings. Each column is split at a point close to
its median by a broken line which runs across the table. All
persons above that line are aiming for jobs which reflect a level
of ambition at or above that characteristic of persons at their
level of origin. We shall designate these persons as "mobiles."
All persons located below the broken line are considered
"non-mobiles." The cluster of cases at upper ends of the columns and the relatively small number of possible "shift" categories make an even dichotomy impossible to achieve, but the
mobile—non-mobile distinction, however gross, will be seen to
have important consequences for school adjustment.

We shall deal with three groups of respondents: mobiles and
non-mobiles as defined above, and a combined group consisting
of persons with no particular work preferences or no specific
expectations. This final category can be termed the "undecideds."
The relative size of these three groups can be seen in Table 19.5.

FEMALES: HOME AND WORK GOALS

For reasons noted above, the decile technique is less efficient
in describing the career plans of females. While some type of ad
hoc occupational classification might be devised to describe the
status level of their goals, the fact that 46 per cent of the girls in
this sample chose not to specify an employment expectation
suggests that any such attempt would have limited relevance.
From a strictly methodological point of view, this is an unhappy

situation. There seems to be no neat way in which to group females in a fashion comparable to the classification developed for males. From a substantive point of view it becomes apparent that the index of anticipated mobility is actually irrelevant to the plans for the future of many girls. For the majority of these respondents it is the performance of their husbands that will achieve whatever mobility they might experience.

From this point of view, we are led to acknowledge the rather obvious fact that the vast majority of these young women will be homemakers. (Only seven girls in this sample expect never to marry.) Many of them will work at various times during their married lives, others will not. We might usefully return to Question-46E(2) and reconsider its wording. The question asked: "What do you think you'll probably end up doing?"

Earlier it was noted that 13 per cent of the girls replied that they would be housewives. Now this does not mean that they will never work at all; it simply means that given the opportunity, 58 persons out of a sample of 447 girls will describe their future role as that of a homemaker. These persons are obvious candidates for a separate category in any classification of anticipated female career lines.

Concerning the balance of the sample, we can look again at the specificity of the job choices made. Virtually all these girls expected to be married, but in addition to the homemaker role, they anticipated and acknowledged the probability of some

---

Table 19.5   Distribution of Mobility Goals for Men

Index of Anticipated Mobility		Per Cent
Mobile		40
Non-mobile		30
Undecided		30
Total per cent		100
N		350
N	350	
NA on SES	16	
Total N	366	

degree of contact with the world of work. The majority of them could identify the job they were moving toward and selected that job title—rather than the term "housewife"—to describe the work they would be doing eventually. The question, of course, was aimed at eliciting a specific job title. Those girls who were able to respond in these terms, even while acknowledging that they expected to be married, are classified as a separate group in our typology of female career expectations.

The remaining group thus contains all girls who expected to be married, but who expressed no definite preference or employment goal when quizzed about their expectations. The relative size of all three groups may be seen in Table 19.6.

To make discussion of these categories less taxing, we reserve the terms "homemakers" and "housewives" for those who described themselves exclusively in those terms. Under the heading "home," we find 14 per cent of all females who expected to be married. The balance of the sample contains the 53 per cent who were able to identify a particular occupational slot that they might fill, even though married, and the 33 per cent who were less specific concerning their employment plans. Some correlates of these choices are discussed below.

CAREER GOALS, AGE, AND SOCIO-ECONOMIC STATUS

In Table 19.3 we noted a tendency for older persons to be both more modest and less specific about their employment

Table 19.6 Distribution of Home and Work Goals for Women

Home and Work Goals	Per Cent
Home and specific work	53
Home and vague work	33
Home	14
Total per cent	100
N	430

N	430	
NA on marry*	17	
Total N	447	

*Includes those who intend never to marry.

goals. The pattern appears again in part *c* of Table 19.7, where, for four-year age groups, we note a drop in the proportion of mobile males and corresponding increases in the percentages of non-mobile and undecided.

A comparable shift occurs when a control for socio-economic status is applied to anticipated mobility goals. Socio-economic status generates an 11 per cent difference within the mobile category, although it should be noted that a large part of this margin is a function of the grossness of our measure of mobility.

Both controls—age and socio-economic status—are applied simultaneously in part *c* of the table, where we find somewhat different patterns of goal shifts by age within each status category. Among high-status males, for example, the tendency is for older persons to abandon high mobility expectations in favor of more modest, but equally specific work goals. Among low-status persons the major shift is from non-mobile expectations to indecision. Thus the movement toward less extreme mobility goals among older males (noted in Table 19.3) seems to be a phenomenon which occurs most often among high-status males; the shift toward less specific goals appears to be more characteristic of those of lower status.

We can apply this same sequence of controls to girls. In part *a* of Table 19.8, for example, we find that the major effect of increasing age among females is to induce a shift from specific to vague work goals. The proportion of girls expecting to be housewives remains constant over both age classes.

Except for a tendency for low-status girls to be less likely to describe themselves only as future homemakers, the pattern of responses noted above repeats itself when socio-economic status is the control variable, as in part *a* of the table. The major shift is again from specific to vague work goals, and in this instance employment uncertainty is concentrated among low-status females.

When we control for age and socio-economic status simultaneously (see part *b*), we find that that the combined effect of both variables induces a sizeable spread within the categories of those acknowledging both specific and uncertain employment plans. In comparison, homemaker goals demonstrate only minor and erratic differences under the dual controls.

Table 19.7 Anticipated Mobility, Age, and Socio-Economic Status

a. Anticipated Mobility among Men by Age

| Age | Index of Anticipated Mobility | | | Total | |
	Mobile (Per Cent)	Non-Mobile (Per Cent)	Undecided (Per Cent)	Per Cent	N
17–20	42	29	28	99	204
21–24	36	32	32	100	145

N	349
NA on age	1
NA on SES	16
Total N	366

b. Anticipated Mobility among Men by Socio-Economic Status

| SES | Index of Anticipated Mobility | | | Total | |
	Mobile (Per Cent)	Non-Mobile (Per Cent)	Undecided (Per Cent)	Per Cent	N
High	45	28	27	100	177
Low	34	32	33	99	173

N	350
NA on SES	16
Total N	366

c. Anticipated Mobility among Men by Socio-Economic Status and Age

| SES | Age | Index of Anticipated Mobility | | | Total | |
		Mobile (Per Cent)	Non-Mobile (Per Cent)	Undecided (Per Cent)	Per Cent	N
High	17–20	49	24	27	100	100
	21–24	39	34	26	99	76
Low	17–20	35	35	30	100	104
	21–24	32	29	39	100	69

N	349
NA on SES	16
NA on age	1
Total N	366

Table 19.8   Home and Work Goals, Age, and Socio-Economic Status

a. Home and Work Goals among Women, by Age

Age	Home and Work Goals			Total	
	Home and Specific Work (Per Cent)	Home and Vague Work (Per Cent)	Home Only (Per Cent)	Per Cent	N
17–20	60	26	14	100	219
21–24	46	40	14	100	211

N	430
NA on marry*	17
Total N	447

b. Home and Work Goals among Women by Socio-Economic Status

SES	Home and Work Goals			Total	
	Home and Specific Work (Per Cent)	Home and Vague Work (Per Cent)	Home Only (Per Cent)	Per Cent	N
High	60	23	17	100	208
Low	48	42	11	101	199

N	407
NA on SES	24
NA on marry*	16
Total N	447

c. Home and Work Goals among Women by Socio-Economic Status and Age

SES	Age	Home and Work Goals			Total	
		Home and Specific Work (Per Cent)	Home and Vague Work (Per Cent)	Home Only (Per Cent)	Per Cent	N
High	17–20	64	20	15	99	104
	21–24	55	26	19	100	104
Low	17–20	55	33	13	101	104
	21–24	40	51	8	99	95

N	407
NA on SES	24
NA on marry*	16
Total N	447

*Includes those who intend never to marry.

Specific work goals are most commonly held by high-status females who are young. They diminish in relative frequency and reach their lowest point among low-status girls twenty-one–twenty-four years of age. Uncertain work goals demonstrate exactly the opposite tendency. A margin of 31 per cent separates the two extremes, and in this instance lower status and higher age seem to be most compatible with indecision.

CAREER GOALS AND ADJUSTMENT TO THE REGULAR SCHOOL SYSTEM

Our measures of school adjustment have been introduced in Chapters 17 and 18. At this point our intention is to employ these variables in an attempt to specify further the career expectations of males and females aged seventeen–twenty-four.

Our expectation, of course, is that the two sets of variables will demonstrate a strong relationship. Part *a* of Table 19.9 describes the mobility goals of males with controls for socio-economic status and adjustment to high school. Among high-status males we find a distinct concentration of mobile respondents among successful school adjusters. According to the second row of the table, a majority of the less successful males inhabit the non-mobile and undecided categories. This pattern is even more pronounced among low-status males, where 72 per cent of all successful high-school students can be described as upwardly mobile in their career expectations, compared to 28 per cent of those less successful in high school.

Part *b* of the table tells a similar story. In this instance we have excluded all current high-school students who are males and dichotomized the current school status of the balance of the sample at the point of exposure to college. (Persons now in high school have not yet had the opportunity to attend school beyond the twelfth grade; the appropriate comparison is thus between individuals who have had the opportunity and who seized it [at least some college], and persons now out of school who terminated their education at or before the twelfth grade [never exposed to college]). In these comparisons we find a more striking correlation between employment goals and school behavior at both social levels. The implication is that throughout the social structure successful adjustment to the regular school system encourages young men to express higher ambitions than their peers. In Chapter 20 we shall report on whatever role adult education might play for such career goals; for the moment let us examine the intentions of females according to our measures of behavior in school.

Part *a* of Table 19.10 shows that within social levels success-ful school adjustment encourages concrete employment goals.

Table 19.9 Anticipated Mobility among Men, by Socio-Economic Status and Adjustment to the Regular School System

a. Anticipated Mobility by Socio-Economic Status and Adjustment to High School

SES	Adjustment to High School	Index of Anticipated Mobility			Total	
		Mobile (Per Cent)	Non-Mobile (Per Cent)	Undecided (Per Cent)	Per Cent	N
High	Successful	63	19	19	101	54
	Less successful	37	33	30	100	123
Low	Successful	72	8	20	100	25
	Less successful	28	36	36	100	148

	N	350
	NA on SES	16
	Total N	366

b. Anticipated Mobility by Socio-Economic Status and Current School Status

SES	Current School Status	Index of Anticipated Mobility			Total	
		Mobile (Per Cent)	Non-Mobile (Per Cent)	Undecided (Per Cent)	Per Cent	N
High	At least some college	71	5	24	100	75
	Never exposed to college	20	46	34	100	65
Low	At least some college	72	13	15	100	46
	Never exposed to college	18	43	40	101	101

	N	287
	NA on SES	16
	NA on school status*	63
	Total N	366

*Includes high-school students.

Table 19.10 Home and Work Goals among Women, by Socio-Economic Status and Adjustment to the Regular School System

a. Home and Work Goals by Socio-Economic Status and Adjustment to High School

SES	Adjustment to High School	Home and Work Goals			Total	
		Home and Specific Work (Per Cent)	Home and Vague Work (Per Cent)	Home Only (Per Cent)	Per Cent	N
High	Successful	64	19	17	100	89
	Less successful	56	26	17	99	119
Low	Successful	57	33	10	100	60
	Less successful	44	45	11	100	139

N	407
NA on SES	24
NA on marry*	16
Total N	447

b. Home and Work Goals by Socio-Economic Status and Current School Status

SES	Current School Status	Home and Work Goals			Total	
		Home and Specific Work (Per Cent)	Home and Vague Work (Per Cent)	Home Only (Per Cent)	Per Cent	N
High	At least some college	79	8	13	100	72
	Never exposed to college	45	35	19	99	118
Low	At least some college	67	23	10	100	40
	Never exposed to college	39	50	10	99	137

N	367
NA on SES	24
NA on school status†	40
NA on marry*	16
Total N	447

*Includes those who intend never to marry.
†Includes current high-school students.

For both high- and low-status females, specific work goals are associated with a history of success in secondary school. However, the impact of school adjustment is, in this case, not sufficient to offset a more general tendency for specific work goals to be endorsed more often by females high in status. This broader pattern can be seen clearly in part *a* of the table. Specific work goals are about as prevalent among low-status girls who did well in high school as among high-status girls who did not match their level of adjustment. Consistent with this pattern we can also observe a tendency for vague work goals to be more characteristic of low-status girls, whatever the character of their adjustment to high school.

Our second indicator of behavior in the regular school system is more consistent with the findings reported for males. When current school status (with high-school students again excluded) is substituted for high-school adjustment as a control variable, 79 per cent of the college-educated high-status girls and 67 per cent of the college-educated, low-status girls report specific work goals. Vague work goals are again more prominent among girls low in status, but exposure to college reduces the frequency of this response to a level below that recorded for high-status girls with less schooling.

In general we can say, for both males and females, that career goals are quite highly correlated with educational attainment. We have chosen to present mobility goals as a dependent variable, but it is obvious that for many persons the causal chain may well operate in the opposite direction, with school adjustment representing an outcome of mobility goals. The nature of our data precludes an exact specification of the direction of influence, although it is quite clear that a strong positive relationship does exist.

A NOTE ON JOB SATISFACTION

Having discussed the relationship between anticipated job placement and school behavior, we can usefully conclude this chapter by considering the characteristics of those respondents who are currently working full time. Only 34 per cent of our sample, or 278 individuals, meet this description, and initially we might try to assess the character of their adjustment to full-time employment. Questionnaire items directed to this problem emphasize a subjective component of work adjustment — the degree of "satisfaction" that a worker feels with his particular line of employment. While job satisfaction does not coincide exactly with the more objective concept of adjustment to full-time employment, it is clearly a major component of such adjustment. In the absence of more complete data we devised an index from the three relevant items which appear in the questionnaire:

[QUESTION 25-E(1)] How well do you like the type of work you're doing?

[QUESTION 25-E(2)] How do you feel about your present salary?

[QUESTION 25-E(3)] How do you feel about the company or employer you work for?

The response categories for each question range from "very satisfied" to "extremely dissatisfied," and the distributions of the answers given appear in the three sections of the Table 19.11. Scanning the entries it can be observed that the greatest degree of satisfaction is with employers; type of work ranks second, and salary third. Assigning one point for each "very satisfied" response recorded, we created the distribution of scores presented in Table 19.12. For purposes of further discussion, persons describing themselves as "very satisfied" on two or three counts are considered "satisfied" workers. According to the table, 29 per cent of the 278 full-time workers meet this criterion.

Full-time workers constitute a distinct minority of the total sample, and, as Table 19.13 suggests, that minority is disproportionately populated by males and by persons low in social status. Many of the females are, as noted earlier, married and homemakers; a relatively large number of persons of high socio-economic status are continuing their education and have yet to enter the labor force on a regular full-time basis.

According to the initial sections of Table 19.14, there seems

Table 19.11 Areas of Job Satisfaction

a. Satisfaction with Type of Work (Question 25-E[1])

	N	Per Cent
Very satisfied	145	52
Moderately satisfied	83	30
A little dissatisfied	27	10
Extremely dissatisfied	11	4
Don't know	1	*
No answer	11	4
Total (working full time)	278	100

b. Satisfaction with Salary (Question 25-E[2])

	N	Per Cent
Very satisfied	85	31
Moderately satisfied	114	41
A little dissatisfied	47	17
Extremely dissatisfied	20	7
Don't know	0	0
No answer	12	4
Total (working full time)	278	100

c. Satisfaction with Employer or Company (Question 25-E[3])

	N	Per Cent
Very satisfied	174	63
Moderately satisfied	66	24
A little dissatisfied	9	3
Extremely dissatisfied	7	3
Don't know	0	0
No answer	22	8
Total (working full time)	278	101

*Less than 1 per cent.

Table 19.12 Index of Job Satisfaction

Number of Indicators	N	Per Cent	Index Description
None	68	24	Less satisfied
One	130	47	Less satisfied
Two	28	10	Satisfied
Three	52	19	Satisfied
Total	278	100	

to be a tendency for persons at a competitive disadvantage on the labor market to report higher levels of job satisfaction. According to the President's Commission on the Status of Women, women in the labor force are said to be less highly rewarded than men, but, according to part *a* of Table 19.14, they are much more likely to express satisfaction with their jobs. Low-status persons enter the labor market with lower levels of education and occupy many of the less desirable jobs, but, according to part *b* of Table 19.14, they are also more likely to express a high level of satisfaction with their employment. Part *c* of the table indicates that when sex and social status are controlled simultaneously, the most satisfied workers of all are those women at the lower half of the social ladder. The magnitude of their performance in this area dwarfs all other differences to be found in the table.

It may well be that low-status women particularly welcome the advantages that full-time employment can yield in terms of the style of life it enables them to enjoy. Whatever the explanation may be for their behavior, their habit of finding particular satisfaction in their work can only handicap us as we pursue the major goal of this section.

Table 19.13   Full-Time Workers

a. Per Cent Working Full Time, by Sex	
Men	Women
50 (366)	21 (447)
Total N	813

b. Per Cent Working Full Time, by Socio-Economic Status	
High	Low
29 (392)	40 (381)
N	773
NA on SES	40
Total N	813

Our intention was to consider the possibility that a positive relationship might exist between adjustment to the regular school system and adjustment to full-time employment. We then hoped to go beyond this point and to examine (in the following chapter) the possibility that both factors, in combination, might significantly affect early patterns of exposure to supplementary education. At this point it is obvious that these aims can be only partially fulfilled.

In the first place, the concentration of low-status persons among those currently employed works against a meaningful

Table 19.14   Job Satisfaction, Sex, and Socio-Economic Status

a. Per Cent Satisfied with Job, by Sex, among Full-Time Workers

Men	Women
24 (182)	39 (96)
Total N (full-time workers) 278	

b. Per Cent Satisfied with Job, by Socio-Economic Status, among Full-Time Workers

High SES	Low SES
25 (113)	34 (153)
N	266
NA on SES	12
Total N (full-time workers)	278

c. Per Cent Satisfied with Job, by Sex and Socio-Economic Status, among Full-Time Workers

Sex	Socio-Economic Status	
	High	Low
Men	21 (70)	27 (104)
Women	30 (43)	49 (49)
N		266
NA on SES		12
Total N (full-time workers)		278

application of our measures of school adjustment, since the majority of these persons have done quite poorly in school and/or are high-school dropouts. Second, when one examines the distribution of job satisfaction under appropriate controls, it becomes evident that one is actually considering the distribution of females throughout the cells of the tabulations. The problem becomes more concrete if we refer to Table 19.15.

At first glance, Table 19.15 tells us that low-status persons who have done well in high school are particularly likely to report a high level of satisfaction with their jobs. The figure (44 per cent) is actually quite misleading, since from earlier data we can infer that the twenty-five cases meeting the two conditions were likely to contain a disproportionate number of girls (because they do much better in high school than boys). As it happens, sixteen of the twenty-five cases (or 64 per cent) are, in fact, girls. Only 26 per cent of the less successful low-status cases are female, and the inference that job satisfaction among low-status workers is influenced by earlier school adjustment is considerably weakened by this information.

At this point the temptation is strong to abandon further discussion of job satisfaction. Upon reflection, however, it becomes apparent that job satisfaction, or, more correctly, lack of satisfaction with one's employment may yet prove to be an important element in decisions to participate in supplementary educational pursuits. We have already inferred that persons

Table 19.15 Per Cent Satisfied with Job, by Socio-Economic Status and Adjustment to High School

SES	Adjustment to High School	
	Successful	Less Successful
High	21 (29)	26 (84)
Low	44 (25)	32 (128)

N	266
NA on SES	12
Total N	278

planning to return to the regular system were disappointed with the environments they had encountered since leaving school. This inference was not tested because the data for such a test are not available. The questions on job satisfaction, for example, were asked only of those persons who did not expect to be attending regular school between September, 1962, and spring, 1963. Thus the returnee's dissatisfaction with his most recent work experience could not be evaluated. An evaluation of this type would have provided at least a partial test of our discussion of the returnee's tendency to rank especially high on practicalism.

The decision to return to the regular school system has many parallels to the decision to seek additional learning through supplementary education. It may be that many young persons who seek training in "irregular" schools will also be found to be high on pragmatism and low on satisfaction with certain aspects of their environment. At the risk of anticipating material reserved for the following chapter, let us present some data on this problem and in the process attempt to salvage some utility for our measure of job satisfaction. Attention is directed to Table 19.16, which indicates the proportions of high- and low-status workers who have ever taken a course in the informal school system in any subject at all. A control is available for job satisfaction.

Table 19.16 Per Cent Who Have Ever Taken a Supplementary Educational Course, by Socio-Economic Status and Job Satisfaction

SES	Job Satisfaction	
	Satisfied	Less Satisfied
High	39 (28)	44 (84)
Low	35 (52)	50 (100)

N	264
NA on SES	12
NA on course	2
Total N (full-time workers)	278

According to the figures in Table 19.16, participation in supplementary education is often related to work adjustment. It is, in fact, dissatisfied workers who have turned most often to the informal school system and this is especially true of persons low in status. Our index of job satisfaction no longer seems to represent wasted effort.

SUMMARY

This chapter discussed selected aspects of the relationship between school and work. Initially, we examined the mobility goals expressed by the sample of persons aged seventeen – twenty-four. Young men revealed a tendency to expect to work eventually in the professional and craft areas. Particularly high goal levels were found among males who were relatively young, unmarried, city dwellers, high in social status, or Negro. There was a general tendency for the specificity of job choices to vary in much the same fashion. An index of anticipated mobility was developed for males, and this measure proved to be quite strongly related to experiences in the regular school system. Mobile youngsters were found in large numbers among successful school adjusters and, in particular, among those who had ever been exposed to college. This pattern was characteristic of both high- and low-status respondents.

A large number of girls were also found to be oriented toward employment at the professional level, and secondary clusters were reported for positions as clerical and private household workers. Thirteen per cent of all girls reported that they expected to be housewives, without offering any other information concerning their eventual employment plans. Because of the unique problems involved in analyzing the career goals of girls (including the fact that many seem to define their primary role as homemaker), a special index was developed to specify their eventual expectations. A majority of girls were found to be planning to combine marriage with paid employment at some specific occupation. Specific work goals of this type were found to be especially prevalent among girls who were young and high in social status. They are especially characteristic of those whose formal schooling included at least some college, and this pattern holds at both social levels.

Roughly one-third of the sample was found to be working full-time; these persons were disproportionately male and tended to be low in status. An attempt to relate job satisfaction to previous adjustment in school was abandoned when it became apparent that a particularly large number of women had expressed a high level of satisfaction with their jobs. On the other hand, a low level of job satisfaction was found to be correlated with participation in supplementary education, especially among those low in status. The following chapter discusses this pattern, and the general question of exposure to supplementary education, in more detail.

20

Patterns
of Early Participation
in Supplementary
Education

All respondents aged seventeen–twenty-four were handed a flash card and asked the following question:

[QUESTION 27] Here is a list of subjects that people sometimes study in addition to regular school work, or after they stop going to school. This includes all kinds of part-time courses, evening classes, correspondence courses, courses given in the army or over television, private leassons–and anything not connected with full-time school work. Have you ever taken a special course in any of these things–or in anything else not listed here?

This chapter presents a profile of responses to this and similar items. In general, our aim is to direct attention to the incidence, the content, and the correlates of exposure to supplementary education among persons aged seventeen–twenty-four.[1]

[1] As noted in the introduction, the term "adult education" is something of a misnomer when applied to the informal school experiences of respondents in the adolescent–young adult phase of the NORC surveys. Many of the learning experiences with which we are concerned occurred well before adulthood and while these persons were still in transit through the regular school system. For this reason the term "supplementary education" is used throughout this section of the monograph to refer to those learning experiences which occurred outside the formal school system. The temporal relationship between formal and informal schooling is not a neat one for (as noted in the Introduction) it is often characterized by overlap, patterns of discontinuity, and shifts from one system to the other. Our data in this area are far from complete, but to afford some leverage on the problem they are being analyzed separately and will be reported in subsequent publications.

RATES OF EXPOSURE TO COURSES IN
SUPPLEMENTARY EDUCATION

Table 20.1 presents a detailed cross-section of those persons in the sample who have ever taken a course unrelated to full-time school work. There are eight sections to the table, which we will examine in turn.

Not unexpectedly, we find a difference in the rates of exposure of younger and older persons. The difference is just large enough to be noticed, and it is reasonable, given the fact that 47 per cent of the entire sample reports at least one exposure.

We should note, however, that this statistic (47 per cent) matches the rate of course-taking in the much larger sample of adults discussed in an earlier section of this report. Among these generally older persons the rate was also 47 per cent. We must, however, note one important limitation on a direct comparison of these figures. Those aged seventeen–twenty-four were asked to consider a list of subjects "that people sometimes study in addition to regular school work, or after they stop going to school." Adults, on the other hand, were asked to respond only in terms of the courses they had taken since leaving regular school. The bases available for comparison are thus somewhat dissimilar; the difference acts to understate the actual exposures of older persons to courses in the informal school system.

However, we should also emphasize that an exposure rate of 47 per cent among persons aged seventeen–twenty-four is an impressive statistic, even in light of the minimized rates of adult participation available for comparison. This figure in no sense compromises the hopes of those adult educators who see a hearty demand for their future services among persons recently attaining maturity.

If part *b* of the table is correct, the previous performance of this age group does not discriminate between the sexes. Participation of males and females in education outside the regular schools is about equal.

Part *c* of the table tells us that persons never married enjoy a cumulative advantage over those who have married, at least at this age level. The difference of 6 per cent is specified when we include a control for sex (part *d*). Apparently most of the margin

Table 20.1 Per Cent Who Have Ever Taken a Course Not Connected with Full-Time School Work, by Selected Social Variables

a. Age	
17–20	21–24
45 (436)	50 (374)

N	810
NA on age	1
NA on courses	2
Total N	813

b. Sex	
Men	Women
48 (364)	47 (447)

N	811
NA on courses	2
Total N	813

c. Marital Status	
Single	Married
50 (438)	44 (373)

N	811
NA on courses	2
Total N	813

d. Sex and Marital Status			
Men		Women	
Single	Married	Single	Married
48 (256)	49 (108)	53 (182)	42 (265)

N	811
NA on courses	2
Total N	813

Table 20.1 *Continued*

e. Community Size			
2,000,000 or More	50,000 – 2,000,000	10,000 – 50,000	Less Than 10,000
61 (180)	49 (315)	43 (134)	35 (182)

N	811
NA on courses	2
Total N	813

f. Region			
Northeast	North Central	South	West
56 (169)	48 (215)	34 (268)	60 (159)

N	811
NA on courses	2
Total N	813

g. Race	
White	Negro
50 (690)	30 (111)

N	801
NA on race*	10
NA on courses	2
Total N	813

h. Socio-Economic Status	
High	Low
55 (391)	40 (380)

N	771
NA on SES	40
NA on courses	2
Total N	813

*Includes Orientals.

can be traced to the behavior of single girls, who seem to be the most eager "informal" school-goers of all.

Part *e* of the table again reminds us of the favored position of city dwellers. The message has been clear throughout this section and, indeed, throughout this volume—living in a large city makes a big difference in the schooling one is likely to receive. Urban residence counts as an advantage.

In line with what we already know of geographical influences on current rates of exposure among adults (cf. Chart 5.3), the figures in part *f* are initially puzzling. Among all adult participants in adult education between June, 1961, and June, 1962, it was noted that "the highest rates of activity are clearly found in the West, the second highest in the South, the third highest in the North Central region, and the lowest in the Northeast." Yet according to the data available in Table 20.1, the rank order of regions is West, Northeast, North Central, and South. Thus the Northeastern and Southern states shift positions when attention is focused upon the cumulative incidence of course-taking among persons aged seventeen–twenty-four.

Among all adults (during June, 1961, to June, 1962), it was demonstrated that the surprisingly high showing of the South was "entirely a function of the more frequent religious study in the South—a sphere of learning not nearly so much affected by educational background as other areas of subject matter." Another pattern, relevant to the problem at hand, is underscored in Table 4.2 of the opening section of this report.

A substantial minority of all persons who study religion are under thirty-five. Of all subject categories, only public affairs attracts a smaller group of younger students.

Taken together, these factors shed some light on the South's shift in position when the two sources of data are compared. Among all possible areas of instruction, southerners are disproportionately represented in the category of religion. But this is a subject favored by older persons and presumably not a field which attracts large numbers of those aged seventeen–twenty-four. When attention is directly fixed upon these younger persons, religious studies decline in importance and we note a decline in overall rates of participation among those located in southern states.

Differential rates of course-taking by race show whites at a much higher level than Negroes. As in rates of participation from June, 1961, to June, 1962, much of this differential can probably be attributed to the level of formal education characteristic of each race. Another contributing factor would be the Negroes' tendency to favor religious study (see Table 5.15) and the already noted concentration of older persons in this subject area. Thus the participation rates of Negroes would be subject to the same forces which depressed the performance of persons aged seventeen – twenty-four in the South. (Many of these Negroes are, in fact, residents of the southern states.)

According to part *h* of the table, socio-economic status is also correlated with participation ranking with community size, region, and race as a predictor capable of generating at least a 15 per cent difference in rates of participation.

SUPPLEMENTARY EDUCATIONAL COURSES
AND INDEPENDENT STUDIES

People also organize programs of study on their own, and although we shall not discuss this practice with the degree of attention accorded to course-taking, we can indicate its general incidence in Table 20.2.

Independent studies are by no means infrequent among persons aged seventeen – twenty-four. Summing the appropriate entries, we find that 52 per cent of the sample employed this approach to further learning; as noted above, 47 per cent were active at least once in course work. Seventy per cent of the sam-

Table 20.2 Per Cent Who Have Taken a Supplementary Educational Course or Organized an Independent Program of Study

Taken a Course	Independent Study	Per Cent
Yes	Yes	29
Yes	No	18
No	Yes	23
No	No	29
Total		99
N		813

ple employed one or the other means, or both. Although comparison with the cumulative experience of the adult sample suffers from restrictions identical to those noted in part *a* above, we can observe, with reference to Table 6.8, that only 61 per cent of the adult sample can claim the same incidence of activity since leaving school.

CONTENT OF EXPOSURE TO SUPPLEMENTARY
EDUCATION AMONG MALES AND FEMALES

We can begin our consideration of differentials in the content of exposures to supplementary education by directing attention to Table 20.3. The table presents the distribution of subject areas sampled by all males and females ever active in informal learning endeavors (both course-taking and independent studies). The fourth column of the table describes subject areas sampled for both sexes combined, and it highlights the impor-

Table 20.3 Subject Matter Studied in All Exposures to Supplementary Education among Persons Aged 17–24, by Sex and for All Participants

Type of Subject	Sex		Observed Difference (Per Cent)	All Participants (Per Cent)
	Men (Per Cent)	Women (Per Cent		
Vocational	39	18	−21	28
White-collar skills	15	14		14
Blue-collar skills	23	4		13
Agriculture	1	0		1
Academic	13	9	− 4	11
Hobbies and recreation	24	29	+ 5	27
Home and family life	2	27	+25	16
Personal development	7	6	− 1	7
Religion	6	3	− 3	5
Public affairs	0	1	+ 1	0
Miscellaneous	8	6	− 2	7
Total	99	99		101
Base	468	586		1,054
No information	3	0		3
Total	471	586		1,057

*The term "exposures to supplementary education" refers both to taking courses and independent studies in this and all subsequent tables.

tance of two areas in particular, vocational studies and hobbies, which together account for 55 per cent of all types of study among persons aged seventeen–twenty-four.

Concerning differences by sex, two subject areas merit special mention: vocational subjects and those dealing with home and family life. Note that the two subjects demonstrating the greatest difference between the sexes also rank among the three areas of supplementary education most often favored by all participants. Among work-related courses we can trace the disparity to the proportionately larger number of males who have studied blue-collar skills. The net effect of this concentration is to give males a substantial edge in vocational training, even though this is an area attracting a considerable number of female students.

In home and family subjects, on the other hand, we find extensive participation among girls, but virtually none among boys. The only area where we can point to figures that are both large and at least roughly equal for the sexes is the hobbies category. For reasons already mentioned, direct comparison with the adult sample is somewhat inappropriate, but it is interesting to reflect on the differences between these figures and those presented in Table 7.2. According to the data concerning adult education after leaving school, the hobbies area is at least relatively dominated by females. The data in Table 20.3 are thus open to two interpretations. Either males are much less likely to take hobbies courses once they leave school, or else proportionately more males have recently been attracted to this type of subject. The data at hand do not permit a conclusive evaluation of either alternative.

EXPOSURE TO SUPPLEMENTARY EDUCATION, SEX, AND ADJUSTMENT TO THE REGULAR SCHOOL SYSTEM

Earlier sections of this volume have emphasized the association of specific social background variables with recent rates of course taking among adults. Educational attainment proved to be a particularly useful indicator of participation between June, 1961, and June, 1962. It should be interesting to examine the proportions of persons aged seventeen–twenty-four who have ever been exposed to supplementary education in terms of their current school status. The relevant comparisons, with a control for sex, appear in Table 20.4.

For both sexes, if we ignore persons currently in high school, we can report a strong bias in participation which favors the better educated. Among those now in secondary school and also among all persons ever exposed to college, females hold a definite edge in the percentage ever exposed to supplementary education.

Since educational attainment is generally related to such exposures, and since we know from previous data that attainment and high-school adjustment are highly correlated, we can pursue this matter more precisely by considering Table 20.5, which indicates for each sex rates of experience with supplementary education among successful and less successful adjusters to high school. A pattern barely suggested in Table 20.4 becomes more explicit with these data: a margin of 8 per cent separates the rates of successful and less successful males; among females the margin is 21 per cent. The participation rates of females aged seventeen – twenty-four are more directly influenced by previous school adjustment than those of males.

Does school adjustment affect the content of the courses of

Table 20.4 Per Cent Who Have Been Exposed to Supplementary Education, by Current School Status and Sex

Current School Status	Sex	
	Men (Per Cent)	Women (Per Cent)
High-school dropouts	58 (70)	59 (102)
High-school students	61 (59)	79 (43)
High-school graduates	74 (107)	67 (174)
At least some college	76 (125)	87 (124)
N	804	
NA on school status	9	
Total N	813	

males and females in a similar fashion? An answer to this question can be gleaned from Table 20.6, where subject areas are tabulated by sex and adjustment to high school.

Scanning the observed differences by school adjustment for each sex, we note that for females the largest margin to be observed (the hobbies category) amounts to only 5 points; among males we can find at least one difference almost three times as large (vocational). Although many of the differences in the table are small, the net impression created is that high-school adjustment has a more decisive influence on the content of the courses taken by young men. For males high-school adjustment is especially critical in influencing exposure to vocational courses, especially at the blue-collar level. Blue-collar courses among male participants who have not done well in high school account for 28 per cent of all subject areas these persons sample, and contribute the major difference to be found in the table.

We might emphasize the fact that no comparable difference in subject area can be found for females. High-school adjustment is an important factor in whether or not they ever participate in supplementary education, but much less of a factor in the type of courses they take. For young males the situation is almost completely reversed: rates of participation are much less affected by high-school adjustment; course content is quite directly affected.

Table 20.5 Per Cent Who Have Been Exposed to Supplementary Education, by Sex and Adjustment to High School

Sex	Adjustment to High School	
	Successful (Per Cent)	Less Successful (Per Cent)
Men	75 (81)	67 (285)
Women	86 (158)	65 (289)
	Total N	813

Table 20.6 Subject Matter Studied in All Exposures to Supplementary Education, by Sex and Adjustment to High School

Type of Subject	Sex					
	Men			Women		
	Adjustment to High School					
	Success-ful (Per Cent)	Less Suc-cessful (Per Cent)	Observed Differ-ence (Per Cent)	Success-ful (Per Cent)	Less Suc-cessful (Per Cent)	Observed Differ-ence (Per Cent)
Vocational	29	43	+14	18	19	+1
White-collar skills	16	14		14	14	
Blue-collar skills	10	28		4	5	
Agriculture	3	1		0	0	
Academic	15	13	− 2	7	10	+3
Hobbies and recreation	29	22	− 7	32	27	− 5
Home and family life	2	2	0	27	28	+1
Personal development	11	5	− 6	7	6	− 1
Religion	7	5	− 2	4	3	− 1
Public affairs	0	0	0	1	0	− 1
Miscellaneous	7	8	+ 1	4	7	+3
Total	100	98		100	100	
Base	123	345		276	310	
No information	1	2		0	0	
Total	124	347		276	310	

EXPOSURE TO SUPPLEMENTARY EDUCATION, SEX, AND SOCIO-ECONOMIC STATUS

According to Table 20.7, socio-economic status is responsible for a 16 per cent differential among young men, favoring those of high status. Among women, the observed difference is only 3 per cent. Note that among low-status respondents, females are 11 per cent more likely to have been exposed to supplementary education.

Considering course content we note, in Table 20.8, that the largest single difference is in the general vocational area for young men. Low status males hold a 10 per cent edge in this area; the largest component of that edge is contributed by blue-collar exposures. Among females it is impossible to find a difference of comparable magnitude. We note, however, that the largest margin to be observed among girls is *also* in the low SES category. Low status girls are more likely to have studied in the area of home and family life by a margin of 6 per cent.

MALES: ANTICIPATED MOBILITY, SOCIO-ECONOMIC STATUS, AND EXPOSURE TO SUPPLEMENTARY EDUCATION

Up to this point we have observed that for males, rates of exposure to supplementary education are responsive mainly to socio-economic status. It seems logical to anticipate that among

Table 20.7 Per Cent Who Have Been Exposed to Supplementary Education, by Sex and Socio-Economic Status

Sex	Socio-Economic Status	
	High (Per Cent)	Low (Per Cent)
Men	77 (177)	61 (173)
Women	75 (215)	72 (208)
	N	773
	NA on SES	40
	Total N	813

Table 20.8 Subject Matter Studied in All Exposures to Supplementary Education, by Sex and Socio-Economic Status

	Sex					
	Men			Women		
	Socio-Economic Status					
Type of Subject	High (Per Cent)	Low (Per Cent)	Observed Difference (Per Cent)	High (Per Cent)	Low (Per Cent)	Observed Difference (Per Cent)
Vocational	36	46	+10	17	19	+2
White-collar skills	14	15		13	15	
Blue-collar skills	21	29		4	4	
Agriculture	1	2		0	0	
Academic	16	11	− 5	8	9	+1
Hobbies and recreation	24	25	+ 1	31	27	− 4
Home and family life	1	3	+ 2	25	31	+ 6
Personal development	8	5	− 3	7	6	− 1
Religion	7	3	− 4	6	1	− 5
Public affairs	0	0	0	1	0	− 1
Miscellaneous	8	7	− 1	5	6	+ 1
Total	100	100		100	99	
Base	271	169		315	243	
No information	1	2		0	0	
Total	272	171		315	243	

low-status males, the highest rates would be found among those most anxious to shift to a higher status. Table 20.9 informs us that mobility goals are indeed correlated with exposure to supplementary education. We find that 81 per cent of all mobile young men report at least one exposure, compared to 67 per cent of the non-mobile and 54 per cent of the undecideds. The percentage difference between the two most extreme types is a substantial 27 points.

In Table 20.10 these proportions are specified by socio-economic status. The 81 per cent of the mobile group noted in Table 20.9, we now find, masks a 16 per cent difference between high- and low-status individuals. Among the non-mobile we find

Table 20.9 Per Cent of Men Who Have Ever Been Exposed to Supplementary Education, by Index of Anticipated Mobility

Index of Anticipated Mobility	Per Cent
Mobile	81 (139)
Non-mobile	67 (106)
Undecided	54 (105)
N	350
NA on SES	16
Total N	366

Table 20.10 Per Cent of Men Who Have Ever Been Exposed to Supplementary Education, by Socio-Economic Status and Index of Anticipated Mobility

SES	Index of Anticipated Mobility		
	Mobile (Per Cent)	Non-Mobile (Per Cent)	Undecided (Per Cent)
High	88 (80)	76 (50)	58 (47)
Low	72 (59)	58 (56)	51 (58)
	N	350	
	NA on SES	16	
	Total N	366	

figures of 76 per cent (high status) and 58 per cent (low status) an 18 per cent margin in favor of high-status persons. A smaller percentage difference obtains in the undecided category, although its direction is consistent with that of the other margins found in the table.

For males, it is quite apparent that social status exercises a strong influence on exposure to supplementary education, whatever the mobility goals' of our respondents. However, within each status category we again note the relative advantage which mobile youngsters hold in exposures to supplementary learning. Among low-status males, in fact, mobile persons exceed the performance of at least one category of high-status persons — the undecideds. Their rate of exposure (72 per cent) is 14 points higher than that of any other group at their own social level.

Turning to the question of areas of study, let us direct attention to Table 20.11, which describes all types of subjects sam-

Table 20.11 Subject Matter Studied on All Exposures to Supplementary Education among Men, by Index of Anticipated Mobility

Type of Subject	Index of Anticipated Mobility					
	Mobile (Per Cent)		Non-Mobile (Per Cent)		Undecided (Per Cent)	
Vocational		34		45		48
White-collar skills	16		13		12	
Blue-collar skills	16		31		35	
Agriculture	2		1		1	
Academic		16		8		15
Hobbies and recreation		24		29		20
Home and family life		2		3		0
Personal development		9		6		3
Religion		5		5		9
Public affairs		*		0		0
Miscellaneous		11		4		4
Total		101		100		99
Base		228		115		97
No information		1		2		0
Total		229		117		97

*Less than 1 per cent.

pled by males with a control for anticipated mobility. Our earlier discussions of course content (cf. especially Tables 20.6 and 20.8) has shown, for males, that the vocational category is especially favored by persons who are low in status and whose careers in high school leave something to be desired. From what is known of the relationship between these items and anticipated mobility, one would predict that non-mobile and undecided respondents would be most likely to have sampled courses in the vocational area. According to Table 20.11, this supposition is correct. And, as we might have inferred from the tables seen earlier, the major factor behind this pattern is the relative reluctance of mobile respondents to expose themselves to skills at the blue-collar level.

Concerning non-vocational exposures, the picture is less clear. It is apparent that mobile respondents predominate in this general area, but consideration of the lower seven types of subjects does not yield any one or two categories in particular which might account for this difference. Miscellaneous subject matter comes closest to offering a sizeable differential in favor of mobile respondents, but the specific items subsumed under that heading are too diverse to discuss under any heading other than "miscellaneous."

Tabulating subject areas by socio-economic status and anticipated mobility would seem to be called for at this point. This has been done and the data examined. There is only one additional point to be made, and rather than reproducing the sixty-six-cell table in full, we shall make it verbally and pass on to other matters: high-status males who are mobile are especially reluctant to expose themselves to training at the blue-collar level and hence, in general, to the overall category of vocational skills.

FEMALES: HOME AND WORK GOALS, SOCIO-ECONOMIC STATUS, AND EXPOSURE TO SUPPLEMENTARY EDUCATION

We turn now to the interplay of career goals and exposure to supplementary schooling for girls. At least one of the findings in Table 20.12 might have been anticipated from earlier data: girls with specific work goals are by far the most active in programs of informal schooling. Ranking second, and sixteen percentage points off the pace, are those who expect only to be housewives. Another margin of 8 per cent separates the homemakers from those with indecisive plans for future employment.

When a control for social background is imposed on these data, as in Table 20.13, we find a reversal of the expected trends. Low-status girls with vague work goals edge out homemakers from their own social level in exposure to informal

Table 20.12 Per Cent of Women Who Have Ever Been Exposed to Supplementary Education, by Home and Work Goals

Home and Work Goals	Per Cent	
Home and specific work	82	(229)
Home and vague work	58	(142)
Home only	66	(59)
N	430	
NA on marry*	17	
Total N	447	

*Includes those who intend never to marry.

Table 20.13 Per Cent of Women Who Have Ever Been Exposed to Supplementary Education, by Socio-Economic Status and Home and Work Goals

SES	Home and Work Goals		
	Home and Specific Work (Per Cent)	Home and Vague Work (Per Cent)	Home Only (Per Cent)
High	84 (124)	58 (48)	67 (36)
Low	80 (95)	63 (83)	61 (21)

N	407	
NA on SES	24	
NA on marry*	16	
Total N	447	

*Includes those who intend never to marry.

schooling and outperform even high-status females with comparable career goals. We shall return to this point in our discussion of course content.

We can open our discussion of areas of participation for females by referring to Table 20.14, which percentages types of
subject studied in terms of home and work goals. The first row
of the table presents us with something of a surprise. Among
informal students, those girls who are most strongly oriented
toward careers in homemaking lead both other categories in
their rate of exposure to vocational skills. Closer examination of
the table informs us that the major reason for this difference is
their impressive performance in the area of white-collar skills.

For girls, adult education in the white-collar sphere means,
basically, training in office skills. It would seem that we have
stumbled upon a rather curious phenomenon. If a sample of the
nation's secretaries and typists were asked to specify their
eventual line of work, one would guess from these data that

Table 20.14 Subject Matter Studied in All Exposures to
Supplementary Education among Women, by Home and
Work Goals

Type of Subject	Home and Work Goals		
	Home and Specific Work (Per Cent)	Home and Vague Work (Per Cent)	Home Only (Per Cent)
Vocational	17	16	24
White-collar skills	13	10	23
Blue-collar skills	4	5	1
Agriculture	0	1	0
Academic	10	4	9
Hobbies and recreation	31	30	21
Home and family life	24	37	37
Personal Development	7	5	5
Religion	5	3	0
Public affairs	0	1	1
Miscellaneous	7	4	1
Total	101	100	98
Base	354	117	65
No information	0	0	0
Total	354	117	65

most would answer, "I'll be a housewife." Indeed, the implication of Table 20.14 is that a good part of the skill training that girls receive at the hands of adult educators is intended to be put to extremely short-term use. For girls these data, taken together with information discussed in Chapter 19 (cf. Tables 19.14 and 19.16), reveal a strategic difference between performance in different types of schools and anticipated career lines. As we learned earlier, girls with specific employment expectations are likely to have adjusted rather well to school and quite often they attend college. It is impossible, of course, to say which came first, but we can say that these girls see a job in their future. Another group of girls have not adapted so well to the regular school system. They turn to the alternate system for skill training and (again, without attempting to specify priority) they seem to see a family in their future. Education, rather than representing a long-term investment with a vocational reward well in the future, appears to these students to be used as a way to maximize short-term gains before homemaking demands a complete commitment.

Returning to Table 20.14 we note that this same category of student is found less often among those engaged in recreational pursuits in the informal system. Their extracurricular learning endeavors, compared to those of others, tend to favor the vocational and homemaking fields.

A final point about female participation merits separate mention. We noted in Table 20.13 that low-status girls outperformed their high-status peers when both were without specific work goals. Glancing back on Table 20.8 we are reminded that among all females, the largest difference that socio-economic status produced was in the homemaking area. Again, this was a difference in favor of low-status respondents. We might follow up on these observations and hypothesize that the unexplained reversal in Table 20.13 is probably due to a heavier concentration of homemaking students among girls with vague work goals.

The difference in homemaking exposures is, in fact, the largest difference which exists between the two vocationally undecided groups of females. As Table 20.15 indicates, it yields a margin of 10 per cent in favor of those of lower status. There is thus some ground for attributing the superior overall performance of low-status girls with vague work goals to their attraction to courses in the home and family sphere.

SUPPLEMENTARY EDUCATION AMONG PERSONS AGED SEVENTEEN – TWENTY-FOUR: A SUMMARY OF FINDINGS ON EXPOSURE AND CONTENT

It is useful to pause and review the ground already covered. The data discussed to this point closely parallel material presented in earlier chapters, although they mainly concern a younger generation. There is of course a difference in definition to remember. We have been dealing with all exposures to supplementary education, not just those which followed the termination of full-time schooling.

In terms of exposure to courses, it was noted that particularly high rates of participation were characteristic of persons who were white, lived in large cities, were high in social status, and came from states in the far West and the Northeast. A large amount of independent study was uncovered; in fact slightly more persons aged seventeen – twenty-four had employed this method of learning than had taken courses. In two instances there were marked differences between the sexes in the subjects they studied. Neither was particularly surprising. Men favored vocational offerings, particularly in the blue-collar field; women were much more likely to have been exposed to subjects in the homemaking category.

Following suggestions implicit in earlier sections of this volume, school adjustment and social status were also employed to specify participation rates for the seventeen – twenty-four-year-

---

Table 20.15 Per Cent Exposed to Home and Family Subjects among Women with Vague Work Goals, by Socio-Economic Status

Socio-Economic Status	Per Cent	
High	31	(49)
Low	41	(68)

old sample. Among this generally younger cohort, it was discovered that a successful adjustment to high school had particular impact on the rates of participation by girls in supplementary education; it did not work nearly so well to specify rates among males. However, it did affect the kinds of courses that young men took; those students who had done less well in high school were most likely to take courses in the informal system in the blue-collar field.

Rates of participation for males were found to be primarily a function of socio-economic status, those of high status participating more often. Social background had a slight impact on the subjects sampled by both sexes. Low-status male students were found to favor courses at the blue-collar skill level; low-status female students took homemaking more often than other girls.

Not unexpectedly, it was found that males who were upwardly mobile were frequent participants in supplementary education. However, they were not particularly interested in vocational offerings. This was particularly true of mobile youngsters who were high in status. For these persons, it would appear that preparation for a career, at least up to age twenty-four, is a service they seek from the regular school system, and not from adult educators. On the whole, these persons have done quite well in school, and the majority have been to college.

Young men without high mobility goals are less likely to turn to the informal school system, and this is especially true of persons low in status. However, when these persons do participate in supplementary education they tend to be especially interested in vocational offerings, particularly at the blue-collar level.

For girls between the ages of seventeen and twenty-four, participation in supplementary education also has much to do with career goals. Those who can report a specific employment expectation are more likely to have been active in the informal school system. This is especially the case for high-status girls, although low-status girls with comparable job plans are also high on participation. It often happens that girls who do poorly in the regular school system (by adapting less well to high school, etc.) take clerical training in informal schools. Many of these are apparently employing this source of white-collar training to prepare for brief office careers that they are quite ready to abandon in favor of homemaking. These girls are also active in the home and family sphere of adult education, an area which also attracts a sizeable number of low-status girls unsure of their future employment goals.

JOB SATISFACTION, PRACTICALISM, AND SUPPLEMENTARY EDUCATION

Persons currently out of school and working full time were initially discussed in the final pages of Chapter 19. At that point we indicated our concern with the decisions these individuals make with regard to supplementary education. A pattern was observed in which the incidence of exposure to supplementary educational courses was found to be greatest among persons relatively dissatisfied with their employment and particularly among dissatisfied workers who were low in social status.

This finding recalled our earlier discussion of decisions to return to the regular school system. Certain characteristics of these returnees suggested that since leaving school they had found reason to be disappointed with their lives as adults and that they had come to the conviction that a more complete education would have certain advantageous consequences for their position in life. These speculations were at least partially supported when it was observed that their decision to return to school could not be accounted for by their previous school adjustment (which was typically less than successful), but that such persons tended to score quite high on an index designed to measure their appreciation of the practical consequences of education (practicalism).

Thus the data we have examined for both types of decisions (to return to the regular system after an absence, and to participate in supplementary education) are not inconsistent with the hypothesis that for many lower-class persons practicalism and dissatisfaction with life chances combine to induce them to seek further educational experiences. For the balance of this chapter wer shall discuss additional data relevant to this hypothesis.

We are concerned primarily with individuals who have some

measure of direct contact with the world beyond the classroom. Persons working full time adequately meet this criterion. As it happens, most of these individuals are low in status and unsuccessful adjusters to high school. These factors place sizeable limitations on the data available for discussion. However, we are also concerned with gaining some leverage on the problem of continuing education among the more "unlikely" groups of candidates—and low-status persons along with less successful adjusters to high school are two of the least likely sources of recruits for extended education.

We have already seen that full-time workers who are relatively low in social origin are more likely to have taken supplementary educational courses if they are less than satisfied with their jobs. Our hunch at this point is that total exposures to adult education in this low-status group will be highest among those less satisfied workers who are highest on practicalism. Table 20.16 contains the relevant data.

According to Table 20.16, the hunch seems to have some relation to fact. Eighty-three per cent of the less satisfied and more practical low-status workers have been exposed to supplementary education. Among workers who are lower on both job satisfaction and practicalism the figure drops to 56 per cent, a margin of twenty-seven points.

Additional data lend further support for this pattern. All respondents who had terminated their schooling and who did not

---

Table 20.16 Per Cent Ever Exposed to Supplementary Education, by Practicalism and Job Satisfaction among Persons Low in Socio-Economic Status*

Practicalism	Job Satisfaction	
	Satisfied (Per Cent)	Less Satisfied (Per Cent)
High	$\overline{}$ (14)	83 (30)
Low	52 (27)	56 (57)

*includes both course work and independent studies.

plan to return immediately to the regular school system were asked:

[QUESTION 24] Do you think you'll ever go back to school either full time or part time?

The question referred to returning to a regular program of studies at some point after September, 1962. Table 20.17, employing the same controls as before, indicates the proportions of low-status workers who eventually expected to return to the formal school system.

The figures in the table are less dramatic than those relevant to supplementary education, but the basic pattern remains unchanged. In this case a margin of eighteen points appears in the intentions of less-satisfied workers, and that difference is a function of practicalism.

Table 20.17 Per Cent Expecting To Return Eventually to the Regular School System, by Practicalism and Job Satisfaction, among Persons Low in Socio-Economic Status

	Job Satisfaction	
Practicalism	Satisfied (Per Cent)	Less Satisfied (Per Cent)
High	– (14)	53 (30)
Low	33 (27)	35 (57)

Table 20.18 Per Cent Expecting To Return Eventually to the Regular School System, by Practicalism and Job Satisfaction, among Persons Adjusting Less Successfully to High School

	Job Satisfaction	
Practicalism	Satisfied (Per Cent)	Less Satisfied (Per Cent)
High	30 (20)	54 (57)
Low	39 (43)	37 (104)

In the area of eventual expectations we can offer additional evidence about the joint effects of job satisfaction and practicalism on patterns of continuing education. In Table 20.18 the relevant universe comprises all full-time workers who have adjusted less than successfully to high school. The control variables are identical to those above; the proportions cited again indicate persons expecting to return eventually to the regular school system.

According to the table, less successful adjusters to high school currently in the labor force are most likely to expect to return to school eventually if they are relatively low on job satisfaction and quick to endorse the practical consequences of advanced education.

In sum the data considered in these three final tables offer some support for our original speculations concerning decisions to return to school. Generally, it would seem that many young persons from relatively disadvantaged backgrounds revise their judgments concerning the adequacy of their educations only after direct (and seemingly disappointing) contacts with the world around them. These are the persons who are most apt to be recruited from the more "unlikely" candidates.

Appendices

Appendix 1

Sample Design and Field Procedures

GENERAL SAMPLE DESIGN FOR THE NATIONAL SURVEYS[1]

The universe which was sampled in this study was the total non-institutional population of the continental United States. The sample was a standard multi-stage area-probability sample.

The primary sampling units (PSU's) employed in this survey derived from NORC's 1953 Master Sample. The PSU's in the Master Sample had been selected with probabilities proportionate to their estimated 1953 populations. Population shifts in the past decade have rendered that set of PSU's a less efficient primary stage than one might desire. Nonetheless, since a well-trained and experienced field force was available in that set of PSU's, it was obviously desirable to update the sample by some procedure which minimized the number of sampling units which needed to be changed. A procedure suggested by Nathan Keyfitz (1951) was employed. This involved the comparison of the desired 1960 probabilities of selection for PSU's with their original 1950 probabilities. If the originally selected PSU had a lower probability than was warranted by its 1960 population, it was retained in the new sample and assigned the desired probability. If the originally selected PSU had a higher probability than was warranted, it was subjected to the possibility of being dropped. The probability of retention for such a PSU was the ratio of its desired probability to its original probability. Replacements for dropped PSU's were made from among those PSU's which had not fallen into the 1953 sample and for which the 1953 probability was lower than that desired in 1960, the

[1]This section of the Appendix was prepared by Seymour Sudman and Jacob J. Feldman.

probability of 1960 selection being a function of the amount of growth the unit had undergone.

Basically, this method preserved the stratification based on the 1950 classifications of geographic regions, size of largest town, median family income, economic characteristics, and, in the South, by race. Counties which the Census Bureau classified as non-metropolitan in 1950 but as metropolitan in 1960 were, however, shifted to metropolitan strata. The restratification completed the computation of selection probabilities, but, in all likelihood, served to increase the efficiency of the sample somewhat.

The current set of PSU's is to be used until the 1970 census is available. For this reason, the 1960 census figures were extrapolated to 1967, the midpoint between the availability of the 1960 and 1970 census reports. For each PSU, the extrapolation was based on its population change between 1950 and 1960.

1. *Selection of Sample within PSU's*

Localities. – Within each selected PSU, localities were ordered according to cities with block statistics, other urban places, and urbanized and non-urbanized Minor Civil Divisions, with the places ordered by 1960 population within each of these categories. Localities were selected from this list by using a random start and applying a designated interval to the cumulative 1960 population. This provided stratification according to size and urban type of locality, and at the same time gave selection with probability proportionate to size.

Cluster size. – Within each locality, a sample of ultimate clusters, or segments, was selected. From the point of view of minimizing the sampling error of estimates from the survey, the smaller the cluster the better. From the point of view of minimizing the interviewing and other field costs, the larger the cluster the better. After weighing these rather contradictory injunctions, it was decided that an average of approximately eight households per segment would be screened in the adult education survey. However, in anticipation of interview losses due to vacancies, demolition, refusals, unavailability, language difficulties, etc., an average of about eleven dwelling units per segment was assigned for screening.

The establishment of the desired sampling ratio for the entire United States, the probability of the particular locality, and the desired cluster size predetermined the number of segments to be selected from any given locality. The actual procedure employed in selecting the necessary number of segments from a particular locality depended on whether or not a recent city directory was available. The street address section of a city directory constituted the sampling frame for about 20 per cent of the localities. These were generally medium-sized cities.

City directory sampling. — The first-stage unit of sampling within a directory was usually a column of addresses. Since it was anticipated that each column from the directory would produce on the average about one and one-third discrete geographic clusters for the final sample, the number of columns to be selected for a given locality was set at three-quarters the number of segments required there. The columns were selected systematically with equal probability.

The overall probability of the column (i.e., the product of the probability of the PSU, the conditional probability of the locality, and the conditional probability of the column) was invariably several times larger than the desired final household probability. Each selected column was therefore divided into several roughly equal-sized groupings of residential directory listings. The number of such groupings in a column was made equal to the integral value nearest to the ratio of the overall column probability to the desired final household probability. One grouping was then randomly selected from each column.

Since different sample columns in a directory contained widely differing numbers of residential listings, the sizes of segments in a given locality was rather variable. In addition, geographic homogeneity was one of the criteria of the allocation of directory addresses into groupings. Thus, when a slight variation in grouping size within a column made for greater geographic homogeneity within one or more of the groupings, such variation was permitted. Even so, many of the groupings did contain (as anticipated) two or more discrete geographic clusters.

Directories in which the street address listings for two or more communities were intermixed were sampled in a somewhat modified fashion. A measurement of the amount of space devoted to the sample locality was made for each column in the directory. A sample of columns was then selected with a column's probability being proportionate to the amount of space devoted within it to the sample locality. Once the columns were selected the procedure followed in the mixed directories was essentially the same as that described above.

In order to correct for the omission of new construction as well as other possible directory errors, a coverage check of the directory listings was conducted for a sample of blocks in one-third of the directory localities. Interviewers canvassed these blocks thoroughly in search of dwelling units omitted from the directory. The sampling ratios employed in selecting blocks and in selecting omitted housing units within blocks were established in such a way that, for any given block, the product of the block's being in the supplementary sample and the sampling ratio employed within the block was exactly equal to the probability which any entry actually appearing in the directory had of falling into the original sample. In other words, housing units appearing in a city directory and those omitted from it were sampled at exactly the same rate.

Sampling in other localities.—Where city directories were not available, 1960 census data were used. In the larger cities, census tract and block data were used. The tracts were ordered according to median income, and selection was made by using a random start and applying a designated skip interval to the cumulative number of households. Blocks were then selected with probability proportional to the number of dwelling units.

In places without block statistics, enumeration districts were selected with probabilities proportional to the number of households. The selected districts were then divided into segments, and estimates of the number of households within each segment were obtained by field counts. The selection of segments was then made with probability proportionate to the number of households.

In each selected segment or block, a listing of households was carried out by interviewers just prior to the start of the study. Households were selected from these listing sheets with probability determined by the ratio of the final sampling ratio of households to the probability with which the segment had been selected.

Sample Execution

A total of 13,293 households were designated for screening. The screening interview lasted about twenty minutes and obtained infor-

Table A—1.1 Results of Screening Interviews

Disposition of Case	Number	Per Cent
Screening interview completed	11,956	89.9
Refusals and break-offs	679	5.1
Not at home	235	1.8
Miscellaneous: deaf, language problems, illness, etc.	374	2.8
Interview completed, but too late to be included	49	0.4
Total	13,293	100.0

mation on adult education activities in the household as well as demographic characteristics. Screener interviews were completed in 11,956 households, or 89.9 per cent of those designated. Table A – 1.1 describes the results in more detail.

Sampling Errors

On the basis of this type of sample design, it was estimated that the sample employed in this study would have an efficiency not less than that of a simple random sample of 8,000 adults. Thus an estimate can also be made of the approximate size of the standard errors which would apply to all population estimates made in this study. This is presented in Table A – 1.2.

The standard error estimates in Table A – 1.2 refer to total United States population. For comparisons of subgroups, Table A – 1.3 is more convenient. It shows the percentage standard error for various sample sizes and percentages. To obtain a standard error of the difference between two independent percentages, find the standard error of each percentage separately, square these standard errors, sum the squares, and take the square root of the result.

For example, to compute the standard error of the difference between 15 per cent of a group of 2,000 and 10 per cent of an independent group of 4,000, first note that the standard errors are respectively 1.0 per cent

Table A – 1.2 Standard Errors for Estimates of Educational Activities

Size of Estimate	One Standard Error (Approximate)
150,000	40,000
200,000	45,000
250,000	50,000
300,000	55,000
400,000	65,000
500,000	85,000
750,000	105,000
1,000,000	120,000
2,500,000	185,000
5,000,000	260,000
10,000,000	360,000
15,000,000	455,000
25,000,000	525,000
35,000,000	585,000

and .4 per cent. Squaring and summing gives 1.16 per cent, and the square root of this is 1.1 per cent, which is the standard error of the difference.

Note that except for very small subsamples, the standard error of the difference will not exceed 4 per cent so that the differences of more than eight percentage points will be statistically significant at the two sigma level.

SELECTION OF RESPONDENTS FOR PERSONAL INTERVIEWS

All results presented in Part II were derived from face-to-face interviews with adults randomly selected from within the households screened in the first phase of the study. Since the design of the national sample has just been outlined, the present section is restricted to a description of how candidates for personal interviews were selected from within these households.

Acutally, two separate samples were drawn in the second phase of the study. First, a random sample of just under 2,000 adults was selected to represent the total adult population of the United States. However, to ensure a substantial number of interviews with persons who had had recent experiences with adult education, an additional sample of over 1,200 persons was drawn from among those who had received instruction in subjects other than Bible studies or traditional religious training during the previous year.

The actual methods by which these two samples were drawn were as follows:

1. *The random sample.*—At the time the national sample was originally drawn for this study, two of every eleven households were se-

Table A–1.3 Percentage Standard Errors for Various Sample Size Groups

Percentage Estimate	Size of Group				
	500	1,000	2,000	4,000	8,000
1	0.5	0.4	0.3	0.2	0.1
5	1.2	0.9	0.6	0.3	.3
10	1.6	1.2	0.8	0.6	.4
15	1.9	1.3	1.0	0.7	.5
20	2.2	1.6	1.1	0.8	.5
30	2.5	1.8	1.2	0.9	.6
50	2.7	1.9	1.4	1.0	0.7

lected for a "long-form personal interview" with some one adult member of the household. The selection of actual respondents within these households was then made by interviewers at the time the screening interviews were administered. To select a respondent, the eligible adults in the household were first listed, and the interviewer then employed the sampling table shown in Figure A–1.1. Interviews were taken only with persons who were either twenty-one or over, married, or the head of a household.

FIRST—List the name and age of every adult who lives in this household in the summary box to the right. Transfer this information from the top of pages 6–7 of this questionnaire. List in order of age (the oldest on the first line) and omit those who are away at college or away in the armed forces.

SECOND—Use the sampling table below to determine which individual to interview. To use this table you will have to remember (*a*) how many people you listed in the box to the right, and (*b*) which letter (A through F) your assignment sheet listed for this household.

	Summary Box	
No.	Name	Age
1		
2		
3		
4		
5		
6		

Sampling Table

And Your Assignment Sheet Contained the Letter	If the Number of Adults Listed Above Is					
	One	Two	Three	Four	Five	Six or More
A. Then interview adult on line	1	2	3	1	5	1
B. Then interview adult on line	No one	1	2	2	4	2
C. Then interview adult on line	1	2	1	3	3	3
D. Then interview adult on line	No one	2	3	4	2	4
E. Then interview adult on line	1	1	2	4	1	5
F. Then interview adult on line	No one	1	1	2	1	6

I must interview the person listed on line _____ in the summary box, using the Survey 447 adult questionnaire.

His/her name is_____

Figure A–1.1 Household Summary and Sampling Table

Of the 23,950 adults enumerated in the screening interviews, 1,974 were selected for personal interviews, of which 1,808 (or 91.6 per cent) were successfully completed. However, since screening interviews were completed in only 89.9 per cent of the households originally selected, the overall completion rate for interviewing on this sample could be represented as only about 82 per cent (91.6 × 89.9 = 82.3 per cent).

2. *The sample of recent participants.* — The additional interviews with recent adult education participants were sampled from among the 9/11 of the total households not used in drawing the random sample. One-half of the recent participants in these households were selected for an interview. This sample was drawn in the office by sampling clerks rather than in the field by interviewers, and interviewers were subsequently supplied with the names and addresses of specific individuals to contact and interview. In some cases, then, several weeks elapsed between visits to a given household. Since none of these interviews could be completed at the time of the original visit to a household, the overall rate of completion for this wave of interviewing was somewhat lower than for the wave in which respondents were selected by the interviewers themselves. Of 1,222 persons selected, 1,037 (84.9 per cent) were successfully interviewed, and the overall completion rate for this portion of the field work was therefore just over 76 per cent (84.9 × 89.9 = 76.3 per cent).

3. *Combining the two strata into a single sample.* — Rather than conduct separate analyses on two different samples of respondents, a weighting procedure was introduced whereby the two subsamples could be combined and treated as a single sample representative of the total adult population. The rationale for this procedure resides in the original sample design and stems from the chances which persons either "active" or "inactive" in adult education during the previous year had of being selected for a long-form interview.

First, since one adult was selected from a random 2/11 of all households in the sample, and since American households contain almost exactly two adults on the average,[2] an adult living in any household in the NORC national sample had just about one chance in eleven of being selected for a long interview. Persons who had taken adult education courses during the previous twelve months, however, could also be selected in the "recent participant" sample, and because of this their total chances of being interviewed were considerably higher. Since

[2] In the first phase of the study, 23,950 adults were located in 11,956 households — a mean average of 2.003 adults per household.

every other recent participant was selected in 9/11 of the total house-holds, these persons had an additional nine chances in twenty-two of being interviewed (1/2 × 9/11 = 9/22). Altogether, then, someone recently active in adult education had a fifty-fifty chance of being se-lected for an interview (1/11 + 9/22 = 1/2). Those not active during the previous year, on the other hand, had just one chance in eleven of falling into the random sample. Recent participants, in other words, were 5.5 times as likely to be interviewed as those not recently active, and the weighting factor which must be introduced to combine the two strata of the sample is therefore a factor of five and one-half.

Altogether, 2,845 different persons were interviewed with the long-form interview schedule, 1,808 in the random sample, and 1,037 in the sample of recent participants. Some of the respondents in the random sample, of course, had been active in adult education pursuits during the previous year, and when the respondents were subsequently classi-fied according to their recent educational experiences, 1,263 turned out to have been "active" while 1,582 were not.

It is between these two aggregates, then, that the differential weights would apply—since in the sampling design the probability of selection rested entirely on one's educational activity during the previous twelve months. When the analysis was conducted, each person in the "inac-tive" stratum was given a weight of 5.5, so that the original sample of 2,845 cases became a weighted sample of 9,964 cases (5.5 × 1,582 + 1,263 = 9,964). All results presented in Part II, then, were calculated from "weighted case bases" rather than from the raw numbers of actual respondents.

While this procedure had the advantage of allowing a consideration of all interviews at each point in the analysis, the method does have disadvantages. Since all the tables in Part II show the "weighted case bases" from which percentages were derived, it is impossible to ap-praise the reliability of any of the estimates reported—that is, to apply directly tests of statistical significance of any percentage differences revealed. In general, of course, no weighted case base could exceed five and one-half times the number of actual cases contained in any cell, and in most instances the increment would be considerably less than this.[3] The main problem, however, is that the "true" case bases cannot be restored by reducing the reported case bases by any constant factor. In tables which distribute the entire sample, the weighting factor was 3.5 times the actual number of respondents (9,964/2,845 = 3.5022). How-

[3]Moreover, the standard procedure was to report no results where the true case base was less than twenty persons.

ever, weights tended to be higher for those segments of the population *less* likely to have been active in adult education pursuits during the previous year. Thus, women were upgraded more than men; older persons more than younger; and persons of low socio-economic status more than those higher up the social class ladder. These differential effects are illustrated in Table A–1.4, where the weights are seen to vary from a low of 2.36 among younger high-status men to a high of 5.10 among older low-status men.

In general, then, where comparisons are based on sex, age, or socio-economic status, quite accurate estimates of the true case bases of cells can be derived by applying the reduction factors shown in Table A–1.4. In other situations, a general reduction by a factor of 3.5 would result in a fairly accurate estimate of the true case base.

SAMPLING PROCEDURES IN THE COMMUNITY STUDIES

As noted in Chapter 13, no systematic sampling procedures were

Table A–1.4 Effects of Weighting Procedure on Respondents of Different Sex, Age, and Socio-Economic Status

Category of Respondent	Actual Number of Respondents	Weighted Case Base	Weighting Factor
Total sample	2,845	9,964	3.50
Sex			
All men	1,334	4,434.5	3.32
All women	1,511	5,529.5	3.66
Age			
Under 30	700	2,063.5	2.95
30–49	1,313	4,328	3.30
50 and over	813	3,504	4.31
Sex, age, and socio-economic status			
Men under 45, low SES	149	594.5	3.99
Men under 45, medium SES	287	845	2.94
Men under 45, high SES	399	943.5	2.36
Men 45 and over, low SES	193	985	5.10
Men 45 and over, medium SES	123	478.5	3.89
Men 45 and over, high SES	164	510.5	3.11
Women under 45, low SES	177	757.5	4.28
Women under 45, medium SES	300	1,110	3.70
Women under 45, high SES	387	999	2.58
Women 45 and over, low SES	288	1,381.5	4.80
Women 45 and over, medium SES	141	584.5	4.16
Women 45 and over, high SES	162	486	3.00

employed to select the cities in which inventories of adult education facilities were to be taken. Once two cities had been chosen for intensive study, however, probability methods were employed to sample the adults in each city who were to receive personal interviews.

The universe which was sampled for these surveys was the total population from twenty-one to sixty-five years of age residing within the urbanized area of each city. Block statistics from the 1960 census of housing were employed to first select sample segments, and after these segments had been listed, specific households were sampled and pre-assigned for contact. The average cluster size within these segments was five.

Once households had been enumerated, respondents were selected by reference to the sampling table shown on page 3 of the Community Studies Interview Schedule (reproduced in Appendix 2). Completed interviews were obtained in 281 of 335 households selected in the first of the two cities (named St. Stevens in the study) and in 265 of 320 selected in the second (Peters), thus representing completion rates of 83.9 and 82.8 per cent, respectively.

SELECTION OF YOUTH FOR PERSONAL INTERVIEWS

For the final phase of the study, a national sample of young people was selected from among the pool of persons in the seventeen–twenty-four age group who had been enumerated in the household screening phase of the national survey. This sample was so drawn as to represent the total population of persons aged seven-

Table A–1.5 Sample Design for the Selection of Young People Aged 17–24

Category of Youth	Portion of Total Sample Used	Selection Rate within Portion of Sample Used	Overall Sampling Rate	Weight Assigned in Ultimate Sample
Single, aged 17–20	All	1/4	1/4	1
Married, aged 17–20	9/11	11/36	1/4	1
Aged 21–24 and still in school	9/11	11/36	1/4	1
Aged 21–24, not in school, and a high-school graduate	9/11	11/72	1/8	2
Aged 21–24, not in school, and not a high-school graduate	9/11	11/36	1/4	1

teen–twenty-four with the exception of those serving in the armed forces and not living within an American household.

Since in two-ninths of the sample households persons either twenty-one–twenty-four or under twenty-one and married had been eligible to receive the adult form of the personal interview, the selection of young people from within these particular categories was restricted to that portion of the original sample not designated for an adult interview. Altogether, five subgroups of youth were identified for purposes of the sample draw, and these groups were sampled in the manner indicated in Table A – 1.5. In effect, then, four of the five subgroups were sampled at the rate of one in four, while the fifth–consisting of all persons aged twenty-one–twenty-four who were no longer in school and who had graduated from high school or better–were selected at the rate of one in eight. Because of this difference in sampling rates, then, it was necessary to assign persons in the latter category a weight of 2 in order to restore the overall representativeness of the sample.

One additional sampling modification was also required, since some youths had also been eligible to receive interviews because they had been recent adult education participants. At the completion of the sample draw, therefore, any youths who had already been interviewed with the adult form of the schedule were dropped from the sample and replaced with the next eligible persons in their category who had also been recent participants, but who had not been interviewed in the second phase of the survey.

Altogether, 865 young people were selected by these methods, and of these, 697 were subsequently interviewed. The overall completion rate was therefore 80.6 per cent. Of the 697 persons interviewed, 116 fell within the stratum sampled at the rate of one in eight, and when these cases were weighted up, the subsequent analysis was carried out on a weighted sample of 813 cases.

Appendix 2

Interview Schedules and Survey Materials

A. THE EDUCATIONAL ACTIVITIES OF AMERICAN
ADULTS: JUNE 1961 – JUNE 1962

NORC 447–448
Confidential

NATIONAL OPINION RESEARCH CENTER
UNIVERSITY OF CHICAGO
Short-Form Household Interview

Identification (58–65)

RESPONDENT'S NAME _____

ADDRESS _____

_____

Segment No. (Six digits)	–
Household No. (Two digits)	

RECORD OF CALLS

	DATE	TIME	RESULTS
1st			
2nd			
3rd			
4th			
5th			
6th			

Notes:

INTRODUCTION

Hello, I'm _____ from the National Opinion Research Center of the University of Chicago. We're conducting a national study of family activities in modern America.

To start, I'd like to list the names of all persons who live in this household. First, who are the adults who live here—from oldest to youngest? Please include all persons either 21 or over or who are married.

(TURN TO PAGE 6)

[Page 2]

CHILDREN 3 TO 16

Are there any persons between the ages of 3 and 16 living here?

NAME _____ | 1 | 1*
RELATION TO HOUSE-
   HOLD HEAD _____ 8 –

  IF NO, CHECK HERE. ☐

  IF YES, RECORD NAMES, RELATION TO HOUSEHOLD HEAD, AGE, AND SEX.

AGE . . ._____ 9 – 10
SEX . . .Male . . . . . . 11 – 1
        Female 2

ASK FOR EACH CHILD 3 TO 6 YEARS OF AGE

1. Was (NAME) enrolled either in school, kindergarten, or nursery school during this past school year—that is, since last September?

No (not enrolled) . . . . 12 – 1
Yes (grade 1+) 2
Yes (kindergarten) 3
Yes (nursery school) . . 4
D.K. . . . . Y
Other (specify) _____

ASK FOR EACH CHILD 7 TO 16 YEARS OF AGE

2. (Next, I'd like to ask about school enrollment during this past school year.) Since last September, has (NAME) been enrolled in school during the whole school year, during only some of it, or not at all?

Whole year (ASK A) . . . 13 – 4
Some of it (ASK A
  and B) 5
Not at all (SKIP TO Q. 3) . 6
D.K. . . . . Y

  IF WHOLE YEAR OR SOME OF IT

A. In what type of school was he/she enrolled—a public school, a private school, or a parochial religious school?

Public . . . . 14 – 7
Private 8
Parochial religious 9
D.K. . . . . Y

  IF ONLY SOME OF IT

B. What was the reason (NAME) was enrolled for just some of the year—

Graduated mid-term . . . 15 – 1
Illness 2

*Due to space limitations, cols. 1-2, 1-3, and 1-4 (all identical to col. 1-1) are not reproduced here. This also applies to cols. 2-2–4 and 3-2–4.—EDITOR.

| did he/she graduate at mid-term, miss school because of illness, drop out during the year, or just what? | Dropped out during year 3
D.K. . . . . Y
Other (specify) _____ |

3. During the past twelve months—that is, since last _____, has (NAME) taken lessons or received instruction in any subject not connected with regular school work including things like music lessons, religious classes, swimming lessons, summer school classes, or anything like that?

    Yes 16–1
    No x
    D.K. . . . . Y

    IF YES
    A. In what subject was the instruction taken? (Anything else?)

    SUBJECTS STUDIED
    1._____ 17–
    2. _____ 18–
    3. _____ 19–

[Page 4]
YOUTH (17 TO 20 AND UNMARRIED)

(i) Are there any unmarried persons between the ages of 17 and 20 living here?

IF NO, CHECK HERE. ☐
IF YES, RECORD NAMES, RELATION TO HOUSEHOLD HEAD, AGE, AND SEX.

NAME _____ |2|1
RELATION TO HOUSE-
HOLD HEAD _____ 8–
AGE . . . ._____ 9–10
SEX . . .Male 11–1
          Female 2

CODE IF LIVING
In school residence . . . 8
On armed forces base . . 9

(ii) Are there any household members this age who are away at school and living in a dormitory, fraternity, or school residence, or who are in the armed forces and living on base or in a camp or barracks?

IF NO, CHECK HERE. ☐
IF YES, RECORD NAMES, RELATION TO HOUSEHOLD HEAD, AGE, SEX, AND WHETHER IN SCHOOL OR IN ARMED FORCES.

TURN TO PAGE 2

ASK FOR EACH YOUTH
4. (Next, I'd like to ask about school attendance during this past school year.) Since last September, has (NAME) been enrolled in school during the whole school year, during only some of it, or not at all?

Whole year (ASK A, B, AND C) 12–1
Some of it (ASK A, B, C, AND D) . . . . –2
Not at all (SKIP TO Q. 5) . 3
D.K. . . . . Y

IF WHOLE YEAR OR SOME OF IT

    A. In what type of school was he/she enrolled—a high school, college, junior college, trade school, business school, or just what?

    B. Was that a public school, a private school, or a parochial religious school?

    C. Was he/she attending school full time or just part time?

IF ONLY SOME OF IT

    D. What was the reason (NAME) was enrolled for just some of the year— did he/she graduate at mid-term, miss school because of illness, drop out during the year, or just what?

High school . . . . . . 13 – 1
Junior college 2
College/university 3
Trade/vocational 4
Business/commercial . . 5
D.K. . . . . Y
Other (specify) _____

Public . . . . 14 – 7
Private 8
Parochial religious 9
D.K. . . . . Y

Full time . . . . 15 – 1
Part time 2
D.K. . . . . Y

Graduated mid-term . . 16 – 1
Illness 2
Dropped out during
    year 3
D.K. . . . . Y
Other (specify) _____

5. During the past twelve months, that is, since last _____, has (NAME) taken lessons or received instruction in any subject not connected with regular school work—including things such as vocational training, music lessons, religious classes, summer school classes (training courses given in the armed forces), or anything like that?

IF YES

    A. In what subject was the instruction taken? (Anything else?)

Yes . . . . 17 – 1
No X
D.K. . . . . Y

SUBJECTS STUDIED
1. _____ 18 –
                       19 –
2. _____ 20 –
                       21 –
3. _____ 21 –
                       23 –

[Page 6]

ADULTS (21 OR OVER OR MARRIED)

(A) ENTER NAME.
(B) What is (NAME'S) relation to the head of the household?
(C) What is (NAME'S) age, please?
(D) RECORD SEX.

NAME _____ | 3 | 1 |
RELATION TO HOUSE-
    HOLD HEAD _____ 8 –
AGE . . . _____ 11 – 1
SEX . . . Male . . . . . . 11 – 1
        Female 2

(E) Are there any other adult members of the household who are away at school living in a dormitory, fraternity or school residence; or in the armed forces and living in a camp or barracks or on a base?

CODE IF LIVING
In school residence . . . 8
On armed forces base . . 9

IF NO, CHECK HERE. ☐
IF YES, ENTER NAME, RELATION TO HOUSEHOLD HEAD, AGE, SEX, AND WHETHER IN SCHOOL OR ARMED FORCES.

TURN TO PAGE 4

ASK IN ALL HOUSEHOLDS

6. Are there any adult members of this household who were enrolled in some type of school or college as full-time students during this past school year —that is, since September? (IF YES: Who?) CODE YES OR NO FOR EACH ADULT.

Yes . . . . 12 – 1
No 2
D.K. . . . . Y

IF YES·

A. In what type of school was he/she enrolled—a high school, college, junior college, trade school, business school, or just what?

High school . . . . 13 – 1
Junior college 2
College/university 3
Trade/vocational 4
Business/commercial . . 5
D.K. . . . . Y
Other (specify) _____

---

7. HAND RESPONDENT YELLOW FLASH CARD,* SIDE 1.

Here is a list of subjects and skills that people sometimes study after they have left school. Would you please read this over and tell me whether during the past twelve months any adult member of the household has received instruction in any of these things—or in any other subjects or skills not listed here? Please include evening classes, correspondence courses, private lessons, lecture series, courses given over television —or anything else like that. How about yourself? (How about NAME?) CODE YES OR NO FOR EACH ADULT.

Yes (ASK 7A – E) . . . . 14 – 1
No X
D.K. . . . . Y

NAME OF SUBJECT OR
SKILL _____ 15 –

CATEGORY NUMBER____ 16 –

IF YES

A. In what specific subject or skill did (you/NAME) receive instruction? IF MORE THAN ONE MENTIONED, RECORD THE ONE STUDIED MOST RECENTLY.

Attended classes . . . . . 17 – 1
Attended lecture series . 2
Attended group discussions 3
Correspondence lessons 4
Private teacher 5
Television 6
On the job training . . . 7
D.K. . . . . Y
Other (specify) _____

*Reproduced at the end of this section—EDITOR.

B. In which category on the card would that subject (skill) best fit?

C. ASK RESPONDENT TO TURN THE CARD OVER.
Of the methods listed on the back of the card, which one best describes how this instruction was received?

IF CODES 1, 2, OR 3, ASK (I) AND (II)
IF CODES 4, 5, 6, 7, OR OTHER, ASK (III)

High school	18 – 0
College/university	1
Private school	2
Business/industry	3
Co-op Extension Service	4
Church/synagogue	5
Armed forces	6
YMCA/community center	7
Library/museum	8
Gov't – federal or state	9
D.K.	Y
Other (specify) _____	

IF 7C was 1, 2, OR 3
(i) What type of school or institution conducted the (classes/lecture/group discussions) – that is, who sponsored them?

[Page 6]
ADULTS (21 OR OVER OR MARRIED)

(A) ENTER NAME.
(B) What is (NAME'S) relation to the head of the household?
(C) What is (NAME'S) age, please?
(D) RECORD SEX
(E) Are there any other adult members of the household who are away at school and living in a dormitory, fraternity or school residence; or in the armed forces and living in a camp or barracks or on a base?
IF NO, CHECK HERE. ☐
IF YES, ENTER NAME, RELATION TO HOUSEHOLD HEAD, AGE, SEX AND WHETHER IN SCHOOL OR ARMED FORCES.

NAME _____	3 | 1
RELATION TO HOUSE-HOLD HEAD _____	8 –
AGE . . . _____	9 – 10
SEX . . . .Male	11 – 1
Female	2
CODE IF LIVING	
In school residence . . .	8
On armed forces base . .	9

TURN TO PAGE 4

[Page 6(b)]
IF YES TO Q. 7 (CONT'D)
IF 7-C WAS 1, 2, OR 3 (CONT'D)
(ii) Approximately how many classes/lessons/discussions did (NAME) attend in connection with this activity?

(SKIP TO 7-D)

IF 7-C WAS 4, 5, 6, 7, OR OTHER

One	19 – 1
Two	2
Three	3
Four	4
Five to eight	5
Nine or more	6
D.K.	Y
1 week or less	20 – 1
2 weeks	2

(iii) For approximately what length of time did (NAME) engage in this study/ training?

3 weeks	3
4 weeks	4
5 to 8 weeks	5
9 weeks or more	6
D.K.	Y

D. Was the instruction taken for "credit" — that is, for some type of degree, diploma, or certificate — or was it "non-credit"?

Credit . . . . 21 – 1	
Non-credit	2
D.K. . . . .`	Y

IF CREDIT
(i) For what type of degree, diploma, or certificate was it taken?

High school diploma . . . 22 – 3	
Bachelor's degree	4
Higher college degree . .	5
D.K.	Y
Other (specify) _____	

E. Did (NAME) receive instruction in any other subjects or skills during the past twelve months?

Yes . . . . 23 – 7	
No	8
D.K	Y

NOTE!! IF YES, GO TO PAGE 10 AND FILL IN DETAILS OF ADDITIONAL SUBJECTS OR SKILLS.

ASK EVERYONE

8. During the past twelve months, has any adult living here been engaged in learning some new subject or skill by means of independent study strictly on his or her own? How about yourself? (How about NAME?) CODE YES OR NO FOR EACH ADULT.

Yes . . . . 24 – 1	
No	2
D.K.	Y

IF YES
A. What was the subject of this study? (Anything else?)

SUBJECTS STUDIED ON ONE'S OWN

1. _____	25 –
	26 –
2. _____	27 –
	28 –

[Page 6]

ADULTS (21 OR OVER OR MARRIED)

(A) ENTER NAME.
(B) What is (NAME'S) relation to the head of the household?
(C) What is (NAME'S) age, please?
(D) RECORD SEX.
(E) Are there any other adult members of the household who are away at school and living in a dormitory, fraternity or school residence; or in the armed forces and living in a camp or barracks or on a base?
IF NO, CHECK HERE. ☐
IF YES, ENTER NAME, RELATION TO HOUSEHOLD HEAD, AGE, SEX AND WHETHER IN SCHOOL OR ARMED FORCES.

NAME _____	3 | 1
RELATION TO HOUSE-HOLD HEAD _____	8 –
AGE . . ._____	9 – 10
SEX . . .Male . . . . . . 11 – 1	
Female	2
CODE IF LIVING	
In school residence . . .	8
On armed forces base . .	9

TURN TO PAGE 4

[Page 6(d)]

ASK IN ALL HOUSEHOLDS: Now to finish up, I'd like just a little more information about the adults in this household.

9. (ASK FOR EACH PERSON UNLESS OB-VIOUS) (Are you) (Is NAME) now married, single, widowed, separated, or divorced?

Married	29–1
Single	2
Widowed	3
Separated	4
Divorced	5
D.K.	Y

10. What (do you) (does NAME) usually do — work full time, work part time (keep house, go to school), or something else?

    IF WORK FULL TIME OR PART TIME
    A. Exactly what type of work do you (does NAME) do?
    B. In what type of business or industry do you (does he/she) work?

Work full-time	30–1
Work part-time only . .	2
Work part-time/keep house	3
Work part-time/school .	4
Keep house only	5
Go to school only	6
Retired	7
D.K.	Y
Other (specify) _____	

TYPE OF WORK _____ 31–

BUSINESS OR INDUSTRY

_____ 32–

CODE IF SELF-EMPLOYED	0

11. What (is your) (is NAME'S) religious preference? IF PROTESTANT: Which denomination?

Protestant	33–1
(Specify denomination)	
Catholic	2
Jewish	3
None	4
D.K.	Y
Other (specify) _____	

12. What was the last grade that (you) (NAME) completed in school?

Never attended school .	34–1
1–4 years	2
5–7 years	3
8 years	4
9–11 years	5
12 years (Finished high school)	6
Some college	7
Completed college	8
Graduate training	9
D.K.	Y
Other schooling in addition (specify) _____	

13. INDICATE THE PERSON THAT YOU INTERVIEWED. . . . . INTERVIEWED THIS PERSON . . . . 35 – 1

| 36 – | 37 – | 38 – | 39 – |

[Page 8]

HOUSEHOLD INFORMATION

14. HAND RESPONDENT INCOME CARD.

Now to finish up, in which of these general groups did your total family income (did NAME's total income) fall last year – before taxes, that is?

RECORD SEPARATELY FOR
EACH FAMILY IN HOUSEHOLD

"YOUR" FAMILY (If more than one family list members)	2ND FAMILY (List members)	3RD FAMILY (List members)
————————	————————	————————
————————	————————	————————
————————	————————	————————
————————	————————	————————
————————	————————	————————

INCOME

	"YOUR" FAMILY	2ND FAMILY	3RD FAMILY
Under $1,000	A . . . 66 – x	A . . . 67 – x	A . . . 68 – x
$1,000 – $1,999 . . .	B . . . 0	B 0	B . . . 0
$2,000 – $2,999 . . .	C . . . 1	C . . . 1	C . . . 1
$3,000 – $3,999 . . .	D . . . 2	D . . . 2	D . . . 2
$4,000 – $4,999 . . .	E 3	E 3	E . . . 3
$5,000 – $5,999 . . .	F 4	F 4	F . . . 4
$6,000 – $6,999 . . .	G . . . 5	G . . . 5	G . . . 5
$7,000 – $7,999 . . .	H . . . 6	H . . . 6	H . . . 6
$8,000 – $9,999 . . .	I 7	I 7	I . . . 7
$10,000 – $14,999 . .	J 8	J 8	J . . . 8
$15,000 or over . . .	K . . . 9	K . . . 9	K . . . 9
D.K.	D.K. . . Y	D.K. . . Y	D.K. . Y

IF REFUSED, CHECK
HERE AND
ESTIMATE . . . . Refused . . ☐   Refused . . ☐   Refused . . ☐

Estimate _____   Estimate _____   Estimate _____

15. SUMMARY OF HOUSEHOLD COMPOSITION
ENTER NUMBER OF ADULTS
IN HOUSEHOLD . . . . TOTAL ADULTS _____ 69 –
ENTER NUMBER OF YOUTH
IN HOUSEHOLD . . . . TOTAL YOUTH _____ 70 –
ENTER NUMBER OF CHILDREN
3 TO 16 . . . . TOTAL CHILDREN _____ 71 –

ASK UNLESS OBVIOUS: Are there any
other children under the age of 3
living here? . . . . NUMBER _____ 72 –
TOTAL PERSONS IN HOUSEHOLD _____ 73 –

16. May I please have your telephone number in
case I have to call back for any reason? TELEPHONE NUMBER _____
Refused . . . . ☐
No telephone . . . . . ☐

COMPLETE THESE ITEMS AS SOON AS INTERVIEW IS FINISHED.
17. RACE OF RESPONDENT: White . . . . 74 – 1
Negro 2
Oriental 3

18. CHECK ONE OF THE FOLLOWING TO SHOW TYPE OF DWELLING UNIT.
Located on farm . . . . 75 – 1
Non-farm: single family house 2
Non-farm: duplex or two-family structure 3
Non-farm: multi-unit structure (e.g., apartment) 4

19. CIRCLE ONE OF THESE TO SHOW LOCATION OF DWELLING UNIT.
Inside the largest city in the primary unit. . . . . 76 – 1
In a suburb of the largest city in primary sampling unit 2
In the outskirts (including nearby small towns of the primary
sampling unit) 3
In open country 4

INTERVIEWER'S SIGNATURE _____

[Page 9]

Notes and Comments

[Page 10]

ADDITIONAL SUBJECTS MENTIONED IN QUESTION 7-A

ASK THE FOLLOWING FOR EACH ADDI-
TIONAL SUBJECT MENTIONED.
RECORD NAME OF PERSON . . . .

NAME OF PERSON _____
_____

A. In what specific subject or skill was the instruction taken?

NAME OF SUBJECT OR
SKILL_____ 40 –

B. In which category on the card would that subject (skill) best fit?

CATEGORY NUMBER
41 _____

C. ASK RESPONDENT TO TURN OVER YELLOW CARD.
Of the methods listed on the back of the card, which one best describes how this instruction was received?

IF CODES 1, 2, OR 3, ASK (I) AND (II).
IF CODES 4, 5, 6, 7, OR OTHER, ASK (III).

Classes . . . . 42 – 1
Lecture series 2
Group discussions 3
Correspondence 4
Private teacher 5
Television 6
On-the-job training . . . 7
D.K. . . . . Y
Other (specify) _____

IF C WAS 1, 2, OR 3
(i) What type of school or institution conducted these (classes/lectures/group discussions) — that is, who sponsored them?

High school . . . . 43 – 1
College/university 2
Private school 3
Business/industry 4
Co-op Extension
  Service 5
Church/synagogue 6
Armed forces 7
YMCA/community
  center 8
Library/museum 9
Gov't — federal or
  state 0
D.K. . . . . Y
Other (specify) _____

(ii) Approximately how many classes/lessons/discussions did (you/NAME) attend in connection with this activity?
(SKIP TO D)

One . . . . 44 – 1
Two 2
Three 3
Four 4
Five to eight 5
Nine or more 6
D.K. . . . . Y

IF C WAS 4, 5, 6, 7, OR OTHER

(iii) For approximately what length of time did (you/NAME) engage in this study/training?

1 week or less . . . . . . 45 – 1
2 weeks 2

3 weeks   3
4 weeks   4
5 to 8 weeks   5
9 weeks or more   6
D.K. . . . .   Y

D. Was the instruction taken for "credit"—that is, for some type of degree, diploma, or certificate —or was it "non-credit"?

Credit . . . . 46 – 1
Non-credit   2
D.K. . . . .   Y
High school diploma . . 47 – 3
Bachelor's degree   4
Higher college degree . .   5
D.K. . . . .   Y
Other (specify) _____

IF CREDIT
(i) For what type of degree, diploma or certificate was it taken?

E. Did (you/NAME) receive instruction in any other subjects or skills during the past twelve months?

Yes . . . . 48 – 7
No . . . .
D.K. . . . .

IF YES: GO TO NEXT COLUMN.
IF NO: GO BACK TO PAGE 6 AND PICK UP WHERE YOU LEFT OFF.

[Page 12]

IDENTIFICATION OF RESPONDENTS TO RECEIVE SUBSEQUENT INTERVIEWS

This page is designed so you can determine which individual should receive a longer interview on Survey 447 (Education).

On Survey 448 (Aging) you interview all individuals aged 65 or over who live in the dwelling unit, and complete the bottom section of this page.

SURVEY 447
USE THIS SECTION ONLY IF YOUR ASSIGNMENT SHEET CONTAINED A LETTER A THROUGH F FOR THIS DWELLING UNIT.

FIRST—List the name and age of every adult who lives in this household in the summary box to the right. Transfer this information from the top of pages 6–7 of this questionnaire. List in order of age (the oldest on the first line) and omit those who are away at college or away in the armed forces.

SECOND—Use the sampling table below to determine which individual to interview. To use this table you will have to remember (a) how many people you listed in the box to the right, and (b) which letter (A through F) your assignment sheet listed for this household.

No.	Summary Box	
	Name	Age
1		
2		
3		
4		
5		
6		

Sampling Table

And Your Assignment Sheet Contained the Letter	If the Number of Adults Listed Above Is					
	One	Two	Three	Four	Five	Six or More
A. Then interview adult on line	1	2	3	1	5	1
B. Then interview adult on line	No one	1	2	2	4	2
C. Then interview adult on line	1	2	1	3	3	3
D. Then interview adult on line	No one	2	3	4	2	4
E. Then interview adult on line	1	1	2	4	1	5
F. Then interview adult on line	No one	1	1	2	1	6

I must interview the person listed on line _____ in the summary box, using the Survey 447 adult questionnaire.

His/her name is_____

SURVEY 448

USE THIS SECTION ON SURVEY 448 IF THERE WAS AN X ON YOUR ASSIGNMENT SHEET FOR THIS DWELLING UNIT.

We will interview each "older person" found in the household.

Complete the following.

☐ I have found no individuals 65 or over and therefore must conduct no interview with an older person here.

☐ I have found _____ individuals 65 and over and therefore must interview all of them. Their names are:

_____   _____

_____   _____

NORC 447
[side one]

Examples of Adult Education Activities

Category Number   Type of Subject

1   Regular school subjects
                    Such as: Great Books
                                History
                                Mathematics
                                Foreign languages
                                Music appreciation

2	Trade, business, or vocational subjects
	Such as: Machine shop
	Typing or shorthand
	Salesmanship
	Office management
	Electronics
3	Any on-the-job training
4	Hobbies and recreations
	Such as: Photography
	Bridge lessons
	Dancing lessons
	Swimming or golf lessons
	Music or art lessons
5	Home and family life
	Such as: Home repairs
	Sewing or cooking
	Gardening
	Infant or child care
6	Personal development
	Such as: Speed reading
	Personality development
	Public speaking
	Physical fitness
7	Religion, morals, or ethics
8	Current events, public affairs, and citizenship
	Such as: International affairs
	Community government
	Democracy
	The dangers of communism
	Citizenship or Americanization
9	Agricultural subjects
0	Other — anything else not covered by these categories
	Such as: Driving lessons

NORC 447
[side two]

How was the instruction taken?
By attending classes
By attending a series of lectures or talks
By attending group discussions
Correspondence lessons by mail
Individual lessons from a private teacher
Lessons given over television
On-the-job training
Some other method (What?)

B. REACTIONS TO CONTINUING EDUCATION

Adult Form

NORC 447—4/62
Confidential

NATIONAL OPINION RESEARCH CENTER
UNIVERSITY OF CHICAGO
Long Form Personal Interview

(1–4)

Identification (5 – 14)

Segment No. (Six digits)	–
Household No. (Two digits)	
Person No. (Two digits)	

NAME _____

ADDRESS _____

RECORD OF CALLS

	DATE	TIME	RESULTS
1st			
2nd			
3rd			
4th			
5th			
6th			

Notes:

About This Person

Before the interview begins, transfer the following information about this individual from the short form household interview.

I. From page 6 or 7 (top)
   A. Age of respondent ——————————————— 15 – 16 –
   B. Sex of respondent   Male . . . . 17 – 1
                                Female   2
   C. Relation to the head of the household ————————————— 18 –

II. From page 6(d) or 7
   D. Marital status   Married . . . . . . 19 – 1
                              Single   2
                              Widowed   3
                              Separated   4
                              Divorced   5

   E. Working status

                              Works full time . . 20 – 1
                              Works part time
                                only   2
                              Works part time/
                                keeps house . . .   3
                              Works part time/
                                school   4
                              Keeps house only .   5
                              Goes to school
                                only   6
                              Retired   7
                              Other (specify)

                              ————————————

   If works full time or part time
                              Type of work done
                              ——————————— 21 –
                              Type of business or
                                industry ————— 22 –
                              Self-employed . . .   0

   F. Religious preference

                              Protestant . . . . . 23 – 1
                              (Specify denomination) ————

Catholic   2
Jewish   3
None   4
Other (specify)

_____

G. Highest grade completed in school

Never attended
school . . . . . . 24 – 1
1 – 4 years   2
5 – 7 years   3
8 years   4
9 – 11 years   5
12 years   6
13 – 15 years (some
college   7
Completed college .   8
Graduate training .   9
Other schooling in
addition (specify)

_____

III. FROM PAGE 8

H. Total family income

Under $1,000	A	25 – x
$1,000 – $1,999	B	0
$2,000 – $2,999	C	1
$3,000 – $3,999	D	2
$4,000 – $4,999	E	3
$5,000 – $5,999	F	4
$6,000 – $6,999	G	5
$7,000 – $7,999	H	6
$8,000 – $9,999	I	7
$10,000 – $14,999	H	8
$15,000 or over	K	9

D.K. . . . .   Y
Refused . . . . □
Estimate _____

NOTE: IF THIS PERSON WAS ENROLLED FULL TIME IN SCHOOL DURING
THE PAST SCHOOL YEAR, HE IS CLASSIFIED AS A "FULL-TIME STUDENT"
IN THIS INTERVIEW (SEE QUESTION 6 ON SHORT FORM).

IF FULL-TIME STUDENT, CHECK HERE. □   26 – 1

The Interview

ASK EVERYONE

1. This interview is mainly about the activities that individuals and families are engaging in these days. Let's start by talking about your own spare time activities and interests.

What things do you enjoy doing most in your spare time—that is, in the time you have left over after work and household tasks are done for the day? (Anything else?)

27 –

---

2. About how much spare time do you find you have these days after your work and household tasks are done—would you say a great deal, some, or hardly any at all?

A great deal	28–0	
Some	1	
Hardly any at all	2	
D.K.	3	

---

3. Do you have about as much spare time as you'd like, or would you rather have more, or less?

As much as I'd like	29–5	
Rather have more	6	
Rather have less	7	
D.K.	8	

---

4. How often do you find yourself with spare time that you don't know quite what to do with—would you say frequently, occasionally, seldom, or never?

Frequently	30–1	
Occasionally	2	
Seldom	3	
Never	4	
D.K.	5	

---

5. People have quite different ideas about the most enjoyable way to spend their spare time. Some people prefer to keep as busy as possible doing different things either at home or out of the home, while others prefer not to do anything in particular and to just take it easy.

A. Which do you think is the better idea about how to spend spare time — keep as busy as possible, or take it easy?

    Keep as busy as possible . . . . . 31 – 1
    Take it easy   2
    D.K.   3

B. How about most other men/women around here — do you think most prefer to keep busy as possible or to take it easy?

    Keep as busy as possible . . . . 32 – 5
    Take it easy   6
    D.K.   7

---

6. Which day of the week do you look forward to most?

    Day* _____ 33 –
    No favorite day   0
    D.K.   x

*IF A FAVORITE DAY
A. Why do you like (DAY) best? (Any other reason?)

    34 –

---

7. And which day do you like the least?

    Day* _____ 35 –
    No least-liked day   0
    D.K.   x

*IF A LEAST-LIKED DAY
A. Why do you like (DAY) the least? (Any other reason?)

    36 –

---

8. Suppose you had to take a complete rest for a month. You wouldn't be sick at all and would be at home and free to move about, but you wouldn't be able to work, engage in much physical exercise, or take part in any social activities outside of your home.

 A. If you found yourself in this kind of situation, what things would be hardest for you to give up among the things you now do? (Anything else?)

 37 –

 B. What would you miss least among the things you now do? (Anything else?)

 38 –

 C. What would you probably do with your time during such a period? (Anything else?)

 39 –

 D. Do you feel that an experience of this sort might be rather pleasant, or that on the whole it would be unpleasant?

 Might be rather pleasant . . . . . 40 – 7
 On the whole unpleasant 8
 D.K. 9

9. HAND RESPONDENT PINK RECREATIONAL ACTIVITIES SHEET AND A PENCIL.

Here is a list of recreational activities that some people enjoy doing and others don't. Whether or not you actually do any of these things now, please check whether you think each one would be a very interesting, slightly interesting, slightly boring, or very boring activity.

Segment No.　　　　Household No.　　　　Person No.

Question 9 Recreational Activities Sheet

Please check for each activity whether you think it would be very interesting, slightly boring, or very boring

Activity	Very Interesting	Slightly Interesting	Slightly Boring	Very Boring
A. Take up some new hobby that you could work on at home	5 – 1	2	3	4
B. Take up some outdoors activity like golf or boating	6 – 5	6	7	8
C. Become active (or more active) in church activities	7 – 1	2	3	4
D. Join a club or other organization in the community	8 – 5	6	7	8
E. Take a course in some subject related to your work or occupation	9 – 1	2	3	4
F. Take a course in some subject not related to your work or occupation	10 – 5	6	7	8
G. Take on do-it-yourself projects around the house	11 – 1	2	3	4
H. Spend time visiting with friends	12 – 5	6	7	8
I. Do volunteer work in the community	13 – 1	2	3	4
J. Watch television	14 – 5	6	7	8
K. Read books	15 – 1	2	3	4
L. Play cards	16 – 5	6	7	8
M. Attend lectures or talks on current events in the world and nation	17 – 1	2	3	4
N. Attend lectures or talks on current events in this part of the country	18 – 5	6	7	8
O. Attend sporting events	19 – 1	2	3	4
P. Attend adult education classes	20 – 5	6	7	8
Q. Attend cultural events such as concerts or art exhibits	21 – 1	2	3	4

10. Hand respondent Card B.

In cities and towns: Next, I'd like to ask some questions about this city/town. Compared with other cities/towns of its size, how would you rate this one as a place to live—outstanding, very good, average, below average, or poor?

In rural areas: Next, I'd like to ask some questions about this neighborhood. Compared with other rural neighborhoods, how would you rate this one as a place to live—outstanding, very good, average, below average, or poor?

Facilities	Outstanding	Very Good	Average	Below Average	Poor	D.K.
A. As a place to live	41–1	2	3	4	5	6
B. How would you rate its recreational facilities for children?	42–1	2	3	4	5	6
C. How about its recreational facilities for adults?	43–1	2	3	4	5	6
D. How about its schools?	44–1	2	3	4	5	6
E. How about its adult education facilities—that is, places where adults can attend classes or can receive instruction in various subjects?	45–1	2	3	4	5	6

11. If an adult living here wanted to take some lessons in how to speak a foreign language, are there any places nearby where he or she might get instruction of this type?

> Yes . . . . 46–1*   ASK A
> No: there are none   2
> No: don't know of any   3

> *IF YES
> A. Where is that? (Is there any place else?)

> High school 47–1
> College or university   2
> College or university extension .   3
> Private school of languages . . .   4
> Private teacher or instructor . .   5
> Other (specify) _____

12. Incidentally, do you yourself speak or read any language other than English?

Yes . . . . 48–1*   ASK A–D
No   x   SKIP TO Q. 13

*IF YES

A. Which language is   IF MORE THAN TWO LANGUAGES
    that? (Any   MENTIONED, ENTER NUMBER HERE_____
    others?)

LIST ONLY THE TWO MOST
RECENTLY LEARNED

	First foreign language____	Second foreign language____
	49–	53–
B. Do you speak (LANGUAGE) fluently, just a little, or not at all?	Fluently . . . 50–1 Just a little . . 2 Not at all . . 3 D.K. 4	Fluently . . . 54–1 Just a little . 2 Not at all . . 3 D.K. 4
C. How well do you read (LANGUAGE) — would you say well enough to read a newspaper, or not quite that well?	Well enough to read a newspaper . . . . 51–6 Not quite that well . . 7 D.K. 8	Well enough to read a newspaper . . . . 55–6 Not quite that well . . 7 D.K. 8
D. Where did you learn to speak/read (LANGUAGE)	At home: grew up with it . . . 52–1 Other firsthand experience (travel; stationed there; friends) . . 2 Studied it in high school. 3 Studied it in college . . . 4 Other (specify) _____	At home: grew up with it . . . 56–1 Other firsthand experience (travel; stationed there; friends) . . 2 Studied it in high school. 3 Studied it in college . . . 4 Other (specify) _____

13. Suppose you had a chance to travel to a foreign country and you decided that before you left you'd try to learn to speak the language of that country. How do you think you would probably go about learning it? (VERBATIM)

57 –

14. HAND RESPONDENT CARD C.

    (i) Of the five methods listed on this card, which one would you prefer if you were learning to speak a foreign language?
    (ii) Which would be your second choice?
    (iii) Which method would you like the least?

Method	First Choice	Second Choice	Would Like the Least
A. Attend regular classes in some sort of school	58 – 1	59 – 1	60 – 1
B. Find a private teacher and take individual lessons	2	2	2
C. Follow lessons given over television	3	3	3
D. Take correspondence lessons by mail	4	4	4
E. Buy a book or some recordings and study it on my own	5	5	5
Wouldn't matter	6	6	6
D.K.	7	7	7

    (iv) Why would you prefer (FIRST-CHOICE METHOD) to any of the others? (Any other reason?)

61 –

15. If you actually were going to learn a foreign language, which language would you most like to learn?

    French . . . . 62 – 1
    Spanish 2
    German 3
    D.K. . . . . Y
    Other (specify) _____

16. Now, to get back to this (CITY/TOWN/NEIGHBORHOOD). Do you know of any places around here or nearby where people no longer in school can attend classes or receive instruction in subjects other than foreign languages?

Yes . . . . 63 – 1*   ASK A – C
No: there are none . . . .   x†   ASK D
No: don't know of any . . . . .   Y†   ASK D

*IF YES
A. Where is that? (Any place else?)

Elementary school . . . . 64 – 1
High school   2
College or university   3
College or university extension .   4
Other (specify) _____

B. What sorts of subjects can be studied there? (Anything else?)
(DO NOT PROBE BEYOND FIVE.)

_____
_____
_____
_____
_____ 65 –

C. How interested do you think most people around here are in attending adult education classes — would you say very interested, mildly interested, or not interested at all?

Very interested . . . . 66 – 0
Mildly interested   1
Not interested at all   2
D.K.   3

†IF NO
D. How interested do you think most people around here would be in attending adult education classes if any were available — would you say very interested, mildly interested, or not interested at all?

Very interested . . . . 67 – 5
Mildly interested   6
Not interested at all   7
D.K.   8

BEGIN DECK 2
FOR FULL-TIME STUDENTS, SKIP TO Q. 18.

17. Thinking back over the time since you left school, have you at any time since then taken an educational course of any sort — including things like evening classes, correspondence courses, lecture series,

discussion groups, courses given over television, home studies, courses given by the armed services, or anything like that?

HAND RESPONDENT YELLOW FLASH CARD (SIDE ONE) AND HAVE HIM RETAIN IT THROUGH Q. 17.

Here is a list of examples that may help you to recall anything of this type.

Yes . . . . 5–1*   ASK A–K

No . . . . x†   ASK L–M

     *IF YES

LIST ALL INSTRUCTION TAKEN SINCE LEAVING SCHOOL, FROM THE MOST RECENT TO THE EARLIEST. ENTER NAME OF EACH SUBJECT STUDIED AND ASK QUESTIONS B AND C FOR EACH SUBJECT ENTERED.

A. Let's start with the most recent—in what subject was that? (Anything before that?)	B. About how old were you when you first enrolled in that?	C. Was that a credit course—that is, was it taken for any sort of certificate, diploma or degree?		
Subject	Age at Time of Enrollment	Yes	No	D.K.
1.				
2.				
3.				
4.				
5.				
6.				
7.				
8.				

For Office Use Only

6–	12–
7–	13–
8–	14–
9–	15–
10–	16–
11–	17–

D. Are you currently enrolled in one of these activities?

Yes . . . . 18 – 1

No . . . . 2*   ASK (1)

*IF NO

(1) About how many years is it since you were last enrolled?

Less than 1 year . . . . 19 – 1

1 – 2 years 2

3 – 5 years 3

6 – 10 years 4

11 – 20 years 5

21 – 30 years 6

More than 30 years 7

D.K. 8

E. How much do you feel you benefited from the course you took most recently – would you say a great deal, some, or not very much?

A great deal . . . . 20 – 1

Some 2

Not very much 3

D.K. 4

F. HAND RESPONDENT CARD D.

(1) In which of the following ways would you say the (course/instruction) was definitely helpful to you? (Any others listed there?)

(2) In which of these ways had you hoped the (course/instruction) would be helpful to you when you first enrolled? (Any others listed there?)

Reasons for Taking Course	It Helped Me	I Had Hoped It Would Help Me
A. On the job I held at that time	21 – 1	22 – 1
B. Prepare for a new job or occupation	2	2
C. In carrying out everyday tasks and duties around home	3	3
D. In carrying out everyday tasks and duties away from home	4	4
E. Spend my spare time more enjoyably	5	5
F. Meet new and interesting people	6	6
G. Get away from the daily routine	7	7
H. Become a better informed person	8	8
None of these	9	9
D.K.	Y	Y

G. Were there any other ways not listed here in which the course was helpful to you?

> Yes . . . . 23–1* ASK (1)
> No   2   SKIP TO H
> D.K.   3   SKIP TO H

*IF YES

(1) In what ways? (Anything else?)

24–

H. Were there any other ways not listed here in which you had hoped the course would be helpful?

> Yes . . . . 25–1* ASK (1)
> No   2   SKIP TO I
> D.K.   3   SKIP TO I

*IF YES

(1) In what ways? (Anything else?)

26–

I. Thinking back to the first course you took, the (SUBJECT) course, could you tell me how you happened to enroll in that?

27–

J. Why do you think you hadn't enrolled in any courses before that time?

28–

K. Have you thought recently that you might like to enroll in some other type of adult education course?

> Yes . . . . 29–1* ASK (1)
> No . . . .   2† ASK (2)
> D.K.   3   SKIP TO Q. 18

*IF YES

(1) What type of subject or course have you thought you might like to take, if it were available? (Anything else?)

————————————————— 30–

†IF NO   SKIP TO Q. 18

(2) Is there any particular reason why not? (What is that?)

31–   SKIP TO Q. 18

†IF NO:

L. Have you ever thought you might like to enroll in an adult education course of some type?

```
Yes . . . . . . . . . . . . . . . 32 – 1*   ASK (1)
No . . . . . . . . . . . . . . .      2     SKIP TO M
D.K. . . . . . . . . . . . . .       3
```

*IF YES

(1) What type of subject or course have you thought you might like to take – if it were available? (Anything else?)

_____ 33 –

M. HAND RESPONDENT CARD E. Suppose you did decide to enroll in some sort of adult education course. In which of the following ways would you most want it to be helpful to you? (Anything else listed there?)

A. On the job that I now hold	34 – 1
B. Prepare for a new job or occupation	2
C. In carrying out everyday tasks and duties around home	3
D. In carrying out everyday tasks and duties away from home	4
E. Spend my spare time more enjoyably	5
F. Meet new and interesting people	6
G. Get away from the daily routine	7
H. Become a better informed person	8
None of these	9
D.K.	Y

*ASK EVERYONE

18. Do you have any relatives, friends, or acquaintances who have attended adult education classes of some sort during the past year or so?

```
Yes, a relative . . . . . . . . . 35 – 1*   ASK A
Yes, a friend . . . . . . . . . . .      2*   ASK A
Yes, an acquaintance . . . . . .         3*   ASK A
No . . . . . . . . . . . . . . . .       4
D.K. . . . . . . . . . . . . . . .       5
```

*IF YES

A. What type of course did (he/she/they) take? (Anything else?)

_____ 36 –

19. Why do you think it is that more people aren't interested in taking adult education courses? (Any other reason?)

37 –

20. HAND RESPONDENT CARD F. Surveys have shown that very few people actually do take adult education courses. Here are some of the reasons people have given for not attending. Please read these over and tell me for each one whether that would apply to you or probably not apply to you.

How about A — would that apply to you or not? (How about B?) (How about C?) (ETC.)

Reasons for Not Taking Courses	Would Apply to Me	Would Not Apply to Me	D.K.
A. I don't think there is anything like that available around here	38 – Y	X	0
B. The things I have heard about don't sound very interesting	39 – 2	3	4
C. I can learn all I need to know without going to classes to do it	40 – 6	7	8
D. I'm usually too tired at night to go out to classes	41 – Y	X	0
E. I'm much too busy with other things and just wouldn't have the time	42 – 2	3	4
F. I'd feel kind of childish going out to classes at night	43 – 6	7	8
G. Although I'm interested in a lot of things, I'm really not the studying type	44 – Y	X	0
H. It would be hard for me to get out of the house at night	45 – 2	3	4
I. Right now I just couldn't afford the money it would cost	46 – 6	7	8
J. I'd probably be too old to start learning new things	47 – Y	X	0

21. In general, do you think that educational classes for adults would be an important thing for your community to spend public money on, or do you think that such money would probably be better spent on something else?

Important thing . . . . 48 – 1
Better spent on something else . 2
D.K. 3

22. Do you think that adult education classes should be offered free of charge to the public, or that those who want to take them should have to pay for them?

Should be free of charge . . . . . 49 – 5
Those who want them should
pay 6
D.K. 7

23. Up to this point we've been talking about enrollment in courses and attendance at classes. Have you ever tried to teach yourself some subject by means of independent study strictly on your own?

Yes . . . . 50–1* ASK A–C

No x   SKIP TO Q. 24

*IF YES

LIST ALL INDEPENDENT STUDY, INCLUDING ANY ENGAGED IN WHILE STILL AT SCHOOL.

A. Let's start with the most recent— in what subject was that? (Was there anything before that?)	B. About how old were you when you first began this study?
Subject	Age
1.	
2.	
3.	
4.	
5.	
6.	

Office Use

51–
52–
53–
54–
55–
56–
57–

C. Are you currently engaged in any studies of this sort?

Yes 58–1   SKIP TO Q. 24

No . . . . 2* ASK (1)

*IF NO

(1) About how many years is it since you were last involved in these studies?

Less than 1 year . . . . 59 – 1
1 – 2 years   2
3 – 5 years   3
6 – 10 years   4
11 – 20 years   5
21 – 30 years   6
More than 30 years   7
D.K.   8

---

24. Most people have things they'd like to learn more about, or would like to be able to do better. Is there anything in particular that you'd like to know more about, or would like to learn how to do better?

Yes . . . . 60 – 1*   ASK A – B
No   2   SKIP TO Q. 25
D.K   3   SKIP TO Q. 25

*IF YES

A. What is that? (Anything else?) DO NOT PROBE BEYOND THREE.

_____ 61 –
_____ 62 –

B. Is there any particular reason why you would like to learn (SUBJECT OR SKILL MENTIONED FIRST)? (Any other reason?)

63 –

---

25. Suppose that a course was being offered on some topic that you were really interested in, and you could study it either by attending classes one evening a week at a nearby school, or by means of home-study lessons which would be mailed to your home once a week. If you had decided to enroll in the course, which of these two methods of study would you prefer — the classes at school, or the lessons mailed to you at home?

Classes at school . . . . 64 – 1*   ASK A
Home-study lessons . . . .   2*   ASK A
D.K   3
Neither of these   4
Wouldn't matter   5

*IF EITHER CLASSES AT SCHOOL OR HOME-STUDY LESSONS

A. Why would you prefer that method to the other? (Any other reason?)

65 –

26. A. Here is a different type of question. From your own experience, or from what you have heard, what types of people would you guess more often attend adult education classes — would you say women or men? (IF D.K.: Which would you guess?)

> Women . . . . 66 – x
> Men 0
> Both 1
> D.K. 2

B. Would you say more often younger people, middle-aged people, or older people? (IF D.K.: Which would you guess?)

> Younger people . . . . 67 – 4
> Middle-aged people 5
> Older people 6
> All age groups 7
> D.K. 8

C. Would you say more often people who have been to college, or people who haven't been to college? (IF D.K.: Which would you guess?)

> Have been to college . . . . . . 68 – 0
> Have not been to college 1
> Both groups 2
> D.K. 3

D. Would you say more often people who want to learn practical things, or people who want to learn about ideas and theories? (IF D.K.: Which would you guess?)

> Learn practical things . . . . . . 69 – 5
> Learn ideas and theories 6
> Both groups 7
> D.K. 8

E. Would you say more often married people or single people? (IF D.K.: Which would you guess?)

> Married people . . . . 70 – 0
> Single people 1
> Both groups 2
> D.K. 3

F. Would you say more often people who are pretty satisfied with life, or people who are a little dissatisfied? (IF D.K.: Which would you guess?)

Pretty satisfied . . . . 71 – 5
A little dissatisfied   6
Both groups   7
D.K.   8

G. And finally, would you say more often people whose main goal
is to get ahead in life, or people whose main goal is to enjoy life?
(IF D.K.: Which would you guess?)

Get ahead in life . . . . 72 – 0
Enjoy life   1
Both groups   2
D.K.   3

---

27. Here is an imaginary situation. Suppose that a man has a chance for
a promotion on his job, but in order to qualify for it he would have to
take a course at night school and be away from home three evenings
a week for about six months. Although he could use the extra money,
his family doesn't really need it, so he doesn't know whether he should
spend this much time away from his family.

A. If you were asked your opinion, would you advise him to definitely take the course, to take the course only if he were sure
of getting the promotion, or to not take the course at all?

Definitely take the course . . . . 73 – 5
Take the course only if he were
sure of getting the promotion .   6
Not take the course at all   7
D.K.   8

B. What do you think most men around here would do in this
situation – do you think most would take the course, or that
most wouldn't?

Most would . . . . 74 – 1
Most wouldn't   2
D.K.   3

C. How do you think most wives would feel about this – do you
think most would want their husbands to take the course, or
not to take the course?

Take the course . . . . 75 – 5
Not to take the course   6
D.K.   7

BEGIN DECK 3

28. ASK UNLESS OBVIOUS. Do you have a TV set in working order?

> Yes 5–4
> No 5

___

29. Is there an educational television station in this area?

> Yes . . . . 6–1* ASK A AND B
> No . . . . x SKIP TO Q. 30
> D.K. . . . . 2 SKIP TO Q. 30

*IF YES

A. Which station is that?

> Channel number _____
> Call letters _____
> City or town _____ 7–

B. Have you ever watched any programs on that station?

> Yes . . . . 8–1† ASK (1)–(3)
> No . . . . x SKIP TO Q. 30
> D.K. . . . . 2 SKIP TO Q. 30

†IF YES

(1) What types of programs have you seen? (Any others?)

> _____ 9–

(2) About how often do you watch programs on that station—almost every day, every other day, once or twice a week, or less often than that?

> Almost every day 10–x
> Every other day 0
> Once or twice a week 1
> Less often than that 2
> D.K. 3

(3) All in all, how would you rate the programs on the educational station in comparison with those on regular television—would you say they are more interesting, less interesting, or about the same?

> More interesting 11–5
> Less interesting 6
> About the same 7
> D.K. 8

30. Suppose that a new educational course was being planned by one of the local television stations, and that the station was going to decide the subject of the course by asking members of the community to make suggestions. If you were asked for your opinion, what kind of a course would you suggest that they give? (Anything else?)

12–

---

31. HAND RESPONDENT CARD G.

   (i) If the choice were narrowed down to the three general themes listed on this card, which one would you vote for – A, B, or C?
   (ii) Which would you vote for second?

Themes	First Choice	Second Choice
A. Practical skills for everyday living	13–0	14–5
B. General knowledge about the world we live in	1	6
C. Interests and hobbies for spare-time use	2	7
D.K.	3	8

32. About how often do you read or glance through a newspaper – would you say almost every day, about every other day, once or twice a week, or less often than that?

Almost every day . . . . 15–x*   ASK A
About every other day . . . . .   0*   ASK A
Once or twice a week . . . . . .   1*   ASK A
Less than that . . . .   2*   ASK A
Never   3   SKIP TO Q. 33
D.K. . . . .   4*   ASK A

*IF OTHER THAN NEVER
A. Is there any particular newspaper that you read regularly?

Yes . . . . 16–6†   ASK (1)
No   7
D.K.   8

†IF YES
(1) Which one? (Any others?)

17–

33. How often do you read or glance through magazines or periodicals —
almost every day, about every other day, once or twice a week, or less
often than that?

Almost every day	18–x*	ASK A
Every other day	0*	ASK A
Once or twice a week	1*	ASK A
Less than that	2*	ASK A
Never	3	SKIP TO Q. 34
D.K.	4*	ASK A

*IF OTHER THAN NEVER

A. Are there any particular magazines that you read regularly?

Yes	19–6†	ASK (1)
No	7	
D.K.	8	

†IF YES

(1) Which ones? (Any others?)

_____ 20–

_____ 21–

34. How often do you watch television — almost every day, every
other day, once or twice a week, or less often than that?

Almost every day	22–x*	ASK A AND B
Every other day	0*	ASK A AND B
Once or twice a week	1*	ASK A AND B
Less often than that	2*	ASK A AND B
Never	3	SKIP TO Q. 35
D.K.	4*	ASK A AND B

*IF OTHER THAN NEVER

A. On an average weekday, about how many hours do you spend
watching television?

Hours _____ 23–

B. In general, would you describe yourself as a heavy viewer, a
moderate viewer, a light viewer, or a non-viewer?

Heavy viewer	24–1
Moderate viewer	2
Light viewer	3
Non-viewer	4
D.K.	5

35. How about radio listening – do you listen to the radio almost every day, about every other day, once or twice a week, or less often than that?

> Almost every day . . . . 25 – x
> About every other day   0
> Once or twice a week   1
> Less often than that   2
> Never   3
> D.K.   4

36. When you read, do you most often read newspapers, magazines, or books?

> Newspapers . . . . 26 – 3
> Magazines   4
> Books   5
> All equally   6
> Never read   7
> D.K.   8

37. About how many books have you read in the past year?

> Number of books _____ 27 –
> D.K.   x

38. Altogether, would you describe yourself as a heavy reader, a moderate reader, a light reader, or a non-reader?

> Heavy reader . . . . 28 – 1
> Moderate reader   2
> Light reader   3
> Non-reader   4
> D.K.   5

39. About how many times have you been to the movies during the past year?

> Number of movies _____ 29 –
> D.K.   x

FOR FULL-TIME STUDENTS, SKIP TO QUESTION 41.

40. About how many years is it since you left school?

> Less than 1 year . . . . 30 – 1
> 1 – 2 years   2
> 3 – 5 years   3

6 – 10 years	4
11 – 20 years	5
21 – 30 years	6
31 – 40 years	7
More than 40 years	8
Never attended school	9
D.K.	x

41. If you were starting over again, how far would you like to go in school?

Not attend at all	31 – 1	
1 – 4 years	2	
5 – 7 years	3	
8 years	4	
9 – 11 years	5	
12 years (finish high school) . . .	6	
Some college	7	
Complete college	8	
Go to graduate school	9*	ASK A
Get other training (specify) _____		
D.K.	x	

*IF GO TO GRADUATE SCHOOL

A. What type of graduate degree would you like to attain?

Type of degree _____ 32 –

FOR FULL-TIME STUDENTS AND PERSONS WHO NEVER ATTENDED SCHOOL, SKIP TO QUESTION 45.

42. When you think back to your own school days, how important was it to you then to study hard and get good grades – was it very important, slightly important, or rather unimportant?

Very important	33 – 5
Slightly important	6
Rather unimportant	7
D.K.	8

43. How important was it to each of your parents that you studied hard and got good grades – was it very important, slightly important, or rather unimportant? How about your father? How about your mother?

	Father	Mother
Very important	34 – Y	35 – 4
Slightly important	X	5
Rather unimportant	0	6
Didn't live with this parent, or parent dead when I attended school	1	7
D.K.	2	8

---

44. How well do you feel you did in school — would you say very well, about average, a little below average, or very poorly?

Very well	36 – 1
About average	2
A little below average	3
Very poorly	4
D.K.	5

Ask everyone

45. A. How far did your father go in school?

B. How far did your mother go in school?

	Father	Mother
Never attended school	37 – 1	38 – 1
Some grade school	2	2
Completed grade school	3	3
Some high school	4	4
Completed high school	5	5
Some college	6	6
Finished college or more	7	7
D.K.	8	8

---

46. A. What kind of work did your father do when you were about 16 years old? (IF NOT LIVING WITH FATHER AT THAT TIME, ASK: What kind of work did he do when you last lived with him?)

Kind of work _____ 39 –

B. In what kind of business or industry was that?

Business or industry _____ 40 –

47. What do you think is the main value of having a good education? (Anything else?)

41 –

48. HAND RESPONDENT CARD H. Of the six things listed on this card, which two do you think are most important in helping a person get ahead the fastest?

Brains	42 – 1
A good education	2
Good luck	3
Hard work	4
Know the right people	5
Personality	6
D.K.	7

49. How important is it to you personally to get ahead in life – would you say very important, moderately important, or rather unimportant?

Very important	43 – 6
Moderately important	7
Rather unimportant	8
D.K.	9

50. Here are some opinions people have expressed concerning the importance of a college education today. Would you agree or disagree that . . .

Statement	Agree	Disagree	No Opinion
A. A college education is less important for a woman than for a man	44 – Y	X	0
B. A college education is less important for a woman who wants to get married right after leaving school than for a woman who plans to have a career. (Would you agree or disagree?)	45 – 2	3	4
C. A college education should be put to use; if you don't use it, why bother with it? (Would you agree or disagree?)	46 – 6	7	8

51. HAND RESPONDENT CARD I.

    (i) Although all of these things are important, which one would you say has given you the most satisfaction in life — A, B, C, or D?

    (ii) Which has given you the second most satisfaction?

    (iii) Which would be third?

Area of Activity	Most Satisfaction	Second Most Satisfaction	Third Most Satisfaction
A. My work	47 – Y	48 – 4	49 – Y
B. My family	X	5	X
C. My friends	0	6	0
D. My hobbies and interests	1	7	1
D.K.	2	8	2

IF RESPONDENT DOES NOT WORK, SKIP TO QUESTION 58.

52. How satisfied are you with your job right now — would you say very satisfied, moderately satisfied, a little dissatisfied, or very dissatisfied?

    Very satisfied . . . . 50 – 1

    Moderately satisfied   2

    A little dissatisfied   3

    Very dissatisfied   4

    D.K.   5

53. A. On the average, how many hours a week, including overtime, do you work during this time of year?

        Average number of hours per week _____ 51 –

    B. How many hours did you work last week?

        Hours worked last week _____ 52 –

54. About how much time do you spend traveling to and from work on an average day during this time of year? (GET TOTAL TRAVELING TIME BOTH WAYS.)

    Hours _____ Minutes _____ 53 –

55. Do you have fairly regular working hours, or do they vary quite a bit?

> Fairly regular . . . . 54–1* ASK A
> Vary quite a bit 2

*IF FAIRLY REGULAR
A. During what hours do you usually work?

> From _____ To _____ 55–

56. How often do you work evenings or nights—frequently, occasionally, seldom, or never?

> Frequently 56–0
> Occasionally 1
> Seldom 2
> Never 3

57. Would you say that you have gone about as far as you can go in your present line of work, or that you can probably go quite a bit further?

> Gone as far as I can go 57–6
> Can go quite a bit further 7
> D.K. 8

58. ASK EVERYONE. In general, how satisfied are you with your life right now—would you say very satisfied, moderately satisfied, a little dissatisfied, or very dissatisfied?

> Very satisfied 58–1   SKIP TO Q. 59
> Moderately satisfied . . . . 2*   ASK A
> A little dissatisfied . . . . 3*   ASK A
> Very dissatisfied . . . . 4*   ASK A
> D.K. 5   SKIP TO Q. 59

*IF LESS THAN VERY SATISFIED
A. What would you want to change about your life right now if you had the chance to change one thing? (VERBATIM)

> 59–

59. Thinking ahead to five years from now, would you estimate that your family income will be higher, about the same, or lower than it is now?

Higher . . . . 60–1*   ASK A
About the same   2   SKIP TO Q. 60
Lower . . . .   3*   ASK A
D.K.   4   SKIP TO Q. 60

*IF HIGHER OR LOWER
A. Would you say considerably higher/lower, or just slightly higher/lower?

Considerably 61–6
Slightly   7
D.K.   8

Now, just a few more questions and we can finish up.

60. A. Where were you born? (state or country)

State in U.S. or country _____ 62–

B. IF BORN IN THE U.S.
Where were your parents born?

	Father	Mother
State in U.S. or country	_____ 63–	_____ 64–

---

61. Were you brought up mainly on a farm, in a small town, a small city, a medium-sized city, or a large city?

Farm or open country 65–1
Small town or village (under
   10,000)   2
Small city (10,000–150,000) . .   3
Medium-sized city (150,000–
   500,000)   4
Large city (over 500,000)   5

---

62. A. How long have you lived in this area?

B. How long have you lived at your present address?

	Area	At Your Present Address
Less than one year	66–1	67–1
1–2 years	2	2
3–5 years	3	3

6 – 10 years	4	4
11 – 15 years	5	5
16 – 20 years	6	6
21 – 25 years	7	7
More than 25 years	8	8
"All my life"	9	9

63. As far as you know, do you expect to be living at this address five years from now, or do you expect to move within that period?

> Expect to be living here . . . . . 68 – 1
> Expect to move . . . . 2* ASK A
> D.K. 3

*IF EXPECT TO MOVE

A. How far away do you expect to move — how many miles, approximately?

> Number of miles _____ 69 –
> D.K. x

64. Do you belong to any groups or organizations here in the community?

> Yes . . . . 70 – 1* ASK A AND B
> No 2

*IF YES

A. Which ones? (Any others?)   B. During the past year have you been active in the group, or not too active?

Name of Organization	Active	Not Too Active
1.		
2.		
3.		
4.			71 –
5.			72 –
			73 –

65. How often do you attend church (or synagogue) services?

Once a week or more . . . . . . 74 – 1
1 – 3 times a month   2
Less than once a month   3
Never   4
N.A.   5

---

66. Quite apart from church (synagogue) going, how important would you say religion is to you — very important, fairly important, or not important at all?

Very important . . . . 75 – 6
Fairly important   7
Not important at all   8
D.K.   9

---

67. Generally speaking, what is your political preference?

Democrat . . . . 76 – 1
Republican   2
Independent   3
D.K.   4

---

68. Do you own this (house, apartment) or do you rent it?

Own house . . . . 77 – 6
Rent house   7
Own apartment   8
Rent apartment   9
Other (specify) _____

---

69. And finally, how many rooms are there in this house (apartment) — not including bathrooms?

Number of rooms _____ 78 –

Length of interview _____
Your signature _____

REMEMBER: GO BACK TO PAGE 2 AND MAKE SURE ALL THE BASIC DATA ARE COMPLETED.

Notes

C. COMMUNITY FACILITIES FOR THE INSTRUCTION OF ADULTS

NORC 447

INFORMANT'S QUESTIONNAIRE

LOCATION
NAME _____
ADDRESS _____
OCCUPATION _____ BUS. PHONE _____ EXT. _____

SECTION ONE

INSTITUTIONS AND GROUPS ACTIVE IN ADULT EDUCATION

Below is a list of the different types of institutions, agencies and groups which offer or sponsor adult education courses in some communities. For each of these, would you please check:

A. whether there were any organizations or institutions of this type which offered or sponsored adult education classes in your community during the past year—that is, since September, 1961, and
B. if there were, how many independent organizations or institutions of this type offered such courses? (NOTE: Do not count two branches of the same institution as two separate agencies. For example, the public library is counted as one independent institution, no matter how many separate branches offered classes.)

Type of Institution and Offering	A. Offers or Sponsors Classes			B. How Many Independent Institutions of This Type Come to Mind?
	Yes	No	Don't Know	Number
1. Public-supported universities or colleges offering adult evening classes for credit				
2. Public-supported universities or colleges offering non-credit adult evening classes				
3. Public-supported universities or colleges sponsoring conferences, workshops, and institutes open to local adults				
4. Public-supported universities or colleges sponsoring lectures and related activities open to local adults				

(Continued)

Type of Institution and Offering	A. Offers or Sponsors Classes			B. How Many Independent Institutions of This Type Come to Mind?
	Yes	No	Don't Know	Number
5. Private universities or colleges offering adult evening classes for credit				
6. Private universities or colleges offering non-credit adult evening classes				
7. Private universities or colleges sponsoring conferences, workshops, and institutes open to local adults				
8. Private universities or colleges sponsoring lectures and related activities open to local adults				
9. Public secondary schools offering adult evening courses for credit				
10. Public secondary schools offering non-credit adult evening classes				
11. Private secondary schools offering adult evening courses for credit				
12. Private secondary schools offering non-credit adult evening classes				
13. Local libraries sponsoring adult education activities				
14. Local museums sponsoring adult education activities				
15. An educational television channel — either UHF or VHF — that is within the range of reception of a majority of households in this city				
16. Government agencies				
17. Fraternal and social groups (such as Masons, Odd Fellows, etc.)				
18. Business groups (such as Chambers of Commerce, etc.)				

(Continued)

(Continued)

Type of Institution and Offering	A. Offers or Sponsors Classes			B. How Many Independent Institutions of This Type Come to Mind?
	Yes	No	Don't Know	Number
19. Civic and political groups (such as political parties, League of Women Voters, etc.)				
20. Labor unions				
21. Religious groups (church-centered groups of any type)				
22. Ethnic groups (such as Sons of Italy, Bavarian Marching Society and Band, etc.)				
23. Veteran's organizations				
24. Recreational and sports groups (such as game clubs, hunting groups, etc.)				
25. Agricultural associations				
26. Cultural organizations (such as drama and music groups)				
27. Community service groups (such as YMCA, Boy Scouts, etc.)				

SECTION TWO

TYPES OF COURSES OFFERED

Below you will find a list of nine general course areas within which a large variety of specific course offerings might be placed. For the moment we are interested in these general categories only. For each category we would like to know whether any courses of this type were offered in your city during the last year. For each type of course, the possible answers are:

A. Yes. (A large number of courses of this type were offered.)
B. Yes. (At least a few courses in this category were offered.)
C. No. (I know of no course fitting this description that was offered.)
D. Don't know. (I'm not sure whether courses of this type were offered.)

Please place a check (✔) beneath the appropriate answer.

Were Courses Offered in This General Category?	Yes, a Large Number	Yes, a Few	No	Don't Know
1. General education subjects: academic subjects of the sort studied as part of a high-school or college education, but excluding all business, trade, vocational, technical, professional or other job-related courses.				
2. How about job-related skills: subjects and skills used in the professional, technical, business, office, clerical and sales spheres?				
3. How about other job-related skills: subjects and skills used in the skilled trades, in semi-skilled occupations and in service occupations?				
4. How about hobbies and recreations: classes dealing with arts, crafts, and skills and interests for spare-time enjoyment?				
5. How about courses dealing with home and family life: topics pertaining to the establishment, maintenance or improvement of a home, and to carrying out household duties and family responsibilities?				
6. How about classes in personal development: subjects and skills aimed at helping people expand themselves in the areas of health, physical fitness, personality development, interpersonal and social skills, and basic reading and writing?				
7. How about classes in religion, morals, and ethics, akin to the notion of "personal development," but concerned exclusively with the area of spiritual, moral, and ethical development?				
8. How about current events, public affairs, and citizenship: topics dealing with current social, political, and economic affairs, courses in Americanization for citizenship, in civic responsibilities, and with general political education?				
9. How about agricultural subjects: all topics related to farming and commercial gardening?				

SECTION THREE

Specific Course Offerings

Finally, we would appreciate some indication of the range of specific course offerings. The format is similar to that of our preceding questions. We have provided you with a sampling of course titles offered by a variety of institutions. For each title we would like you to indicate whether or not it (or something very similar) was among those offered to local adults in your community last year.

There are three possible answers:

A. Yes. (I definitely know this was offered in the past year.)
B. No. (This subject was not offered by any local institution in the past year.)
C. Don't know. (I'm not sure whether or not this was offered by anyone last year.)

Please check the appropriate answer.

Specific Course Offerings	Yes, Was Offered	No, Was Not Offered	Don't Know
Planning for marriage			
Do-it-yourself repairing			
Speed reading			
Personal hygiene			
Great Books courses			
Introductory German			
Repairing TV sets			
Welding			
Typing or shorthand			
Office management			
Art lessons			
Bridge lessons			
Animal husbandry			
Plant disease control			
Your Congress and how it works			
Communism and world conquest			

(Continued)

Specific Course Offerings	Yes, Was Offered	No, Was Not Offered	Don't Know
History of the Unitarian movement			
Philosophical foundations of Christian thought			
Landscaping			
Care of the retarded child			
Dale Carnegie courses			
Yoga			
Solid geometry			
Geology			
Piano tuning			
Repairing airplane equipment			
Blueprint reading			
Data processing systems			
Leather crafts			
Short-wave radio operation			
Commercial gardening			
Breeding minks for profit			
Political climates of underdeveloped nations			
The Common Market and European federation			
Religious thought in the Orient (Zen Buddhism, teachings of Confucius, etc.)			
The Apocalypse: an exegesis			

NATIONAL OPINION RESEARCH CENTER
SURVEY 447

ADULT EDUCATION RESOURCES INVENTORY FORM

1. Name of institution contacted _____

2. Address _____

3. Category No. _____ 4. How contacted: in person ( ) phone ( )
   other (explain) _____

5. Source of information _____

6. Position _____

7. Institution does ( ) does not ( ) offer adult education classes.

8. Institution does ( ) does not ( ) sponsor non-classroom adult educational activity.
9. List of classroom courses is appended ( ) does not apply ( ).
10. Total adult classroom enrollment: ____ students. Does not apply ( ).
11. List of non-classroom activities is appended ( ) does not apply ( ).

1. Name of institution contacted _____
2. Address _____
3. Category No. _____ 4. How contacted: in person ( ) phone ( ) other (explain) _____
5. Source of information _____
6. Position _____
7. Institution does ( ) does not ( ) offer adult education classes.
8. Institution does ( ) does not ( ) sponsor non-classroom adult educational activity.
9. List of classroom courses is appended ( ) does not apply ( ).
10. Total adult classroom enrollment: ____ students. Does not apply ( ).
11. List of non-classroom activities is appended ( ) does not apply ( ).

Survey 447 – CS
April 1963
Confidential

NATIONAL OPINION RESEARCH CENTER
UNIVERSITY OF CHICAGO

Personal Interview

_____
(1 – 3)

_____
Segment Number
(Two digits)

_____
Household Number
(One digit)

_____

RESPONDENT'S NAME _____
STREET ADDRESS _____
CITY _____ STATE _____

INTRODUCTION

Hello, I'm _____ from the National Opinion Research Center of the University of Chicago. We're conducting a survey of family activities in modern America.

In order to determine which person in your household I'm to interview, I have to list the names of all persons who live here.

HOUSEHOLD ENUMERATION

I. First, how many people are there living in this household?
(INCLUDE ALL CHILDREN, PEOPLE TEMPORARILY AWAY, ROOMERS, ETC.)

Number of people _____

II. NAMES OF HOUSEHOLD RESIDENTS
1. Are there any persons over 65 living here?
(IF YES, ENTER NAMES IN BOX A.)
2. Who are the other persons 21 or over living here – from oldest to youngest? (ENTER NAMES IN BOX B.)

3. Are there any married persons under 21 living here?
   (IF YES, ENTER NAMES IN BOX B.)
4. Are there any other persons under 21 living here?
   (IF YES, ENTER NAMES IN BOX C.)

III. ASK THE FOLLOWING FOR EACH PERSON LISTED
   5. What is (NAME'S) relation to the head of the household?
   6. How old was (NAME) on (his/her) last birthday?
   7. RECORD SEX OF PERSON: M FOR MALE AND F FOR FEMALE.

Name		Relation to Head	Age	Sex	Indicate Respondent
Box A Adults over 65	1				
	2				
	3				
Box B Adults 21–65 and married persons under 21	1				
	2				
	3				
	4				
	5				
	6				
Box C Children and unmarried persons under 21	1				
	2				
	3				
	4				
	5				
	6				

Sampling Table

And Your Assignment Sheet Contained the Letter	If the Number of Adults Listed in Box B Is					
	One	Two	Three	Four	Five	Six or More
A. Then interview adult on line	1	2	3	1	5	1
B. Then interview adult on line	1	1	2	2	4	2
C. Then interview adult on line	1	2	1	3	3	3
D. Then interview adult on line	1	2	3	4	2	4
E. Then interview adult on line	1	1	2	4	1	5
F. Then interview adult on line	1	1	1	2	1	6

I must interview the person listed on line _____ in Enumeration Box B. His/her name is _____

☐ Check here if there are no eligible respondents in this household.

Office Use

7 –	8 –	9 –	10 –	11 –	12 –	13 –	14 –	15 –	16 –

THE INTERVIEW

1. This interview is mainly about the activities that individuals and families are engaging in these days.

What things do you enjoy doing most in your spare time — that is, in the time you have left over after work and household tasks are done for the day? (Anything else?)

17 –

2. A. About how much spare time do you find you have these days after your work and household tasks are done — would you say a great deal, some, or hardly any at all?

       A great deal . . . . 18 – 0
       Some 1
       Hardly any at all 2
       Don't know 3

   B. Do you have as much spare time as you'd like, or would you rather have more, or less?

       As much as I'd like . . . . 19 – 5
       Rather have more 6
       Rather have less 7
       Don't know 8

3. How often do you find yourself with spare time that you don't know quite what to do with — would you say frequently, occasionally, seldom, or never?

       Frequently . . . . 20 – 1
       Occasionally 2
       Seldom 3
       Never 4
       Don't know 5

4. Now, I'd like to ask about your family.
   What is your marital status?

Single: never married	21 – 1
Married	2
Widowed	3
Separated	4
Divorced	5

---

5. About how many close relatives do you (and your husband/wife) have living in or around (NAME OF CITY)?

   Number of close relatives _____ 22 –

---

6. Do most of your relatives live around (NAME OF CITY) or do most live farther away?

Most live here	23 – 1
About half live here	2
Most live farther away	3

---

7. Now, how about friends other than relatives? About how many close friends would you say you have here in (CITY) – that is, people you feel free to talk with about personal things?

   Number of close friends _____ 24 –

---

8. Do most of the people you consider as close friends live here in (CITY) or nearby, or do most of them live farther away?

Most live here	25 – 5
About half live here	6
Most live farther away	7

---

9. During the past two weeks, about how many times did you get together with the people you know – I mean things like going out together or visiting in each other's homes?

Not at all	26 – 0
Once	1
Twice	2
Three times	3
Four times	4
Five or more times	5

10. Do most of your friends here in (CITY) know each other?

> Yes . . . . 27 – 1   *ASK A
> Some do, some don't   2   *ASK A
> No   3   SKIP TO Q. 11
> Don't know   4   SKIP TO Q. 11

*IF YES OR "SOME DO"

A. Do you and your friends ever get together and do things as a group?

> Yes . . . . 28 – 1   †ASK B–C
> No   2   SKIP TO Q. 11
> Don't know   3   SKIP TO Q. 11

†IF YES

B. About how many times a month do you get together?

> Number of times _____ 29 –

C. What types of things do you do when you get together? (Anything else?)

> 30 –

11. HAND RESPONDENT CARD A.

Here is a list of different kinds of groups that people sometimes join. Do you belong to any organizations, clubs or groups of the type listed there – or to any others not listed there?

> Yes . . . . 31 – 1   *ASK A – C
> No   2   SKIP TO Q. 12

*IF YES

A. What Are the Names of the Groups You Belong To? (Any Others?)	B. During the Past Year Were You Active in That or Not Too Active?		C. Did You Hold Any Office in That Group Last Year?	
Name of Group or Organization	Active	Not Too Active	Yes	No
1.				
2.				
3.				32 –
4.				33 –
5.				34 –
6.				35 –

12. ASK EVERYONE

Are any of your close friends active in any of the groups or organizations listed on that card?

Yes . . . . 36 – 1   *ASK A

No 2   SKIP TO Q. 13

Don't know 3   SKIP TO Q. 13

*IF YES

A. What are the names of the groups they belong to? (Are there any others?)

1. _____

2. _____

3. _____   37 –

4. _____   38 –

5. _____

6. _____   39 –

13. How long have you lived in (CITY) or nearby?

Less than one year . . . . 40 – Y

1 – 2 years X

3 – 5 years 0

6 – 10 years 1

11 – 20 years 2

More than 20 years 3

"All my life" 4

14. Do you think of (CITY) as your real home – the place where you really belong, or do you think of it as just a place where you happen to be living?

My real home . . . . 41 – 6

Just a place 7

Don't know 8

15. Suppose that (CITY) was left several million dollars by some wealthy ex-resident on condition that the money be spent on some worthwhile public project. In your opinion, what would be the best thing for (CITY) to spend the money on? (Does any other project come to mind?)

42 –

16. HAND RESPONDENT CARD B. Let's say that a special election was held to decide how the money would be spent.

    (i) If the money had to be spent on one of the four things listed on this card, which one would you vote for?
    (ii) Which would be your second choice?
    (iii) Which would you vote for third?

Project		1st Choice	2nd Choice	3rd Choice	4th Choice	Don't Know
A. A new civic auditorium	43 –	1	2	3	4	5
B. Renewing the downtown area	44 –	1	2	3	4	5
C. A new public center for adult education	45 –	1	2	3	4	5
D. A new sports arena	46 –	1	2	3	4	5 47 –

17. HAND RESPONDENT CARD C. Compared with other cities of its size, how would you rate (CITY) as a place to live—outstanding, very good, average, below average, or poor?

Facilities		Out-standing	Very Good	Average	Below Average	Poor	D.K.
A. As a place to live?	48 –	1	2	3	4	5	6
B. How would you rate its recreational facilities for children?	49 –	1	2	3	4	5	6
C. How about its recreational facilities for adults?	50 –	1	2	3	4	5	6
D. How about its schools?	51 –	1	2	3	4	5	6
E. How about its adult education facilities—that is, places where adults can attend classes or receive instruction in various subjects?	52 –	1	2	3	4	5	6

18. Do you know of any places in or around (CITY) where people no longer in school can attend classes or receive instruction in any subject at all?

        Yes . . . . 53 – 1   *ASK A
        No, I don't know of any   2
        No, there are none   3

*IF YES
A. Where is that? (Any place else?) ENTER SPECIFIC NAMES.

54 –
55 –
56 –
57 –
58 –
59 –
60 –
61 –
62 –
63 –
64 –

19. HAND RESPONDENT CARD D. Here is a list of subjects that adults sometimes take courses in after they leave school. Can you think of anywhere at all around (CITY) where a person no longer in school could take courses in these things?

Subject		Yes	No	If Yes: Where Is That? (Any Place Else?)
A. How about typing and shorthand?	65 –	Y	X	1. 2.
B. How about auto mechanics?	66 –	2	3	1. 2.
C. How about dancing lessons?	67 –	6	7	1. 2.
D. How about elementary mathematics?	68 –	Y	X	1. 2.
E. How about advanced mathematics?	69 –	2	3	1. 2.
F. How about cooking or home-making?	70 –	6	7	1. 2.
G. How about public speaking?	71 –	Y	X	1. 2.
H. How about music appreciation?	72 –	2	3	1. 2.

(Continued)

Subject		Yes	No	If Yes: Where Is That? (Any Place Else?)
I. How about swimming lessons?	73–	6	7	1. 2.
J. How about how to manage a business?	74–	Y	X	1. 2.
K. How about speed reading?	75–	2	3	1. 2.
L. How about politics and government?	76–	6	7	1. 2.
M. And how about different religions of the world?	77–	Y	X	1. 2.

20. ASK MEN ONLY. Suppose you wanted to take a course related to your own line of work. Would there be any place here in (CITY) where you could take it?

          Yes . . . . 78–2* *ASK A
          No   3   SKIP TO Q. 21
          Don't know   4   SKIP TO Q. 21

     *IF YES
     A. Where is that? (Any place else?)

          1.
          2.

BEGIN DECK 0 + 2 _____
                    (1–3)

21. ASK EVERYONE. About how many years is it since you last attended school full time?

          Respondent is still attending
               school full time . . . . 4–0 SKIP TO Q. 23
          Less than 1 year . . . .   1 ⎤
          1–2 years . . . .   2 ⎥
          3–5 years . . . .   3 ⎥
          6–10 years . . . .   4 ⎬ ASK Q. 22
          11–20 years . . . .   5 ⎥
          More than 20 years . . . .   6 ⎥
          Never attended school . . . . . .   7 ⎦

22. ASK EVERYONE EXCEPT FULL-TIME STUDENTS. Thinking back over the time since you left school, have you at any time since then taken an educational course of any sort—including things like evening classes, correspondence courses, private lessons, lecture series, courses given over television, on-the-job training courses, or anything like that?

HAND RESPONDENT YELLOW FLASH CARD. Here are some other examples that may help you to recall anything of this type.

Yes	5–1	*ASK A–J
No	x	†ASK K–L

*IF YES: LIST ALL INSTRUCTION TAKEN SINCE LEAVING SCHOOL, FROM THE MOST RECENT TO THE EARLIEST. ENTER THE NAME OF EACH SUBJECT STUDIED, AND ASK QUESTION B, C, AND D FOR EACH SUBJECT ENTERED.

A. Let's Start with the Most Recent—in What Subject Was That?	B. About How Old Were You When You First Enrolled in That?	C. Was That a Credit Course—That Is, Was It Taken for Any Type of Certificate, Diploma, or Degree?			D. Where Did You Take That Course—What School or Organization in (City) Sponsored It?
	Age	Yes	No	D.K.	Name of Organization (If Outside of City, Indicate Location)
1.					
2.					
3.					
4.					
5.					
6.					
7.					
8.					

For Office Use Only

6–	7–	8–	9–	10–	11–	12–	13–

14–	15–	16–	17–	18–	19–	20–	21–

E. Are you currently enrolled in one of these activities?

    Yes . . . . 22 – 1   †ASK (1)
    No   2   SKIP TO F.

    †IF YES
    (1) Which subject is that?

    Name of subject(s) ——————— 23 –

F. Were you enrolled in any of these activities between September and December of last year?

    Yes . . . . ·. . 24 – 1   †ASK (1)
    No   2   SKIP TO G.

    †IF YES
    (1) Which subject was that?

    Name of subject(s) ——————— 25 –

G. How much do you feel you benefited from the course you took most recently—would you say a great deal, some, or not very much?

    A great deal . . . . 26 – 5
    Some   6
    Not very much   7
    Don't know   8

H. HAND RESPONDENT CARD E.
    (i) In which of the following ways would you say your most recent course was definitely helpful to you? (Any others listed there?)
    (ii) In which of these ways had you hoped the course would be helpful to you when you first enrolled? (Any others listed there?)

Reasons for Taking Course	It Helped Me	I Had Hoped It Would Help Me
A. On the job I held at that time	27 – 0	28 – 0
B. Prepare for a new job or occupation	1	1
C. In carrying out everyday tasks and duties around home	2	2
D. In carrying out everyday tasks and duties away from home	3	3
E. Spend my spare time more enjoyably	4	4
F. Meet new and interesting people	5	5
G. My religious life	6	6
H. Get away from the daily routine	7	7
I. Become a better informed person	8	8
None of these	9	9
Don't know	Y	Y

I. HAND RESPONDENT CARD F. Here are some people you may have talked to just before you took your last course.

  (i) Was it from someone on this list that you first heard about the course? (IF YES: Who?)
  (ii) Was there anyone you talked to who encouraged you to take that course? (IF YES: Who?) (Anyone else?) CIRCLE ALL THAT APPLY.
  (iii) Was there anyone you talked to who thought it wasn't a good idea for you to take that course? (IF YES: Who?) (Anyone else?) CIRCLE ALL THAT APPLY.
  (iv) Was there anyone you knew who actually took that same course at the time you did? (IF YES: Who was that?) (Anyone else?) CIRCLE ALL THAT APPLY.

Person	First Heard About It	Encouraged Me To Take It	Thought I Shouldn't Take It	Took the Course When I Did
No, none of these persons	29 – Y	30 – Y	31 – Y	32 – Y
My husband or wife	1	1	1	1
Someone else in my family	2	2	2	2
My employer	3	3	3	3
Someone else I knew at work	4	4	4	4
A close friend	5	5	5	5
A neighbor	6	6	6	6
A member of my church	7	7	7	7
A member of some club or organization I belonged to	8	8	8	8
Someone else (Who?)				

J. Have you thought recently that you might like to enroll in some other type of adult education course?

      Yes . . . . 33 – 1   *ASK (i) – (ii)
      No   2   †ASK (iii)

*IF YES

  (i) What type of subject or course have you thought you might like to take? (Anything else?)
  (ii) Where would you like to study that — at what school or organization here in (CITY)?

      (i) Subject or course   (ii) School or organization
  1.   1.
  2.   2.
  3.   3.

SKIP TO Q. 23.

†IF NO

(iii) Is there any particular reason why not? (What is that?)

34 –
35 –
36 –
37 –
38 –
39 –
40 –
41 –
42 –
43 –
44 –
45 –
46 –

SKIP TO Q. 23

†IF NO TO Q. 22

K. Have you ever thought you might like to enroll in an adult education course of some type?

Yes . . . . 47 – 1   †ASK (i) – (ii)
No 2   SKIP TO L

†IF YES

  (i) What type of subject or course have you thought you might like to take? (Anything else?)

  (ii) Where would you like to study that – at what school or organization here in (CITY)?

(i) Subject or course   (ii) School or organization

1.   1.
2.   2.
3.   3.

48 –
49 –
50 –
51 –
52 –
53 –
54 –
55 –
55 –
56 –
57 –
58 –
59 –

L. HAND RESPONDENT CARD G. Suppose you did decide to enroll in some sort of adult education course. In which of the following ways would you most want it to be helpful to you? (Anything else listed there?)

A. On the job I now hold 60–0
B. Prepare for a new job or
    occupation   1
C. In carrying out everyday
    tasks and duties around
    home   2
D. In carrying out everyday
    tasks and duties away
    from home   3
E. Spend my spare time more
    enjoyably   4
F. Meet new and interesting
    people   5
G. My religious life   6
H. Get away from the daily
    routine   7
I. Become a better informed
    person   8
    None of these   9
    Don't know . . . .   Y

ASK EVERYONE

23. Do you have any relatives, friends, or acquaintances who have attended adult education classes of some sort during the past year or so?

Yes, a relative 61–Y
Yes, a friend   X
Yes, an acquaintance   0
No   1
Don't know   2

---

24. How interested would you say most people around here are in attending adult education classes – would you say very interested, mildly interested, or not interested at all?

Very interested 62–5
Mildly interested   6
Not interested at all   7
Don't know   8

25. Why do you think it is that more people aren't interested in taking adult education courses? (Any other reason?)

63 –

26. HAND RESPONDENT CARD H. Surveys have shown that very few people actually do take adult education courses. Here are some of the reasons people have given for not attending. Please read these over and tell me for each one whether that would apply to you or probably not apply to you.

How about A: would that apply to you or not? (How about B?) (How about C?) Etc.

Reasons for Not Taking Course		Would Apply to Me	Wouldn't Apply to Me	Don't Know
A. I don't think there is anything like that available around here	64 –	Y	X	0
B. I'm usually too tired at night to go out to classes	65 –	2	3	4
C. I'd feel kind of childish going out to classes at night	66 –	6	7	8
D. Although I'm interested in a lot of things, I'm really not the "studying" type	67 –	Y	X	0
E. Right now I just couldn't afford the money it would cost	68 –	2	3	4
F. I'd probably be too old to start learning new things	69 –	6	7	8
G. I'd feel like a stranger – I wouldn't know anyone taking the course	70 –	Y	X	0
H. I'm much too busy with other things and just wouldn't have the time	71 –	2	3	4

27. In general, do you think that educational classes for adults are an important thing for (CITY) to spend public money on, or do you think that such money would probably be better spent on something else?

Important thing . . . . 72 – 1
Better spent on something
    else 2
Don't know 3

28. Do you think that adult education classes should be offered free of charge to the public, or that those who want to take them should have to pay for them?

Should be free of charge . . . . 73 – 5
People should pay for them . . .   6
Don't know   7

BEGIN DECK 0 + 3 _____
(1 – 3)

29. Up to this point we've been talking about enrollment in courses and attendance at classes. Have you ever tried to teach yourself some subject by means of independent study strictly on your own?

Yes . . . . 4 – 1   *ASK A – C
No X   SKIP TO Q. 30

*IF YES
LIST ALL INDEPENDENT STUDY INCLUDING ANY ENGAGED IN WHILE STILL AT SCHOOL.

A. Let's Start with the Most Recent — in What Subject Was That? (Was There Anything Before That?) (Subject)	B. About How Old Were You When You First Began To Study That? (Age)	
		5 –
		6 –
		7 –
1.		8 –
2.		9 –
3.		10 –
4.		11 –
5.		12 –
6.		

C. Are you currently engaged in any studies of this type?

Yes . . . . 13 – 1   SKIP TO Q. 30
No 2   †ASK D

†IF NO
D. About how many years is it since you were last involved in these studies?

Less than 1 year . . . . 14 – 1
1 – 2 years 2
3 – 5 years 3
6 – 10 years 4
11 – 20 years 5
More than 20 years 6

30. HAND RESPONDENT CARD I.

(i) Here's a different type of question. Suppose you decided to take an evening course on the subject of politics and government. If the same course was being offered at each of the five places listed on that card, and if the cost and travel time were the same in each case, where would you prefer to take the course?

(ii) Suppose the course was in music appreciation. Which do you think would be the best place to study that?

(iii) What if it was a subject like speed reading? (Where would you prefer to study that?)

(iv) How about a course on different religions of the world? (Where would you prefer to study that?)

(v) What about a course related to the line of work you're in—or to some line of work you're interested in? (Where would you like to study that?)

(vi) FOR MEN: And finally, what if the course was in how to do your own home improvements? (Where would you prefer to study that?)

FOR WOMEN: And finally, what if the course was in cooking or homemaking? (Where would you prefer to study that?)

Place	Politics and Government	Music	Speed Reading	Religions of The World	Line of Work	Home
College or university	15 – 1	16 – 1	17 – 1	18 – 1	19 – 1	20 – 1
Local high school	2	2	2	2	2	2
Church	3	3	3	3	3	3
YMCA/community center	4	4	4	4	4	4
A private school	5	5	5	5	5	5
Wouldn't matter	6	6	6	6	6	6
Don't know	7	7	7	7	7	7

Office Use

21 –
22 –
23 –
24 –
25 –

31. Do you have a TV set in working order?

> Yes 26–7
> No 8

32. Is there an educational television station in this area?

> Yes . . . . 27–1 *ASK A
> No . . . . 2 SKIP TO Q. 33
> Don't know . . . . 3 SKIP TO Q. 33

> *IF YES
> A. Which station is that?
>
> > Channel number _____
> > Call letters _____
> > City or town _____ 28–

33. HAND RESPONDENT CARD J.

> (i) About how often do you read or glance through a newspaper?
> (ii) How often do you read or glance through magazines?
> (iii) How often do you watch television?
> (iv) How about radio listening—about how often do you listen to the radio?

Frequency	Newspapers	Magazines	Television	Radio
A. Almost every day	29–1	30–1	31–1	32–1
B. About every other day	2	2	2	2
C. Once or twice a week	3	3	3	3
D. Sometimes—but less than once a week	4	4	4	4
E. Never	5	5	5	5
Don't know	6	6	6	6

34. IF "NEVER" WATCH TELEVISION: SKIP TO Q. 35. On the average weekday, about how many hours do you spend watching television?

> Hours _____ 33–

35. ASK EVERYONE. When was the last time you read a book—either a hard cover or a soft cover—all the way through?

> 34–

36. In general, do you prefer games and sports where you keep score and play to win, or where you don't keep score and play just to have fun?

> Keep score and play to win . . . 35-6
> Don't keep score: play to have
> > fun 7
> Don't know 8

37. Now, here are some questions which might be used on a radio or television quiz program. Some of them are fairly hard: let's see how many you can answer.

36-

A. What ocean would you cross in going from the United States to England?

_____ ☐ Don't know 37-

B. Just your best guess. What is the population of the United States?

_____ ☐ Don't know 38-

C. In what year did the United States enter the *first* world war?

_____ ☐ Don't know 39-

D. What team won the National League baseball pennant last year?

_____ ☐ Don't know 40-

E. How many senators are there from each state?

_____ ☐ Don't know 41-

F. Will you tell me who Plato was?

_____ ☐ Don't know 42-

G. What mineral, or metal, is important in the making of the atom bomb?

_____ ☐ Don't know 43-

H. What author wrote *War and Peace?*

_____ ☐ Don't know 44-

38. What do you usually do — work full time, work part time, keep house, go to school, or just what?

566

Volunteers for Learning

Work full time . . . . 45 – 1   *ASK A – D
Work part time   2   *ASK A – D
Keep house   3   †ASK E
Go to school   4   †ASK E
Other (specify) _____   5   †ASK E

*IF WORKS
A. What type of work do you do?

Type of work _____ 46 –

B. In what type of business or industry do you work?

Business or industry _____ 47 –

C. How satisfied are you with your job right now – would you say
very satisfied, moderately satisfied, a little dissatisfied, or very
dissatisfied?

Very satisfied . . . . 48 – 1
Moderately satisfied   2
A little dissatisfied   3
Very dissatisfied   4
Don't know   5

D. Would you say that you've gone about as far as you can go in
your present line of work, or that you can probably go quite
a bit farther?

Gone as far as it can go . . . . . 49 – 7
Can go quite a bit farther   8
Don't know   9   SKIP TO Q. 39

†IF KEEP HOUSE, SCHOOL, OR "OTHER"
E. Did you ever work for pay?

Yes . . . . 50 – 1   ‡ASK F – G
No   2   SKIP TO Q. 39

‡IF YES
F. What type of work did you do when you worked?

(JOB HELD LONGEST) _____ 51 –

G. In what type of business or industry was that?

_____ 52 –

39. ASK EVERYONE. How tired are you each day after you've finished your regular work and tasks? Do you usually have some energy left for other things, or are you usually pretty worn out?

        Have some energy left . . . . . . 53 – 7

        Pretty worn out   8

40. A. What was the highest grade you completed in school?
    B. If you were starting over again, how far would you like to go in school?
    C. How far did your father go in school?
    D. How far did your mother go in school?

Highest Grade	Respondent's Schooling	If You Were Starting Over	Respondent's Father	Respondent's Mother
Never attended school	54 – 0	55 – 0	56 – 0	57 – 0
1 – 4 grades/years	1	1	1	1
5 – 7 grades/years	2	2	2	2
8 grades/years	3	3	3	3
9 – 11 grades/years	4	4	4	4
12 grades/years	5	5	5	5
13 – 15 years (some college)	6	6	6	6
16 years (completed college)	7	7	7	7
More than 16 years (beyond college graduation)	8	8	8	8
Don't know	9	9	9	9

41. A. What kind of work did your father do when you were about 16 years old? (IF NOT LIVING WITH FATHER AT THAT TIME, ASK: Well, what about the person who contributed the most to your support in those days?)

        Kind of work _____ 58 –

    B. In what kind of business or industry did he work?

        Business or industry _____ 59 –

42. What do you think is the main value of having a good education? (Anything else?)

                              60 –

43. Taken all together, how would you say things are these days — would you say that you are very happy, pretty happy, or not too happy?

Very happy . . . . 61 – 6
Pretty happy   7
Not too happy   8

---

44. Now, just a few more questions and we can finish up.
    A. Where were you born?

    (STATE IN U.S. OR COUNTRY)

    _____ 62 –

    B. IF BORN IN THE U.S.
    Where were your parents born?

    Father (STATE IN U.S. OR COUNTRY)

    _____ 63 –

    Mother (STATE IN U.S. OR COUNTRY)

    _____ 64 –

---

45. HAND RESPONDENT CARD K. Were you brought up mainly on a farm, in a small town, a small city, a medium-sized city, or a large city?

Farm or open country . . . . . . 65 – 1
Small town or village (under
  10,000)   2
Small city (10,000 – 150,000) . .   3
Medium-sized city (150,000 –
  500,000)   4
Large city (over 500,000)   5

---

46. A. How closely do you follow local news – the things that happen here in your city – would you say very closely, fairly closely, or not too closely?
    B. What about the news of the world – do you follow international news very closely, fairly closely, or not too closely?

	Local news	News of the world
Very closely	66 – 0	67 – 5
Fairly closely	1	6
Not too closely	2	7

---

47. As far as you know, do you expect to be living at this address five years from now, or do you expect to move within that period?

Expect to be living here . . . . . 68 – 1
Expect to move   2   *ASK A
Don't know   3

*IF EXPECT TO MOVE
A. How far away do you expect to move – how many miles, approximately?

Number of miles _____ 69 –
Don't know . . . .   Y

---

48. What is your religious preference?

Protestant . . . . 70 – 1   *ASK A
Catholic   2
Jewish   3
None   4
Other (specify) _____

*IF PROTESTANT
A. Which denomination?

Denomination _____ 71 –

---

49. How often do you attend church (synagogue) services?

Once a week or more . . . . . . 72 – 1   *ASK A
1 – 3 times a month   2   *ASK A
Sometimes, but less than once
    a month   3   *ASK A
Never   4
Don't know   5

*IF OTHER THAN "NEVER" OR "DON'T KNOW"
A. What is the name of the church (synagogue) you usually attend?

Name of church
    (synagogue) _____
                                   73 –
                                   74 –

---

50. Quite apart from church (synagogue) going, how important would you say religion is to you – very important, fairly important, or not too important?

Very important . . . . 75 – 5
Fairly important   6
Not too important   7
Don't know   8

---

51. Generally speaking, what is your political preference?

Democrat . . . . 76 – 1
Republican   2
Independent   3
None   4
Don't know   5

---

52. HAND RESPONDENT CARD L. Now to finish up, in which of these general groups did your total family income fall last year – before taxes, that is?

A. Under $1,000 . . . . 77 – X
B. $1,000 – $1,999   0
C. $2,000 – $2,999   1
D. $3,000 – $3,999   2
E. $4,000 – $4,999   3
F. $5,000 – $5,999   4
G. $6,000 – $6,999   5
H. $7,000 – $7,999   6
I. $8,000 – $9,999   7
J. $10,000 – $14,999   8
K. $15,000 or more   9
Don't know . . . .   Y
Refused ☐ Interviewer estimate:
    Category _____

Length of Interview _____
Your signature _____

---

53. CHECK RACE OF RESPONDENT.

White . . . . 78 – 1
Negro   2
Oriental   3

D. THE CONTINUING EDUCATION OF AMERICAN YOUTH

Youth Form

NORC 447
8/62
Confidential

NATIONAL OPINION RESEARCH CENTER
UNIVERSITY OF CHICAGO

_____

(1 – 3)

Identification (4 – 13)

Segment No. (Six digits)
Household No. (Two digits)
Person No. (Two digits)

NAME _____

ADDRESS _____

_____

RECORD OF CALLS

	DATE	TIME	RESULTS
1st			
2nd			
3rd			
4th			
5th			
6th			

Notes

About This Youth

This information has been transferred from the short-form household interview (SFHI). If any items are not completed, complete them during this interview.

I. Age of respondent

Seventeen	14 – 7
Eighteen	8
Nineteen	9
Twenty	0
Twenty-one	1
Twenty-two	2
Twenty-three	3
Twenty-four	4

II. Sex, plus special office code

Male	15 – 1
Female	2
FOR OFFICE USE ONLY	Y

III. Relation to head of household

Son or daughter	16 – 1
Head	2
Wife of head	3
Other (specify) _____	

IV. Marital status

Single	17 – 1
Married	2
Other (specify) _____	

V. School attendance last year (Complete either A or B)

A. If entered as a youth (Q. 4)

Whole year	18 – 1
Some of it	2
Not at all	3
D.K.	4

B. If entered as an adult (Q. 6)

Yes	18 – 6
No	7
D.K.	8

VI. Total family income

Under $1,000 . . . . 19–x	
$1,000–$1,999	0
$2,000–$2,999	1
$3,000–$3,999	2
$4,000–$4,999	3
$5,000–$5,999	4
$6,000–$6,999	5
$7,000–$7,999	6
$9,000–$9,999	7
$10,000–$14,999	8
$15,000 or over	9
D.K.	Y
Refused . . . . □	
Estimate _____	

YOUTH INTERVIEW

1. The first part of this survey is about school. Will you be going to school at all this year—or will you be working (or keeping house) or just what?

Going to school . . . . 20–1 ⎫
Going to school and working . . 2 ⎬ SKIP TO
Going to school and keeping ⎪ SECTION I
house . . . . 3 ⎭

Not going to school—working . 4 ⎫
Not going to school—keeping ⎬ SKIP TO
house . . . . 5 ⎪ SECTION II
Other (specify) _____ 6 ⎭
Undecided about school . . . . . 9* ASK A AND B

*IF UNDECIDED ABOUT SCHOOL

A. Why is it you might not attend school this year? (Any other reason?)

21–

B. Right now, would you say it's more likely you will go, or more likely you won't?

More likely I will 22–1   ASK SECTION I
More likely I won't 2   SKIP TO SECTION II
D.K. 3   ASK SECTION I, AND ALTER PHRASING OF QUESTIONS TO READ: "IF YOU DO GO BACK TO SCHOOL. . . ."

SECTION I

ONLY FOR YOUTH ATTENDING SCHOOL THIS YEAR

2. Will you go (to school) full-time or just part-time this year?

Full-time . . . . 23 – 1
Part-time 2
D.K./Undecided 3

---

3. A. What school will you be going to?

NAME OF SCHOOL _____

B. Where is that?

CITY OR TOWN, AND
STATE _____

---

4. A. What type of school is that? (Is it a high school, a college, junior college, vocational school, business school, or just what?)

Junior high school . . . . 24 – 1
Regular high school 2
Junior college 3
College or university 4
Vocational or trade school . . . 5
Business or commercial
school 6
Other (specify) _____ 7

B. Is that a public, a private or a parochial religious school?

Public . . . . 25 – 1
Private 2
Parochial religious . . . . 3*   ASK C
D.K. 4
Other (specify) _____ 5

*IF PAROCHIAL RELIGIOUS
C. Which religious group runs it?

Roman Catholic . . . . 26 – 6
Lutheran 7
Jewish 8
Other (specify) _____ 9

---

5. What type of course are you taking there?

If in high school	If in college	If other than high school or college
General . . . . . . Y	Liberal arts . . . . Y	Type of course
College prepara-	Science/math . . . x	_____
tory x	Business 0	
Trade/vocational . 0	Engineering (or	
Business/	pre-) 1	
commercial . . . 1	Medicine (or	
Other (specify)	pre-) 2	•
_____ 2	Law (or pre-) . . . 3	
	Education 4	
	Agriculture 5	
	Nursing 6	
	Other (specify)	
	_____ 7	27 –
		28 –

---

6. What grade (school year) will you be in this year?

8th grade or less . . . . 29 – Y
9th grade, high school   X
10th grade, high school   0
11th grade, high school   1
12th grade, high school   2
1st year, college   3
2nd year, college   4
3rd year, college   5
4th year, college   6
Beyond 4th year, college   7
Other or ungraded course
  (specify) _____   8* ASK A

*IF OTHER OR UNGRADED COURSE
A. What was the last regular school grade that you completed?

8th grade or less . . . . 30 – Y
9th grade, high school   X
10th grade, high school   0
11th grade, high school   1
12th grade, high school   2
1st year, college   3

2nd year, college	4
3rd year, college	5
4th year, college	6
Beyond 4th year, college	7

7. Do you think you'll stay in school (college) until you graduate, or that you'll probably leave before you graduate?

Stay until graduation	31 – 1*	ASK A AND B
Leave before graduating	2†	ASK C
D.K.	3	

*IF STAY

A. When do you expect to graduate?

Year _____ Month _____ 32 –

B. What type of diploma, degree, or certificate will you get then?

High-school graduation diploma	33 – 1
Bachelor of arts degree	2
Bachelor of science degree	3
Other (WRITE OUT NAME IN FULL: DO NOT USE INITIALS) .	4

†IF LEAVE

C. Why do you think you'll leave before you graduate? (Any other reason?)

34 –

8. How far do you plan to go in school, altogether?

Less than high-school gradua- tion	35 – 0
High-school graduation	1
1 – 3 years of college	2
Graduate from college	3
Professional or graduate school after college	4
D.K.	5
Other (specify) _____	6

9. SHOW CARD A.

A. Are there any persons on here, or anyone else, who you've talked to recently about your school plans? (Who was that?) (Anyone else?)

B. Which persons on here would think you're doing the right thing to stay in school this year? (Anyone else?)

C. Are there any persons on here, or anyone else, who think you'd be better off to leave school this year?

Person	Talked to About School Plans	Thinks I Should Stay in School This Year	Thinks I'd Be Better Off To Leave School
No: none of these persons	36 – Y	37 – Y	38 – Y
D.K.	x	x	x
My father or mother	0	0	0
A brother or sister	1	1	1
A friend still in school	2	2	2
A friend out of school	3	3	3
A teacher at school	4	4	4
A school counselor	5	5	5
My employer	6	6	6
Girl friend, boy friend or fiancé	7	7	7
My husband or wife	8	8	8
Someone else (specify) _____	9	9	9

10. Will you be working at all while at school this year?

    Yes . . . . 39 – 1*   ASK A – C
    No   2   SKIP TO Q. 11
    D.K.   3   SKIP TO Q. 11

*IF YES

A. What kind of work will you be doing?

   Kind of work _____ 40 –

B. Where will you be working—for what type of company or business?

   Type of company or
   business _____ 41 –

C. About how many hours a week will you work there?

   Hours per week _____ 42 –

11. How about last year—were you in school last year, or working, or just what?

    School . . . . 43 – 1
    School and working   2
    School and keeping house   3

Not in school — working . . . . .   4* ASK A AND B

Not in school — keeping house . .   5* ASK A AND B

Not in school — other

(specify) _____   6* ASK A AND B

*IF NOT IN SCHOOL LAST YEAR

A. How long has it been now since you last attended school?

Length of time: Years _____

months _____ 44 –

B. How old were you when you last attended?

Age _____ 45 –

---

12. Let's go back now to when you first started school. What sort of elementary school did you go to — a public, private or parochial religious school? (IF MORE THAN ONE TYPE OF ELEMENTARY SCHOOL ATTENDED, CIRCLE ALL THAT APPLY.)

Public . . . . 46 – 1

Private 2

Parochial religious 3*

Other (specify) _____ 4

*IF PAROCHIAL RELIGIOUS

A. Which religious group ran it?

Catholic . . . . 47 – 6

Lutheran 7

Jewish 8

Other (specify) _____ 9

---

13. How many different elementary schools did you attend?

None . . . . 48 – 0

One 1

Two 2

Three 3

Four 4

Five 5

Six 6

More than six 7

---

14. Altogether, how many different schools have you attended since you left elementary school?

None . . . . 49 – 0
One . . . . 1*⎤ SKIP TO SECTION
Two . . . . 2*⎥ III
Three . . . . 3*⎥ ASK A, B, AND
Four . . . . 4*⎬ C FOR EACH
Five . . . . 5*⎥ SCHOOL AT-
Six . . . . 6*⎥ TENDED (UP TO
More than six . . . . 7*⎦ SIX)

*IF ONE OR MORE SCHOOLS ATTENDED SINCE ELEMENTARY SCHOOL

A. How about the first (second, etc.) one – what type of school was that?

> MAIN TYPES OF SCHOOL
>   (WRITE IN BELOW)
> Junior high school
> High school
> Vocational, trade or technical
>   school
> Business or commercial school
> Junior college
> College, or university
> If other, specify

B. Which grades did you complete there? (IF AN UNGRADED COURSE, ENTER NUMBER OF YEARS ATTENDED.)

C. Was that a public, a private or a parochial religious school? (IF PAROCHIAL RELIGIOUS: Which religious group ran it?)

Type of School (Write In)	Grades Completed There	Sponsorship of School		
		Public	Private	Religious (Specify)
1st				
2nd				
3rd				
4th				
5th				
6th				

Office Use Only

SKIP TO SECTION III

50–	51–	52–	53–	54–	55–

SECTION II

ONLY FOR YOUTH NOT ATTENDING SCHOOL THIS YEAR

15. How about last year—were you in school at all last year?

        Yes 56–1
        No . . . .   2* ASK A AND B

*IF NO

A. How long has it been now since you last attended school?

        Length of time: Years _____
                Months _____ 57–

B. How old were you when you last attended?

        Age _____ 58–

16. Next, I'd like to go back to when you first started school. What sort of elementary school did you go to—was it a public, a private or a parochial religious school? (IF MORE THAN ONE TYPE OF ELEMENTARY SCHOOL ATTENDED, CIRCLE ALL THAT APPLY.)

        Public 59–1
        Private   2
        Parochial religious . . . .   3* ASK A
        Other (specify) _____   4

*IF PAROCHIAL RELIGIOUS

A. Which religious group ran it?

        Catholic 60–6
        Lutheran   7
        Jewish   8
        Other (specify) _____   9

17. How many different elementary schools did you attend?

        None 61–0
        One   1
        Two   2
        Three   3
        Four   4
        Five   5
        Six   6
        More than six   7

18. Altogether, how many different schools did you attend after you left elementary school?

None	62–0*	ASK A
One	1†	
Two	2†	ASK B, C, AND
Three	3†	D FOR EACH
Four	4†	SCHOOL AT-
Five	5†	TENDED (UP TO
Six	6†	SIX)
More than six	7†	

*IF NO SCHOOLS ATTENDED AFTER ELEMENTARY SCHOOL

A. What was the highest grade you completed in school?

   Highest grade completed _____   SKIP TO Q. 19

†IF ONE OR MORE SCHOOLS ATTENDED SINCE ELEMENTARY SCHOOL

B. How about the first (second, etc.) one — what type of school was that?

   MAIN TYPES OF SCHOOL
     (WRITE IN BELOW)
   Junior high school
   High school
   Vocational, trade or technical
     school
   Business or commercial
   Junior college
   College or university
   If other, specify

C. Which grades did you complete there? (IF AN UNGRADED COURSE, ENTER NUMBER OF YEARS ATTENDED.)

D. Was that a public, a private or a parochial religious school? (IF PAROCHIAL RELIGIOUS: Which religious group ran it?)

Type of School (Write In)	Grades Completed There	Sponsorship of School		
		Public	Private	Religious (Specify)
1st				
2nd				
3rd				
4th				
5th				
6th				

Office Use Only

63–	64–	65–	66–	67–	68–

79–Y,1	80–4,7

END OF DECK Y,1

BEGIN DECK Y,2 _____
                     (1–3)

19. A. What was the name of the last school you attended?

   Name of school _____

   B. Where is that?

   City or town, and state _____

   _____

20. When you last went there, were you attending full-time or just part-time?

   Full-time 4–1
   Part-time   2

21. When you left there had you graduated from your course, or did you
leave before you graduated?

> Graduated . . . . 5 – 1* ASK A AND B
> Left before graduating . . . . . . 2† ASK C
> Other (specify)_____ 3

*IF GRADUATED

A. What sort of diploma (certificate, or degree) did you get when
you graduated?

> Regular high school diploma . . 6 – 1
> Other (WRITE OUT NAME IN
>   FULL: DO NOT USE INITIALS)
> _____ 2

B. At that time, had you thought at all that you might go further
with your education?

> Yes . . . . 7 – 1‡ ASK (I) AND (II)
> No . . . . 2 SKIP TO Q. 22
> D.K. . . . . 3 SKIP TO Q. 22

‡IF YES

(i) What type of course had you thought you might take?

> 8 –

(ii) What was the main reason you didn't take it? (Any other
reasons?)

> 9 – SKIP TO Q. 22

†IF LEFT BEFORE GRADUATED

C. (i) What was the main reason you left school then?

> 10 –

(ii) Were there any other reasons?

> 11 –

22. SHOW CARD B. Here are some reasons other people have given for leaving school. Did any of these apply to you at the time you left school? How about A? How about B? (Etc.)

Reason		Applied to Me	Did Not Apply to Me	D.K.
A. I felt I had as much education as I needed	12 –	Y	X	0
B. I was just tired of going to school	13 –	2	3	4
C. I thought I might go back eventually, but I wanted to get some practical experience first	14 –	6	7	8
D. I felt I could get the kind of job I wanted without any further schooling	15 –	Y	X	0
E. My grades weren't good enough to go any farther	16 –	2	3	4
F. I had financial problems	17 –	6	7	8
G. I wanted to get married	18 –	Y	X	0
H. School was a real drag for me and I was glad to get out	19 –	2	3	4

23. SHOW CARD C. Here is a list of persons you may have talked to at about the time you left school.

A. Is there anyone on here, or anyone else, who at that time thought you should stay in school and get more education? (Who?) (Anyone else?) (CIRCLE AS MANY AS APPLY.)

B. Is there anyone who thought it was a good idea for you to leave school when you did? (Who?) (Anyone else?) (CIRCLE AS MANY AS APPLY.)

C. Is there anyone you've talked to recently who thinks it would be a good idea for you to go back to school sometimes? (Who?) (Anyone else?) (CIRCLE AS MANY AS APPLY.)

Person	Wanted Me To Stay in School	Thought I Should Leave When I Did	Thinks I Should Go Back to School
No: None of these persons	20 – Y	21 – Y	22 – Y
D.K.	X	X	X
My father or mother	0	0	0
A brother or sister	1	1	1
A friend still in school	2	2	2
A friend out of school	3	3	3
A teacher at school	4	4	4
A school counselor	5	5	5
My employer	6	6	6
Girl friend, boy friend or fiancé	7	7	7
My husband or wife	8	8	8
Someone else (specify) _____	9	9	9

24. Do you think you'll ever go back to school either full time or part time?

    Yes — full-time . . . . 23 – 1* ASK A – D
    Yes — part-time . . . . 2* ASK A – D
    No . . . . 3 SKIP TO Q. 25
    D.K./not sure . . . . 4 SKIP TO Q. 25

*IF YES

A. When do you think you'll go back? (PROBE FOR A SPECIFIC DATE.)

    Sooner than January, 1963 . . . 24 – 0
    January – April, 1963 1
    May – August, 1963 2
    September – December, 1963 . . 3
    January – April, 1964 4
    May – August, 1964 5
    September – December, 1964 . . 6
    January, 1965, or later 7
    D.K. 8

B. What kind of school will you go to when you go back?

    Regular high school . . . . 25 – 1
    Junior college 2
    College or university 3
    Other (specify) _____ 4

C. What type of course would you take there?

If going to high school	If going to college or university	If other than high school or college
General . . . . . . Y	Liberal arts . . . . Y	Type of course
College preparatory X	Science/math . . . X	_____
Trade/vocational . 0	Business 0	
Business/commercial . . . 1	Engineering (or pre-) 1	
Other (specify) ___ _____ 2	Medicine (or pre-) 2	
	Law (or pre-) . . . 3	
	Education 4	
	Agriculture 5	
	Nursing 6	
	Other (specify) _____ 7	

26–

D. Altogether, how far do you think you'll go in school?

Graduate from high school . . . . 27 – 1
1 – 3 years college   2
Graduate from college   3
Professional or graduate school
    after college   4
D.K.   5
Other (specify) _____   6

---

25. Right now, are you working full time, part time, or not at all?

Full time . . . . 28 – 1*   ASK A – L
Part time . . . .   2†   ASK M – Q
Not at all . . . .   3‡   ASK R

*IF WORKING FULL TIME
A. What kind of work do you do?

Kind of work _____ 29 –

B. In what type of business or industry is that?

Type of business or industry
_____ 30 –

C. On the average, how many hours a week, including overtime, do you work?

Average hours per week _____ 31 –

D. How long have you been working at that job?

Years _____ months _____
    weeks _____ 32 –

E. SHOW CARD D.
    1. How well do you like the type of work you're doing?
    2. How do you feel about your present salary?
    3. How do you feel about the company or employer you work for?

Rate of Satisfaction	Type of Work	Salary	Company or Employer
Very satisfied	33 – 1	34 – 1	35 – 1
Moderately satisfied	2	2	2
A little dissatisfied	3	3	3
Extremely dissatisfied	4	4	4
Don't know	5	5	5

*IF WORKING FULL TIME

F. How good are your chances for advancement on your job—
    would you say very good, fair, or poor?

> Very good . . . . 36 – 1
> Fair   2
> Poor   3
> D.K.   4

G. Does your job give you a chance to do the kind of work you do
    best?

> Yes . . . . 37 – 1
> No . . . .   2§ ASK (1)
> D.K.   3

§IF NO
(1) What kind of work do you feel you can do better?

                                    38 –

H. How did you learn your job—did you take some kind of training
    course when you started, or did you learn it more or less by
    starting right in and doing it?

> Training course . . . . 39 – 1# ASK (1)
> Learned by doing it   2
> Both . . . .   3# ASK (1)
> Other (specify) _____   4

#IF A TRAINING COURSE WAS TAKEN
(1) How long was your training course?

> Length of course _____ 40 –

I. Altogether, how long did it take you to learn how to do the work
    on your job?

> Length of time _____ 41 –

*IF WORKING FULL TIME
J. How much do you make a week?

> Average weekly pay _____ 42 –

K. Would you like to keep your present job, or would you rather
    get another one if you could?

> Like to keep present job . . . . 43 – 1
> Like to get another job . . . . .   2** ASK (1) AND (2)
> D.K.   3

**IF GET ANOTHER JOB
(1) What's the main reason you'd like to leave your job?

44 –

(2) What kind of job would you rather get?

45 –

L. In a year from now, do you think you'll be working at the same job?

Yes . . . . 46 – 1   SKIP TO Q. 26
No . . . .   2†† ASK (1)
D.K. . . . .   3†† ASK (1)

††IF NO OR DON'T KNOW
(1) What do you think you'll be doing a year from now?

47 –   SKIP TO Q. 26

†IF WORKING PART TIME
M. What kind of work do you do?

Kind of work _____ 48 –

N. In what type of business or industry is that?

Type of business or
industry _____ 49 –

O. About how many hours a week do you work, on the average?

Average hours per week _____ 50 –

P. How much do you make a week?

Average weekly pay _____ 51 –

Q. Right now, are you trying to find a full-time job?

Yes . . . . 52 – 1‡‡ ASK (1)–(3)
No   2   SKIP TO Q. 26

‡‡IF YES
(1) About how long have you been looking for one?

Length of time _____ 53 –

(2) What would you say is the main reason why you haven't found one yet?

54 –

(3) Are there any other reasons why not?

55–   SKIP TO Q. 26

‡IF NOT WORKING AT ALL

R. Right now, are you trying to find either a full-time job or a part-time job?

```
Yes, full-time job . . . . . . . . 56–1§§ ASK (1)–(3)
Yes, part-time job . . . . . . .      2§§ ASK (1)–(3)
Yes, either (or "anything") . . .     3§§ ASK (1)–(3)
No . . . . . . . . . . . . . . . .     4  SKIP TO Q. 26
```

§§IF YES

(1) About how long have you been looking for a job?

Length of time _____ 57–

(2) What would you say is the main reason why you haven't found one yet?

58–

(3) Are there any other reasons why not?

59–

---

26. ASK ALL YOUTH WHO ARE NOT GOING TO SCHOOL THIS YEAR.

IF RESPONDENT WORKS: Besides your present job, how many other full-time or part-time jobs have you had since you left school?

IF RESPONDENT DOES NOT WORK: Altogether, how many different full-time or part-time jobs have you had since you left school?

```
None . . . . . . . . . . . . . . 60–0  SKIP TO SEC-
                                       TION III
One . . . . . . . . . . . . . .    1*  ASK  A,  THEN
                                       SKIP TO SEC-
                                       TION III
Two . . . . . . . . . . . . . .    2†

Three . . . . . . . . . . . . .    3‡ ⎤
Four . . . . . . . . . . . . . .   4‡ ⎥
Five . . . . . . . . . . . . . .   5‡ ⎥
Six . . . . . . . . . . . . . .    6‡ ⎬ ASK A, B, AND C
Seven . . . . . . . . . . . . .    7‡ ⎥
Eight . . . . . . . . . . . . .    8‡ ⎥
Nine or more . . . . . . . . . .   9‡ ⎦
```

*†‡A. First job after leaving school

   (1) Let's start with the first job you had after you left school. What kind of work did you do on that job?

   Kind of work _____ 61 –

   (2) In what type of business or industry was that?

   Type of business or
     industry _____ 62 –

   (3) How soon after leaving school did you start that job?

   Length of time _____ 63 –

   (4) How much did you make a week on that job?

   Average weekly pay _____ 64 –

   (5) How long did you do that?

   Length of time _____ 65 –

   (6) How did you happen to leave that job – did you quit or were you laid off, or just what?

   Quit . . . . 66 – 1
   Laid off   2
   Fired   3
   Other (specify) _____   4

*†B. Second job after leaving school

   (1) What kind of work did you do on your second job?

   Kind of work _____ 67 –

   (2) In what type of business or industry was that?

   Type of business or
     industry _____ 68 –

   (3) How soon after leaving your first job did you start on that?

   Length of time _____ 69 –

   (4) How much did you make a week on that job?

   Average weekly pay _____ 70 –

   (5) How long did you do that?

   Length of time _____ 71 –

(6) How did you happen to leave that job?

    Quit . . . . 72 – 1
    Laid off   2
    Fired   3
    Other (specify) _____   4

*†‡C. Most recent job

   (1) What kind of work did you do on your most recent job (on the job you held before your present one)?

       Kind of work _____ 73 –

   (2) In what type of business or industry was that?

       Type of business or
          industry _____ 74 –

   (3) How soon after leaving your previous job did you start on that one?

       Length of time _____ 75 –

   (4) How much did you make a week on that job?

       Average weekly pay _____ 76 –

   (5) How long did you do that?

       Length of time _____ 77 –

   (6) How did you happen to leave that job?

       Quit . . . . 78 – 1
       Laid off   2
       Fired   3
       Other (specify) _____   4

Office Use

| 79– Y, 2 | 80–4, 7 |

END OF DECK Y, 2

SECTION III

ASK ALL YOUTH

27. SHOW BLUE FLASH CARD.[1] Here is a list of subjects that people sometimes study either in addition to regular school work, or after they stop going to school. This includes all kinds of part-time courses, evening classes, correspondence courses, courses given in the army or over television, private lessons—and anything else not connected with full-time school work.

Have you ever taken a special course in any of these things—or in anything else not listed here?

Yes . . . .   4-1*   ASK A-G FOR
                                            EACH COURSE TAKEN
No   x   SKIP TO Q. 28

*IF YES

A. FIRST SUBJECT: Let's start with the   Name of subject or skill
most recent—in what subject was
that?

OTHER SUBJECTS: In what subject
was that?
                                                            5-
                                                            6-

B. ASK RESPONDENT TO TURN CARD   Method of study
OVER. Which of those methods de-
scribes how you studied that?
                                                            7-

C. What type of school or institution   Type of school or institution
gave that? (Where did you take it?)
                                                            8-

D. How old were you when you first   Age _____   9-
took that?

E. About how long did you study it?   Length of time   10-

---

[1]Reproduced at the end of this section—Editor.

F. Was that a "credit" course for some kind of diploma, degree, or certificate, or was it "non-credit"?

Credit . . . . 11 – 1† ASK (1)
Non-credit . . . 2
D.K. 3

†IF CREDIT
(1) For what kind of diploma, degree, or certificate?

Type of credit

12 –

G. Did you take any other courses before that?

Yes 13 – 1 GO TO NEXT
No . . . x COLUMN
SKIP TO Q. 28

ADDITIONAL SUBJECTS STUDIED

2nd subject	3rd subject	4th subject
Name of subject or skill	Name of subject or skill	Name of subject or skill
14 –	23 –	32 –
15 –	24 –	33 –
Method of study	Method of study	Method of study
16 –	25 –	34 –
Type of school or institution	Type of school or institution	Type of school or institution
17 –	26 –	35 –
Age _____	Age _____	Age _____
18 –	27 –	36 –
Length of time	Length of time	Length of time
19 –	28 –	37 –
Credit . . 20 – 1† ASK (1)	Credit . 29 – 1† ASK (1)	Credit . 38 – 1† ASK (1)
Non-credit . 2	Non-credit . 2	Non-credit . 2
D.K. . . 3 GO TO NEXT COLUMN SKIP TO Q.28	D.K. . . 3 GO TO NEXT COLUMN SKIP TO Q.28	D.K. . . 3
Type of credit	Type of credit	Type of credit
21 –	30 –	39 –
Yes . . . 22 – 1	Yes . . 31 – 1	Yes . . 40 – 1
No . . . 2	No . . . 2	No . . . 2

28. Have you ever tried to teach yourself something strictly on your own?

Yes . . . . 41–1* Ask A–B

No . . . . 2 skip to C

*If yes: list all subjects studied (up to six).

A. What was that? (Was there anything else before that?)	B. About how old were you when you started to study that?
Subject	**Age**

1.

2.

3.

4.

5.

6.

C. For persons still attending school, skip to Q. 29. Surveys have shown that very few people take special courses once they leave school. Here are some reasons people have given for not taking more courses. Would any of these statements apply to you? How about this one? (Read each statement.)

Reasons for Not Taking Course		Would Apply to Me	Would Not Apply to Me	D.K.
1. I'd be interested in taking some type of course, but there's nothing like that available around here. (Would that apply to you or not?)	42–	Y	X	0
2. The courses I've heard about sound pretty dull. (Would you agree with that, or not?)	43–	2	3	4
3. I can learn all I need to know without taking courses to do it. (Would you agree with that, or not?)	44–	6	7	8
4. I'm much too busy with other things right now, and just wouldn't have the time. (Would that apply to you, or not?)	45·	Y	X	0
5. I'm interested in a lot of things, but I really don't enjoy studying. (Would you agree with that, or not?)	46–	2	3	4
6. Right now, I just couldn't afford it. (Would that apply to you, or not?)	47–	6	7	8
7. I've never thought about taking a special course. (Would that apply to you, or not?)	48–	Y	X	0

29. Many people have things they'd like to learn more about, or would like to know how to do better. Is there anything you'd like to learn more about, or learn how to do better?

Yes . . . . 49 – 1* ASK A – B

No . . . . 2 SKIP TO Q. 30

Don't know . . . . 3 SKIP TO Q. 30

*IF YES

A. What is that? (Is there anything else?) Do NOT PROBE BEYOND THREE.

B. Why would you like to learn that? (Any other reason?)

Name of subject — Reasons for learning it

1st subject

50 –   51 –

2nd subject

52 –   53 –

3rd subject

54 –   55 –

---

30. If you were starting over again, how far would you like to go in school?

Not attend at all . . . . 56 – 1

1 – 4 years 2

5 – 7 years 3

8 years 4

9 – 11 years 5

12 years – finish high school . . . 6

13 – 15 years – some college . . . 7

16 years – complete college . . . 8

Go to graduate school . . . . . . 9* ASK A

D.K. . . . . Y

Get other training (specify)

————————————— X

*IF GO TO GRADUATE SCHOOL

A. What type of graduate degree would you like to get?

Type of degree ——————— 57 –

IF RESPONDENT NEVER ATTENDED HIGH SCHOOL, SKIP TO QUESTION 41.

31. SHOW CARD E.
    (i) When you think back over your high-school days, how impor-
    tant was it to you then (has it been to you) to study hard and
    get good grades — would you say A, B, C, or D?
    (ii) How about most other students in your high school — how im-
    portant was it to them to study hard and get good grades?
    (iii) How important was it to your parents that you studied hard —
    how about your father?
    (iv) How about your mother?

Rate of Importance	Importance to Me	Importance to Most Other Students	Importance to My Father	Importance to My Mother
A. Extremely important	58 – Y	59 – 4	60 – Y	61 – 4
B. Slightly important	X	5	X	5
C. Not very important	0	6	0	6
D. Couldn't have cared less	1	7	1	7
Don't know	2	8	2	8

32. At high school, were your grades more often in the upper third of
your class, in the middle third, or in the lower third?

> Upper third . . . . 62 – 1
> Middle third 2
> Lower third 3
> D.K. 4

33. How close were you to the center of the student activities that went
on at your high school — were you pretty close to the center, a little on
the outside, or completely outside of things?

> Pretty close to the center . . . . 63 – 1
> A little on the outside 2
> Completely outside of things . . 3
> D.K. 4

34. Did you belong to any clubs, organizations, or athletic teams in
high school?

> Yes . . . . 64 – 7* ASK A
> No 8

*IF YES

A. Which ones? (Any others?) (WRITE IN FULL NAME OF CLUB, ORGANIZATION, OR TEAM: DO NOT ENTER INITIALS.)

1. _____
2. _____
3. _____
4. _____
5. _____
6. _____
7. _____
8. _____

$$65-$$
$$66-$$
$$67-$$

---

35. About how many students were at your high school?

  Under 100 . . . . 68 – 1
  100 – 299 2
  300 – 499 3
  400 – 749 4
  750 – 999 5
  1,000 – 1,499 6
  1,500 – 1,999 7
  2,000 or more 8
  D.K. 9

---

36. SHOW CARD F. Which one of these statements best describes what most of the teachers were like in your high school — would you say A, B, or C?

  A. They were good teachers,
    and pretty sharp . . . . . . 69 – 4
  B. They were all right as teach-
    ers, but were kind of
    square 5
  C. They were pretty poor all
    around 6
  None of these 7
  Don't know 8

---

37. Were most of the students in your high school pretty easy to get to know or pretty hard to get to know?

> Pretty easy to get to know . . . 70 – 1
> Pretty hard to get to know . . .   2
> Don't know   3

---

38. Were there any subjects that you really liked well in high school?

> Yes . . . . 71 – 1* ASK A
> No   2
> D.K.   3

   *IF YES
   A. Which ones? (Any others?)

> 72 –
> 73 –

---

39. All in all, what were the things you liked best about high school? (Anything else?)

> 74 –

---

40. What things did you like least about it? (Anything else?)

> 75 –

79–Y, 3	80–4, 7

END DECK Y, 3
BEGIN DECK Y, 4 _____
       (1 – 3)

41. ASK EVERYONE. What do you think is the main value of a good education? (Anything else?)

> 4 –

---

42. SHOW CARD G.

> (i) How important is it to have a college education in order to get a good paying job around here – would you say A, B, C, or D?

> > A. Absolutely necessary . . . . 5 – Y
> > B. It helps but isn't necessary .   x
> > C. Doesn't matter one way or
> >   the other   0
> > D. You're better off without it .   1
> > D.K.   2

(ii) How important is it to have a college education in order to be respected and looked up to by most people around here?

    A. Absolutely necessary . . . .   6 – 4
    B. It helps but isn't necessary .   5
    C. Doesn't matter one way or
        the other   6
    D. You're better off without it .   7
        D.K.   8

---

43. SHOW CARD H. Of the six things on this card, which two do you think are most important in helping a person get ahead?

    Brains . . . .   7 – 1
    A good education   2
    Good luck   3
    Hard work   4
    Know the right people   5
    Personality   6
    D.K.   7

---

44. A. How far did your father go in school?

    B. How far did your mother go in school?

	Father	Mother
Never attended school	8 – 1	9 – 1
1 – 4 grades	2	2
5 – 7 grades	3	3
8 grades	4	4
9 – 11 grades	5	5
12 grades/high-school graduate .	6	6
1 – 3 years college	7	7
4 years college	8	8
Graduate school	9	9
D.K.	Y	Y

---

45. A. What kind of work does your father do?
    IF DECEASED: What was your father's main occupation during most of his lifetime?

    Type of occupation _____ 10 –

    B. In what type of business or industry is (was) that?

Type of business or
industry _____ 11 –

---

46. Is there any particular line of work that you'd really like to get into eventually?

      Yes . . . . 12 – 1* ASK A – E
      No . . . . 2 SKIP TO Q. 47
      D.K. . . . . 3 SKIP TO Q. 47

*IF YES
  A. What is that?

      Line of work _____ 13 –

  B. What is it about that line of work that you'd like best?

                    14 –

  C. What do you have to do to get into that? (Anything else?)

                    15 –

  D. Do you know anyone who does that type of work?

      Yes . . . . 16 – 1† ASK (1)
      No 2
      Don't know 3

    †IF YES
    (1) Who is that? (Anyone else?)

                    17 –

  E. Do you think you'll actually end up in that line of work?

      Yes . . . . 18 – 1 SKIP TO Q. 47
      No . . . . 2‡ ASK (1) AND (2)
      Don't know . . . . 3‡ ASK (1) AND (2)

    ‡IF NO OR DON'T KNOW
    (1) What might keep you from getting into that? (Is there anything else?)

                    19 –

    (2) What do you think you'll probably end up doing?
                    20 –

---

47. SHOW CARD I. Here are three different types of jobs. If you had your choice, which one would you pick?

A. A job which pays a moderate
   income but which you are
   sure of keeping . . . . . . 21 – 1
B. A job which pays a good income, but which you have
   a 50-50 chance of losing   2
C. A job which pays an extremely good income, if
   you make the grade, but in
   which you lose almost
   everything if you don't
   make it   3
Don't know   4

---

48. SHOW CARD J. How would you rank these five things as things to look for on a job?

Job Advantages	Which Would Be First	Which Would Be Second?	Third?	Fourth?	Fifth	Office Use
A. Steady work	1	2	3	4	5	22 –
B. Chance for advancement	1	2	3	4	5	23 –
C. Interesting work	1	2	3	4	5	24 –
D. Friendly people to work with	1	2	3	4	5	25 –
E. A high income	1	2	3	4	5	26 –
Check if D.K.						

49. In general, do you think that pay increases on a job should be based more on a person's age and experience, or more on how well he or she does on the job?

Age and experience . . . . 27 – 1
How well he or she does on the
   job   2
D.K.   3

---

50. Next I'd like to talk about your spare-time activities and interests. What things do you like doing in your spare time? (Anything else?)

28 –

51. How often do you have spare time that you don't know what to do with—would you say frequently, occasionally, seldom or never?

Frequently 29–1
Occasionally 2
Seldom 3
Never 4
D.K. 5

52. People have different ideas about the best way to spend spare time. Some like to keep as busy as possible doing things, while others like to just take it easy.

A. Which do you think is the better idea about how to spend spare time—keep as busy as possible, or take it easy?

Busy as possible 30–1
Take it easy 2
D.K. 3

B. What about most other people your age around here—do you think most of them prefer to keep as busy as possible, or to take it easy?

Busy as possible 31–5
Take it easy 6
D.K. 7

53. In general, do you prefer games and sports where you keep score and play to win, or where you don't keep score and play just to have fun?

Keep score and play to win . . . 32–6
Don't keep score and play to
have fun 7
D.K. 8

54. Which day of the week do you look forward to most?

Day _____ 33 –   *ASK A
No favorite day 8
D.K. 9

*IF A FAVORITE DAY
A. Why do you like (DAY) best? (Any other reason?)

34–

55. And which day do you like the least?

> Day _____ 35 –   *ASK A
> No least liked day   8
> D.K.   9

*IF A LEAST LIKED DAY
A. Why is that? (Any other reason?)

36 –

---

56. SHOW CARD K.

(i) Around here how common or rare is it for young people to quit school before finishing high school – would you say A, B, C, D, or E?

(ii) How common is it for young people around here to go to college?

(iii) How common is it around here for boys to get married before they're 21?

(iv) How about girls – how common is it for girls around here to get married before they're 21?

(v) How common is it for young people around here to get into trouble with the police?

Frequency	Quit School	Go to College	Boys Get Married before 21	Girls Get Married before 21	Trouble with Police
A. It's the usual thing – practically everyone does	37 – 1	38 – 1	39 – 1	40 – 1	41 – 1
B. About three out of four do	2	2	2	2	2
C. About half do	3	3	3	3	3
D. About one in four does	4	4	4	4	4
E. It's very rare – practically no one does	5	5	5	5	5
Don't know	6	6	6	6	6

---

57. Do you usually go around with a large group of friends, one or two close friends, or do you usually stay pretty much to yourself?

> Large group of friends . . . . . . 42 – 1
> One or two close friends   2
> Stay pretty much to myself . . .   3
> D.K.   4

IF MARRIED, SKIP TO Q. 59.

58. How soon do you think you'll get married?

Less than 1 year	43 – 1*	
About a year	2*	
About 2 years	3*	GIRLS ONLY:
About 3 years	4*	ASK A
4 – 5 years	5*	
6 – 10 years	6*	
Later than 10 years	7*	
Never expect to marry	8	
Don't know	9	

*ONLY FOR UNMARRIED GIRLS WHO DO EXPECT TO MARRY SOME-
TIME

A. After you get married, will you probably work until you have
a family, not work at all, try to combine working with a family,
or just what?

Work until I have a family . . .	44 – 1
Not work at all	2
Combine work with a family . .	3
Don't know	4
Other (specify) _____	5

---

59. ASK UNLESS OBVIOUS. Do you have a TV set in working order?

Yes	45 – 4
No	5

---

60. Is there an educational television station in this area?

Yes	46 – 1*	ASK A AND B
No	x	SKIP TO Q. 61
D.K.	2	SKIP TO Q. 61

*IF YES

A. Which station is that?

Channel number _____
Call letters _____
City or town _____ 47 –

B. Have you ever watched any programs on that station?

Yes	48 – 1†	ASK (1) – (3)
No	x	SKIP TO Q. 61
D.K.	2	SKIP TO Q. 61

†IF YES

(1) What types of programs have you seen? (Any others?)

_____ 49 –

(2) About how often do you watch programs on that station
—almost every day, every other day, once or twice a week,
or less often than that?

Almost every day	50 – x
Every other day	0
Once or twice a week	1
Less often than that	2
D.K.	3

(3) All in all, how would you rate the programs on the educational station in comparison with those on regular television
—would you say they are more interesting, less interesting,
or about the same?

More interesting	51 – 5
Less interesting	6
About the same	7
D.K.	8

---

61. Suppose that a new educational course was being planned by one
of the local television stations, and that the station was going to decide
the subject of the course by asking members of the community to make
suggestions. If you were asked for your opinion, what kind of a course
would you suggest that they give? (Anything else?)

52 –

---

62. SHOW CARD L.
(i) If the choice were narrowed down to the three general topics
listed here, which one would you vote for—A, B, or C?
(ii) Which would you vote for second?

	First choice	Second choice
A. Practical skills for everyday living	53 – 0	54 – 5
B. General knowledge about the world we live in	1	6
C. Interests and hobbies for spare time use	2	7
D.K.	3	8

---

63. SHOW CARD M.

   (i) About how often do you read or glance through a newspaper?

   (ii) How often do you read or glance through magazines?

   (iii) How often do you watch television?

   (iv) How about radio listening—how often do you listen to the radio?

Frequency	Newspaper	Magazines	Television	Radio
A. Almost every day	55–1	56–1	57–1	58–1
B. About every other day	2	2	2	2
C. Once or twice a week	3	3	3	3
D. Sometimes—but less than once a week	4	4	4	4
E. Never	5	5	5	5
Don't know	6	6	6	6

IF "NEVER" WATCH TELEVISION, SKIP TO Q. 65.

64. On an average weekday, about how many hours do you spend watching television?

       Hours _____ 59 –

IF "NEVER" READ MAGAZINES, SKIP TO Q. 66.

65. When you're reading a magazine and come across puzzles or quizzes, do you usually stop and try them, or usually not?

       Usually stop and try them . . . 60–7

       Usually not 8

       D.K. 9

66. Which do you read most often—newspapers, magazines, or books?

       Newspapers 61–1

       Magazines 2

       Books 3

       All equally 4

       Never read anything 5

       D.K. 6

67. About how many books have you read in the past year?

       Number of books _____ 62 –

       Don't know . . . . Y

68. About how many movies do you go to in a month?

> Number of movies ———————— 63 –
> Don't know . . . .   Y

---

69. If you had your choice of where to live, would you choose to live in this area or somewhere else?

> In this area . . . . 64 – 1
> Somewhere else . . . .   2* ASK A
> Don't know   3

> *IF SOMEWHERE ELSE
> A. Why is that — why would you like to leave here? (Any other reason?)
>
> 65 –

IF MARRIED, SKIP TO Q. 72.

70. SHOW CARD N. As you know, people your age often disagree with their parents. Do you ever disagree with them on any of the following things? (Which ones?) (Anything else listed there?)

> No: None of these things . . . . 66 – Y
> Don't know   X
> My parents aren't living   0
> A. Staying out late at night . . .   1
> B. Who I go out with on dates .   2
> C. The friends I go around
>   with   3
> D. What I do in my spare time .   4
> E. Not trying hard enough at
>   school   5
> F. The amount of time I
>   study   6
> G. Leaving school   7
> H. Going back to school   8
> I. The kind of job I have   9
> J. The line of work I want to
>   get into . . . . 67 – 1
> K. Not having a job   2
> L. Getting married   3
> M. Religion   4
> N. Politics   5

71. Do you ever disagree with them on anything else not listed here?

> Yes . . . . 68 – 1* ᴀsᴋ A
> No 2
> Don't know 3

*ɪғ ʏᴇs
A. What is that? (Anything else?)

> 69 –

---

72. Taking all things together, how happy are you with your life right now—would you say very happy, pretty happy, or not too happy?

> Very happy . . . . 70 – 6
> Pretty happy 7
> Not too happy 8
> Don't know 9

---

73. What would you change about your life right now if you had the chance to change one thing?

---

74. A. Where were you born?

> State in U.S. or country _____ 72 –

B. Where were your parents born?

> | | Father | Mother |
> |---|---|---|
> | State in U.S. or country | _____ 73 – | _____ 74 – |

---

75. A. How long have you lived in this area?
B. How long have you lived at your present address?

> | | Area | Present address |
> |---|---|---|
> | Less than one year . . . . | 75 – 1 | 76 – 1 |
> | 1 – 2 years . . . . | 2 | 2 |
> | 3 – 5 years . . . . | 3 | 3 |
> | 6 – 10 years . . . . | 4 | 4 |
> | 11 – 15 years . . . . | 5 | 5 |
> | More than 15 years, or "all my life" . . . . | 6 | 6 |

79 – ʏ,4 | 80 – 4,7

END OF DECK ʏ,4

For Office Use

6-	7-	8-	9-	10-	11-	12-	13

BEGIN DECK Y,5 _____
                    (1–3)

76. How my younger brothers and sisters do you have?

Number _____ 4–

---

77. How many older brothers and sisters?

Number _____ *

*IF NONE, SKIP TO Q. 78.

*IF ONE OR MORE, ASK A–E FOR EACH OLDER BROTHER OR SISTER (UP TO SIX)

ASK A–E FOR EACH OLDER BROTHER/SISTER   Oldest[1]

A. What are the names of your older brothers/sisters?   Name _____

B. RECORD SEX

Male 1
Female 2

C. How old was (NAME) on his/her last birthday?   Age _____

D. What was the highest grade in school that (NAME) completed?

Never attended 1
1–4 grades 2
5–7 grades 3
8 grades 4
9–11 grades 5
12 grades 6
Some college 7
Finished college 8
Graduate school 9
Other (specify) _____ 0

E. What was (NAME) doing last year— going to school, working, or just what?

Going to school 1*
Working . . . . 2†
Keeping house 3
Other (specify)_____ 4

[1]For reasons of space, cols. 2–6, asking the same questions for the second through sixth oldest child, have been omitted.—Editor.

*IF GOING TO SCHOOL

(1) How far does (NAME) plan to go in school?

Less than 12 grades 1
12 grades 2
1 – 3 years college 3
Finish college 4
Graduate school 5
D.K. 6
Other (specify) _____ 7

†IF WORKING

(2) What type of work does he/she do?

Type of work

(3) In what type of business or industry is that?

Business or industry

---

78. Do you belong to any clubs, organizations or teams around here?

Yes . . . . 14 – 1* ASK A
No 2
D.K. 3

*IF YES

A. Which ones? (Any others?) ENTER FULL NAME OF CLUB, OR-GANIZATION, OR TEAM — DO NOT ENTER INITIALS.

1. _____
2. _____
3. _____
4. _____
5. _____
6. _____

15 –
16 –

---

79. What is your religious preference?

Protestant . . . . 17 – 1
(Which denomination?) _____
Catholic 2
Jewish 3
None 4
Other (specify) _____ 5

18 –

80. How often do you attend church (or synagogue) services?

Once a week or more . . . . . . 19 – 1
1 – 3 times a month   2
Less than once a month   3
Never   4
D.K.   5

81. Apart from church (synagogue) going, how important would you say religion is to you – very important, fairly important, or not important at all?

Very important . . . . 20 – 6
Fairly important   7
Not important at all   8
D.K.   9

82. If you could have voted in the 1960 election, would you have voted for Kennedy or for Nixon?

Kennedy . . . . 21 – 1
Nixon   2
Don't know   3
Other (specify) _____   4

83. Just one more question. Who did your parents vote for in the last election – Kennedy or Nixon?

	Father	Mother
Kennedy	22 – Y	23 – 4
Nixon	X	5
They didn't vote	0	6
Don't know	1	7
Not living then	2	8
Other answer (specify) _____	3	9

THANK YOU

To the interviewer: Complete the following questions at the end of the interview.

84. Race of respondent

White 24–1
Negro   2
Oriental   3

---

85. Was the respondent cooperative during the interview?

Yes – very cooperative 25–1
Yes – mildly cooperative   2
Rather uncooperative   3
Very uncooperative   4

---

86. Was anyone else present during the interview?

Yes 26–1*
No   2

*IF YES
Who, and for which parts of the interview?

---

87. Were there any questions which the respondent appeared to have difficulty in answering?

Yes 27–1*
No   2

*IF YES
Which questions?

---

88. Do you think the respondent gave truthful answers at all times during the interview?

Yes 28–1
No 2*

*IF NO
On which questions are you doubtful?

---

89. Length of interview

Hours _____ Minutes _____

---

90. Your signature _____

NORC 447
[side one]

Examples of Special Courses

Category	Subject
1	Extra courses in regular school subjects Such as: Mathematics History English composition Foreign languages
2	Trade, business, and vocational subjects Such as: Auto mechanics Machine shop Typing or shorthand Salesmanship Electronics
3	Any on-the-job training
4	Hobbies and recreation Such as: Photography Dancing lessons Swimming lessons Music or art lessons Handicrafts Sports
5	Home and family skills Such as: Home repairs Sewing or cooking Baby sitting
6	Personal skills Such as: Speed reading Remedial reading Personality development Public speaking Physical fitness
7	Any religious training
8	Current events, public affairs, or citizenship Such as: International affairs Community government

Democracy
The dangers of communism
Citizenship or Americanization

9   Any agricultural subjects

0   Other—anything else not covered here
Such as: Driving lessons

NORC 447
[side two]

Methods of study

Attended classes
Attended a series of lectures or talks
Attended group discussions
Correspondence lessons by mail
Individual lessons from a private teacher
A course given over television
On-the-job training
Some other method? (What?)

References

References

Adult Educ. J. 1945. Vol. IV, No. 2.

COLEMAN, J. S. 1961. *The adolescent society.* New York: Free Press of Glencoe.

DAVIS, A. 1951. *Social class influence upon learning.* Cambridge, Mass.: Harvard University Press.

DUNCAN, O. D. 1961. In A. J. REISS, JR. *Occupations and social status.* New York: Free Press of Glencoe. Pp. 109–61.

EDITORS OF "FORTUNE." 1955. *The changing American market.* Garden City, N.Y.: Hanover House.

ELECTRONIC INDUSTRIES ASSOCIATION. 1962. *Television set activity report.* Washington, D.C.

FLANAGAN, J., DAILY, J., SHAYCROFT, D., GORHAM, W., and GOLDBERG, I. 1960. *Designing the study.* Pittsburgh: Project Talent, University of Pittsburgh. Mimeographed.

———. 1962. Studies of the American high school. Pittsburgh: Project Talent, University of Pittsburgh. Mimeographed.

———. 1963. Studies of a complete age group—age 15. Pittsburgh: Project Talent, University of Pittsburgh. Mimeographed.

GREENE, B. I. 1962. Continuing education and the high-school dropout. *Adult Educ.,* XII, 76–83.

HOGGART, R. 1957. *The uses of literacy.* London: Chatto and Windus.

HOULE, C. O. 1961. *The inquiring mind.* Madison, Wis.: University of Wisconsin Press.

HYMAN, H. 1953. The value systems of different classes. In R. BENDIX and S. M. LIPSET (Eds.). *Class, status, and power.* Glencoe, Ill.: Free Press. Pp. 426–42.

HYMAN, H., and SHEATSLEY, P. 1947. Some reasons why information campaigns fail. *Publ. Opin. Quart.,* XI, 412–23.

KATZ, E., and FELDMAN, J. J. 1962. The Kennedy-Nixon debates: A survey of surveys. *Stud. publ. Communications,* No. 4.

KEYFITZ, N. 1951. Sampling probabilities proportional to size. *J. Amer. statist. Ass.,* XLVI, 105–9.

LIPSET, S. M., and BENDIX, R. 1960. *Social mobility in industrial society.* Berkeley: University of California Press.

LONDON, J., *et al.* 1963. Adult education and social class. Survey Research Center, University of California. Multilith.

LUNDBERG, G. A., *et al.* 1934. *Leisure: A suburban study.* New York: Columbia University Press.

PRESIDENT'S COMMISSION ON THE STATUS OF WOMEN. 1963. *American women: Report of the commission.* Washington, D.C.: U.S. Government Printing Office.

RCA ETV NEWS. 1958. No. 24.

RIVERA, R. J. 1963. The sociology of adolescence: A selective review of the literature. Chicago: National Opinion Research Center. Multilith.

RIESMAN, D. 1958. Leisure and work in post-industrial society. In E. LARRABEE and R. MEYERSOHN (Eds.). *Mass leisure*. Glencoe, Ill.: Free Press.

RIESSMAN, F. 1962. *The culturally deprived child*. New York: Harper and Row.

SALEEM, B. L., and MILLER, S. M. 1961. The neglected dropout: The returnee. Syracuse, N.Y.: Syracuse University Youth Development Center. Mimeographed.

SEXTON, P. 1963. Negro career expectations. *Merrill-Palmer Quart.*, IX, 303 – 16.

SCHRAMM, W. 1955. Telecourses: Preliminary reports. *NAEB Television Research Fact Sheet,* Ser. IV.

SCHRAMM, W., LYLE, J., and POOL, I. D. S. 1963.*The people look at educational television*. Stanford, Calif.: Stanford University Press.

STEINER, G. A. 1963. *The people look at television*. New York: Alfred A. Knopf.

TAEUBER, C., and TAEUBER, I. 1958. *The changing population of the United States*. New York: John Wiley and Sons.

U.S. DEPARTMENT OF COMMERCE. 1961. *Statistical abstract of the United States, 1961*. Washington, D.C.: U.S. Government Printing Office.

––––––. 1962. *Statistical abstract of the United States, 1962*. Washington, D.C.: U.S. Government Printing Office.

––––––. 1963. *Statistical abstract of the United States, 1963*. Washington, D.C.: U.S. Government Printing Office.

U.S. DEPARTMENT OF COMMERCE, BUREAU OF THE CENSUS, 1960. *United States census of housing, 1960*. Washington, D.C.: U.S. Government Printing Office.

––––––. 1962a. *Current population reports: School enrollment, October 1961*. Ser. P-20, No. 117, July 11. Washington, D.C.: U.S. Government Printing Office.

––––––. 1962b. *United States census of population, 1960: General social and economic characteristics*. Washington, D.C.: U.S. Government Printing Office.

––––––. 1963. *Current population reports: Population characteristics*. Ser. P-120, No. 121, Feb. 17. Washington, D.C.: U.S. Government Printing Office.

U.S. DEPARTMENT OF HEALTH, EDUCATION AND WELFARE. 1958. *Health statistics*. Washington, D.C.: U.S. Government Printing Office.

––––––. 1959. *Participation in adult education*. Circular No. 539. Washington, D.C.: U.S. Government Printing Office.

WHITE, R. C. 1955. Social class differences in the uses of leisure. *Amer. J. Sociol.*, LXI, 145 – 50.

Index

Index

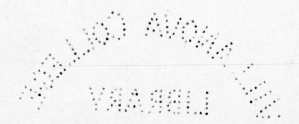